WHITE SPACE, BLACK HOOD

WHITE SPACE, BLACK HOOD

OPPORTUNITY HOARDING AND SEGREGATION IN THE AGE OF INEQUALITY

SHERYLL CASHIN

BEACON PRESS, BOSTON

BEACON PRESS
Boston, Massachusetts
www.beacon.org

Beacon Press books
are published under the auspices of
the Unitarian Universalist Association of Congregations.

24 23 22 21   8 7 6 5 4 3 2 1

This book is printed on acid-free paper that meets the uncoated paper
ANSI/NISO specifications for permanence as revised in 1992.

Text design and composition by Kim Arney

Library of Congress Cataloging-in-Publication Data
Name: Cashin, Sheryll, author.
Title: White space, black hood : opportunity hoarding and segregation
in the age of inequality / Sheryll Cashin.
Description: Boston : Beacon Press, [2021] | Includes bibliographical
references and index.
Identifiers: LCCN 2021015657 (print) | LCCN 2021015658 (ebook) |
ISBN 9780807000298 (hardcover) | ISBN 9780807000373 (ebook)
Subjects: LCSH: Community development, Urban—United States. | African
American neighborhoods—United States. | Equality—United States. |
United States—Race relations.
Classification: LCC HN90.C6 C383 2021 (print) | LCC HN90.C6 (ebook) |
DDC 307.1/4160973—dc23
LC record available at https://lccn.loc.gov/2021015657
LC ebook record available at https://lccn.loc.gov/2021015658

For descendants,
with love

CONTENTS

STORIES THEY TOLD
THEMSELVES AND A NATION

Why not . . . incorporate the blacks into the state . . . ? Deep rooted prejudices entertained by the whites; ten thousand recollections, by the blacks, of the injuries they have sustained [and] the real distinctions which nature has made . . . This unfortunate difference of colour, and perhaps of faculty, is a powerful obstacle to the emancipation of these people.

—THOMAS JEFFERSON, 1788[1]

Two totally different races, as we have before seen, cannot easily harmonize together, and although we have no idea that any organized plan of insurrection or rebellion can ever secure for the black the superiority, even when free, yet his idleness will produce want and worthlessness, and his very worthlessness and degradation will stimulate him to deeds of rapine and vengeance; he will oftener engage in plots and massacres, and thereby draw down on his devoted head, the vengeance of the provoked whites.

—THOMAS R. DEW, professor of history, metaphysics
and political law, William & Mary College, 1832[2]

Never before has the black race of Central Africa, from the dawn of history to the present day, attained a condition so civilized and so improved, not only physically, but morally and intellectually. It came among us in a low, degraded, and savage condition, and in the course of a few generations it has grown up under the fostering care of our institutions, reviled as they have been, to its present comparatively civilized condition. This, with the rapid increase of numbers, is conclusive proof of the general happiness of the race, in spite of all the exaggerated tales to the contrary.

—JOHN C. CALHOUN, US senator, 1837[3]

We hear much of the civilization and christianization of the barbarous tribes of Africa. In my judgment, those ends will never be attained, but by first teaching them the lesson taught to Adam, that "in the sweat of his brow he should eat his bread," and teaching them to work, and feed, and clothe themselves.

—ALEXANDER H. STEPHENS,
vice president of the Confederacy, 1861[4]

There are eight millions of white people and four millions of negroes in juxtaposition. The latter are, in domestic subordination and social adaptation, corresponding with their wants, their instincts, their faculties, the nature with which God has endowed them. They are different and subordinate creatures, and they are in a different and subordinate social position, harmonizing with their natural relations to the superior race, and therefore they are in their normal condition.

—J. H. VAN EVRIE, doctor and author, 1861[5]

[T]he common white people of the country are at times very much enraged against the negro population. They think that this universal political and civil equality will finally bring about social equality . . . There are already instances . . . in which poor white girls are having negro children.

—WHITE NORTH CAROLINA MAN, 1871[6]

[P]utting colored men into office, in positions of prominence, will gradually lead them to demand social equality, and to intermingle by marriage with the whites.

—WHITE MISSISSIPPI POSTMASTER, 1871[7]

We consider the underlying fallacy of the plaintiff's argument to consist in the assumption that the enforced separation of the two races stamps the colored race with a badge of inferiority. If this be so, it is not by reason of anything found in the act, but solely because the colored race chooses to put that construction upon it. . . . If one race be inferior to the other socially, the Constitution of the United States cannot put them upon the same plane.

— HENRY BROWN, Supreme Court Justice,
majority opinion in *Plessy v. Ferguson*, 1896

The white people of the country, as well as I, wish to see the colored people progress . . . Segregation is not humiliating but a benefit, and ought to be so regarded by you gentlemen. If your organization goes out and tells the colored people of the country that it is a humiliation, they will so regard it, but if you do not tell them so, and regard it rather as a benefit, they will regard it the same. The only harm that will come will be if you cause them to think it is a humiliation.

—WOODROW WILSON, 1914[8]

The sun is never allowed to set on any niggers in Glendive.

—GLENDIVE (MONTANA) INDEPENDENT, 1915[9]

The general objectives of . . . planning are to conserve human resources and maintain the nation and the race . . .

—ALFRED BETTMAN, director of the National
Conference on City Planning, 1933[10]

I'm not prejudiced, but I'd burn this building down before I'd sell it to any damned nigger.

—WHITE CHICAGO MAN, 1945[11]

Today in the urban slums, the limits of responsible action are all but invisible.

—RICHARD NIXON, 1967[12]

We don't mind being accused of police brutality. They haven't seen anything yet. . . . [W]hen the looting starts, the shooting starts.

—WALTER E. HEADLEY, police chief,
Miami, Florida, 1967[13]

There's a woman in Chicago. . . . She has 80 names, 30 addresses, 12 Social Security cards and is collecting veterans' benefits on four nonexisting deceased husbands. And she's collecting Social Security on *her cards. She's got Medicaid, getting food stamps, and she is collecting welfare under each of her names. Her tax-free cash income alone is over $150,000.*

—RONALD REAGAN, 1976[14]

Today I reject United States Sentencing Commission proposals that would equalize penalties for crack and powder cocaine distribution by dramatically reducing the penalties for crack. . . . Trafficking in crack, and the violence it fosters, has a devastating impact on communities across America, especially inner-city communities. Tough penalties for crack trafficking are required because of the effect on individuals and families, related gang activity, turf battles, and other violence.

—WILLIAM J. CLINTON, 1995[15]

A new generation of street criminals is upon us—the youngest, biggest and baddest generation any society has ever known.

—WILLIAM J. BENNETT, JOHN J. DIIULIO,
AND JOHN P. WALTERS, 1996[16]

He was acting like a thug, not like a gentle giant. He certainly didn't deserve to be shot for it.

—BILL MAHER, 2014[17]

We need law and order. If we don't have it, we're not going to have a country. . . . Our inner cities, African Americans, Hispanics are living in hell because it's so dangerous. You walk down the street, you get shot.

—DONALD J. TRUMP, 2016[18]

These THUGS are dishonoring the memory of George Floyd. . . . Any difficulty and we will assume control but, when the looting starts, the shooting starts.

—DONALD J. TRUMP, 2020[19]

WHITE
SPACE,
BLACK
HOOD

INTRODUCTION

O n Memorial Day 2020, New Yorkers headed outdoors, emerging after months of COVID-19 isolation. Two of them encountered each other in the Ramble, a woodland of Central Park that attracts hundreds of bird species and people devoted to watching them. Amy Cooper and Christian Cooper (no relation) were both graduates of elite universities; she from the University of Chicago, he from Harvard. They both used civil language as their encounter descended. Amy, wearing a standard white PPE mask, said: "Sir, I am asking you to stop recording me." Christian said: "Please don't come close to me." More than forty million people watched the viral video of an ancient and dangerous American script.

The video opened with the tension between characters already heated. Christian, a board member of the New York City Audubon Society, had asked Amy to leash her dog, which was the park rule and of particular concern in the Ramble to avid birders like him. When Amy declined to comply, Christian admitted later that he told her, "Look, if you're going to do what you want, I'm going to do what I want, but you're not going to like it." He attempted to lure the dog to him with a treat.[1] Amy was incensed. Christian refused to stop recording her. She could have leashed her dog and walked away. Instead, she warned him that she would call the police. "I am going to tell them there is an African American man threatening my life," she said, after Christian had asked her three times not to approach him.

Amy Cooper was a finance professional, donated to Democrats, and used the phrase "African American man" twice, rather than "nigger" or "thug." She followed through on her threat, called 911, and worked herself into hysteria as Christian continued to film her from a social distance. She preferred to struggle and yank her beloved cocker spaniel by the collar—making dog lovers wince—rather than surrender her power to weaponize her status. Her advance warning suggested she knew that police were primed to hear a fake distress call from a white female that tapped hoary stereotypes of Black men as predators.

Multiply this interaction and other macroaggressions each day, all day, across the land, and you will begin to understand why being Black in America is exhausting. Amy operated as if the Ramble was her space in which she could choose who belonged and whether to comply with posted rules. A Black man, telling her what to do, was threatening and needed to be expelled. Later, Amy apologized, and Christian, though resolutely opposed to racism, expressed concern and reservations about the swift, mob-like destruction of Amy's life as she became a social media example.[2] Christian also refused to participate in a prosecutor's investigation of a misdemeanor charge against Amy for filing a false report, and the charge was dropped after she completed a therapeutic program with instruction on racial bias.[3] In a fantasy version of the story, the Ramble could have been a public commons for easier talk, even disagreement, among equals—a space not for white power but dialogue, more than once, maybe daily, as citizens tried to build a new, transformative American community. Not then, not yet.

The same Memorial Day, in Minneapolis, Derek Chauvin, a white officer kneeled on George Floyd's neck for more than nine minutes. Floyd was handcuffed, lying facedown, begging, "Please . . . I can't breathe." Bystanders beseeched the four officers, including Chauvin, to relent, to get off his back and neck. Chauvin was impassive, nonchalant, hands in his pockets, so determined, it seemed, to show citizens who was in power that he remained on Floyd's neck after Floyd had stopped moving, with no pulse.

Floyd had called out: "Mama, mama, mama, mama. . . . I love you. Tell my kids I love them. I'm dead." He was polite to the end. His last words showed up on protest signs, including in Lafayette Square—a park in Washington, DC, named for a key French ally of the American Revolution, and once the grounds of a slave market. Citizens reinvigorated it as a space for free expression before a barricaded White House.[4] Before death, Floyd spoke, though, like Christ crucified, asking God why he was forsaken, his pleas were not answered:

> I can't breathe. I can't breathe. Ah! I'll probably just die this way.
> I can't breathe my face.
> I can't breathe. Please, [inaudible]
> I can't breathe. Shit.
> I will, I can't move.
> My knee. My neck.
> I'm through, I'm through. I'm claustrophobic. My stomach hurts. My neck hurts.
> Everything hurts. I need some water or something, please. Please? I can't breathe, officer.
> You're going to kill me, man.
> Come on, man. Oh, oh.
> I cannot breathe. I cannot breathe. Ah! They'll kill me. They'll kill me. I can't breathe. I can't breathe! Oh!
> Ah! Ah! Please. Please. Please.[5]

Chauvin, who had eighteen previous misconduct complaints, could not muster any empathy or surrender his learned power to dehumanize. The nation and world convulsed in protests because seventeen-year-old Darnella Frazier recorded the entirety of Floyd's execution for all to see. It felt biblical, a sacrifice of a beloved Black son and father, to expose truth. Millions rose up across the globe. With a new lens for systemic racism, they began to see it everywhere.

Floyd was killed after allegedly using a counterfeit twenty-dollar bill he may not have even known about. "Forgery for what? For what?" he had said at the beginning of his encounter with the police.[6] Christian Cooper was surveilled, perhaps, for being an uppity Black man. The twin viral episodes of Memorial Day 2020 converged, and a battle for narrative about Black Lives ensued over a summer thick with Black deaths—from COVID-19, police shootings, and yes, a seasonal rise in Black-on-Black homicides. It was #BlackLivesMatter versus "law and order." An indecent president tried to distract the country from his failed response to COVID-19 and the nearly two hundred thousand people who had died from the virus on his watch by then. President Trump followed an old playbook of American politics, invoking myths that cast himself as defender of white Americans and their suburban way of life. He was honest and transparent in his pro-segregation leanings. White space was meant to be protected. The "infested" cities, particularly inner cities, rioters, and looters were meant to be policed.

Trump's desperate weaponization of racial justice uprisings, his defense of white space and white nationalism, mirror a tension that has been at the center of American politics since the nation's founding. Each time the United States seems to dismantle a peculiar Black-subordinating institution, it constructs a new one and attendant myths to justify the racial order. Thomas Jefferson agonized in *Notes on the State of Virginia* about whether and how to incorporate sable Africans into the polity. Early generations of white property-owning men, those allowed to be leaders, told stories of Black inferiority to justify slavery. Later generations alleged sexual predation of white women by Black men to justify Jim Crow and residential segregation. Men and women of the so-called greatest and silent generations, as well as baby boomers from Bill Clinton to Donald Trump, fabulized about the people in the hood. Always and forever, anti-Black rhetoric was critical to uniting whites in politics.

This book aims to make processes of American residential caste transparent. A basic move, of creating and maintaining Black-subordinating institutions to confer value on affluent whites, has not changed, though the mechanics and propaganda have metastasized. I argue that policy decisions made in the early twentieth century, to construct ghettos, have profound consequences for producing *current* inequality. I also contend that geography is now central to American caste, a mechanism for overinvesting in affluent white space and disinvesting and plundering elsewhere. Geography helps to construct social and racial distinctions that justify the way things are.

I call the Black people trapped in high-poverty neighborhoods "descendants," in recognition of an unbroken continuum from slavery. Occasionally, I also use this honorific to describe Black Americans like myself, who do not live in the hood but descend from the long legacy of slavery. Descendants are typecast and consigned to the bottom of the social order. Denizens of poverty-free, very-white spaces enjoy entrenched advantages, and everyone else struggles to access opportunity in real estate markets premised on exclusion begun a century before to contain descendants. The residential caste system I describe is not only about the iconic hood. It is about power, politics, and distribution of resources *away* from those who most need public goods *to* people and communities with more than enough.

Non-descendants should care, because exclusion and opportunity hoarding harm the vast majority of people who cannot buy their way into bastions of affluence, and because geography as caste is destroying America. Physical segregation, constructed at the outset to contain then-Negroes, is the progenitor of our broken, gerrymandered politics. Descendants were powerless to change their reality in large part because of myths told about them. Mythologizing about "pathological" Black people helped perfect broad skepticism about government and anti-tax fanaticism.

Of course, there are other strains of American oppression and dog-whistling rhetoric. Pervasive contemporary stereotypes of immigrants and Americans of color, of Muslims, and of Black Americans imply divergence from a presumed norm of American Christian whiteness. That norm, sometimes stated plainly by avowed white nationalists, was the organizing plank for regimes of oppression essential to American capitalism and expansion—from the conquest of Indigenous and Mexican people to slavery to the exclusion of Asian and other immigrants and, later, to Jim Crow. Ancient and current stories of oppression along myriad dimensions need to be told and retold to hasten the day when a critical mass of whites rejects the idea of white dominance and joins an ascending coalition to dismantle regimes borne of supremacy.[7]

I am writing about the geography and dogma of anti-Black oppression because I care about descendants and because geography as caste ensnares us all. Under the old Jim Crow, Blackness was the primary marker for discrimination and exclusion. American caste now exists at the intersection of race, economic status, and geography, and this system of sorting and exclusion has been hardening. It thrives on certain cultural assumptions—that affluent space is earned and hood living is the deserved consequence of individual behavior.

Like race, "ghetto" is a social construct. At some point, this word used to describe high-poverty neighborhoods became pejorative, as powerful as the N-word. To paraphrase sociologist Elijah Anderson, American society is very invested in the ghetto as a dangerous place, where people at the bottom of the social order live.[8] Our words and mechanisms for subordination have changed. The problem of Black belonging continues, but it is most felt by descendants in the hood.

Descendants are the group least likely in American society to experience the accoutrements of citizenship. Exit from the hood and from the bottom of the social order is improbable. Among the modern state action designed to contain descendants are militaristic policing in which Blackness itself becomes the pretext for stopping people, mass incarceration, the criminalization of poverty, a school-to-prison pipeline, and housing and school policies that invest in, rather than discourage, poverty concentration.

Less understood is that concentrated Black poverty facilitates poverty-free affluent white space and habits of favor and disfavor by public and private actors. White space would not exist without the hood and government at all levels created and still reifies this racialized residential order. In particular, this book illuminates three anti-Black processes that undergird the entire system of American residential caste—boundary maintenance, opportunity hoarding, and stereotype-driven surveillance. Many people acquiesce in or participate in these processes. Yet the practices necessary to maintaining residential caste also undermine most non-Black people. The successful have seceded from the struggling. Highly educated and affluent people tend to live in their own neighborhoods and support policies like exclusionary zoning and neighborhood school assignments that lock others out and concentrate advantage.[9]

As with slavery and follow-on institutions like peonage and convict leasing, the hood is a source of wealth extraction and exploitation that benefits American capitalists—from the prison industrial complex to Opportunity Zones that enabled investors, through loopholes, to shelter 100 percent of capital gains in luxury properties rather than distressed hoods the program was marketed to help. In another example, in the 2000s, predatory lenders targeted segregated Black neighborhoods for their most usurious subprime mortgages. This predation culminated in a foreclosure crisis that eviscerated Black and Latinx wealth, reduced the Black homeownership rate to 1968 levels, and eliminated gains of the civil rights revolution in housing.[10] White homeownership rebounded while the rate of Black homeownership continued to decline under unchecked financial processes that disparately harmed. By 2020, the Black-white homeownership gap had widened to a chasm not seen *since 1890*.[11] And yet we don't tell stories that encourage the prosecution and jailing of white-collar criminals who steal Black wealth and create national financial crises. We have a pervasive narrative about Black "thugs" but no similar policy-driving story about corporate criminals.

While state and private actors plunder, extract, surveil, and contain in the hood, they overinvest in and protect white space. Apologists have constructed many modern stereotypes to support the status quo and retain the benefits of exclusion and exclusivity—from golden schools, neighborhoods, and infrastructure to artisanal food. The idea that descendants belong apart from everyone else is the often-unspoken-but-sometimes-shouted-out-loud norm animating most fair housing and school integration debates. Stereotypes also hide the fact that concentrated poverty is by no means solely a Black problem. The footprint of concentrated poverty is expanding; the percentage of Blacks, Latinx, and whites who live in such conditions is rising. Concentrated poverty grows fastest in the suburbs.[12] Yet it is far easier for politicians and media figures to stoke division among those mutually locked out of opportunity than to build multiracial coalitions that transcend division and demand fairness from elites.

Ultimately, I argue for abolition of the processes of anti-Black residential caste and *repair,* the building of new institutions of opportunity for descendants, and the nation. The goal should be to transform the lens through which society sees residents of poor Black neighborhoods, from presumed thug to presumed citizen, and to alter the relationship of the state with these neighborhoods, from punitive to caring. I offer positive examples of places that are beginning to do this. I also call on the state at all levels to cease and desist from habits borne of white supremacy.

This work will be difficult, perhaps as arduous and long-arced as the movements for abolition of slavery and modern civil rights. There is cause for hope. Black voters mattered in 2020. Joe Biden centered racial equity and justice in his presidential campaign and won decisively. Black voters mobilized in Georgia for Senate runoff races and helped clinch a governing, though bare, majority for Democrats in Congress, with the tie-breaking privileges of the first Black, South Asian, and woman to be vice president, Kamala Harris. A plurality of whites and sizeable majorities of Asian, Black, Indigenous, and Latinx people prevailed in politics. This coalition can grow and pursue saner, just policies both nationally and locally. Despite backlash and fatigue, Black Americans have more allies than they have ever had in US history. Together, we must first understand the processes of residential caste, then dismantle them.

CHAPTER 1

BALTIMORE

A Study in American Caste

The Black Butterfly and *the White L.* A public health researcher coined these monikers for distinct cultural spaces in the city that invented racial zoning but also inspired descendants like Frederick Douglass and Thurgood Marshall to chart paths for justice.[1] Baltimore is illustrative of a wider pattern, of a past and present of investing in exclusionary areas and disinvesting in Black neighborhoods. Other metropolitan regions with large populations of descendants are caught in the same vicious cycle.

At the onset of the Civil War, Baltimore was home to the nation's largest free urban Black population. About 90 percent of its twenty-seven thousand Blacks were free in 1860. Like other strains of humanity that found their way to Baltimore—Jewish, Polish, Czech, Slovak, Italian, Irish—African Americans lived in small enclaves adjacent to other groups. Public places, including parks, theaters, hotels, restaurants, and department stores, were open to Blacks as late as 1905, though attitudes were changing. White Baltimoreans who had lived with a sizeable population of Negroes for generations suddenly could no longer tolerate proximity to them in any realm. With the rise of eugenics, there was a growing intolerance among the wealthy for anyone who diverged from affluent protestant whiteness. Exclusion and exclusivity secured property values and social status.[2]

The movement for racial zoning began when Blacks moved to McCulloh Street, two blocks from the graceful mansions of Eutaw Place. A prominent Black lawyer, W. Ashbie Hawkins, purchased a house at 1834 McCulloh and rented it to his brother-in-law and law partner, George W. F. McMechen. McMechen had graduated from what is now Morgan State University and Yale Law School. Other Blacks with solid incomes, including a postal clerk and school teachers, rented houses on McCulloh. Blacks occupied the west side of the block and whites remained on the east side.

White residents took umbrage at their new neighbors. They formed the McCulloh Street–Madison Avenue Protective Association, resolving: "The colored people should not be allowed to encroach on some of the best residential streets in the city and force white people to vacate their homes." Whites threw stones and bricks into the McMechens' new home and dumped tar on their steps. One particularly incensed white neighbor campaigned for a new city ordinance that would criminalize Blacks moving to a majority-white block and vice versa and the city council embraced it.[3]

Mayor J. Barry Mahool, known nationally as a progressive social-justice reformer signed the law. "Baltimore Tries Drastic Plan of Race Segregation," a *New York Times* headline hollered on Christmas Day 1910. The mayor, interviewed at length for the article, bemoaned that Baltimore had about one hundred thousand "colored" people or one-sixth of the city's population, and that well-to-do Blacks were buying property in white neighborhoods, unlike their allegedly more deferential brethren in the Deep South, who knew their place. On many blocks, Mahool complained, whites were forced to live with Blacks, and panicked whites often sold. Elsewhere, Mahool made his position and racial ideology clear: "Blacks should be quarantined in isolated slums in order to reduce the incidents of civil disturbance, to prevent the spread of communicable disease into the nearby White neighborhoods, and to protect property values among the White majority."[4] The *Times* featured an image of the handsome, dapper, and presumably disease-free McMechen.[5]

Racial zoning was born, and numerous southern and midwestern cities followed suit. W. Ashbie Hawkins fought Baltimore's law for the next seven years. He, too, was a descendant. His father, up from slavery, had served as a reverend. Hawkins became an advocate for racial equality. An alumnus of historically Black Morgan State, he had enrolled at the University of Maryland School of Law in 1889. A year later, the school succumbed to demands from white students, forcing him and another Black student to leave. After completing his legal education at Howard University, Hawkins immediately began to agitate.

On August 20, 1892, the 273rd anniversary of the arrival of enslaved Africans at Jamestown, Hawkins wrote a column for a new Black-owned paper, *The Afro-American*, under the headline "An Alarming Condition." He decried "the very poor facilities provided . . . for the education of colored children." Their schoolhouses and equipment were "a disgrace," their school terms "too short." And the state showed "reckless disregard of the character" and professional training of their teachers. He wrote a few years before the US Supreme Court endorsed the fiction in *Plessy v. Ferguson* that separate could be equal for Black people. Hawkins anticipated the Negro's fraught legal position: "We have a right to every facility offered others, but unfortunately for us we do not seem to have the power to enforce it."[6]

This did not stop Hawkins from trying. He was a leader in the Niagara Movement, founded by W. E. B. Du Bois and others. Hawkins filed lawsuits challenging residential segregation, unequal pay for Negro teachers, and segregation and unequal conditions on trains and boats. In one case, a Negro woman, Dr. Julia P. H. Coleman, wrote the National Association for the Advancement of Colored People, or NAACP, headquarters in New York in 1918, reporting that she had attempted to enter the ladies' car of a train in Baltimore, bound for Washington, DC. Conductors had barred her and pushed her to the pavement. "I went to the nearest telephone and called up Mr. Ashby [sic] Hawkins," she wrote. She insisted on bringing a test case "for the benefit of the race" and asked the NAACP to lend its support.

Together, she and Hawkins prevailed. Hawkins explained in a letter to the NAACP that they had won an initial judgment and one cent in damages, but he appealed and won additional damages and reaffirmation from the Baltimore courts "that this railroad had no authority to segregate interstate passengers." He vowed to keep filing cases against the railroad predicting it would "get tired of undertaking to keep up this segregation." Hawkins became Thurgood Marshall's hero and a model for the NAACP's new legal department.[7]

Hawkins also challenged the racial zoning ordinance that was enacted in Baltimore. He filed a lawsuit and succeeded in having early versions set aside, though a fourth version of the law survived. Hawkins was undeterred. As lawyer for the NAACP, he filed a brief opposing a racial zoning ordinance in Louisville, Kentucky, in *Buchanan v. Warley,* in which the Supreme Court struck down all racial zoning, in 1917. The posture of that case surely helped. A white property owner who wished to sell to a Negro succeeded, with the assistance of the NAACP, in convincing the Court that this violated his property rights. Hawkins continued to fight residential restrictions for Black Americans until he died in 1941. He also agitated through politics, running as an independent for US Senate in 1920. It was a protest campaign for "race representation," he said, to force the Republican Party of Lincoln to which Blacks hewed to support Negro candidates in local and legislative races and respond to Black community interests.[8] In his final campaign plea to Black voters, published in 1920, again in an opinion piece in *The Afro-American,* Hawkins articulated inequities endured by descendants:

> For fifty years we have religiously supported the candidates of the Republican Party . . . and it is an open secret that our reward for this loyalty is nothing more nor less than studied neglect. . . . the local Republican party has done nothing to remedy the miserable condition of our rural school system . . . it has connived at "Jimcrow" regulations . . . it has refused to compel the transportation companies to abide by the law . . . The letter of the law provides for equal accommodations . . . and still no State agency can be induced to compel compliance therewith. . . . what use is this party to us?[9]

Hawkins then argued that Maryland counties controlled by white Republicans taxed colored families and used those funds solely for white schools. "Not a cent of local taxes is spent on the education of colored children," he protested. "We are expected to do the voting and nothing else . . ." Negroes, he argued, were not allowed to have

Hawkins, left, and McMechen were brothers-in-law who practiced law together until Hawkins died in 1941. A high school in Baltimore is named after McMechen.

positions of responsibility or material rewards that whites did not want them to have. He called on Black voters to show "race pride" and vote their interests.[10]

Though Hawkins succeeded in eliminating racial zoning, Baltimore's segregationists turned to exclusionary tools deployed in every American city with a sizeable Black population. Wealthy Roland Park, at the northern edge of Baltimore, became one of the first streetcar suburbs in the United States to insert restrictive covenants in property deeds, which constrained owners from renting or selling to Blacks. But the Roland Park covenants included one exception. In the subsection titled Nuisances, deeds typically stated: "At no time shall . . . said tract or any part thereof, or any building erected thereon, be occupied by any negro or person of negro extraction. This prohibition, however, is not intended to include occupancy by a negro domestic servant."[11] Though white Baltimoreans enforced restrictive covenants throughout the city, they did not resort to acute violence, as whites did in places like Chicago.[12]

A common practice of denying credit to African Americans spread when the Home Owners' Loan Corporation (HOLC) mapped Baltimore during the Great Depression, applying the "hazardous" D rating to virtually every neighborhood where Blacks predominated or had "infiltrated." This practice, known as "redlining," institutionalized a two-tiered system of traditional lending and investment in white areas, predatory lending by speculators, and disinvestment in Black areas. Negroes were "dangerous" and "undesirable," a "detrimental influence," according to HOLC's eugenics-infused underwriting standards. Jews were also marked as threatening to property values.

Yet Black Baltimore had strengths. Sandtown-Winchester is currently associated with its felled native son, Freddie Gray, and grimness both real and imagined. In its heyday, this West Baltimore neighborhood was known as Baltimore's Harlem. It brimmed with Black-owned businesses and nightclubs where Billie Holiday, Cab Calloway, and others wowed audiences. After the neighborhood received the D rating from HOLC, it could not attract private investment for homes, and the city decided to place public housing intended solely for Black people there.[13]

Only two Black neighborhoods evaded the D rating. W. Ashbie Hawkins lived in Wilson Park, a small enclave, restricted, ironically, to educated Blacks. A mile away, Black luminaries like W. E. B. Du Bois resided in tiny Morgan Park. These two strivers' islands surrounded by whites, garnered the B, or "still desirable," rating.[14] Forever and always, the so-called Black community suffered class tensions, evident in a 1915 *The Afro-American* article, typical of the newspaper's decades of crusading against segregation and exclusion. Under the heading "Segregation a Boon to Real Estate Sharps," an unnamed reporter wrote that those Negroes who wanted to buy "desirable property" were forced to pay at least 20 percent more than whites and that, in segregated sections, colored folk paid extortionate rents for houses with falling ceilings and other badly needed repairs. The reporter observed that Negroes who were "conservative housekeepers, intelligent and . . . homeowners" would avoid declining areas that were attracting "unintelligent" renters and "undesirable persons."[15]

HOLC's D rating tracked Baltimore's Black population, which was contained in the west and east by restrictive covenants. HOLC gave color codes to each rating: A was green ("Best"), B was blue ("Still Desirable"), C was yellow ("Definitely Declining"), and D was red ("Hazardous"). Maps 1.1 and 1.2 of Baltimore, which appear in the insert of color-coded maps in this book, show how whiteness was valued, and Blackness devalued. Restrictive covenants and HOLC ratings worked in tandem to construct the "Black Butterfly" and the "White L" at the city center—geographically opposed places and identities that produce racial inequality to this day.

During World War II, speculators made fortunes by buying properties in declining white areas adjacent to Black neighborhoods and reselling them to Blacks for as much as 80 percent more. They saddled Black buyers with substandard properties, in need of intense capital improvements for which no traditional banks would make loans. Descendants who wished to buy or improve their properties were relegated to the exploitive financing terms of speculators. Syndicates of private investors turned substandard housing into gold, providing the financing for usurious rent-to-buy land installment contracts to Negroes, who often never succeeded in gaining ownership, much less the funds to fix deteriorated housing.[16]

Blockbusting was the broadly used term for the practice of enticing panic selling by whites by stoking fear of a Black invasion and extracting extraordinary markups from Black buyers. Among the blockbusters who stoked white fear for profit in Baltimore were some Black speculators who also intended to advance the frontier of housing options for Black people. In 1955, two hundred blockbusters descended on Edmondson Village in West Baltimore after a few Blacks arrived. A working-class area of redbrick row houses transitioned from white to Black with the pace of a night following day. Blockbusters divided row houses into rental units to make more profit. Sometimes Black buyers divided their homes and rented space out to others in order to cover steep installment payments. Greed speeded overcrowding and deterioration.[17]

Most Blacks lived in West Baltimore, but blockbusters also helped to "Blacken" the east side, where Morgan State is located. A once-small community of southern Black migrants grew as blockbusters manipulated white economic and racial fears. As the east and west wings of the Black Butterfly expanded, shops and services that white Protestant and Jewish communities had enjoyed soon disappeared from what became all-Black neighborhoods.[18] As middle-class Blacks moved in, middle-class whites fled to the suburbs, propelled by Federal Housing Administration (FHA)-backed mortgages that were denied to Blacks and federally sponsored interstate highways. The first metropolitan beltway in the country, Interstate 695, sprouted prosperous edge communities in suburban counties. Baltimore's white population plunged by one-third between 1950 and 1970.[19]

By 1968, Baltimore was 46 percent Black. Black Americans were underrepresented on a racially gerrymandered city council; all citywide elected officials were white.[20] Baltimore's Black neighborhoods had suffered from major development decisions made for them by others. An east-west expressway had been planned as early as the 1930s. Over three decades, state highway builders procured and demolished thousands of Black-occupied homes along the Franklin-Mulberry corridor in the Harlem Park neighborhood though the expressway was never built. In the 1940s, descendants in East and West Baltimore formed a "Movement Against Destruction" to resist demolition by the highway builders.

Harlem Park, the spiritual and cultural center of Black life in the city, was home to historic churches and institutions and striving Black professionals and civil rights activists, including Parren Mitchell. Like W. Ashbie Hawkins, Mitchell was an alumnus of Morgan State, and he wanted to continue his education at the University of Maryland. Mitchell assented when Thurgood Marshall and other lawyers for the NAACP Legal Defense and Education Fund (LDF) recruited him to sue. Together, they forced the university to admit Mitchell to its graduate program in sociology, which he completed with honors. Mitchell also seemed to share Hawkins's belief that Black Americans could represent themselves. In 1970, on his second try, he beat a ten-term incumbent, becoming the first Black elected to Congress from Maryland. His brother, Clarence Mitchell Jr., chief lobbyist for the NAACP for three decades, helped secure federal civil rights laws that propelled the second Reconstruction.

Harlem Park, economically integrated and proud, declined after the revival of a proposal for an east-west highway in the 1960s. Once the area was targeted for a cut-through, residents ceased investing in their homes and many buildings deteriorated or were abandoned. Despite community protests, highway builders condemned parts of Rosemont, a middle-class Black neighborhood, though the expressway was ultimately canceled.[21] Such decisions by road builders and those empowered to shape development devastated Black communities in Baltimore and nationally. Road building provided an opportunity to clear out inner-city "blight," though that really meant undesired people. The road builders used highways to insulate white communities with concrete, with ramparts of four to eight lanes. Vital Black neighborhoods like Sweet Auburn in Atlanta, also called "the richest Negro street in the world" for its concentration of Black commerce, were intentionally cut in two by freeways.[22]

Former US senator Barbara Mikulski famously began her public career opposing an interstate link through Canton and Fells Point. These majority-white neighborhoods were spared any demolition. Black neighborhoods in West Baltimore, at the stub end of a 1.4-mile abandoned "Highway to Nowhere," were not so fortunate. More than 1,500 residents were permanently displaced from a multiblock swath cleared for the abandoned road, which destroyed 971 homes and 62 businesses. The highway itself was a sunken six-lane ditch with no off-ramps.[23]

It was an assault on Blackness. Highways and urban renewal displaced about a tenth of Baltimore's population. Most of those uprooted were descendants, and the shock of displacement increased instability and abandonment. Those in charge of public housing development added to the misery. The city bulldozed homes for highways or "renewal" and then moved the poor Blacks it had displaced into public or subsidized housing in neighborhoods that mounted the least resistance. This created pockets of intense poverty, social dysfunction, and discontent. After Dr. King was assassinated in 1968,

"The Road to Nowhere"

disempowered descendants rioted and set Baltimore on fire. Widespread damage was self-inflicted, but the urban decay associated with Baltimore's Black neighborhoods predated the riots and traced back to HOLC's D ratings, the exploitation of blockbusters, and poverty-concentrating development that moved Negroes.[24]

URBAN RENEWAL AND
HIGHWAYS AS "NEGRO REMOVAL"

The University of Richmond's Digital Scholarship Lab mapped the location of urban renewal projects in Baltimore and the nation. Nearly all were in areas previously rated D by HOLC, a cumulative attack on Black neighborhoods. In Baltimore, urban renewal displaced 8,678 families, 74 percent of which were of color, by the 1960s.[25] The Highway to Nowhere, running east-west just a few blocks below a renewal project in Harlem Park, added to the neighborhood's trauma.

In the wake of the 1968 riots, white flight to suburban Baltimore County continued, as did that county's virulent opposition to open housing or any development that invited or retained Black residents. The county used federal urban renewal funds and its police and zoning powers to target and remove poor Black settlements in what MIT urban studies scholar Yale Rabin called "expulsive zoning." It systematically displaced low-income Black families by rezoning Black residential areas for business or industry and sparing nearby white areas. Compensation was rare; most of those displaced were forced to seek housing in Baltimore. Baltimore County razed its four public housing projects by 1954 and adamantly refused to comply with the new Fair Housing Act of 1968. It also left Black hamlets with unpaved streets and scant public investment while adjacent white developments received paved streets and better improvements.[26]

Descendants were left behind in a wounded, extremely segregated city much poorer than the surrounding suburbs. After the riots, disinvestment, especially in redlined West Baltimore, continued. Middle- and upper-income African Americans and some of the historic churches they attended scattered, often decamping from Baltimore to segregated Black areas in suburban counties. With deindustrialization, a city once buoyed by the Port of Baltimore, Bethlehem Steel, and manufacturing hemorrhaged more than one hundred thousand factory jobs. The steel mill and a General Motors plant closed, as did others. The port fell from the second- to eleventh-busiest in the nation.[27] Gone were the jobs that enabled Baltimoreans without a college degree to "make good money," as Black folk would say, through work. In the poorest neighborhoods, the drug trade filled the vacuum. Meanwhile, public-policy makers made matters worse.

Housing policies continued to contain descendants in high-poverty neighborhoods. As a federal court found in *Thompson v. US Department of Housing and Urban Development* (HUD), the federal government concentrated public housing almost exclusively in the city of Baltimore, bypassing surrounding counties. As of 2018, Baltimore had the fifth-highest public housing density but was only twenty-sixth in population among US cities. Despite this history of intentionally concentrating Black poverty, Senator Mikulski led the effort to eliminate funding for HUD's Moving to Opportunity program. The demonstration program would have moved fewer than

a thousand Baltimore public housing residents to middle-class lo-
cales across a multicounty region. Mikulski sided with suburban opponents who were misinformed. Working-class whites in an eastern
Maryland suburb that already had its fair share of low-income housing were most vocal, though they weren't even likely to be impacted.[28]

In 1987, Baltimore native Kurt Schmoke became the city's first
elected African American mayor. Like virtually every first Black
mayor in an American city, he inherited ghettos created by white supremacy. By then, Baltimore was a majority-Black city. Across the region, stark patterns of light and dark, affluent and poor, advantaged
and denied, were entrenched.

Schmoke, a Rhodes scholar and graduate of Yale College and
Harvard Law School, gained national attention when he proposed
decriminalization as an alternative to the War on Drugs. The drug
trade and related epidemics of violence, heroin, and AIDS roiled the
city. "How could we improve communities without a war on drugs?"
he asked in a *Baltimore* magazine interview in 2018. "We didn't
seem to be getting anywhere. Law enforcement would make a show
of the drugs and money they seized, but the problem persisted." He
reasoned, based on his years as a drug-warring prosecutor and careful attention to data, that drug prohibition actually increased crime
and violence without reducing addiction. He wanted a conversation
about alternatives but was met with national outrage. The country
would later catch up to his views.[29] During the height of crack and
the drug war, it took courage to resist constructed myths and advocate for evidence-based solutions—like a needle-exchange program
for addicts, which Schmoke convinced the legislature to support.[30]
Though he served as mayor for three terms and had some successes,
segregation and the ravages of deindustrialization remained.

Schmoke and developer James Rouse partnered to try to counter
these forces. Together, they channeled $130 million in public and
private investment into Sandtown-Winchester. The initiative built or
renovated more than a thousand affordable homes and launched education and health services. But new homes and well-intentioned services did not enhance residents' possibilities for finding work, nor did
they attract new jobs or businesses to the area. This one-time infusion
was not able to counter eight decades of intention in quarantining

descendants.[31] Schmoke also couldn't overcome suburban indifference or hostility to the majority-Black city.[32] That polarization would contribute to another betrayal of Baltimore in the 2000s.

THE RED LINE

Maps tell stories. The city of Baltimore's health department produced one for a community health assessment; it appears as Map 1.3 in the insert. In its pointillist digital painting, each resident is rendered as one colored dot. Blacks are purple; whites are peach; Asians are blue; Latinx, a difficult-to-discern aqua; mixed-race people, red; and Indigenous people, unfortunately, invisible. The resulting Butterfly, a dense purple, dominates the landscape and the White L, a peachy mixture, persists at the city's center. Blacks are still a majority, about 63 percent, of the city's population. Asian, Latinx, and mixed-race residents complicate the picture of persistent segregation. Asians are clustered mainly near whites. Latinx and mixed-race people straddle both majority-Black and majority-white neighborhoods. The city's health department acknowledged the historic policies that produced segregation and attendant environmental differences that contribute to pronounced health disparities across neighborhoods.[33] It did not mention disparities in access to transportation, which loom large in Baltimore.

In 1965, planners envisioned six rapid-transit lines radiating from downtown Baltimore to the suburban edges.[34] Two years later, the Baltimore Regional Planning Council suggested a similar plan including an east-west line through Black neighborhoods.[35] Suburbanites opposed these lines; racial fear was the explicit or implied subtext. Anne Arundel County, a very white county south of Baltimore, home to Annapolis, resisted any rail routes. One vocal group in Anne Arundel complained, "The Metro would enable poor, inner-city blacks to travel to the suburbs, steal residents' TVs and then return to their ghettos in Baltimore." Light rail garnered the dog-whistling moniker "Loot Rail."[36]

Because of fierce public opposition, a single subway line was laid, a Metro "system" with only one spoke and no wheel. Opened in 1983, it runs fifteen miles northwest from Baltimore to Owings Mill,

Maryland. A light rail line was eventually laid that followed the north-south route of the original 1965 plan. Opened in 1992, it runs from northern Baltimore County through downtown Baltimore and south to the Baltimore/Washington International Thurgood Marshall Airport. Two affluent white neighborhoods, Ruxton and Riderwood, succeeded in vetoing stops on this line. The light rail route largely served whites in the northern reaches of the city and suburbs who wished to travel south to Baltimore's tourist-centered Inner Harbor and the retro-style Camden Yards baseball stadium, which also opened in 1992. This route traversed the vertical corridor of the White L and didn't even connect with the lone subway line.[37]

In the absence of a comprehensive transit system, people without cars, particularly low-income descendants concentrated in West Baltimore, were forced to depend on a woefully scattered and maddeningly slow bus system operated by the Maryland Transit Administration, known as MTA. Ramelle McCall told a *ProPublica* reporter what he endured to escape the odds of living in Sandtown-Winchester. As a teenager in the 1990s, McCall rose at 5 a.m. for the two-hour commute to an arts magnet high school in the county. Later, he attended a commuter college outside the I-695 beltway; he road bus to rail to bus again, sharing the journey ad nauseam with Black domestics heading to work in suburban castles. They waited for buses that scorned published schedules, passed them by when filled, and, once they did board, crawled along clogged routes. This young Black man must have had supernatural strengths. He became an Episcopal priest and returned to minister to a depopulated, mostly Black church in the city's heart.[38]

More recently, an investigative reporter for WBAL-TV Channel 11 tried to ride MTA buses from West Baltimore to a new Amazon fulfillment center in southeast Baltimore seven miles away. Had she driven a car, the commute would have taken twenty-three minutes. She boarded the number twenty-one MTA bus on West Lafayette Avenue, which borders Sandtown-Winchester, at 5:30 a.m. At 6 a.m., she got on the packed number eight bus, headed downtown. A descendant chuckled when she told him where she was going, "Oh my . . . okay, good luck," he offered. She then boarded the number twenty-six bus and endured fifteen stops before arriving at

Amazon. The trip took ninety-five minutes. Had she been an employee trying to make the 7 a.m. shift, she would have been late, underscoring a brutal statistic. Less than one in three Baltimoreans can get to work in under ninety minutes on public transportation. Meanwhile, according to bus riders, in low-wage, high-turnover service jobs, employers regularly fire employees after three tardy arrivals of more than fifteen minutes. They call it a transit dismissal. In the service and shipping industries clustered near BWI Marshall Airport, bus riders often have to walk the last mile of their commute; employer-provided shuttles can be sporadic. With businesses reluctant to invest in West Baltimore, and burgeoning development in the southeastern part of the region, carless descendants in the west were cut off from opportunity.[39]

Sorely missing was the long-planned east-west transit route to major employment hubs and other rail lines. For decades suburbanites resisted transit as well as open housing. Plans for a comprehensive rail system remained a paper dream. A movement toward New Urbanist walkable living and a route that didn't reach much into the suburbs improved the odds for transit in Baltimore. In 2002, Governor Parris Glendening, an advocate of smart growth, supported new planning for what would be called the Red Line. It is an ironic name for a proposed corridor in which the majority of residents are African Americans living in historically redlined neighborhoods.[40]

The proposed 14-mile line included a 3.4-mile tunnel that would have allowed the public to glide under congested downtown streets where cars crawled at six to twelve miles per hour during peak periods. The planned route ran from suburban Woodlawn just beyond the city's western edge through struggling West Baltimore to downtown, the Inner Harbor, gentrifying Fells Point and Canton, and struggling East Baltimore, ending at the Johns Hopkins Bayview Medical Center. Planned stops included other major employers like the Centers for Medicare and Medicaid Services and the Social Security Administration in Woodlawn and the downtown central business district, where 160,000 employees converged every weekday. Stops were also planned for Edmondson Village, Rosemont, Harlem Park, and other Black neighborhoods that would finally benefit from rather than be degraded by robust infrastructure development.

Planners also proposed stops connecting to Amtrak/MARC train routes and the subway and light rail lines, to create a comprehensive rail system. Baltimore was more than a century overdue for racial healing, and the city was going to be united, at least physically, through transit.

The planning process also began to repair trust and relations between the city and its Black neighborhoods, and between those neighborhoods and predominantly white ones. Federal, state, and city transportation agencies, a host of organizations and citizens worked together for twelve years to plan for, design, and approve the Red Line. The MTA was inclusive as it tried to build community support. Government actors met repeatedly with citizens and stakeholder organizations. Together, they hammered out a written document that summarized state and city commitments to Baltimoreans. The Red Line Community Compact was a blueprint for ensuring Baltimore residents and businesses participated in construction, the Red Line improved the environment, and citizens had a voice in fostering community-centered development. Dozens of individuals, organizations, and state and local government officials signed this compact.[41] West Baltimore communities denuded of commerce were rezoned for mixed uses, anticipating new economic and civic activity around each station. Each proposed station had an advisory committee to help shape their neighborhood's renewal. Edmondson-Westside High School, for example, was going to train local adults and students to enter jobs in construction, maintenance, and transit operations. One elder advocated for new trees to beautify their station.[42] Citizens planted many ideas—the kind of civic roots, if allowed to grow, that social scientists suggest discourages violence in poor neighborhoods.[43]

By 2015, all planning, engineering, environmental- and health-impact assessments, financing, and political compromise related to the Red Line route had been completed. The state of Maryland had spent $288 million on planning and right-of-way acquisitions. The Maryland General Assembly had approved a gas-tax increase to fund the project, and the state had committed $1.235 billion from its Transportation Trust Fund for its share of construction costs. The federal Department of Transportation had approved a "New Starts" grant of $900 million for the Red Line. It was coming to fruition.

Until Larry Hogan, the newly elected Republican governor, canceled the Red Line.

Hogan forfeited the $900-million federal grant and reallocated *all* of the state money earmarked for the first phase of Red Line construction—$736 million—to road projects in exurban and rural areas. In Hogan's imagination, transportation funds were meant for roads and Baltimore's didn't even exist. He released his plan for transportation funding reallocations, entitled the Highways, Bridges, and Roads Initiative, with a map that did not include the state's largest city on it. Like supporters of African colonization for freed slaves in earlier eras, Hogan had willed a fantasy, that the city and its problems could disappear.[44]

Anyone paying attention to Hogan's statements during his 2014 campaign for governor could have predicted this outcome. Hogan, an Anne Arundel County resident and founder of an eponymous commercial real estate business, was an established skeptic of transit rail, which he deemed too expensive, and a believer in highway asphalt. In his first bid for governor, Hogan argued against light rail and strenuously advocated for roads. Rail, no; roads, yes—polar positions that advanced his campaign. Proposed transit projects with large price tags for a majority-Black city (the Red Line) and for affluent Washington suburbs (the Purple Line) provided an easy context for tapping into resentment in outlying areas. Hogan didn't need a racial dog whistle to draw the contrast. In a debate with opponent Black Democrat Anthony Brown, Hogan all but promised to kill the Red and Purple Lines and put state transportation funds into roads.[45]

Once in office, Hogan canceled the Red Line but not the Purple Line, though he did reduce its budget. The light-rail Purple Line, dogged by cost overruns and construction delays, will run, when completed, through Prince George's and Montgomery Counties in the suburbs of Washington, DC, and connect to the Washington Metro subway system.[46] Montgomery County has the highest per-capita income among all counties in the Maryland. Although Hogan did not include the Purple Line on his original list of infrastructure priorities,[47] the then-new Trump administration included the transit system on its list of possible projects to support.[48] When asked about his commitment to the Purple Line after being elected, Hogan evaded: "Yeah, we're going to be talking about that during transition."[49]

In contrast, Hogan called the Red Line "a wasteful boondoggle" and defended rescinding it because he "oppose[d] wasteful and irresponsible spending on poorly conceived projects." The planned 3.4-mile tunnel provoked him the most. He viewed it as a costly indulgence, though running the Red Line under the worst of Baltimore traffic in order to facilitate "rapid" transit was a central feature of a system designed to dramatically reduce commute times.[50]

Hogan's conclusions seemed to be based on political calculation rather considered deliberation. Nonprofit supporters of the Red Line invoked a state statute guaranteeing freedom of information and demanded evidence of the Hogan administration's written reanalysis of the Red Line. The state's vacant response suggests there was no such analysis, much less any consideration of the racial impact of rescinding the Red Line.[51]

Transit activists concluded that Hogan didn't care about the effect on Black people or Baltimore generally. It was "a 'fuck you' to Baltimore," activist Richard Chambers told a reporter.[52] With Black Democrats who opposed Hogan concentrated in Baltimore, there was no political cost and much potential gain in his decision to cancel transit only for Baltimore. Hogan garnered very high vote margins in Baltimore County and the overwhelming majority of rural areas.[53] The fact that the decision to rescind the Red Line came two months after uprisings in Baltimore over the death of Freddie Gray added to transit advocates' suspicions of Hogan's motives.

Gray, a twenty-five-year old African American man, lived in Gilmor Homes, a large though low-rise public housing complex erected in Sandtown-Winchester in 1942. In 2015, the year Gray died, the complex was a ragged, trash-strewn place engulfed in drugs, drug dealing, and prosaic shootings that would try any soul. Within months of Gray's death, Baltimore paid women residents of Gilmor Homes a damage settlement because they had been pressured by city maintenance men to perform sex acts in exchange for repairs on their apartments. The women had to live with rodents, mold, risk of electrocution, and no heat if they refused.[54]

The same year, Baltimore ranked lowest in the nation on Harvard economist Raj Chetty's rankings for social mobility of poor children, especially Black boys. Freddie Gray was one of them, a product of concentrated poverty, lead-exposure, a school system that regularly fails its children, and the social codes of Baltimore's poorest streets. Gray was arrested after running when he locked eyes with a policeman; a switchblade that police found on him provided pretext for taking him into custody, though he didn't wield it at officers.[55] Another urban drama opened.

Descendant citizens videotaped the arrest. Multiple officers tackled Gray's small body, though he had stopped running of his own accord.[56] Something seemed to snap, the young man who had been running could no longer walk. He roared with pain, and the officers had to lift his limp torso, legs swinging like damaged twigs, into the paddy wagon. The officers did not buckle Gray up for safety and this devalued man's spinal cord was nearly severed during the ride.[57] He died seven days later, the impetus for an uprising, though Baltimore officialdom enhanced conditions for it by canceling buses and the subway at Mondawmin Mall just as high school students were departing school, leaving thousands of stranded and frustrated youth on the streets.[58] No one died in the uprising, though 380 properties were damaged and global press made much of a burned CVS drugstore. The city incurred approximately $20 million in costs for police, firefighter, and other assistance and damage to public property.[59]

Baltimore mayor Stephanie Rawlings-Blake and city council president Bernard "Jack" Young both castigated "thugs" for vandalism and looting, as did President Obama, who denounced "the handful of criminals and thugs who tore up the place," "destroying and undermining opportunities and businesses in their own communities."[60] All three leaders were Black. After being criticized for using the word, Rawlings-Blake and Young retreated.[61] Obama spokesman Josh Earnest affirmed that the president did not regret his choice of words.[62] Governor Hogan also called protestors "thugs" after meeting with President Obama to discuss the crisis: "He [Obama] supports our actions 100 percent. We talked about the fact that . . . we need to get to the answers and resolve this situation, the concern that everybody has about what exactly happened in the Freddie Gray incident. [But] lawless gangs of thugs roaming the streets, causing damage to property and injuring innocent people, . . . we're not gonna tolerate that."[63] Freddie Gray, too, was cast as a thug by some on social media, as if he deserved to die because he had a criminal record that included drug offenses.[64] Stereotypes filled the vacuum created by historical amnesia and squelched possibilities for nuanced public understanding, for building public support for repair of the conditions that led to revolt.

Governor Hogan visited Baltimore neighborhoods after the uprising, though he complained about what the state had had to spend in response and all but used the extra cost to further justify canceling the Red Line.[65] In a news conference, he claimed, "There's no place in the state where we invest more money than Baltimore City . . . Last week I just announced $7.3 million extra funding for the city. We just spent $14 million extra money on the riots in Baltimore City a few weeks ago."[66] Black activists and signatories to the Red Line Community Compact interpreted his actions as punitive. They filed a civil rights complaint with the US Department of Transportation. Among their many arguments, they had this to say about Hogan's motivations:

> The Governor's decision to cancel the Red Line was issued just 60 days after what became known locally as the "uprising," when Baltimore was still reeling, appeared to many as a gesture of contempt. At the moment when our city most needed courageous leadership and strategic support, what it got instead from the state's highest authority was a kick in the teeth. The perception among many African Americans in Baltimore is that the Governor values incarceration of black people over their education, and prioritizes highways for white rural and suburban people over investing in access to opportunity for the black and brown people of Baltimore city.[67]

Hogan earned this perception with Black Baltimoreans through words and deeds. Upon taking office, he declared that Baltimore was "declining rather than improving" and cut $36 million from its schools budget but approved $30 million to build a youth jail in the city.[68] Baltimore public school children froze in winter, heating crises borne of decades of underinvestment in the oldest school buildings in the state and a $3-billion backlog of needed capital improvements.[69] Hogan also eliminated or lowered tolls on suburban highways and bridges even as Baltimoreans endured fare increases on buses, rail, and commuter lines.[70] He supported expensive road projects of dubious necessity in sparsely populated rural areas while not scheduling road projects for Baltimore.[71] Worse, an investigative reporter found that Hogan advanced major transportation and road projects that potentially raised property values for nearby properties owned by *his* commercial real estate business.[72]

The NAACP Legal Defense and Education Fund (LDF) and other civil rights organizations also filed a complaint with the US Department of Transportation, on behalf of Earl Andrews, a Baltimore resident who depended on public transit, and BRIDGE, an interfaith coalition for equity. Like W. Ashbie Hawkins a century before, LDF took up the unequal conditions that Black Americans faced in transportation. Modern civil rights lawyers have a potentially powerful tool. Title VI of the Civil Rights Act of 1964 prohibits discrimination on the basis of race, color, or national origin in any program or activity receiving federal financial assistance. Prohibited racial discrimination may be intentional or the result of facially neutral practices that have a "disparate impact" on a racial group. LDF offered statistical and qualitative evidence of disparity created by rescinding the Red Line and reallocating funds.[73]

Less than 2 percent of jobs in Baltimore were in the Black neighborhoods with planned Red Line stops. Nearly all residents of distressed places would have to travel elsewhere to get to work, whether in the city or the suburbs. Yet in some of these neighborhoods the majority of residents had no vehicle, as did the carless 44 percent of residents along the planned corridor. They had to ride the bus, and their commutes were withering. About one-fifth to one-quarter of residents at proposed stops were unemployed, compared to a city unemployment average of 14 percent.[74] The distressed hoods of East and West Baltimore along the proposed corridor, on average, were

80 percent Black, 30 percent poor, and 65 percent female-headed.[75] Single Black mothers with no car, and children that needed to get to and fro, desperately needed reliable public transit.

While the majority of the population along the Red Line route was African American, of the five most expensive road projects that received reallocated funds under Hogan's transportation plan, only about 14 percent of the population of adjoining census tracts were Black. In addition to losing the opportunity for nearly halving commute times, Black Baltimoreans lost a grasp at one of more than ten thousand new jobs projected and the potential upsides of transit-oriented development at each station.[76] A transportation economist found that *whites received a 228 percent net increase in benefits from the reallocation while African Americans lost benefits, at −124 percent.*[77]

The harm to poor Black communities in Baltimore was even more pronounced. Lost was the opportunity for a new start, a reversal of chronic disinvestment. In particular, the Red Line offered a chance to ameliorate the harms of the Road to Nowhere, on which the Red Line would overlie, offering descendants a ride to opportunity rather than a neighborhood-destroying express route for others.[78] Lost, too, was the chance to reduce air pollution for the city with the state's poorest air quality and highest rates of pediatric asthma.[79]

Despite ample evidence and arguments presented in the two civil rights complaints, the Trump administration closed the case without making a finding. In lieu of an investigation of the joined complaints, it said it would conduct a comprehensive review of Maryland's transportation programs, for compliance with Title VI.[80]

The Georgetown Law Civil Rights Clinic filed freedom of information statutory requests to find out what happened with the promised comprehensive review. The Maryland Department of Transportation (MDOT) disclosed a trove of documents and emails while the Trump administration delayed, blaming the COVID-19 pandemic. Most telling were email communications between US and Maryland officials in 2018. Federal transportation officials did open a "corrective action" and informed MDOT that it would conduct a comprehensive Title VI analysis of its transportation spending. They rejected MDOT's initial response, saying it had "simply provided a conclusion that disparate impacts did not exist." MDOT tried again; in a subsequent email, it claimed no disparate impact violation because "large amounts of both State and federal funded investments in transit and other transportation modes closely correlated with the Census tracts with higher minority population." In its answer, MDOT did not quantify what these "large amounts" were, for what projects, or which minority communities allegedly benefited, nor did it analyze whether the alleged "large amounts" made up the difference from the cancellation of the Red Line. Despite these deficiencies, the Trump administration accepted MDOT's answer at face value and closed the corrective action without any explanation of its reasoning.[81]

In other words, the Trump and Hogan administrations never gave a considered response to the Title VI petitioners' core claim: In canceling the Red Line and reallocating its funds to other projects, Hogan and Maryland favored white areas to the detriment of Black citizens. The citizens who toiled for more than a decade planning the Red Line, building trust and a multiracial coalition for renewal, deserved a published response that a federal court might review to determine if the agency's logic was arbitrary or evaded the demands of Title VI. There was no opportunity for *any* public accountability.

Closing the case without findings was also insulting, a message that the civil rights claims of Black Americans don't warrant a response. In the words of Samuel Jordan, a signatory to the Community Compact and the attendant complaint filed with the US Department of Transportation (DOT), canceling the Red Line amounted to an "aggressive assertion of the status quo" and "the status quo for Black people is always punitive." Jordan is president of the Baltimore Transit Equity Coalition, formed after Hogan's cancellation to advocate reinstating the Red Line. They continue to fight for the people of the city who suffer "transit detention," said Jordan.[82]

Two years after rescinding the Red Line, Hogan offered Baltimore a consolation, $135 million for BaltimoreLink, an ostensibly revamped bus system that was hardly a substitute for a $2.9 billion rail system. Hogan claimed the new bus system would be "transformative," but angry riders complained that commutes worsened as bus lines were eliminated.[83] For some, a one-bus commute became a two- or three-bus commute. Earl Andrews, whom LDF represented in his complaint filed with DOT, did not own a car. In his sixties, the African American resident of East Baltimore road buses to church, his job as an accountant at a luxury hotel, and evening seminary classes for a master's in theology. He told a *Washington Post* reporter that he had to transfer buses after BaltimoreLink began, adding ten minutes to his already lengthy work commute. A Saturday shopping trip to Arundel Mills Mall took him four hours because the BaltimoreLink bus never came.[84]

Carless residents of Black neighborhoods weren't the only ones complaining. Among the animated online comments to the *Post* article were these:

Richard Gilpin
7/17/2017 10:41 AM EDT

BaltimoreLink has reduced residents' links to jobs and the region's subway, light-rail and MARC commuter rail lines. One out every three bus routes have been deleted in some areas. For example, with the deletion of bus route 31, there is no direct Inner Harbor bus service from Boston Street and Fleet Street. Truly a disaster—now many of us have returned to driving downtown.

trejean
7/16/2017 10:57 AM ED

. . . communities across the US are investing in rapid transit because people are now demanding it. Cities like Denver, Houston, and others are using rapid transit improvements like Light Rail and Bus Rapid Transit (BRT) to draw people into their cities. . . .

The bus lines on the busiest lines in Baltimore are very overcrowded. Even with the new Service, it's standing room only. Sometimes the buses are so crowded they can't pick up new passengers. If your routes are this popular and you have done all tweaks possible to improve regular bus service, it only makes sense for one to looks at a more robust system to serve passengers.

But there were also comments in this vein:

suburb lifer
7/17/2017 1:56 PM EDT

Go away. No one wants any transportation system or station near the suburbs, look at all the crime data, then in a flash your neighborhood becomes the city . . .

Several commenters also seized on statements in the article from Earl Andrews, who appeared in a picture, riding transit in a khaki business suit, as coiffed and sartorially splendid as George W. F. Mc-Mechen had been in 1910. Andrews, who rides transit by choice, noted that the Red Line would have improved the lives of "disenfranchised people" in the neighborhoods where the 2015 uprising had occurred and that it was "not a good feeling" to see the Purple Line go forward "while our hopes are dashed here." Negative commenters cast Andrews's reserved statement of frustration as a Black man asking for a handout for himself and all of Black Baltimore. Andrews also had pro-transit allies and defenders among the commenters, some of whom named the racism they saw in disparate treatment for Baltimore.[85]

Earl Andrews

It was a familiar clash of worldviews, between the dexterous and nondexterous, between people willing to rub shoulders with a rainbow of humanity on buses or rail and those trapped by myths and fear. Among the myths that opponents circulated about the Red Line was Baltimore taking from taxpayers elsewhere in the state. The purveyors of this narrative were oblivious or indifferent to a long history of state and federal government investing in roads and infrastructure in racially exclusive suburbs, along with mortgage tax deductions and FHA-backed loans not available to Blacks. This state-sanctioned order, borne of supremacy, has not been dismantled and the resulting segregation pits heavily white, Republican-leaning areas against multiracial, Democrat-leaning areas in a zero-sum competition for scarce public resources. Predominantly Black, Latinx, and poor areas fare worst in this competition.

Maryland spent $2.4 billion (not including ongoing bond interest payments) to build a nineteen-mile outer beltway that connects Washington, DC, suburbs, the same ones that will receive a Purple Line. This "Intercounty Connector" is lightly used, and because its toll revenues are far lower than projected, the rest of the state subsidizes it and other costly road projects it struggles to afford, with an increased gas tax.[86] And Governor Hogan, for all his complaints about the cost of the Red Line, supported a $9 billion proposal to relieve traffic congestion on highways by adding more lanes, including express toll lanes that affluent people would be more likely to use. The planned relief was car centric, and tolls would not begin to cover the costs. Completely absent from this vision was investment in rapid rail or buses to reduce traffic by enabling individuals to get out of cars, much less offering transportation relief to carless Marylanders.[87]

This architecture of redistribution, overinvesting in predominantly white space and disinvesting in predominantly Black, poor space, also occurs within the city of Baltimore. The spared, intact neighborhoods of Fells Point and Canton became points of downtown revival and upscale development that woos urban professionals. This development or gentrification was stimulated and subsidized by public investment and tax breaks for private developers *because* of proximity to high-poverty neighborhoods. In other words, an Enterprise Zone, a tax-incentive program designed to stimulate investment in places that private markets would otherwise bypass, was deployed primarily in majority-white areas rather than the poor Black areas that have been on the receiving end of state plunder. Baltimore-based public health researcher Lawrence Brown and legal scholar Audrey McFarlane underscored the dichotomy in their scholarship. The White L, saturated with Enterprise Zones, received hundreds of millions in tax increment financing, a free Charm City Circulator shuttle, new loft apartments, courteous policing, well-resourced public schools, and amenities that delight. The Black Butterfly received more than its fair share of public and subsidized housing, school closures, aggressive policing, and punishment.[88] Plainclothes officers preyed on residents in the hood, conducting "jump outs," ostensibly looking for guns. Anyone could be targeted, but these officers did not answer citizen calls, an approach to policing that is not effective and damages rather than protects the community.[89]

It did not matter that five of the last six mayors were Black, that Blacks were a majority on the city council, or that the police chief and chief prosecutor were Black. Segregation perpetuates disparities. Black city leaders never dismantled segregation and would have been stymied if they tried because it would have required sacrifice from majority-white areas that were low-poverty *because* Black poverty had been concentrated elsewhere. Across the nation, Black leaders who inherited ghettos largely followed the same punitive policies as other places in response to drugs and crime—harsh policing and sentencing.[90] Mass incarceration was the result, and neighborhoods like Sandtown-Winchester arguably were harmed rather than improved by this policy. Sandtown-Winchester/Harlem Park is the highest incarceration community in the city; 3 percent of residents of this area are in prison.[91] Taxpayers, too, are harmed. Prisons and jails in Baltimore cost almost $300 million a year—annual incarceration of residents of Sandtown-Winchester/Poplar Hill cost $17 million annually.[92]

Black neighborhoods continued to draw economic predators. In the 2000s, while the White L got traditional banking and mortgages, residents of the Black Butterfly were targeted for subprime loans with exploding interest rates and exorbitant prepayment penalties. Black middle-class neighborhoods were devastated by the wave of foreclosures, and descendants who lost their homes were forced to move into apartments in high-poverty areas.[93]

Racial segregation produced other systemic inequalities that are only beginning to be revealed as Black leaders, like former city councilmember and current mayor Brandon Scott, and the public forced city agencies to undergo a racial equity analysis. The city planning department found that of $670 million in recently budgeted capital projects, white neighborhoods were slated to receive almost twice as much as Black areas of the city.[94] Another analysis found Baltimore neighborhoods that are less than half Black receive nearly four times the investment than neighborhoods that are overwhelmingly Black.[95]

Lately, a $5.5 billion public-private waterfront development on a south Baltimore peninsula known as Port Covington is emerging. The project was conceived by Under Armour founder and billionaire Kevin Plank and initiated by his real estate company. The formerly industrial 235-acre area will be transformed over two decades into an innovation hub of cybersecurity and biotech firms, gleaming new residences for their workers, and retail and other amenities to serve them. Governor Hogan's administration designated the project as an Opportunity Zone, marking it as a federal tax shelter for investors. The riches of Port Covington will be well-insulated from the rest of Baltimore by an I-95 border and otherwise surrounded by water. Its developers received $660 million in tax increment financing, far exceeding support given by the fiscally challenged city to other projects, and only a portion of the $1.1 billion of public financing the Port Covington developers intend to secure. In return, the city received promises that 20 percent of the fourteen thousand housing units to be built would be affordable, though it is unclear and doubtful that the people of the Butterfly will benefit much from this new Emerald City.

This is America and the new American caste. It is not based solely on race or on class. Geography—physical segregation—is the key mechanism for the redistribution of resources from taxpayers toward affluent majority-white areas and away from poor ones. The vicious cycle continues in metropolitan Baltimore and everywhere that ghettos were constructed. Perhaps Baltimore suffers more from hoary, race-tinged division because it had more Black people in 1860, 1910, and 1960 than other places, and government invested mightily in segregation to contain them. And yet the noose that still strangles West Baltimore also constrains the entire region.

Education, a ladder of social mobility, remains separate and unequal in Baltimore and elsewhere in America. In 2020, Governor Hogan vetoed a bill known as the Blueprint for Maryland's Future that would have been a down payment on recommendations from the public Kirwan Commission to transform Maryland public education from mediocre to world-class. According to Maryland's Department of Legislative Services, Baltimore City Public Schools are underfunded by $342 million annually, causing its children to endure among the highest student-to-teacher ratios in the state. All told, the Kirwan Commission's proposals, after a ten-year phase-in, were estimated to cost $4 billion annually. Hogan condemned the Kirwan proposals, dubiously claiming the plan would demand $6,000 in taxes from every Maryland family. Then the COVID-19 pandemic gave him a blunt fiscal defense for his veto. In February 2021, Maryland Democratic lawmakers overrode Hogan's veto and approved a digital-advertising tax to begin funding the Kirwan plan.

COVID-19 killed Black people proportionate to their numbers in majority-Black Baltimore. Gun homicides also spiked with the pandemic. Headlines about violence, whether a prosaic shooting or a public-school child attacking a teacher, continue in Baltimore. A people disempowered will find ways to rebel and get attention. More of the same, quarantine and punish, results in more of the same. Why should we be surprised when disinvestment and containment produce such outcomes? No other neighborhoods in Baltimore were subjected to the cumulative, blunt-force trauma of decades of racist and flawed public and private action. In a city plagued by segregation and its effects, a chance for a reboot, for a new Red Line that might help heal and unify rather than punish and isolate, was not taken.

CHAPTER 2

WHITE SUPREMACY BEGAT "THE GHETTO"

M y great-great-grandmother, Lucinda Bowdre, was a woman of African and possibly other heritage. Born in Augusta, Georgia, in 1819, she may or may not have been enslaved. She became a seamstress and mother to seven children fathered by an Irish American dry goods merchant and slaveowner named John Cashin. In Augusta, apparently, they were a family, though perhaps a clandestine one.

By 1860, Lucinda was living as a widow on Clifton Street in Philadelphia with a gaggle of children named Cashin. The census taker listed her as head of household and identified the entire family as Black, free inhabitants. They were part of a steady stream of Black Americans who came to the Quaker City, often via the Underground Railroad. In the mid- and late-nineteenth century, Philadelphia had the largest population of Blacks of any northern city. It was the nation's center of Black intellectual and institutional life.

Lucinda and her oldest daughter, Virginia, worked as seamstresses out of the home, as was the practice of many Black women in the city. Virginia's husband, William Dorsey, a scion of a prominent Black family, worked as a waiter in his family's catering business. The Dorseys were at the very top of a guild of Black caterers who evolved from house servants, butlers, and cooks to masters of the culinary arts. For a while, white elites were content to hire them. Together, Lucinda, Virginia, and William provided for a house full of minors. The neighborhoods below South Street, which had been populated by waves of Irish immigrants a generation before, were becoming the province of many Blacks, fugitive slave and free, who were pouring into the city in search of opportunity. Industrial jobs were reserved mainly for European immigrants. Blacks struggled to make their way, often undertaking the most menial labor.[1]

Living on Clifton Street, just below South Street, placed Lucinda and family near the Black community's institutional heart. Two of her children attended the Institute for Colored Youth, a Quaker school that provided a free classical education for talented Negro children. My great-grandfather, Herschel V. Cashin, was one them, and this exposure began a family tradition of academic striving and political agitation that would reverberate for generations.[2]

The institute, which ultimately became Cheyney University of Pennsylvania, was a source of community pride—the only school in the city led by Black administrators and faculty. Its annual oral examinations in Latin, Greek, and mathematics were open to the public, as was the school's library. It offered a series of public lectures by "colored" greats, including Frederick Douglass. A stone's throw from the institute was Mother Bethel, the first Black church in the city, founded in 1794, and the progenitor of the nation's first Black denomination, African Methodist Episcopal. The *Christian Recorder* newspaper, an abolitionist organ of the AME church, was published blocks away.

During young Herschel's years at the institute, the head of the boys' department was Octavius Valentine Catto, a man of outsized talents and ambitions for his people. He was the main force behind the eleven colored Union regiments that were raised, trained, and sent from the region to fight in the Civil War. He was a leader in the Equal Rights League. Like its civil rights successors in the South a century later, the league protested segregation of Philadelphia's streetcars and advocated for Black voting rights. Catto and other league militants orchestrated a nonviolent campaign in which men and women blocked streetcars with their bodies and filled them with Christian ministers, sick children, pregnant women, and wounded war veterans. When police and conductors ejected these sympathetic riders from the cars, the ensuing publicity converted many. It took a successful court battle in 1867 to clinch victory. Voting equality for men was supposed to come with ratification of the Fifteenth Amendment to the Constitution. On the first day of the first Philadelphia city election in which Black men exercised their new voting rights, Irish immigrant gangs rioted against Black voters to prevent radical Republicans from taking over city government. A Democratic Party operative shot Octavius Catto in the back and killed him.[3]

Lucinda died in 1865, and Virginia and William continued to reside at Clifton Street for a year before moving to Locust Street, nearer the extended Dorsey family and catering business. Virginia and William cared for the younger Cashins and raised six Dorsey children of their own. When their thirty-year marriage collapsed in 1890, Virginia moved into her own abode. She continued to work as a dressmaker, claiming to be a widow for the remainder of her days.[4]

In 1896, a young W. E. B. Du Bois set out to document the people and institutions in Philadelphia's Seventh Ward, the institutional heart where many descendants had landed. In *The Philadelphia Negro,* Du Bois noted about forty thousand Blacks were scattered throughout Philadelphia, although they were often relegated to the worst dwellings by reason of "race prejudice." The one-quarter of Philadelphia Negroes who lived in the Seventh Ward also resided near whites, although usually in clusters.[5]

This was a common pattern of Negro settlement in northern cities in the 1890s. Blacks tended to live among whites, though they might be segregated at the block level. Ghettoization, the extreme concentration of nearly all Negroes into designated quarters, had not yet begun.[6]

The Philadelphia Negro was the first comprehensive sociological examination of a Black community in America. Throughout the twentieth century, other African American social scientists built stellar reputations by carefully documenting conditions in Black ghettos, inspired perhaps by Du Bois's example. Du Bois used the word "slums" to name the pockets of Black poverty he observed in the Seventh Ward. He was unflinching in describing "vicious" criminals, "gamblers," "prostitutes," and "thieves" living among the honest, penniless Blacks who landed on the worst, deteriorated blocks. Yet

Du Bois sensitively analyzed the environmental conditions that encouraged crime. He took pains to distinguish the small numbers of Blacks that constituted the semipermanent criminal class from the poor Black laborers that formed the "great mass" of the Negro population in the ward.

According to Du Bois, most Black laborers were good-humored churchgoers. As descendants of slavery, they had limited skills. They were locked out of industrial jobs by racist trade unions and were charged higher rents than whites for the worst accommodations. Du Bois concluded it was the conditions thrust on the Negro, not Negroes themselves, that were the main cause of social problems. Du Bois lamented that even the most educated and qualified Negroes were denied jobs on the grounds of color—a caste system that a fortunate few Blacks evaded when an individual white employer decided to be fair. As Du Bois presciently predicted in his classic 1903 essay collection *The Souls of Black Folk,* the problem of the twentieth century would be "the problem of the color line," although he did not anticipate its looming geographic dimensions.[7]

When Du Bois wrote *The Souls,* the vast majority of American Negroes lived in the South under the stifling institutions and social controls that replaced slavery—Jim Crow, peonage, sharecropping on the masters' terms, and violence. It was a world where every white male child could demand to be called Mister and every Negro man was a boy, where false accusations of rape sparked lynching pageants and actual rape of Black women could be excused or ignored.[8] Between 1900 and 1930, about 1.6 million Blacks moved; this exodus would be called the First Great Migration.

The great migrants were descendants of slavery. As they left the South to escape oppression and find opportunity, whites in the rest of the country resorted to violence and began a multidecade process of constructing Black ghettos. The ghetto, originated as a place for housing Jews in sixteenth-century Venice, was a phenomenon brutally replicated by Nazis in German-occupied Europe. In the United States, the ghetto became "a space for the intrusive social control of poor blacks."[9]

World War I accelerated migration as labor shortages fueled African American dreams. Everywhere migrants went, they met white

resistance, though some places were more violent than others. Cleveland, Ohio, allowed African Americans to live in relative peace and
some integration between 1870 and 1900. Once a bastion of abolitionism and a major stop on the Underground Railroad, Cleveland
enjoyed a reputation for positive race relations, particularly between
its small population of middle-class Blacks and the white neighbors
they typically lived among.

The life of a prominent Black Clevelander testifies to the "strange
career" of American color lines.[10] George A. Myers, born in Baltimore
to free Black parents, migrated in 1879 to Cleveland, where he found
work as a barber at one of the city's leading hotels. Black Americans
dominated the barber trade, and Myers rose on skill and close friend-
ships he formed with upscale clients like Mark Hanna, who later became a US senator. Another client was Liberty E. Holden, publisher
of the *Cleveland Plain Dealer*. When Holden decided to open a new
hotel, Hollenden House, he loaned Myers the bulk of what he needed
to open his own barbershop on the premises.

Hollenden Barber Shop and the hotel that housed it became legendary luxury establishments. The barbershop, which famously had
a telephone installed at every barber chair, was a mecca for politicians, industrialists, and celebrities, including Mark Twain. Myers
personally coiffed eight presidents, from Hayes to Harding. By 1920,
he had more than thirty employees, including barbers, hairdressers,
manicurists, and pedicurists. The staff was Negro, the clientele apparently only white, and Myers, who participated in both all-Negro
and predominantly white civic institutions in Cleveland, did not
seem to have any misgivings about de facto racial exclusion in the
barber trade as he and his employees prospered from its exclusivity.[11]

Myers became an activist in Republican politics, serving as a lieu-
tenant to Mark Hanna, who in turn was at the right hand of Ohioan
and future US president William McKinley. Hanna tapped Myers to organize southern Black Republicans to support McKinley, and Myers
became the premier Black Republican in the state, attending three national conventions as a delegate. In Myers's archives, I found correspon-
dence between him and my great-grandfather, Herschel V. Cashin, who
had moved to Alabama and became a Reconstruction legislator, lawyer,
Republican activist, and national convention regular. Herschel wrote

The famed Hollenden Barber Shop

*George A. Myers,
proprietor*

fondly of their "acquaintance begun when we were both advocates of the matchless McKinley . . . whom we were happy to crown at St. Louis in 1896." Both men believed in American democracy and the Negro's rightful place in it but endured the bitter reversals of segregation and resurgent white supremacy.

In Cleveland, white attitudes began to change in the 1910s as Black migrants became a multitude. Myers wrote about the influx in a letter to his close friend James Ford Rhodes, a white American historian and retired industrialist. He informed Rhodes that Cleveland's small Black minority had tripled and that many of the migrants "are of the lowest and most shiftless class." Myers's conservatism and classism showed, but still, he decried: "Where Cleveland was once free of race prejudice, it is now anything but that . . ." He would grow militant in his politics and advocacy for colored folk as segregation spread.[12]

By 1916, whites had perfected methods of exclusion. Another prominent Black Clevelander complained that in some sought-after neighborhoods, realtors would not sell or rent to Negroes "no matter how much money we have to pay for the desired property." A growing reluctance of white property owners outside the Central Avenue district to sell to Negroes became unofficial policy as restrictive covenants were increasingly inserted into property deeds.[13]

The great migrants were not the only immigrants to Cleveland. Peach- and olive-skinned Europeans also found their way to this American industrial powerhouse. One historian attributed racist resistance to Negro neighbors by Poles, Hungarians, Italians, and other white ethnic groups in Cleveland to "status anxieties." They spurned proximity to Blacks because American society had designated this group as inferior and they feared perhaps they would get caught in the Negro's undertow. Such attitudes, whatever their origin, helped to create ghettos.[14]

Because of this racism, most Black newcomers to Cleveland were forced to live in circumscribed areas. Jane Edna Hunter, a nurse, said she endured "the despairing search for decent lodgings—up one dingy street and down another, ending with the acceptance of the least disreputable room we encountered." The sections designated for Blacks in Cleveland were adjacent to vice districts that enticed a racially diverse array of sinners with money to spend. The editor of a Negro weekly, the Cleveland *Gazette,* bemoaned the "speakeasies, gambling and questionable houses" proliferating in a decaying section of Hamilton Avenue. According to Hunter, brothels there engaged in "wholesale organized traffic in black flesh." This pattern of locating vice districts near Negroes, or the other way around, was repeated in many, if not most, northern cities with neighborhoods that catered to the lustful. The association of Black neighborhoods and Black people with loose morals and vice became a self-fulfilling prophecy in the minds of many whites.[15]

George Myers was able to purchase a home in the predominantly Jewish Glenville neighborhood. However, he wrote with despair to Booker T. Washington about emerging separation in the city. Washington was the dominant Black voice in the country at the time, having called on Negroes to cast down their buckets in the commercial world, use their hands to work, and accept exclusion from politics and social equality in his famous Atlanta Compromise speech. Myers disagreed with his friend. In his letter to Washington, he declared,

"Segregation here of any kind to me is a step backward and will ultimately be a blow to our Mixed Public Schools." In ensuing years, Myers would use his influence to protect Negroes in their use of a public swimming pool and the same City Hospital that whites used. He and allies also successfully campaigned for hospital privileges for colored medical interns and nurses.[16]

Yet physical segregation took root in Cleveland, and the footprint of Blackness slowly expanded. Langston Hughes, who resided in Cleveland in this period, wrote in his autobiography that "the Negro district was extremely crowded" and that during his high school years he lived "either in attic or basement, and paid quite a lot for such inconvenient quarters." "As always," he continued, "the white neighborhoods resented Negroes moving closer and closer—but when the whites did give way, they gave way at very profitable rentals."[17] When restrictive covenants failed, or a white owner decided to sell to a Negro, some whites turned to thuggery to protect themselves from a feared invasion. In 1917 and 1919, white mobs attacked the homes of Negroes who migrated.[18]

Cleveland suburbanites were even more vicious in their response to a rare Negro migrant. When Arthur Hill purchased a home for his family in Garfield Heights in 1924, a mob of two hundred whites surrounded the home and demanded that they vacate within ten days. Hill asked the mayor for police protection. The mayor refused, citing costs, and declared that "colored people had no right to purchase such a nice home." The Hills abandoned their house after enduring months of threats by white mobs. When E. A. Bailey, a Black physician, moved to an even more exclusive Cleveland suburb, Shaker Heights, whites threw stones, fired shots into his house, and set flame to his garage. Dr. Charles Garvin, one of Negro Cleveland's most prominent citizens, built a home near the border of Cleveland Heights in 1925, prompting whites to circulate a pointed handbill:

> Certain niggers have recently blackmailed certain residents of . . .
> Cleveland Heights . . . They are now trying to erect a house at 11114
> Wade Park Avenue to blackmail us. But they will not. The residents
> of the Neighborhood will not give one cent to those blackmailers.

Appoint your committees to oppose and eradicate this group of black gold diggers. Let them know we can duplicate [the] riots [that took place] in Tulsa, St. Louis, Chicago, and Baltimore.[19]

Such anti-Black violence and hatred were common throughout the country, as were race riots. And it didn't matter whether Negroes were upright or uncouth. Blackness itself was a provocation, especially when a Negro achieved something. The Tulsa pogrom of 1921 was ignited by a claim that a Black shoeshine, Dick Rowland, assaulted a white female elevator operator. In the nonhysterical account, he accidentally stepped on her foot as he entered the elevator and she screamed.[20] She did not press charges, but the clarion call of rape brought a mob of whites to the county jail that held Rowland. Some armed Black men arrived to protect Rowland, a shot was fired, and the mob and complicit state actors proceeded to burn, loot, and bomb from the air a thriving Black community.

Blacks had moved to Oklahoma Territory before it became a state. Their hope and prayer had been to be left alone to build something for themselves, apart from the strictures of supremacy. They tried to use the railroad tracks that separated the white and Negro sides of Tulsa as a barrier of protection. In Greenwood, they erected schools, a library, and a hospital, in addition to many businesses. Unlike the fictional people of Wakanda, they could not hermetically seal themselves from dangerous invaders.

The Greenwood business district, aka Negro Wall Street, was then America's most prosperous concentration of Black entrepreneurs, home to nearly six hundred Black-owned businesses, including grocery stores, hotels, restaurants, law offices, pharmacies, and movie theaters. Over eighteen hours, crazed individuals and state actors destroyed more than one thousand homes and businesses and killed hundreds of Blacks. The local white paper called Greenwood "Niggertown" and condoned its destruction.[21] Reportedly, the first bombs ever dropped on American soil fell on Greenwood, in one of the nation's worst domestic terror attacks.[22] Eyewitnesses reported that "the scope of the attack was equal to warfare: homeowners shot dead in their front yards, planes dropping turpentine bombs onto buildings, a machine gun firing bullets on a neighborhood church."[23]

The *New York Times* quoted Adjutant General Charles F. Barnett, who commanded the Oklahoma National Guard brought to the city to quell the violence: "Twenty-five thousand whites, armed to the teeth, were ranging the city in utter and ruthless defiance of every concept of law and righteousness. [Motor cars swept through,] their occupants firing at will."[24]

White supremacy was resurging. In 1915, D. W. Griffith's infamous film, *The Birth of a Nation*, was America's first box-office blockbuster. The three-hour movie dramatized the founding of the Klan after the Civil War, depicted Reconstruction legislators as buffoons, and showed a white woman leaping to her death to flee a Black man played by a white actor in blackface. It also showed the Klan lynching that character. President Woodrow Wilson watched the movie at a White House screening. Wilson, a Virginian, had sanctioned the introduction of segregation in federal agencies, a serious retrenchment in opportunities and dignity for Negro federal workers.[25]

In Ohio, George Myers launched a letter campaign against screening the movie, without much success. Nationally, the NAACP protested

Greenwood burning, Tulsa Riot, June 1921

the film and whites flocked to see it. In several cities, some viewers left movie theaters and attacked Blacks. The film inspired others to reconstitute the Klan the same year. At least one-third of new Klan members lived in cities throughout the country.[26] The Fox Film Corporation competed for white audiences with a popular film called *The Nigger*. According to the Black-owned Cleveland *Advocate* newspaper, the film depicted "huge mob scenes and race riots," "the crack of the white man's whip and the scream of blacks."[27] Race riots broke out in three dozen cities during what would be called the Red Summer of 1919. Some whites were incited by false claims of Black men assaulting white women. But the real tinder seemed to be white World War I veterans who disembarked in America, alongside Black veterans, and could not accept the suggestion of racial equality or integration. The collective death toll of the riots was in the hundreds.[28]

The process of ghettoization, of defining Black space and attributing declining conditions caused by such containment to the allegedly innate character of Negro people, did not improve race relations which, by design, were quite broken in the 1920s. As described, this self-fulfilling process had begun in Cleveland. Myers blamed property owners who refused to rent or sell decent housing to Negroes for the squalid housing conditions in Cleveland's Black neighborhoods. In a letter to Judge George S. Adams, he wrote, "While I do not condone crime, (all criminals look alike to me), the negro, morally and otherwise, is what the white man has made him, through the denial of justice, imposition and an equal chance."[29]

Myers could not protect his employees from racism. Hollenden House management informed him that, when he retired, they would be replaced with white people. Myers delayed retiring for as long as his weakening heart would allow. He died on January 17, 1930, the very day he planned to tell his staff that he had sold the barbershop to Hollenden management and that they would be let go. At lunchtime, he sought to purchase a ticket for a vacation. Before he could return to the shop to give his employees notice, he collapsed, as his heart failed.[30]

. . .

Ghettoizing proceeded at varying paces throughout the North. As Charles Hamilton Houston and Thurgood Marshall were chipping away at the southern regime of Jim Crow through court litigation, whites elsewhere were institutionalizing the Black ghetto as much as possible or, in the case of sundown towns, excluding Blacks from living in or being present in their localities after sunset. Ghettos were erected much faster and with extreme precision in cities like Chicago and New York, likely because of the sheer numbers of Negroes there that whites felt compelled to avoid. In Cleveland and western cities like Omaha, Minneapolis, and Los Angeles, and in most southern cities, the process was slower. But ghettos, orchestrated with great intention, became the predominant response to Black people, wherever they existed in large numbers.[31]

The ideology of supremacy animated not only ghettoization but also eugenics laws authorizing state-enforced sterilization of undesired populations, and a 1924 federal law that banned or severely restricted immigration for all nationalities except people from northern Europe. Discriminatory immigration, sterilization, and segregation policies would continue for much of the twentieth century. White supremacy was embedded in American culture, and politicians easily tapped it for their own purposes.[32] Unlike European ethnic migrants, who whitened and ultimately were incorporated as equal citizens, the great migrants would be treated quite differently. Their ghettos were more extreme, enduring, and damaging to American race relations. Many African American social scientists would later grapple with the iconic ghetto and its consequences, including St. Clair Drake and Horace Cayton, covering Chicago through the 1930s, Kenneth Clark in Harlem in the 1960s, William Julius Wilson in Chicago and nationally, beginning in the 1970s, and Elijah Anderson in Philadelphia in the 1980s.[33]

In *Black Metropolis*, Drake and Cayton noted that Blacks in the first great wave of migration to Chicago were largely confined to an eight-square-mile area they referred to as the Black Belt. Later generations referred to it generally as the South Side, future home to Michelle Robinson, who became Michelle Obama. Black neighborhoods also emerged on the West Side.

Violence was a favored tool for containing Black Chicagoans. Between 1917 and 1921, nearly sixty homes were firebombed when Negroes dared to move into a white neighborhood. The restrictive covenant also systemically blocked Blacks from purchasing near whites and forbade willing whites from selling to them. White terrorists even occasionally firebombed the homes of white realtors or other allies that facilitated a sale to a Negro family.[34]

Ghettoization was the process of working out the physical mechanism of white supremacy. Racism begat the Black ghetto and the ghetto, in turn, begat more racism. Drake and Cayton noted the "vicious circle" in which whites feared economic loss and social isolation if their neighborhood became "all-Negro." This concern, coupled with "race prejudice," made residential segregation, fear, and racism mutually reinforcing. If segregation had not been chosen in the first place, the authors surmised, the vicious circle would not have been set in motion. Negroes put constant pressure on housing markets adjacent to the Black Belt because they had nowhere else to move, yet the vast majority of whites preferred segregated housing. Drake and Cayton cited a *Fortune* magazine opinion poll in which 77 to 87 percent of respondents from sections across the country favored it.[35]

This was a produced result. Negative stereotypes about the Negro had been inscribed in American culture, and they were readily available to shape housing markets. In Chicago, property owners' associations sponsored mass meetings to arouse whites about the peril of Negro "invasion." "They published scathing denunciations of Negroes branding them arrogant, ignorant, diseased, bumptious, destructive of property and generally undesirable," wrote Drake and Cayton.[36]

The *Black Metropolis* authors also underscored how conditions in the ghetto hardened white attitudes as well as the perimeter between Black and white space. In the Black Belt of Chicago, descendants were forced to live *ninety thousand residents per square mile* compared to whites living a mere *twenty thousand residents per square mile.* They were confined to the worst housing, where disease festered due to extreme overcrowding; the city purposely provided poorer services; and schools, inferior and overcrowded, ran on shifts. Drake and Cayton attributed social ills they observed, like juvenile delinquency, to segregation and argued, per the vicious circle, that whites tended to blame Negroes for the conditions in the ghetto that concentrated segregation caused. Blacks, in turn, were deemed "unfit" to be included in American society, and therefore, whites felt justified in keeping them "quarantined behind the color line."[37]

While invisible to most whites, African Americans could see the beauty and genius in their Black world. Drake and Cayton, like Du Bois before them, documented the entire strata of Negroes, their pursuit of happiness, the vital Black culture and institutions they created, the "race men" and women who uplifted their people. The authors used the glowing name Bronzeville, alternatively the "Black Metropolis," when describing these positive aspects of life in the segregated Black Belt.[38] For Drake and Cayton, "ghetto" was a descriptor of extreme residential segregation, not a pejorative label about Blackness itself.

Gunnar Myrdal in *An American Dilemma* also recognized a vicious circle in American race relations, although he predicted that whites would evolve.[39] Drake and Cayton were pessimistic. They argued that the color line persisted because whites did not live by the civic ideals of "democracy, freedom, equality, fair play" that they professed to believe in.[40]

Government supported and reified whites' desire to live apart from Black folk. It acted with great intention in creating ghettos and encouraging residential segregation, although multiple actors contributed. This history has been written comprehensively by several authors.[41] Here I offer only the litany of government policies and practices that rendered physical segregation the American way.

Violence and restrictive covenants were not as efficient nor respectable as zoning. As great migrants traversed the Upper South, several cities, including Baltimore and Louisville, enacted racial zoning to impose a stark residential segregation that did not exist when land use was unregulated. Again, the Supreme Court prohibited that strategy when it decided *Buchanan v. Warley* in 1917.

It was a limited victory. In 1926, the Supreme Court ruled on the landmark case *Village of Euclid v. Ambler Realty,* condoning what is now referred to as Euclidian zoning. The Court endorsed the idea that certain uses of land, like duplexes, were "parasitic" on single-family homes and the people who lived there and therefore should be separated from these idealized neighborhoods. In ensuing decades, thousands of new suburban governments would form, enabling middle- and upper-class whites to wield the zoning power to exclude types of housing, and therefore, certain populations.

The federal government decided in the 1930s that it was economically risky and not appropriate for people of different races to live together. The Home Owners' Loan Corporation (HOLC) invented redlining, encoding unacceptable categories of neighborhoods in red ink, and lending elsewhere, preferably in newly developing white areas. It redlined more than two hundred American cities, giving majority-Black neighborhoods the lowly D rating. The D rating marked Black neighborhoods, in many cases vibrant, as "hazardous" to lending institutions. The A rating went only to "homogenous" white neighborhoods. That decision reverberated and became destiny. Blacks could not get loans to buy or invest in their homes. Starving whole neighborhoods of credit discouraged outsiders from investing there. A 2019 Federal Reserve study examined those neighborhoods and found current effects of the D rating eighty years ago. The D rating correlated with present disinvestment and decline. It increased Black segregation and depressed homeownership and property values. It accounted for 40 percent of the gap in home values between D- and C- rated neighborhoods by 1980, and untold differences in value compared with A-rated neighborhoods.[42]

Major federal policies supported expanding and demarcating segregated Black space and exclusionary white space. The Federal Housing Administration (FHA) insured the thirty-year mortgage to bring homeownership to the white masses. Thanks to low down payments and interest rates, buying a home became cheaper than renting, for those who could qualify for an FHA-guaranteed loan. The FHA insured mortgages primarily for white suburbia, creating and reifying white space while refusing to invest in Black communities or underwrite mortgages for Blacks who sought to buy there. The Veterans Administration operated its mortgage-assistance programs in the same racially discriminatory manner. African Americans, cut out of the government's largest wealth-building programs and traditional mortgages, were preyed on by avaricious speculators.[43]

In his influential essay "The Case for Reparations," Ta-Nehisi Coates wrote of unbroken kleptocratic plunder, of Black bodies and Black-owned land in the South, and of the meager savings African Americans accumulated in the North. His essay featured Clyde Ross. Mississippi authorities seized his parents' forty-acre farm and animals on a claim of unpaid taxes that the family was powerless to defend. It was part of a widespread phenomenon of state theft of Black-owned land. The once-independent family was forced into share-cropping. Clyde Ross left the South. After fighting for the freedom of others in World War II, he sought his own in Chicago. Ross was part of the second wave of migration, hastened by World War II, that continued through 1970. About six million Black people moved in seven decades, like a steady exodus from Egypt. Ross and others wanted homes and, with rare exception, the only way they could acquire them was through installment contract purchases that conveyed no equity or ownership until the last usurious payment was made. Predatory speculators bought houses cheaply from panicked whites, sold them to Black folk like Clyde Ross at exorbitant prices, and evicted anyone who couldn't make payments—relentless plunder that made speculators fortunes by cheating Black people.[44]

In the 1940s and 1950s, Chicago was a laboratory for segregation strategies that would shape future federal policy. Violence also continued to be a tool for containing the Negro. White Chicagoans used bombs, arson, and mob violence in the 1940s and less explosive tactics in the 1950s, against Black migrants. Whites also sparred with Blacks to keep them out of favored schools, parks, and beaches. The Irish in Englewood, the Czechs and Poles in Cicero and Trumbull Park, and others learned to think of neighborhood and public space in all-or-nothing terms, and they resorted to blows to try to hold it all. White ethnics developed cultural myths to justify virulent racial hatred. According to Drake and Cayton, local newspapers "boast[ed] that it was Southern and Eastern Europeans who really built this country while Negroes were 'swinging in trees,' 'eating each other.'"[45]

The Windy City's political and business leaders catered to white racism by maintaining and expanding swaths of Blackness. Chicago's "second ghetto," as historian Arnold Hirsch called it, was vertical.

Many thousands of descendants were placed in an "unbroken wall of high-rise public housing" constructed along State Street from Twenty-Second to Fifty-Fifth Streets. This mammoth density of Black poverty was something new—a government-sponsored institution that served the interests of ordinary whites and the speculators who wished to exploit Blacks and fearful whites in housing markets. Once this new concentrated poverty was in place, white hysteria would only grow, and the vicious circle continued.[46]

Major federal policies mirrored the Chicago method of expanding and demarcating both segregated Black space and exclusionary white space. The interstate highway program, the world's largest public works program when it was built, facilitated white flight from cities and walled off the Black side of town that whites learned to fear. Under a congressionally enacted urban-renewal program for "slum clearance," which James Baldwin and others called "Negro removal," the federal government subsidized the local destruction of nearly four hundred thousand mostly Black-occupied homes, erasing Blackness from downtown centers in the 1950s through the early 1960s. Most of those displaced were moved to public housing or more marginal neighborhoods. The federal government paid local housing authorities to build public housing and acquiesced when locals intentionally assigned Blacks and whites to separate and unequal housing projects.[47] Like the ghetto itself, notorious public high-rises where every family was Black and poor incubated misery and disinvestment, although the occupants of the housing were usually blamed.

St. Louis, Missouri, for example, created an urban oasis that became a monster. The Pruitt-Igoe projects housed twelve thousand very low-income Black people in thirty-three high-rise buildings. It became a national symbol of "failed" public housing, and its residents were often cast as villains in the mythical story of its demise. Left out of this tale in which modern design succumbed to garbage, urine, stench, broken windows, crime, and vandalism are the racist policies of state and federal government and the external force of deindustrialization. The more accurate story is that city leaders eagerly used public housing funded by the federal government to isolate poor Blacks. The project collapsed financially because St. Louis's once-vital industrial economy plummeted. Industrial jobs disappeared from the central city; newly jobless tenants could not afford the rents to maintain the buildings. In hindsight, it was a bad idea to build complicated high-rises without allocating funds for their maintenance. The Pruitt-Igoe residents wanted and demanded upkeep that was not forthcoming. Ultimately, Pruitt-Igoe was torn down, its detonation aired on national television. It became a mythic symbol of the mistakes, recrimination, and tension that would play out wherever ghettos were constructed.[48]

These cumulative public investments in segregation produced intended results. Rates of Black-white residential segregation rose in every decade from the 1920s to the 1970s. Hypersegregation of poor Blacks emerged in more than fifty metropolitan areas before the civil rights movement began to change housing policy.[49] Demographers define hypersegregation as experiencing very high levels of isolation along multiple technical measures. In the twentieth century, no other racial or ethnic group was subjected to such apartheid.[50]

Middle- and upper-income African Americans were also segregated. My family experienced this racism in Huntsville, Alabama, in the mid-1960s. Our ancestor Lucinda Bowdre, née Cashin, died as the Civil War ended and Emancipation began. Four generations later, descendant Cashins resisted the color line in the heart of Dixie on myriad fronts. My parents began with public accommodations. My mother, Joan Carpenter Cashin, sat down at a Walgreens lunch counter and demanded to be served. She intentionally got herself arrested with her four-month-old baby, me, in her arms. This bit of psychological warfare was a turning point in Huntsville's sit-in movement. After Black Huntsvillians won the right to eat and shop where they wanted, my parents and fellow agitators turned to desegregating schools and politics. They were integration pioneers, trying to reconstruct the South as Herschel Cashin's radical Republican generation had also tried to do.

My parents also confronted the color line in housing. Only one elementary school in Huntsville had programs for deaf children; my parents tried for two years to buy a home in its district for the benefit of my hearing-impaired brother. No one would sell to a multi-degreed Black dentist, my father, Dr. John L. Cashin Jr., who had run for mayor in a bid to encourage Blacks to register to vote. Restrictive covenants and the attitudes that animated them persisted in the early 1960s, even after the 1948 Supreme Court case *Shelley v. Kramer* determined they were unenforceable. My father improvised, recruiting whites from the Unitarian church we attended to purchase a house for us with his money. Most of our new neighbors were welcoming, although telephone cowards threatened us constantly, and once someone shot a bullet through our front picture window as we slept.[51]

After Congress enacted the Fair Housing Act in 1968, more Black families became integration pioneers. Southern white representatives in Congress massively resisted this law, and it passed only after the assassination of Martin Luther King Jr. As grieving and aggrieved Blacks rioted and cities burned, some moderate Republicans decided to join other legislators to support the law. The act penalized racial discrimination in housing but had no meaningful enforcement mechanisms. The law did open housing markets, and most nonpoor Black Americans exited ghettos.

Thankfully, levels of segregation between Blacks and whites have declined considerably since 1970. But the footprint of concentrated poverty has exploded since 2000. The truly disadvantaged descendants of slaves are Black Americans stuck in neighborhoods that higher-income Blacks fled.

The civil rights movement worked a transformation in Black class structure. Before the movement, the majority of Blacks were poor. Today, a large majority of Black Americans are *not* poor.[52] But racial disparities persist.

Blacks perennially lag whites in average wages. Acquiring more education does not change Black-white wage gaps, which exist at the lowest—and highest—education and wage levels. Black families are much less likely than white families to own a home, and for every dollar of wealth held by a median white family, a median Black family holds eight cents. Black students perennially lag whites in achievement, high school graduation, and completion of college. Blacks and whites use drugs at similar rates, but African Americans are 6.5 times as likely to be imprisoned by states for drug charges.[53]

These unequal conditions are not mere aftereffects of slavery. Generations of intentionally racist policies imposed on slavery's descendants play a role, particularly the decision to create and maintain segregation. Segregation is still the defining feature of Black American life. Most Black American children attend separate and unequal schools. Most middle- and even upper-class Black Americans live near poor Black neighborhoods and experience an exposure to poverty that most whites and Asians avoid.[54]

Black progress is fragile. In families with little household wealth, any emergency can become a financial disaster. Segregation for Black Americans also means living in neighborhoods with very different possibilities and a distinct, if predatory, relationship with the state. Black neighborhoods, like those that received the D rating nearly a century ago, still garner less of everything, with the exception perhaps of policing. Meanwhile, the key holdover of the supremacist regime that has never been dismantled is the concentrated-poverty hood; it persists, as do stereotypes. The vicious circle of attributing conditions there to the alleged character of descendants continues, as does a nefarious distributional politics.

CHAPTER 3

SEGREGATION NOW

The Past Is Not Past

During World War II, defense contractors on the West Coast began to hire African Americans, and descendants moved west as well as north for opportunity. In Los Angeles, white racism and restrictive covenants limited migrants' housing choices, and many African Americans landed in Watts. This neighborhood in South LA had been thoroughly integrated but became nearly all-Black in the 1960s largely because the federal government insisted on siting segregated public housing there.[1] Watts burned in 1965. A roadside traffic stop led to an altercation between white police and a Black family, a matchstick that incited five days of rioting. Thirty-four people died, a thousand were injured, and the property damage rose to $40 million. An aerial shot of Watts burning in 1965 looked a lot like Tulsa burning in 1921.

The clash in Watts was not dissimilar to the race riots of the 1910s, 1920s, and 1940s. The actors and script may have varied, but the fault line was the same, white dominance versus Black insurgence. In Watts, an LA police department with a reputation for racism and brutality among Negroes were the frontline enforcers of law and order in a social order built on segregation. Similar clashes between Black citizens and the police erupted in the summers of 1966 and 1967. "Burn, baby, burn!" became a mantra for discontented residents of

Burning buildings during Watts riots, August 1965

poor Black neighborhoods. In 1966, eleven cities burned. In the long hot summer of 1967, scores more cities burned. By the end of that tumultuous year, more than 160 revolts had erupted in cities large and small, although 75 percent of them were minor. The nation was riveted by the riots that roiled major cities, most lethally in Detroit and Newark. In the Motor City, undercover police raided an unlicensed Black-owned bar in the ungodly hours of a Sunday morning. Black Vietnam veterans were celebrating coming home and didn't appreciate the disruption and disrespect. The raid set off a five-day revolt that ended in forty-three deaths, over one thousand injuries, and damage to two thousand buildings.[2] The news media televised scenes of pillage, looting, arson, and the National Guard engaging against an implied domestic enemy.

President Lyndon Johnson created the National Advisory Commission on Civil Disorders, popularly known as the Kerner Commission, after its chairman, Illinois governor Otto Kerner. Johnson asked the commission to investigate the causes of urban uprisings and make recommendations. He handpicked moderate establishment figures, all but two of whom were white, as commissioners and expected them to issue a report praising his Great Society programs. The commissioners overcame Johnson's intentionally limited budget. They held lengthy hearings with experts and local officials. They visited many cities, talked to people in Black neighborhoods, and read the scholarship of historians and social scientists on race and the Negro. Shocked by the conditions they saw, they wanted to awaken whites to the truth of ghetto isolation. They noted the growth of white segregationist and Black separatist groups and worried that growing polarization would tear the country apart.[3] They foresaw Black urban majorities, surrounded by white exclusionary suburbs, and wanted to forestall an America divided into "two societies, one black, one white—separate and unequal," as the Kerner Report famously prophesized.

The Kerner Report, issued on Leap Day, February 29, 1968, surprised everyone with a scathing indictment of "white racism" and the segregation it wrought. It focused on institutional and structural forces rather than the behavior of individual rioters and became an instant bestseller. Among other broadsides, the report stated:

> Segregation and poverty have created in the racial ghetto a destructive environment totally unknown to most white Americans. What white Americans have never fully understood—but what the Negro can never forget—is that white society is deeply implicated in the ghetto. White institutions created it, white institutions maintain it, and white society condones it.[4]

The Kerner Report even suggested that Black rioters had learned about violence from white people. "A climate that tends toward approval and encouragement of violence as a form of protest," it alleged, "has been created by white terrorism directed toward nonviolent protest; by the open defiance of law and Federal authority by state and local officials resisting desegregation."

White terrorism had been on full display in the South. Less known today are the thousands of individual acts of menace outside the South by whites resisting Black people moving toward them. In Boston, for example, in the early 1960s, acts against new Black residents included "damaged cars, ignited papers thrust under apartment doors, fecal material at doorways, racial epithets on their doors, . . . rocks, bricks, bottles, and other debris thrown through their windows, . . . Molotov cocktails, arson, and shootings."[5]

In 1966, Dr. King had joined the Chicago open housing movement, rented an apartment on the West Side, and participated in marches through white neighborhoods, sparking hostility and sometimes violence. When King led a group of seven hundred marchers through Marquette Park on the South Side, thousands of whites tried to thwart them. They jeered, threw rocks, bottles, and firecrackers. In video footage, King ducks as sounds like gunfire ring through the air. A racist David landed a stone on King's head; the pacifist kneeled for a moment among supporters before rising to resume his nonviolent resistance. "I have seen many demonstrations in the South, but I have never seen anything so hostile and so hateful as I've seen here today," King later told reporters.[6] He had become convinced that housing segregation was the critical mechanism for unequal distribution of public services—schools, hospitals, housing code enforcement, garbage collection, parks and recreation—and the Kerner Report would validate that sentiment.[7]

The report did not condone violence. It did, however, amplify the sources of Black grievance. Black ghettos convulsed with frustration about police brutality, rampant unemployment, substandard housing with unaffordable rents, sorry schools, racism and disrespect from whites, weak or nonexistent public services, and powerlessness to change anything. First among deeply held frustrations were police practices, which the commission subjected to withering scrutiny:

Police have come to symbolize white power, white racism and white repression. And the fact is that many police do reflect and express these white attitudes. The atmosphere of hostility and cynicism is reinforced by widespread belief among Negroes in the existence of police brutality and in a "double standard" of justice and protection—one for Negroes and one for whites.[8]

A confrontation with police was often the last straw that ignited a revolt.

Social psychologist Kenneth Clark, in his book *Dark Ghetto*, an independent study of Harlem in the early 1960s, interviewed many residents. One, identified only as "Man, age about 33," testified to how descendants experienced the police as something akin to overseers. "The white cops, they have a damn sadistic nature," he said. "A bunch of us could be playing some music, or dancing, which we have as an outlet for ourselves. We can't dance in the house, we don't have clubs or things like that. So we're out on the sidewalk . . . Right away here comes a cop. 'You're disturbing the peace!' . . . Everyone is enjoying themselves . . . and he'll want to chase everyone. And gets mad. I mean, he gets mad! We aren't mad. He comes into the neighborhood, aggravated and mad."[9]

The Kerner Report criticized the media for reporting on the disorders without communicating to its majority-white audience "a sense of the degradation, misery, and hopelessness of living in the ghetto." The report explained that the typical rioter was a young male, lifelong resident, high-school dropout, though better educated than his nonrioting neighbor, and usually employed in a menial job. "He was proud of his race, extremely hostile to both whites and middle-class Negroes and, although informed about politics, highly distrustful of the political system." He was seeking "fuller participation in the social order and the material benefits enjoyed by the majority of American citizens." "Rather than rejecting the American system," the report concluded, rioters "were anxious to obtain a place for themselves in it."

In other words, Black rioters were ordinary Americans, as ordinary as an earlier generation of white participants in lynch mobs or a new generation of white terrorists who bombed, killed, or attacked civil rights protestors and integration pioneers. The commissioners feared that America was lurching toward permanent separation and inequality and that racial polarization would lead to the destruction of democracy. In the report, they argued that the nation had three choices: continue present policies, enrich the ghetto, or integrate Black Americans into the society outside the ghetto. They concluded the country had to choose and vigorously pursue integration although they also called for immediate investments in ghetto neighborhoods. "The primary goal must be a single society, in which every citizen will be free to live and work according to his capabilities and desires, not his color," the report concluded.

The commissioners' recommendations, bold and comprehensive, aimed to dismantle segregation. On the housing front, they declared all federal housing programs "must be given a new thrust aimed at overcoming the prevailing patterns of racial segregation." They called for a comprehensive federal open-housing law and the construction of six million new units of affordable housing outside the ghetto. They also recommended creating two million new jobs, sharply increasing federal funding to eliminate de facto school segregation and provide year-round quality compensatory education in disadvantaged schools, increasing police training, and transforming welfare to a viable income-support system.

Many whites resisted the Kerner Report's accusations of racism and complicity. An irritated President Johnson ignored its recommendations with one exception. Johnson did follow through on its call to create more police intelligence units, and they were used to surveil Black Power organizations like the Black Panthers.[10] After declaring a War on Crime in 1965, he had begun to devote greater resources to policing than the War on Poverty, as uprisings across the nation unfolded. In an important 2016 book, Yale historian and law professor Elizabeth Hinton describes how the Johnson administration abandoned direct investment in grassroots programs that empowered Black citizens to solve community problems. Its early investments in policing were borne of a lens of pathology and delinquency applied to Black urban youth and a profound fear of more uprisings. Black youth and radical activists that were stereotyped as prone to collective violence and criminality were marked for surveillance and social control. Johnson's War on Crime initiated law-and-order investments that marked the beginning of the federal turn toward a punitive, carceral approach to urban problems, Hinton showed.[11] Richard Nixon used the Kerner Report as a messaging prop in his campaign for the presidency. He protested that the report "blames everybody for the riots except the perpetrators of the riots."[12] Nixon rode to the presidency on a law-and-order rhetoric, and the liberal cross-racial coalition that had supported the New Deal, civil rights, and Great Society programs soon collapsed.

AFTER 1968

As the Kerner Report suggested, the processes of ghettoization and segregation were entrenched by 1968. Dr. Martin Luther King Jr. was assassinated a month after the report was issued and more than one hundred cities ignited in fire, riots, and despair. The Fair Housing Act of 1968, which King's death and urban immolation propelled to passage, was a weak law with no meaningful enforcement mechanisms until it was amended in 1988. The act did allude to the idea, championed in the Kerner Report, that the federal government should change its entire direction to fund integration rather than segregation. The law required HUD to administer its programs "in a manner affirmatively to further" the act's goal of housing integration. This "affirmatively further" fair-housing requirement has been held to apply not only to HUD but its state and local grantees.[13]

George Romney, father of 2012 Republican presidential candidate Mitt Romney, served as Nixon's first secretary of Housing and Urban Development. A devout Mormon, the pro-civil-rights Republican, as governor of Michigan, had been deeply affected by the deadly Detroit riot. He championed passage of a state fair housing law in its aftermath. As HUD secretary, he pursed housing integration like the missionary he had once been.

Secretary Romney wrote a confidential memo to his staff, outlining his plan to use HUD's funding to force suburbs that were a "high-income white noose" around Black ghettos to change. He did not alert the White House when he announced his Open Communities initiative. Mayors were used to receiving HUD grants to help pay for roads, sewers, and other infrastructure, the bones for any new residential development. Romney's initiative conditioned HUD assistance on building affordable nonsegregated housing and stopping exclusionary zoning. Communities that were denied funds complained to the White House. Nixon forced Romney to release funds to resistant suburbs. In a private memo to his domestic policy advisor John Ehrlichman and chief of staff H. R. Haldeman, Nixon wrote, "I am convinced that while legal segregation is totally wrong that forced integration of housing or education is just as wrong."[14]

Nixon told Haldeman to keep Romney at a distance. In a letter to Nixon in which he sought a meeting to defend his Open Communities program, Romney wrote and underlined these words: "It is becoming increasingly clear that the lower, middle income and the poor, white, Black and brown family, cannot continue to be isolated in the deteriorating core cities without broad scale revolution."[15] Nixon refused to meet with Romney and forced him to abandon the initiative. After Nixon's reelection in 1972, Romney was pressured to resign. He told a friend of his disappointment: "I don't know what the president believes in. Maybe he doesn't believe in anything."[16]

When Romney, the son, campaigned for president in 2012, he committed to closing HUD altogether.[17] Speaking to a group of wealthy donors, Mitt Romney disdained an alleged "47 percent" of Americans, Obama voters, "who are dependent upon government, who believe that they are victims, who believe that government has a responsibility to care for them, who believe they are entitled to health care, to food, to housing, to you-name-it."[18] By then, the narratives often accompanying small-government, anti-tax conservatism were entrenched. And yet, six years later, following George Floyd's death, US senator Mitt Romney donned an N-95 mask and marched with protestors in Washington, DC, and tweeted his image with three simple words, "Black Lives Matter."[19]

To date, George Romney is the only HUD secretary to have pressured and penalized segregated communities for their sins of racial exclusion. In ensuing decades, the "affirmatively further" requirement was violated regularly by HUD and local governments. HUD distributed billions to localities for community and housing development with few strings attached, the result of "New Federalism" block grants first championed by Nixon. While the new Biden administration has promised to promote fair, inclusive housing, as of February 2021, HUD continues its practice of distributing about $5.5 billion annually in grants for community development, parceled among more than one thousand local jurisdictions nationwide, with no meaningful accountability for affirmatively furthering integration.[20]

Under Nixon's direction, the federal government also declared a moratorium on funding public housing construction. With the exception of a program to replace the worst, concentrated public housing with smaller, mixed-income developments, the federal government retreated from the business of funding construction of new public housing. Instead, it uses the tax code to incentivize private investment in affordable housing. The Low-Income Housing Tax Credit program costs the federal government about $10 billion annually for affordable housing construction primarily in poor communities that already have more than their fair share of affordable housing.[21]

HUD also funds housing vouchers for low-income tenants, although only one in four eligible persons actually receives such assistance. Formerly known as Section 8, the Housing Choice Voucher Program does not alter the racially and economically segregated housing market that voucher holders face. Historically, whites fare better than Black and Latinx people in moving to opportunity. According to census data, more than half of Black and nonwhite Hispanic voucher holders landed in low-opportunity areas where 20 percent or more residents are poor. Meanwhile, nearly two-thirds of white voucher holders rented in areas where less than 20 percent of residents are poor.[22] In other words, the federal government continues to invest in segregation.

Descendants trapped in thickets of poverty that HUD and others created have often sued. In rulings issued from the 1970s through the 2000s, federal courts found that HUD and local governments knowingly and willingly promoted and maintained segregated public housing. Courts also found that HUD and localities failed to "affirmatively further" integrated housing. In 2005, for example, after almost a decade of litigation, a judge castigated HUD for rendering Baltimore "an island reservation for use as a container for all of the poor of a contiguous region."[23]

Courts approved remedies for intentional segregation in Baltimore, Boston, Buffalo, Chicago, Dallas, East Texas, New Haven, New York, and beyond. Even where victories were won, HUD and defendants often delayed complying with court orders. While descendants and their lawyers managed to file lawsuits in about twenty places, in the rest of the nation, HUD and locals felt no pressure to give up their segregation-promoting ways. Because of its long history in funding public housing and local development, HUD is part of the story of segregation in *every* American metropolitan area.[24]

Dorothy Gautreaux, lead plaintiff

The first major legal victory for public housing tenants was *Gautreaux v. Chicago Housing Authority*. The Chicago Housing Authority (CHA) had located more than 99 percent of public housing in the city in poor Black neighborhoods. Dorothy Gautreaux, a resident of the Altgeld Gardens housing project, was part of a small band of tenant organizers who helped push housing issues onto the civil rights agenda in the city. Warmth, intensity, and a laser-like focus on specific tactics were her hallmarks. When Gautreaux applied to live in public housing, she and her husband were desperate to move their four children out of a single-bedroom apartment. She rightly believed that waiting for placement in a white or rare mixed project would be futile. So she accepted a prompt assignment into Altgeld Gardens, an overwhelmingly Black venue that would become a training ground for a young community organizer named Barack Obama decades later. She and tenants at other housing projects wanted to challenge racial exclusion. They had a lawyer, Alex Polikoff, who stuck with the case for twenty-six years. Gautreaux died in 1968, at age forty-one of kidney failure, the result of years of hypertension. She did not live to see the impact of the case that bore her name.[25]

In its 1976 *Gautreaux* decision, the Supreme Court sanctioned a metropolitan-wide remedy that opened white and integrated suburbs to low-income Black movers because HUD, the national government, was also liable. This decision came two years after the Court, in *Milliken v. Bradley,* had virtually eliminated metropolitan-wide school desegregation remedies. After *Milliken,* involving the Detroit area, white suburban school districts everywhere were free to remain segregated, which added incentives to white flight and secession from urban school districts.

Gautreaux did work wonders for the twenty-five thousand low-income people who received housing vouchers to move to more than one hundred communities as a result of this lawsuit. Social scientists demonstrated improved employment for parents and college education for children compared to the trajectories of families who opted to stay in high-poverty Chicago neighborhoods.[26] The case gave birth to similar court-ordered or federally sponsored housing mobility programs in other regions and the innovation of "scattered site" public housing in which units are dispersed throughout a city. Ironically, because of fierce legal resistance from descendants like Dorothy Gautreaux, the city that had created a national model for concentrated Black public housing also spawned a model for deconcentrating poverty.[27]

HUD learned somewhat from the lawsuits brought against it. The Clinton administration made some strides to support mobility strategies for low-income tenants. In the 1990s, HUD nudged its grantees to plan for integrated housing although they were never held accountable for results. Enforcement of the Fair Housing Act's ban on discrimination in sales and rentals typically lagged with Republican administrations. But antidiscrimination enforcement under Democratic administrations could not undo entrenched patterns of segregation. After decades of lobbying and lawsuits from civil rights organizations, in 2015, the penultimate year of the Obama administration, HUD finally completed a regulation to "affirmatively further fair housing."[28]

The Affirmatively Furthering Fair Housing (AFFH) rule required localities across America to analyze their housing patterns for racial bias, disclose those patterns to the public, and set goals for how they will reduce identified segregation. Obama's HUD held out the threat of withholding funds for noncompliance, but it also offered a spirit of cooperation, technical assistance, and data to help communities promote integration. In January 2018, HUD secretary Ben Carson, himself a descendant, whose parents had migrated from the South to Detroit, suspended the AFFH rule after fewer than one hundred communities had undertaken compliance. The Trump administration retracted other modest rules and practices the Obama administration had put in place to encourage integration in housing and education.[29]

Infamously, President Donald Trump attempted to weaponize the already suspended AFFH rule in his reelection bid. In the revolutionary summer of 2020 as many whites were grappling anew with systemic racism, Trump tweeted:

> I am happy to inform all of the people living their Suburban Lifestyle Dream that you will no longer be bothered or financially hurt by having low income housing built in your neighborhood. . . . Your housing prices will go up based on the market, and crime will go down. I have rescinded the Obama-Biden AFFH Rule. Enjoy![30]

Some conservatives had criticized the AFFH rule for not directly pressuring localities to deregulate and change their exclusionary zoning codes. Carson had claimed he wanted to make housing markets more inclusive through local deregulation.[31] Instead, Trump used the suspended rule as one more arrow in his quiver of white identity politics. This was a move not seen in post-civil-rights America. The president of the United States actively promoted economic segregation and, by inference, racial segregation. This may have been a learned family tradition. Trump's father was successfully sued for racial discrimination against Black renters in his apartment complexes; Donald Trump was also named as a defendant.[32]

So-called blue states like California have not done much better in eliminating exclusion. To date, the California legislature has failed to pass a critical bill suspending local single-family zoning in order to encourage density and help solve the state's massive affordable housing crisis.[33] Racial integration remains deeply contested. Sociologists theorize that segregation perpetuates itself on the social habits and networks it creates. Segregation engenders daily habits and ingrains biases of comfort and discomfort. Social networks, particularly for whites, tend to be racially homogenous and greatly influence where people choose to live.[34]

Indifference to fair housing law, from the 1970s to the present, was not the only problem descendants faced. As William Julius Wilson wrote in his seminal book *The Truly Disadvantaged,* those

trapped in inner cities did not benefit from the civil rights movement. Equality never came to them. He argued that their plight was
worsened by deindustrialization, the exit of semiskilled, living-wage
jobs from cities, *and* the exit of middle-class and professional Blacks
from poor neighborhoods. By the 1980s, descendants were much less
likely to find work and were more isolated socially, deprived of the
stabilizing influence of their better-off Black brothers and sisters.[35]

SEGREGATION NOW

The Kerner Report's prediction of chocolate cities surrounded by va-
nilla white-flight suburbs came to pass and lasted for a while. It was
inevitable. The suburban dream, in which buying a split-level castle
in a planned community on a thirty-year mortgage for less than it
cost to rent in the city, was too good to pass up for the white masses
who were offered this ticket. White flight accelerated in the 1960s
on the general desire to avoid Blacks and urban turmoil. The Fair
Housing Act and fair credit laws enacted in the 1970s made it easier
for Black American strivers to move to suburbs too. Many former
white-flight suburbs like Black Jack, Missouri, became very Black;
about half of metropolitan Blacks currently live in suburbs, although
poverty tends to follow them.

In 1965, Congress reformed immigration law, eliminating preferences for northern and western Europeans and restrictions on people
from places replete with color. This radically changed the complex-
ion of the country. With mass immigration, by 2000, Hispanics were
the largest minority, and Asian Americans and multiracial people
are currently the fastest-growing demographic groups. The American metropolis became a prism of many colors. It also became a
place of economic sorting and zero-sum competition between high-,
medium-, and low-opportunity communities. Before the COVID-19
pandemic, wealthy and highly educated people were moving toward
the diverse metropolis rather than away from it, although they tend
to live in bubbles of affluence. It is unclear whether the pandemic will
cause a lull in that pattern or a shift back to suburban or exurban
living for those with choices. Whatever the dynamic, concentrated
affluence persists, as does racial segregation.

Each demographic subgroup experiences racial segregation differently. In the classic *American Apartheid,* Douglas Massey and Nancy Denton popularized a measure of segregation known as dissimilarity. In 1970, Black-white dissimilarity stood at 78 across 287 metropolitan areas, meaning that 78 percent of Blacks would have to move in order to be evenly distributed among white people, reflecting their overall percentage of the population in every neighborhood. In 2010, Black-white dissimilarity had fallen to 60, and this measure has been falling modestly with each passing decade since 1970. However, dissimilarity above 60 is considered high, and Blacks remain the group most segregated from whites. Levels for Latinx or Hispanics have increased slightly as this population has grown, to 49, which is considered moderate segregation. And levels of Asian American dissimilarity from whites have remained the same, about 40, or very moderate. Whites, however, tend to be quite spatially isolated from others. The average white person lives in a neighborhood that is 76 percent white.[36] While the vast majority of whites reject segregation in public opinion surveys, in practice, their willingness to enter or remain in a neighborhood declines sharply as the percentage of Black neighbors increases.[37]

Indigenous people are usually invisible in assessments of segregation because their numbers are so small. Four centuries ago, as English colonizers arrived, an estimated fifteen million Indigenous people inhabited North America above what is now Mexico. According to the 2010 census, the total population that identified solely as Native American or Alaskan was about three million. Millions of Native Americans did not magically disappear. European colonizers annihilated them—a massive act of genocide. While this book is about anti-Black systemic oppression, this history must be acknowledged because American origin stories tend to erase the actions of white supremacy. Native peoples, too, were subjected to inferiorizing myths. US courts and society participated in the racist myth of the allegedly superior European Christian discoverer to the "heathen" or "savage," justifying murder and taking of ancestral land from highly organized Indigenous nations.[38] In some countries that acknowledge a past history of violation of human rights, *current* policy attempts to ameliorate and reconcile that past.[39] In the US, the project of awakening and acknowledging racism and its ancient and current structures continues.

For the majority of Black Americans, segregation and exposure to poverty continue to be a lived reality. About half of all Black metropolitan residents live in highly segregated neighborhoods.[40] Black American descendants of slavery tend to be more segregated from whites than recent Black immigrants.[41] This underscores a basic claim: Only Black Americans were subjected to massive forced servitude that endured for centuries. Other groups historically placed below white Anglo-Saxons certainly endured and continue to endure harsh forms of discrimination. The descendants of slavery and Jim Crow, however, were subjected to a regime of extreme, massive residential segregation that uniquely defines the Black American experience. In other words, Black Americans have endured a series of peculiar institutions designed by the state specifically to oppress them, and the hood and its attendant processes of predation, containment, and disinvestment continue.

While a majority of Blacks no longer live in the hood, high-poverty Black neighborhoods persist, as does the architecture of segregation. Intentional segregation of Blacks in the twentieth century shaped development and living patterns *for everyone* and put in place an infrastructure for promoting and maintaining segregation. The past is not past. Racial steering in real estate markets, discrimination in mortgage lending, exclusionary zoning, a government-subsidized affordable housing industrial complex that concentrates poverty, local school boundaries that encourage segregation, plus continued resistance to integration by many but not all whites—all contribute to enduring segregation. All of these practices also happen to produce profits and enormous wealth for a small cadre of mainly white investors, institutions, and corporations.[42]

In metropolitan areas with large Black populations that were very overt in creating ghettos, the main trend is stasis or as some demographers put it "stalled integration."[43] Milwaukee, Cleveland, Chicago, Detroit, New York, Birmingham, Philadelphia, and Flint are among the twenty-one metro areas that remained hypersegregated as of the 2010 census. Massey and Denton explained this concept. Hypersegregated neighborhoods experience high levels on at least four of five distinct measures of segregation. In a hypersegregated Black neighborhood, one can walk several blocks in any direction and not spy a white person.[44] In the Milwaukee metro area, about 80 percent of African Americans would have to move in order to be evenly distributed. To summarize, while rates of Black-white segregation have declined, in hypersegregated areas, a basic architecture of containment, particularly of poor Black Americans, continues.

In 2010, roughly one-third of all metropolitan Blacks were hypersegregated, down from 61 percent in 1970.[45] This progress should be acknowledged. But while fewer people live in the hypersegregated spaces, the hood as a place and an institution of caste remains, with outsized consequences for descendants and American race relations.

Metropolitan areas with large numbers of Black people still have neighborhoods of concentrated Black poverty and the unequal state and private practices that attach to them. Headline-grabbing events involving disparate treatment of Black people happen regularly in segregated Black neighborhoods or regions that have them.[46] A metro area need not meet the technical definition of hypersegregation for anti-Black systemic forces to operate. A history of Black ghettoization and the continued presence of high-poverty Black neighborhoods may be sufficient.

Affluent Black Americans who can afford it buy their way into premium neighborhoods. Economic segregation is rising fastest among Black and Latinx people. Black and brown one-percenters are moving to high opportunity, although when they do, that usually means moving to predominantly white spaces. For Blacks with resources, the African American Dream is fraught with dilemma. Real estate markets often present extremes: majority-Black neighborhoods near pockets of poverty *or* very white spaces where a nondexterous neighbor may call the police, say, when they spy a Black man attempting to enter his own house.[47] Only about 4 percent of advantaged, majority-Black neighborhoods are surrounded by other advantaged neighborhoods.[48]

Mary Patillo, a professor of sociology and African American studies, documented the proximity of Black middle-class neighborhoods in Chicago to disadvantaged poor Black neighborhoods, a pattern that has been replicated nationally.[49] Predominantly Black neighborhoods, even relatively elite ones with households earning at least $100,000, are usually spatially linked to Black communities of concentrated disadvantage. Try as they might, most Black American strivers do not fully escape "the hood" or segregation. About two-thirds of majority-Black census tracts share a border with a severely disadvantaged census tract, compared to only 35 percent of Latinx tracts and only 8 percent of white tracts.[50] Put differently, Black Americans making $100,000 tend to live in neighborhoods with amenities akin to neighborhoods occupied by whites making $40,000.[51]

Between 1970 and 2005 to 2009, the percentage of middle-class or affluent Blacks who lived in islands of advantage grew from 12 percent to 34 percent. If this is progress, as some would argue, it also underscores that descendants trapped in the hood are ever more isolated from Black models of success. Through her fieldwork, sociologist Karyn Lacy documented the phenomenon of economic sorting. Escaping "the ghetto" and its perceived undertow was very much on the minds of Blacks who moved to affluent spaces. Yet, as sociologist and criminologist Patrick Sharkey has documented, the "most common residential environment of middle- and upper-income African Americans continues to be a disadvantaged neighborhood that is surrounded by other disadvantaged neighborhoods."[52] The options are much worse for poor Black folk.

Experts define ghettos today in terms of concentrated poverty, not race. Paul Jargowsky, a public policy scholar, analyzed neighborhood characteristics and concluded that where 40 percent or more of families in a neighborhood have incomes below the federally defined poverty level, this is a rough measure of a high-poverty ghetto. Many academics and policy advocates use this 40 percent threshold for "high" or "concentrated poverty" and so will I.[53] Despite the decline in number of hypersegregated metropolitan areas, the number of high-poverty census tracts rose by 50 percent after 2000. Jargowsky noted in 2013 that there were more zones of concentrated poverty than had ever been recorded.[54] As of 2016, there were 4,058 high-poverty census tracts. About half were predominantly a mixture of Black and Latinx, and about one-quarter were predominantly Black.[55]

After declining in the 1990s, the number of people living in high-poverty neighborhoods nearly doubled, from roughly seven million to fourteen million, between 2000 and 2013. The footprint of concentrated poverty spread and shifted in many areas, often landing in older suburbs. In the Detroit metro area, for example, the number of high-poverty tracts tripled, from 51 to 184, between 2000 and 2013. Maps convey this story better than words. Maps 3.1 and 3.2 in the insert of colored maps show the disappearance of middle-class people, the spread of concentrated poverty, and the increasing concentration of affluence in Chicago, from 1970 to 2017. The economic ravages of the COVID-19 pandemic may well entrench more concentrated poverty.

Concentrated affluence tracks heavily with predominantly white space. Concentrated poverty leans Black and Latinx.[56] Stark lines between white space and Black and brown hoods create political polarization and constant battles over resources and who the city will serve. In Chicago, the wealthy and highly educated gravitate to the North Side. Rising housing prices and rents and a winnowing of middle-class jobs drive out ordinary folk who used to call the city theirs.

In the summer of 2020 in Chicago, and elsewhere, these battles or uprisings spilled out into the streets. A police shooting, or a rumor about one, caused some young people to rampage in Chicago on the Magnificent Mile, a high-end retail district on the North Side. Some broke windows, vandalized, and looted. *I do not condone criminal behavior.* But I understand where these emotions come from. Kimberly Jones, an author and activist, broke it down in a viral video. In a summer of uprisings and protest, she summarized plainly that responders to police killings included peaceful protestors, rioters, and looters; she defended all three responses. She called on those focused on looters to consider, "Why are people that broke . . . that food insecure . . . that clothing insecure that they feel like their only shot [is] walking through a broken glass window to get what they need." She asserted that the social contract was broken and used the metaphor of the game Monopoly. After 400 rounds of Monopoly in which you had to play for someone else and give them everything you earned to build wealth for them, and then another 50 rounds "where everything you gained and earned was taken from you—that was Tulsa

[and] Rosewood," economically self-sufficient places that whites burned to the ground. Then, after 450 rounds, she continued, "finally they allow you to play and they say catch up, but you can't win, the game is fixed." She concluded, with barely contained rage, that if poor Black people don't own anything, "as far as I'm concerned, they can burn this bitch to the ground."[57] The Kerner Commission's nightmares, it seemed, had come true.

Chicago is not alone in these stark patterns and civil discord. In the twenty-first century, descendants still rise up—in Cincinnati, Ferguson, Baltimore, Milwaukee, St. Louis, and beyond—often for the same reasons the Kerner Commission identified in 1968. People segregated into low-opportunity, high-poverty neighborhoods may revolt when harassed, beaten, or killed by the police. Since the Kerner Report was issued, life chances have grown worse for the descendants left behind in very poor places. Economic inequality has increased, racial and ideological polarization has grown, segregation in neighborhoods and schools are a persistent feature of American life. And democracy and our democratic values are threatened in a political system in which popular will is regularly subverted by racial partisan gerrymandering and voter suppression.

Meanwhile, concentrated poverty is much more complex than it used to be. Single-race high-poverty census tracts are less common. Although Black people are most exposed to concentrated poverty, followed by Hispanics, white exposure grew fastest in the 2000s.[58] The stereotype of the ghetto hides this complexity.

Where high levels of Black segregation persist, researchers have found that it was actively promoted by zoning laws that restricted density and by high levels of anti-Black prejudice, particularly in places with large numbers of Blacks with lower incomes and education levels than most whites.[59] Old habits persist. Those who feel justified in their prejudices about descendants are not likely to know or care about intentional state action in creating and sustaining segregation and pols have pandered to those prejudices for decades.

CHAPTER 4

GHETTO MYTHS
THEY TOLD A NATION

She did not look especially Black, except perhaps to those skilled at discerning hints of African. Linda Taylor, one of many aliases deployed in a life of putting on identities, was a mixed-race woman born to a white mother. She was sufficiently pale to be listed as white by census takers in Arkansas in 1930 and 1940, an era when the state prized and protected whiteness by criminalizing interracial sex. Family lore and outrage had it that Taylor's father was a Black man. Her mother denied it. As an adult, Taylor escaped the oppressions of color lines through disguise and flight. She was a migrant, though not a great or honest one. She left the South for California and passed as white, Hawaiian, Filipino, "Spanish," as needed. Segregation facilitated her deceptions. She "whitened" when she lived in white spaces and "Blackened" when she moved to a neighborhood on the South Side of Chicago.

Taylor was arraigned for welfare fraud in 1974 and dressed the part of "welfare queen," the name the *Chicago Tribune* gave Taylor as it dramatized her to its readers. She seemed to relish the role. In a photograph, Taylor was super-fly, sporting a double-breasted fur coat and a studded, wide-brimmed hat tipped to the side. A fact-drenched book, *The Queen*, depicted reporters, politicians, and law enforcement so obsessed with Taylor's potential abuse of social programs that the state did not pursue evidence that may have convicted her of kidnapping and murder.[1]

How did this extraordinary con artist and probable psychopath, a biracial woman unusually skilled at fooling states and eight (purported) husbands, become a stereotype of Blackness that ultimately justified shredding the social safety net?[2] This American story speaks to the power of convenient narrative over fact. It is also an exemplar of a particular kind of racist mythmaking that I call "ghetto mythology."

Ronald Reagan was not sparking much interest in his first run for president in 1976. As Taylor's real-life soap opera emerged in the press, Reagan, the actor, found that her story and his repeated use of it got him traction with audiences. Taylor became the star of his stump speech. She was cheating not just on welfare but food stamps, Social Security, and veterans benefits from ostensibly dead husbands to collect an annual tax-free income of $150,000, Reagan claimed, as the audience gasped. That figure was grossly inaccurate. In his prodigious search for the truth, Josh Levin, author of *The Queen*, found that Taylor's cumulative fraudulent take over decades, not annually, was estimated at $40,000. She was charged and convicted of stealing less than nine thousand dollars from taxpayers in 1976, the year Reagan ran with Taylor's story.[3] Though the *Tribune* coined the term "welfare queen," Reagan subsequently used it in a radio address, claiming that Taylor's "take" from government was "at a million dollars," an even more exaggerated and untrue sum.[4]

Reagan did not refer to Taylor's race. She was simply "a woman" "in Chicago." Black ghettos and the social connotations that were constructed along with them enabled Reagan to imply Blackness with ease. The late Lee Atwater, a key Republican operative who worked on Reagan's two successful presidential campaigns attested to Republican intentions. He became Reagan's political director, then chairman of the Republican National Committee. In a much-quoted interview, Atwater spoke about how Republicans wooed white voters. He admitted, "Anyway you look at it, race is . . . on the back burner." Atwater was a South Carolina protégé of arch segregationist Strom Thurmond and admirer of Richard Nixon's "Southern

Strategy." He explained: "You start out in 1954 by saying, 'Nigger, nigger, nigger.'"[5] In connecting this brand of explicit racist politics to the year 1954, when *Brown v. Board of Education of Topeka* was decided, Atwater implied that the aim was to exploit white outrage about the possibility of integration with Black people. He invoked the nuclear N-word perhaps as a metaphor, in the vein of George Wallace's vow after losing a gubernatorial race that he would never be "out-niggered" again. When asked about his transition from racial moderate to segregation hardliner, Wallace once said, "You know, I tried to talk about good roads and good schools and all these things that have been part of my career, and nobody listened. And then I began talking about niggers, and they stomped the floor."[6]

"By 1968 you can't say 'nigger'—that hurts you," Atwater continued, though he did not explain why overt supremacist politics began to backfire.[7] George Wallace ran for president as an independent that year, opposing school integration and using law-and-order rhetoric. The Republican winner, Richard Nixon, also used law-and-order codes to appeal to Wallace supporters. After 1968, the language got more sophisticated. Atwater explained, "So you say stuff like forced busing, states' rights and all that stuff. You're getting so abstract now, you're talking about cutting taxes . . . it is getting that abstract and that coded, that we are doing away with the racial problem one way or the other."[8]

The "racial problem" meant Black people, the descendants who white people had been taught they were entitled to live apart from. Reagan may have been surprised at how simple it was to whistle and woo voters to an ideology of government shrinkage and tax cuts. Created during the Depression, Aid to Families with Dependent Children (AFDC), was initially marketed with wholesome images of coiffed blonds holding their fair children. They were the sympathetic mothers who deserved social supports in times of need.[9] The program, known to the nation as "welfare," would "Blacken" in the public's imagination in the decades that hypersegregated ghettos and separate white space were constructed.[10]

On the campaign trail, Reagan painted a picture of the Cadillac-driving welfare queen who stole without remorse from taxpayers and got ahead of hardworking, impliedly white people who played by the rules. He also tried out other tropes. The food stamp program helped "some young fellow ahead of you to buy a T-bone steak" while "you were in line waiting to buy a hamburger," he pandered on the campaign trail. In the South, Reagan had called that "young fellow" a "strapping young buck" before he decided to use a less overt dog whistle. But a government that helped unworthy, impliedly Black people get ahead of industrious, impliedly white people was the unmistakable message that Reagan pedaled to engender hostility to the entire project of government.[11]

Ronald Reagan won the presidency in 1980, infamously launching his general election campaign in the Mississippi county where civil rights workers James Chaney, Andrew Goodman, and Michael Schwerner were murdered by the Klan sixteen years before. "I believe in state's rights," he crowed to an adoring white crowd of thousands at the Neshoba County Fair. In the North, Reagan told ghetto myths about Linda Taylor, and many whites bought his lies. Macomb County, Michigan, just north of very Black Detroit, for example, went from being the most Democratic suburban county in the country in 1960, voting 63 percent for Kennedy that year, to voting 66 percent for Reagan in 1984. In focus groups, Democratic pollster Stanley Greenberg found racial resentment animated much of the switch:

> Blacks constitute the explanation for their vulnerability for almost everything that has gone wrong in their lives. [They see] the federal government "as a black domain where whites cannot expect reasonable treatment." . . . There was widespread sentiment . . . that the Democratic party supported giveaway programs, that is, programs aimed primarily at minorities."[12]

Legal scholar Ian Haney López explains in his book *Dog Whistle Politics* how Democratic and Republican politicians and presidents used veiled racial appeals to convince whites to support policies that benefited the superrich and opposed their own economic interests. In analyzing the effectiveness of Reagan's dog-whistling, Haney López connected tropes about welfare recipients to white fear of integration with Blacks. He wrote:

> When Lyndon Johnson declared his War on Poverty, he extended the benefits of social welfare to nonwhites. In the process, this effort targeted segregation, for obviously poverty in nonwhite communities was deeply tied to racially closed workplaces, schools, and housing. As a result, welfare and integration became tightly linked, and hostility toward integration morphed into opposition to welfare. . . .
>
> Reagan's campaign against welfare helped make the case for tax cuts by successfully using social programs like welfare, and its implicit connection to integration, to convince voters that the real danger in their lives came from a looming, intrusive government.[13]

When Reagan ran in 1976, levels of segregation in northern and midwestern cities between whites and Blacks were near their highest levels in the twentieth century. A coded dog whistle can't work unless the humans to which these messages are targeted are already primed to hear at that frequency. An established racial order gives racial meaning to supposedly neutral codes. Seven decades of ghetto building certainly helped to create hoary stereotypes of Blackness to tap into.

Reagan differed from race-coding predecessors Wallace and Nixon, however. He was the first US president to deploy ghetto mythology to alter both the welfare state and the US tax structure. President Reagan invoked tropes of welfare dependency as he promoted cuts to programs for the poor.[14] In 1981, he successfully championed a federalism package that utilized nine block grants to consolidate seventy-seven categorical programs, terminated sixty-two additional programs, and included a multiyear cut of $130 billion in domestic initiatives—a 25 percent reduction in funding.[15] The Reagan administration also promulgated new rules that denied cash assistance and Medicaid (healthcare for poor people) to millions of working families and cut their food assistance. People who wanted to work and did work could no longer qualify for assistance even if their income did not exceed official poverty levels. The savings from these cuts and the federalism package helped pay for Reagan's tax revolution.[16]

Reagan moved aggressively in 1981 to cut taxes for the richest one percent of taxpayers, reducing the top marginal tax rate from 70 to 28 percent. In the 1980s, this amounted to about $1 trillion in tax relief, and the antigovernment orthodoxy Reagan set in motion conferred another $1 trillion each following decade.[17] Tying dramatic tax cuts to dramatic spending reductions in services to help pay for them became a way for voters to express hostility to a government that was allegedly helping Black people and hurting white people. Stories told about descendants were central to the Reagan revolution. His arsenal of coded messages included attacks on affirmative action, "forced busing," and hostility to civil rights. Wedge issues worked to move many white Democrats from the coalition that had supported the New Deal and Great Society programs to the Republican, tax-cutting column.[18]

The "ghetto" became "the inner city" in public discourse and while that designation was more forgiving in its connotations, the Reagan administration's rhetorical and actual assault on antipoverty policies erased the history of government constructing and maintaining poor Black space from public memory, even as it continued that legacy. Civil rights cases against segregation in schools or housing that traditionally had been filed by the Justice Department virtually disappeared in Reagan's first term.[19] The Reagan administration largely ceased enforcing fair housing law and acquiesced in public and private discrimination to contain descendants.[20]

Instead of mitigating the harms of state-sponsored segregation, Reagan used the culprit of personal behavior and family breakdown to jettison or downgrade urban policies.[21] His cuts to HUD were particularly egregious. From 1980 to 1988, federal spending for housing shrank from about $28 billion to $10 billion.[22]

Reagan deployed ghetto mythology on another front. In the same campaign speeches in which he weaponized the "welfare queen," he used the word "predator" to talk about crime. The criminal Reagan conjured was "a staring face—a face that belongs to a frightening reality of our time: the face of the human predator."[23]

President Reagan announced his War on Drugs in 1982. As Michelle Alexander notes in her groundbreaking book *The New Jim*

Crow: Mass Incarceration in the Age of Colorblindness, Reagan's war increased military and law enforcement funding to fight drugs more than tenfold while dramatically cutting spending for drug treatment, prevention, and education.[24] To justify and build public support for a drug war, the Reagan administration sponsored a media campaign that sensationalized crack use in inner-city neighborhoods and private media outlets embraced this narrative. Alexander wrote:

> Thousands of stories about the crack crisis flooded the airwaves and newsstands, and the stories had a clear racial subtext. The articles typically featured black "crack whores," "crack babies," and "gangbangers," reinforcing already prevalent racial stereotypes of black women as irresponsible, selfish "welfare queens," and black men as "predators"—part of an inferior and criminal subculture.[25]

Other scholars have pointed out that state and local actors, including cities controlled by Black Americans, also massively incarcerated, in response to violent crime as well as drugs.[26] But they do not contest that the federal drug war was propelled by and itself perpetuated pervasive stereotypes of inner-city residents. The footage associated with crack, like the news coverage of urban uprisings of the sixties, reseeded ghetto images into the American psyche. Many institutional actors and individuals, of all political persuasions and races, at all levels of government, participated in the demonization of descendants and this, in turn, justified punitive forms of policing.[27]

US penal policy changed dramatically in the decades following the civil rights revolution. In 1986, the House of Representatives proposed a fifty-to-one disparity in sentences between Black-associated crack and white-associated cocaine powder, and the Senate doubled the disparity to one-hundred-to-one with no deliberation as to why the doubling down was necessary.[28] As with Johnson's War on Crime, government continued to retreat from humane policies that might help descendants overcome ghetto isolation *and* to militarize law enforcement in their neighborhoods.[29]

Ghetto myths begat punitive policies at all levels of government, and incarceration grew like kudzu. The American inmate population ballooned by 700 percent above what it was in 1970, to 2.3 million incarcerated persons, with no correlation to growth in population or crime. With only 5 percent of the global population, the US houses nearly a quarter of the world's prison population.[30] Alexander argued that this new system of social control of Black people was constructed in response to white resentment of civil rights gains and to the economic dislocation that poor Blacks were experiencing in deindustrializing cities. Republicans and Democrats competed with each other to exploit white attitudes about Black folk. Mass incarceration and attendant bans on ex-offenders from voting or receiving federal housing, student loans, and other assistance constituted a new Jim Crow, she argued.[31]

The drug war also deepened certain processes of American caste: predation in Black hoods, denigration of Black people, and masking of capitalist plunder. In previous eras, slumlords and block-busting speculators benefited from fear-inducing ghetto mythology. In the new era of mass incarceration, companies extracted wealth from a mushrooming prison industrial complex. For-profit companies, backed by private equity investors, dominate the market for correctional services. With rampant privatization of correctional services, there are about four thousand companies that receive revenues from the roughly $80 billion spent annually in America for prisons.[32]

The peculiar Black-subordinating institutions of the ghetto and mass incarceration were supremely damaging to the families and individuals ensnared by them. And the myths constructed and propagated to justify these institutions also inflict harm independent of the institutions. As Bryan Stevenson, the acclaimed public interest lawyer, has argued, the ideology of supremacy may have been more harmful than the institutions it justified because the ideology endures.[33] Ghetto myths performed a political function—justifying policies that criminalized being poor, cut antipoverty spending, and encouraged segregation and tax cuts that exacerbated income and wealth inequality.[34] What is less obvious is the connection of modern ghetto mythology to our nation's original sin. Slavery launched an endless war over narrative, and anti-Black mythology has been central to American politics for centuries.

GHETTO MYTHS AS A LEGACY OF WHITE SUPREMACY

In his masterful, definitive history of racist ideas in America, *Stamped from the Beginning*, Ibram X. Kendi shows that racism progressed and morphed across centuries even as anti-racist people offered anti-racist ideas and resistance in every era. Kendi identifies tropes propagated about poor Blacks in poor neighborhoods, beginning in the 1960s—essentially the ghetto myths presented in this chapter—as part of this multicentury continuum.[35] I agree and explain here the operational connection of ghetto myths to previous eras of supremacist mythology.

Powerful classes tend to explain and accept the unearned benefits that flow from social hierarchies, a habit that is universal in human history. Most societies construct a pecking order. Founding fathers, and it is nearly always fathers, construct origin stories or what scholars call "hierarchy-enhancing myths" that encourage stereotyping. National mythology promotes patterns of behavior that constitute culture. National culture, in turn, reifies hierarchical institutions, like slavery and segregation. Once created, such institutions tend to endure over generations. Those who benefit tend to defend discrimination as they defend their preferred institution. There are hierarchy-attenuating myths and practices, like abolitionism, civil rights, and human rights. But once a hierarchical structure is in place, it is much easier to maintain inequality than attenuate it.[36]

Thomas Jefferson authored the beautiful words of the Declaration of Independence, and those self-evident truths of universal human equality are central to our American origin story. He also wrote words in *Notes on the State of Virginia* that traded in white supremacy, speculating aloud about the alleged inferiority of Africans, effectively apologizing for, if not justifying, slavery.[37] Racial essentialism, ascribing character traits to particular phenotypes, was a new phenomenon in the late eighteenth century. German philosopher Immanuel Kant, like Jefferson, compared so-called races to each other. Kant ascribed to the Negro "a silly natural aptitude," and consequentially, "no real culture." He asserted that Black people were devoid of an essential human character, the ability to make independent judgments. The Negro culture, according to Kant, was that of slaves who "allow themselves to be trained."[38] Kant also denigrated Indige-nous people, describing them as having only a "half-extinguished life power," and as a group that has "still not fully acclimated."[39] While Kant later disavowed slavery and colonialism, in a world where os-tensibly enlightened white elites and their nations benefited from slavery and conquest, the ideas needed to justify these institutions flourished, especially in America, with "such quantities of land to waste as we please," as Jefferson wrote.[40]

Jefferson's struggle between self-evident truths and convenient, slavery-supporting mythology of Black inferiority, was America's struggle. Future generations of Americans were inculcated in white supremacy as preferred follow-on institutions to slavery were created and justified.[41] New institutions required new myths to justify them. Poor white men in the Jim Crow South could overlook how they, too, were disenfranchised by poll taxes or regressively taxed and often economically exploited by their bosses. The common man's fanfare was "Dixie" and other siren songs that propagated stereotypes first uttered by his economic superiors: inferior, nigger, rapist, thug.

Division and supremacy were central to American culture, forever and always benefiting a small class of elites. With the distance of time and culpability, it is easy to see and acknowledge the role of racial myths in propping up institutions like slavery and the old Jim Crow that we now profess to abhor. But can we acknowledge how modern stereotypes—"thug," "ghetto"—supplanted "rapist" or "nigger" to perform a similar political function in post–civil rights America?

Ghetto mythology is the latest iteration of anti-Black stereotyp-ing that distracts white voters from capitalist plunder. As sociologist and social anthropologist Loïc Wacquant argues in *Urban Outcasts*, since the 1970s, "the tale of the 'underclass' masks and thus absolves regressive choices made by the federal and local authorities (irrespec-tive of party affiliation)."[42] Underclass was a term popularized by William Julius Wilson in *The Truly Disadvantaged*. Wacquant, who studied under Wilson, argued that this ultimately derogatory label was forced on poor Blacks by "specialists in symbolic production—journalists, politicians, academics and government experts—for pur-poses of controlling and disciplining."[43] That even progressive Black intellectuals like Cornel West used the term "underclass" attested "to the degree to which the ghetto [became] an alien object."⁴⁴ The rhetoric of the "underclass" was a testament to classism on the part of all non-descendants.

Infamous in the annals of ghetto stereotyping is Daniel Patrick Moynihan's leaked 1965 report, *The Negro Family: The Case for National Action*, in which he wrote: "The evidence—not final, but powerfully persuasive—is that the Negro family in the urban ghettos is crumbling." Moynihan was serving as an assistant secretary in the US Department of Labor and did not write the report for public consumption. It was an internal call to action to convince President Johnson and others in the administration to boldly address an ongoing and expanding crisis. He wrote of the divergence between a reported half the Negro population that constituted a stable and growing Black middle class and the other half that was a "disadvantaged lower class." Moynihan, a scholar and policy wonk, wrote that because of housing segregation Black middle-class children grew up in or adjacent to slums and were "therefore constantly exposed to the pathology of the disturbed group." In his rendering, everyone in the ghetto was pathological. And yet his analysis was more nuanced than his conclusions.

Moynihan acknowledged that the American slavery from which Negroes descended was the cruelest system of bondage in human history, one that stripped the enslaved of any rights or autonomy, rendering them utter chattel for owners. He cited Black American sociologist E. Franklin Frazier's 1939 book, *The Negro Family*, and what Frazier wrote about the effects on Black families of living in "city slums." He acknowledged the lack of employment in those neighborhoods and cited data showing that Black families were stronger in rare years of low Black male unemployment. He acknowledged "deep-seated structural distortions" visited upon Black people over "three centuries of injustice." But he concluded that these external forces had resulted in a "tangle of pathology" for the disadvantaged that was "capable of perpetuating itself without assistance from the white world." Showing his sexism and that of the times, he argued that federal policy should aim to fix the allegedly broken, matriarchal Black family structure, to help Black men find work so that they could return to their rightful place as heads of households. Unlike the Kerner Commission report that would come, Moynihan's report did not suggest the federal government should attack the "structural distortions" it and white America had supported, like segregation.[45]

The Moynihan Report reverberated for half a century. Progressive scholars and voices castigated Moynihan for "blaming the victim."[46] Conservative thinkers and pundits endorsed what the report had to say about "pathology," and allegations of welfare dependency, single Black motherhood, drugs, and violent thuggery became regular conservative fodder. Each generation had public intellectuals and private armchair mythologists who offered versions of these tales to explain a status quo of racial inequality. Among them, Charles Murray, author of anti-welfare polemics in the 1980s and '90s, argued that the "underclass" and Black people were less intelligent than others and that this intellectual inferiority and social welfare programs encouraging dependency explained their disadvantaged status. He advocated for a eugenic ethno-fatalism in which the state would abolish social welfare programs and once even recommended containing impliedly pathological people in their own zones and allowing disease, suicide, and homicide to reduce this undesired population.[47] Some of Murray's critics accused him of being a white supremacist and white nationalist.[48] Certainly his arguments mirrored the inferiorizing that accompanied slavery and Jim Crow. Murray and others who pathologized the ghetto poor were enormously influential, helping to shrink social welfare spending even as government largesse to affluent spaces continued.[49]

Black intellectuals, though often more empathetic to their poorer brethren, struggled with classism. Ever since W. E. B. Du Bois published *The Philadelphia Negro*, Black elites had to reconcile their own status as talented, aspiring, ostensibly "new" Negroes with the "old" Negroes of the agrarian South who made their way north, with shabby clothes and country habits. Social distancing and anguish as well as trying to live apart were part of the response.[50] In the twentieth and into the twenty-first century, Black sociologists and academics struggled to understand and interpret the persistence of inequality in high-poverty Black neighborhoods. Some, like William Julius Wilson, identified structural forces as dominant while acknowledging culture, others, like Orlando Patterson, stressed culture.[51] In the height of the drug war when levels of violent crime soared, Black intellectuals and policy elites debated about how to respond to the few descendants who were shooting and menacing. Distinguished legal scholar Randall Kennedy and Justice Clarence Thomas aligned their writing and judgments with protecting the interests of the law-abiding Black people who were victimized by violent Black criminals, even if that meant ceding more power to law enforcement and narrowing individual liberties.[52] A young lion law professor and former prosecutor, Paul Butler, argued that Black jurors should refuse to convict nonviolent Black offenders because of the justice system's ingrained racism and that Black people should coalesce to solve community problems.[53]

At some point "ghetto" became an adjective with distinct cultural meaning that distinguished its style, dress, speech, and social codes from middle-class respectability.[54] Sometimes middle- and upper-class Black people participate in this othering. Even in Washington, DC, where Democrats outnumber Republicans by about twelve to one, and where Black Americans, for many years, controlled government, political leaders pursued punitive laws that fueled mass incarceration and filled DC prisons with young Black men.[55] The same Black political leadership was also slow to adopt an inclusionary zoning ordinance that requires mixed-income development and instead pursued policies that displaced many poor residents from the city. Whatever cultural forces operate in poor Black spaces, real or imagined, here my purpose is to show that politicians weaponized stereotypes in ways that masked unequal treatment and distribution of resources. And US presidents and politicians campaigning for that highest office have been the greatest players in this performance art.

PRESIDENTS AND PRESIDENTIAL ASPIRANTS AS GHETTO MYTHMAKERS

George H. W. Bush won the presidency in no small part through dog-whistling. Bush's supporters cast William R. Horton as the villain in a thirty-second television advertisement that they produced to attack Democratic presidential nominee Michael Dukakis in 1988. In the ad, a narrator described the heinous deeds for which "Willie"

Horton was convicted though he had never used that nickname. The camera lingered on a grainy prison picture taken after Horton had emerged from weeks of solitary confinement. A dark-skinned, Afroed Black man with a wildly overgrown beard stared back as the narrator announced that "Willie" Horton had been convicted for killing a young man by stabbing him nineteen times. Despite a life sentence, he was granted weekend furloughs from a Dukakis-backed program. Horton absconded, the narrator continued, to repeatedly rape a woman and stab her boyfriend. In that era, all fifty states deployed prison furlough programs to ease convicts' inevitable reentry into society. As governor of California, Ronald Reagan had defended his state's program as overwhelmingly effective after two furloughed prisoners committed murder.[56]

Though the Bush campaign denied involvement the Willie Horton ad, it created its own commercial criticizing the Massachusetts furlough program without mentioning Horton. On the campaign trail, Horton became for Bush what the welfare queen had been for Reagan. Bush pounded the Willie Horton narrative throughout the general election, mentioning him in speeches almost daily. Lee Atwater, Reagan's former operative and Bush's presidential campaign manager, had learned through focus groups that he could turn white Democrats away from Dukakis with the Horton story. "By the time we're finished, they're going to wonder whether Willie Horton is Dukakis' running mate," Atwater said.[57]

It worked. Dukakis's seventeen-point lead in August 1988 evaporated, and Bush won the election handily.[58] It was a watershed low in overt racial appeals that presaged the racial toxicity of the Trump era. Future candidates like Bill Clinton felt the need to establish their tough-on-crime bona fides with white voters. The ensuing frenzy of political competition fueled mass incarceration and locked government into a punitive relationship with descendants that endures.[59]

President George H. W. Bush also used ghetto mythology to dramatically escalate spending on the drug war. In his first address from the Oval Office, on live television, he raised a baggie filled with crack cocaine and told the nation it had been purchased mere blocks from the White House. It was an orchestrated stunt and policymaking as performance. An undercover Drug Enforcement Administration

(DEA) agent had lured Keith Jackson, a student at historically segregated Spingarn High School, to sell him crack in Lafayette Park.
Jackson was under investigation as part of a wider effort to indict
drug kingpin Rayful Edmond III. Jackson, so isolated in his northeast DC neighborhood, did not even know what or where the White
House was and had to be directed there by the DEA agent.

Bush's desire to dramatize and escalate the drug war set this
farce in motion. He told his audience that the solution to drugs was
"more prisons, more jails, more courts, more prosecutors," and he
announced a $1.5 billion increase in federal police spending, the larg-
est single increase in the history of drug enforcement. The crack that
Jackson supplied in Lafayette Park was a useful prop for a president
who also announced that he was assigning the US military a new
role in fighting drug traffickers internationally. The Cold War was
ending, and ghetto myths helped fill the vacuum to justify perpetual
militarized policing at home and abroad. By the end of Bush's term,
the Pentagon's counter-narcotics budget was 100,000 percent higher
than it had been when Reagan declared the drug war in 1982.[60]

In his first run for the presidency, Bill Clinton felt the squeeze of
generations of political pandering to white voters. Clinton ran as a
"New Democrat" and alternated between speaking to all Americans
and trying to appeal to white racial conservatives through rhetoric
and policy positions that harmed Black people. He left the campaign
trail to oversee the execution of mentally impaired Black American
Ricky Ray Rector, subsequently observing "No one can say I'm soft
on crime."[61] He used a forum hosted by Jesse Jackson to attack rap-
per Sister Souljah, who had said publicly of gang violence in LA that
young nihilists should consider being ecumenical in their killing and
take white lives for a week. Whatever Souljah's motives, Clinton was
criticized for cynically using the moment to signal to whites the limits
of his oneness with Jesse Jackson and Black people.[62]

Worse, Clinton sponsored and championed an extremely punitive $30 billion crime bill in 1994 that kick-started a prison-building
boom and, among other things, ended Pell Grants for prisoners who
sought to better themselves through education.[63] He advocated for
the one-hundred-to-one sentencing disparity between crack and powder cocaine charges. He backed an unforgiving "three-strikes law."

He supported laws that would deny federal student financial aid, welfare, and food stamps to individuals with drug convictions. He allowed public-housing institutions to refuse to provide housing to anyone with a criminal past. With this cumulation of harshness, Michelle Alexander argued, Clinton relegated many Black Americans to a "permanent second-class status eerily reminiscent of Jim Crow."[64]

Together, President Bill Clinton and House Speaker Newt Gingrich ended welfare as the nation had known it. The Clinton administration and the Gingrich Congress replaced AFDC, a cash assistance entitlement to individuals who met poverty criteria, with Temporary Assistance to Needy Families. But most of this TANF aid was sent to states as block grants with much state discretion on how to spend the funds. Under Clinton and Gingrich, "welfare reform" denied food stamps to childless adults. Plenty were willing to work, trying and failing to find a job, but they could starve under new rules because of their failure to work.[65]

The Reagan administration had pushed people who found *any* work off the rolls, and now cash assistance and food stamp recipients were being castigated for not working. Clinton invoked rhetoric of personal responsibility, declaring that in dismantling AFDC and instituting TANF, he would end the "cycle of dependence" and "achieve a national welfare reform bill that will make work and responsibility the law of the land." Newt Gingrich whistled louder, claiming: "It is impossible to maintain civilization with 12-year-olds having babies, 15-year-olds killing each other, 17-year-olds dying of AIDS, and 18-year-olds getting diplomas they can't even read. Yet that is precisely where three generations of Washington-dominated, centralized-government, welfare-state policies have carried us."[66] Again, the main beneficiaries of cuts to these programs for the poor were rich taxpayers who received more tax cuts.[67]

Why did Clinton, a man who had Black friends, who so understood and reveled in Black culture that author-laureate Toni Morrison crowned him our "first Black president," take such harsh positions that harmed Black Americans?[68] Though Clinton personally liked and promoted Black folk in his administration, his success in politics depended on a dichotomy between middle- and upper-class "respectable" Blacks and inner-city residents whom he and previous presidents pathologized. In a speech that was very well received when it was delivered in November 1993, Clinton spoke of communities "where there are no families, where there is no order, where there is no hope." He was addressing an audience of Black ministers in the hallowed pulpit in which Dr. Martin Luther King Jr. gave his last sermon. Clinton wondered aloud how they would explain to King, were he to reappear, "that we gave people the freedom to succeed and we created conditions in which millions abuse that freedom to destroy the things that make life worth living and life itself?" In the speech, Clinton applauded the achievements of the Black middle class, then castigated violent youth and alleged "millions" who were abusing the freedoms King died fighting for. Clinton channeled King, claiming that the slain leader would say:

> I did not live and die to see the American family destroyed. I did not live and die to see 13-year-old boys get automatic weapons and gun down nine-year-olds just for the kick of it. I did not live and die to see young people destroy their own lives with drugs and then build fortunes destroying the lives of others. . . . I fought for freedom, he would say, but not for the freedom of people to kill each other with reckless abandonment, not for the freedom of children to have children and the fathers of the children to walk away from them and abandon them . . .[69]

The speech was considered among the best of Clinton's presidency in an era when urban gun violence was dramatically higher than it is today.[70] To his credit, Clinton bemoaned an epidemic that would make an eleven-year-old girl plan her own funeral, so sure she was that she would not live long in the world she knew. As he touted his crime bill, he also championed its ban on assault weapons and emphasized that in addition to policing and law enforcement he was trying to invest more in education and get a health care bill passed that would guarantee access to drug treatment.[71] The stereotype of young Black teens toting assault weapons and killing other Black babes, however, drove his march to harsh penalties and more incarceration. Clinton refused, for example, to follow the recommendations of the expert Sentencing Commission to reduce disparities in penalties between crack and powder cocaine and in doing so, once again, invoked the image of a violent inner city.[72]

Hillary Clinton also deployed ghetto mythology to defend the crime bill. "They are often the kinds of kids that are called 'super-predators,'" she said in 1996, "no conscience, no empathy, we can talk about why they ended up that way, but first we have to bring them to heel."[73] In her own run for the presidency two decades later, she would recant this statement and champion prison reform as she wooed Black and brown voters.[74]

The theory of super-predators, promoted in a book by William J. Bennett, John J. DiIulio Jr., and John P. Walters, has since been debunked. They fabulized that inner-city children, surrounded by delinquents, were becoming increasingly "radically impulsive" and "brutally remorseless"—criminals who would "murder, assault, rape, rob, burglarize, deal deadly drugs, join gun-toting gangs and create serious communal disorders."[75] Though this philosophy initially gained traction, it was soon discredited and DiIulio himself, after having an epiphany while praying in church, renounced it.[76]

This debunking mirrors ongoing national trends and a bipartisan consensus that both mass incarceration and the drug war were designed and perpetuated in error. In 2015, a number of influential leaders, including Bill Clinton, Hillary Clinton, Marco Rubio, and Ted Cruz offered essays and reforms designed to rectify excesses in the criminal justice system.[77] Some argue that these attempts at amelioration are motivated more by fiscal concerns than a desire to achieve true justice. Michelle Alexander warns, "the racial ideology that gave rise to these laws remains largely undisturbed."[78] In 2010, President Obama signed a bill reducing the disparity in sentencing for crack cocaine versus powder cocaine from one hundred to one to eighteen to one, which begs the question of why any disparity was allowed to persist.[79]

Barack Obama, the erudite community organizer who once worked with and for descendants on the South Side of Chicago, did not invoke overt ghetto stereotypes to shape policy during his presidency, though he did use the word "thugs" to describe vandals in the Baltimore uprisings and regularly lectured Black people. There was a common theme to the lectures, whether delivered from a pulpit of a Black church, a Morehouse College graduation, or some other very Black venue. In his first memoir, biracial Barry came of age and ultimately chose African American for his identity, becoming Barack Obama.[80] When addressing the collective family he married into, Obama often used the language and admonishment of personal responsibility.[81]

Campaigning in Beaumont, Texas, in February 2008, Obama told a predominantly Black audience that they should not give "cold Popeyes" to their children for breakfast, provide a bag of potato chips for lunch, or let them drink eight sodas a day. In chiding Black parents for these alleged nutritional failings, he did not mention food deserts that tend to plague Black neighborhoods nor offer any proposal to redress them. He also accused them: "When that child comes home, you got the TV set on, you got the radio on, you don't check their homework, there is not a book in the house, you've got the video game playing."[82] The same year, he gave a Father's Day address on the South Side of Chicago at the Apostolic Church of God—twenty thousand members strong. He decried "the national epidemic of absentee fathers" and pledged to address it with legislation to step up child support enforcement. He drew on his personal mythology as a boy whose own father was absent and presented it as broader truth. Obama said of "too many" impliedly Black "AWOL" fathers: "They have abandoned their responsibilities, acting like boys instead of men. And the foundations of our families are weaker because of it."[83]

Prolific author and professor of African American studies, Michael Eric Dyson had taken comedian Bill Cosby to task in a book three years before, calling him out for his public crusade against the alleged failings of poor Black parents.[84] The day after Obama gave his Father's Day speech, Dyson criticized him in *Time*, suggesting it was aimed at ambivalent white voters and grounded in stereotypes that had endured since the Moynihan Report. Dyson cited a study by social psychologist Rebekah Levine Coley showing that Black fathers who did not live with their children were more likely than fathers of any other race or ethnicity to maintain contact with their offspring.[85] In 2013, the Centers for Disease Control and Prevention released a report that found Black fathers were more involved on a daily basis with their children than white and Hispanic fathers, the other groups studied. Black fathers do naturally what society stereotypes them as not doing.[86] Obama could have told a different, more nuanced story, of those who fall down in the face of systemic forces and the heroic efforts of those who father despite all challenges. Some of President Obama's second-term policies would begin to attack structural forces descendants face. But campaigning on Father's Day in 2008, it was mainly the absent Black daddy's fault.

One critic argued that when Obama lectured Black folk, he was inoculating himself, perhaps, from appearing too aligned with Black Americans, still president of all the people, as he regularly said.[87] Obama had to overcompensate for being a Black man in the White House. He, too, was constrained by long-established national habits and ideas about Blackness. On those occasions when he mildly entered Black pain, noting that if he had a son, he would have looked like slain Trayvon Martin or stating that the police behaved "stupidly" when they arrested Dr. Henry Louis Gates on his own front porch, many whites took umbrage.[88]

Obama was caught between the optimistic possibilities for multiracial coalition that propelled him into office and an old politics animated by anti-Black feeling. After being elected to a second term, he was emancipated, and his administration took steps to chip away at the follow-on institutions of supremacy, though he did not talk about it in this manner. He was the first modern president to visit a prison. He promoted policies of decarceration and reentry and the federal prison population began to decline on his watch. In the final two years of his presidency, his secretary of Education, John King, began to actively promote and incentivize school integration, and the US Department of Housing and Urban Development issued a series of regulations designed to promote residential mobility and integration. Obama also granted commutations and pardons to more inmates than any president since President Harry Truman—1,927 by the time he left office.[89] And his Department of Justice founded the Smart on Crime Initiative that, among other efforts, instructed federal prosecutors to pursue fewer low-level drug offense cases.[90]

Donald Trump was perhaps the most transparent president to use ghetto mythology to benefit very rich people. A Twitter president, with eighty-eight million followers in 2020, he used his cellphone-pulpit to bully. Of course, he was ecumenical in attacking individuals and institutions that did not serve his personal interests, including the press, national security agencies, the Federal Reserve, and the FBI. He frequently stereotyped entire groups and in his first three years in office attacked minorities more than 850 times on Twitter.[91]

Among numerous calumnies, he cast Mexicans as "rapists" in his first speech as candidate for president. He regularly described asylum seekers at the Mexico-US border as dangerous invaders, words invoked by a domestic terrorist who shot at a crowd of people at an El Paso Walmart—injuring twenty-six and killing twenty-two.[92] He repeatedly used stereotypical and inciting language to describe the Islamic community, once declaring on NBC: "They are not assimilating . . . They want sharia law. They don't want the laws that we have." He said Jews who vote for Democrats were "very disloyal to Jewish people and very disloyal to Israel," which is insulting to Jews who lean Democratic and trades on an anti-Semitic stereotype that Jews pledge allegiance first to Israel.[93] In a closed-door meeting with congressional leaders about immigration reform, Trump said that he did not want more immigrants from Africa and Haiti, which he categorized as "shithole countries," and said that he preferred more immigrants from places like Norway.[94] Racist stereotypes animated and propelled some of Trump's most discriminatory or inhumane policies, including caging immigrant children at the southern border and travel bans targeted at Muslim countries.

And Trump's inhumanity included a particularly long history of trading in ghetto mythology. Arguably the Central Park Five case of 1989, in which a white woman jogger was brutally beaten and raped and five teens of color were wrongly accused, marked Trump's entry onto the national political stage. He ignited hysteria when he placed a full-page advertisement in four New York newspapers including the *New York Times,* under the outsized, bold heading "Bring Back the Death Penalty. Bring Back Our Police!" "What has happened to law and order," he queried in the advertisement. He painted a picture of New Yorkers held hostage "to a world ruled by the law of the streets, as roving bands of wild criminals roam our neighborhoods." In addition to demanding reinstatement of the death penalty, Trump called on politicians like Mayor Ed Koch to "unshackle" law enforcement "from the constant chant of 'police brutality.'" In Trump's advertisement, "thugs" were not "citizens," and they deserved brutal treatment.

Even after the Central Park Five were exonerated, after the actual perpetrator, an adult serial rapist and murderer, confessed and his DNA matched that at the crime scene, Trump persisted with myths, asserting that "these young men do not exactly have the pasts of angels."[95] And yet none of them had ever been arrested prior to the jogger's tragic case. The facts did not matter. He lied to suit his ends, a habit on full display during his presidency.[96]

When questioned about the case in June 2019, President Trump refused to apologize. There were "people on both sides of that," he said, siding with a much-criticized prosecutor and police detectives.[97] This utterance was eerily similar to what he said after a white nationalist plowed his car into a multiracial crowd in Charlottesville, Virginia, killing Heather Heyer. "You also had some very fine people on both sides," he said.[98] Trump's signature politics required demarcating lines, nodding, signaling, or screaming out loud to those people he was with about those he was impliedly against.

In his first and second campaigns for president, Trump invoked "law and order," the dog whistle Nixon had used in the wake of the urban uprisings of the 1960s. In the 2016 campaign, Trump associated all Blacks with the inner city, painting a vivid image: "Our inner cities are a disaster. You get shot walking to the store. They have no education, they have no jobs."[99] At a campaign rally, he encouraged police to be "rough" with "thugs" they arrest.[100] The Black Lives Matter movement, rising in 2016, gave him a perfect foil to signal his cultural and racial affinities. At campaign rallies, "all lives matter" was his consistent response to BLM protestors or anyone who had the temerity to express concern about police brutality.[101]

As president, Trump was particularly withering in his comments about Baltimore. On Twitter, he called now-deceased congressman Elijah Cummings's district "dangerous & filthy" and a "disgusting, rat and rodent infested mess." He also said of Baltimore, "No human being would want to live there." Trump once called the Atlanta district of the now-deceased civil rights saint Congressman John

Lewis "crime infested" and instructed him to focus on "the burning and crime-infested inner-cities of the US." He tweeted that the four congressional women of color and American citizens known as the Squad—Alexandria Ocasio-Cortez, Ayanna Pressley, Ilhan Omar, and Rashida Tlaib—should "go back [to] the totally broken and crime infested places which they came from."[102] *New York Times* columnist Charles Blow contended that Trump's rhetoric linking Blackness to criminality and "infestation" were part of his larger project of maintaining a supremacist hierarchy in which nonwhites are subhuman and whites are superior.[103]

Beyond Twitter rants, as with prior presidents, ghetto mythology shaped harsh policy decisions. The Trump administration proposed to eliminate food assistance for people stuck in high unemployment places who could not find a job, a new rule that would cut seven hundred thousand people from SNAP (the Supplemental Nutrition Assistance Program). Though this policy would hurt many poor whites in struggling areas, ghetto myths rendered the people on food assistance Black in the public's mind and this likely insulated Trump from criticism from his base for proposing such cuts.[104]

The Trump administration also announced a vague plan to lower the official federal poverty line, a stealth move that, if established, would purge millions from safety-net programs like Medicaid, free-school meals, and energy assistance. David Super, a legal scholar and expert on social welfare policy, claimed that the only discernible motive for such cruelty to poor people, including children, was to help pay for a $2 trillion tax cut, mainly for the super wealthy and corporations, that our nation could not afford.[105] Trump proposed to obliterate the social safety net by cutting $4.4. trillion in government expenditures over ten years.[106]

In addition to tearing at an already tattered social safety net, as described previously, the Trump administration repealed or suspended housing rules that the Obama administration put in place to promote residential integration. The Trump administration also proposed deregulatory "reforms" that steered investment and lending away from historically redlined, disadvantaged communities to luxury development, benefiting wealthy investors and corporate interests. From Reagan to Trump, mythologizing to promote tax cuts for rich people, deregulation, and government shrinkage, except for military spending and border walls, became vulgarly transparent.

To his credit, Trump did support and sign the First Step Act of 2018, a bipartisan effort to reduce the size of the federal prison population and improve outcomes for returning citizens. The act retroactively reduced mandatory-minimum sentences and the harshest penalties for nonviolent drug offenses and gave judges more discretion to depart from the mandatory-minimum, three-strike harshness that fueled mass incarceration. Trump celebrated this achievement as a correction of the excesses of the 1994 Crime Bill that Bill Clinton championed. President Trump invited a rainbow of beneficiaries of the act to the White House and humanized their stories, showing that he was capable of applying a different lens than "thug" to formerly incarcerated people.[107]

And yet Trump leaned on law-and-order tropes in his 2020 reelection bid, more like George Wallace than Richard Nixon in stoking racial division. Trump deployed federal jackboots against citizen protestors, inciting tensions to orchestrate the reality show he wanted. Whether raising a Bible after a night in which federal forces tear-gassed citizens protesting for Black lives, sending forces to duel with protestors in Portland, Oregon, or unconditionally defending Kenosha, Wisconsin, police who shot an unarmed Black father, Jacob Blake, seven times at point-blank range as his three sons watched, Trump cast himself to suburban white voters as their protector against anarchy, riots, and racial integration of their neighborhoods.

Democratic presidential contender Joe Biden had been a lead drafter and shepherd of the 1994 Crime Bill and had a lengthy record of supporting tough criminal policies. In 2020, candidate Biden pointed to the 1994 Crime Bill's ten-year assault weapons ban, prohibitions on violence against women, and funding for drug treatment and background checks for gun purchases.[108] Biden, historically a political moderate, also made racial reconciliation and racial justice a central tenet of his campaign. We reached a tipping point, it seemed, in Democratic Party politics. Anti-Black dog-whistling was now a political nonstarter rather than de rigueur for the party that had once dominated the South as a defender of white supremacy. The choice for voters in 2020 was stark, pitting an emerging multiracial coalition open to racial reckoning against an enduring contingent prone to vote their resentments. For five decades, and centuries, whether and how to incorporate descendants as equal, valued citizens remained a central subtext of American politics. Antitax, racial capitalism wrought profound inequality, and Trump attempted to tap the rage of those locked out, which is most people, not with dog whistles but a bullhorn. That Biden won—with a record eighty-one million votes—along with Kamala Harris, suggests real possibilities for a multiracial democracy that values Black lives and brings all people along.

BELIEFS VS. FACTS

Despite politics, empirical evidence frequently debunks ghetto myths. According to an extensive body of social science research, many people associate Blackness with criminality.[109] Social and political scientists document how local crime stories, particularly local news outlets prime watchers to conflate violence with being Black, activating subconscious fear and loathing of Black people.[110] Not surprisingly, public beliefs about Black criminality far surpass reality. The vast majority of Black people are not violent criminals and rates of violent crime fell sharply after the mid-1990s, especially in poor Black neighborhoods. By 2010, rates of violent crime were half of what they had been at their peak.[111] Inconveniently for mythologists, by 2015, whites in America were committing the largest percentage of violent crime.[112] And yet the Trump administration intentionally downplayed the rise of white supremacist domestic terrorist groups and defunded law enforcement and national security investigation of them.[113]

Those who worry about violent crime should most fear their own race, particularly men they know.[114] Most violent crime occurs between people of the same race. But discarding the lens of fear of Black people requires discerning which Black individuals, based on their individual behavior, actually warrant precaution—mental work regularly done for white individuals.

The facts also defy damaging stereotypes about who uses public assistance. Pre-COVID, in 2017, 28.0 percent of TANF recipients were white, 28.4 percent were Black, and 37.4 percent were Hispanic, with use of the program by Native American, Asian, Native Hawaiian or Pacific Islander, or multiracial groups at roughly 1 to 2 percent respectively.[115] These relative percentages of the rainbow of TANF beneficiaries have been fairly consistent since fiscal year 2011.[116] Though historically Black participation in "welfare" has been higher, this historic discrepancy was not large, and "welfare" was never a majority-Black program. Meanwhile, since at least fiscal year 2010, white families have greatly outnumbered Black families in receiving SNAP food aid, comprising on average 36 percent of SNAP families. Black families are the second-largest group assisted by SNAP, comprising on average since 2010, 24.7 percent of SNAP families.[117] Post-COVID, the US Department of Agriculture's Food and Nutrition Service reported difficulty getting reliable data from states on SNAP usage because of the pandemic.

Out-of-wedlock births are heavily associated with Black women and the alleged breakdown of the Black family. Despite this narrative, births to unmarried Black females have dropped dramatically since 1970. Black teenage birthrates, which dropped by 63 percent between 1991 and 2013, are currently at an all-time low. Unmarried Black women are doing what conservatives have lectured them to do, having fewer children. Married Black couples have cut back on childbearing even more; it is their restraint that skews the ratio of married to unmarried Black births, making it appear that out-of-wedlock childbearing has been on the rise among Black Americans when in fact such births have been falling precipitously.[118]

Thankfully, a growing cohort of Americans has awakened and rejects stereotyping. Recent research suggests a gap of perception between culturally dexterous and nondexterous people. Cultural dexterity, a phrase I coined, is the quality of being able to accept, if not welcome, racial and cultural difference and not insist that one's own cultural norms or race be dominant.[119] A culturally dexterous white person accepts the loss of centrality of whiteness in America and is willing to work at accommodating if not embracing a variety of cultural and social norms. Culturally dexterous whites practice pluralism. They see race, or at least don't pretend that they do not see it. The dexterous, in my view, are also willing to see and name racism.

Some go further and actively resist it. A dexterous person has friends or loved ones of a different race, and this experience humanizes others in ways that can debunk stereotypes. Younger whites are more apt to be dexterous than their parents or grandparents, though it is easy enough to find images of white collegiate partiers dressing "ghetto" for the thrill of it.[120]

Gaps of perception about the prevalence of racism and structural barriers that hold Black Americans back show up in opinion polls. A 2019 study by Pew Research Center found that 68 percent of Blacks and 55 percent of whites believed that being Black generally hurts a person's ability to achieve social and economic progress.[121] Partisan identity influenced whether whites were willing to acknowledge structural barriers. White Democrats who acknowledge Black disadvantage identify racial discrimination (70 percent), less access to good schools (75 percent) or high-paying jobs (64 percent) as major obstacles while white Republicans tend to blame family instability, lack of good role models or lack of motivation to work hard.[122]

White conservatives, particularly Republicans, are much more likely to deny obstacles and discrimination against Black Americans in a land where obstacles to descendants are abundant. White conservatives, especially evangelicals, are more likely to perceive discrimination against whites, that is themselves, than to acknowledge racial discrimination against Black people.[123] Social scientists find that racial resentments drive whites who harbor them to repudiate government interventions because they attribute racial inequality to personal behavior and not systemic discrimination. Racial resentment, which is not the same as racism, remains the strongest predictor of white attitudes toward policies to redress racial inequality and has been since the 1980s.[124]

The characteristics that some whites attribute to Blacks as the reasons for their failings—lack of good role models, lack of motivation to work hard, and lack of family stability—mirror ghetto myths and reinforce a social order that prioritizes affluent whites. Widespread denial of anti-Black discrimination and pathologizing of poor Black people explains why it is so difficult to dismantle or mitigate concentrated poverty. Resistance to facts among a political minority, coupled with racial and political gerrymandering, and an electoral college that accords disproportionate power to states where racial conservatives dominate, entrenches an unacceptable status quo: gross economic and racial inequality and a broken social contract. In a society premised on separation and hoarding in advantaged places and containment of descendants elsewhere, only an advantaged few can win.

CHAPTER 5

OPPORTUNITY HOARDING

Overinvest and Exclude, Disinvest and Contain

On an April afternoon in Philadelphia, 2018, another urban op-era unfolded. Entrepreneurs Rashon Nelson and Donte Robinson sat down in a Starbucks coffeehouse to wait for another local businessman to arrive. They were both twenty-three-years young, friends since grade school, and excited to be pursuing their dreams and a potential real estate deal. Nelson asked to use the restroom as they waited and a barista declined, telling him that only patrons could use it, if they wished to order anything. The men informed her that they were waiting for someone to begin a meeting. Minutes later, police officers arrived and told Nelson and Robinson to leave, im-mediately. They refused, in a low-key way. Melissa DePino, a white customer and citizen-journalist in that moment, posted a video on Twitter that traveled the globe. Woke viewers saw two calm Black men acquiescing in being handcuffed and arrested, as seven police officers crowded a fabricated crime scene.[1]

Rittenhouse Square, the highest-income neighborhood in Phila-delphia, is also more than 80 percent white. It gained some notoriety as the locale where Nelson and Robinson were arrested for "waiting while Black." Elijah Anderson, the sociologist and leading urban eth-nographer, refers to such turf as "white space" as does legal scholar, Elise Boddie, in her theory of racial territoriality.[2]

Despite the civil rights movement, Anderson writes, American society "is still replete with overwhelmingly white neighborhoods, restaurants, schools, universities, workplaces, churches and other associations, courthouses, and cemeteries, a situation that reinforces a normative sensibility in settings in which black people are typically absent, not expected, or marginalized when present." Anderson argues that where Black and white homogeneous spaces appear on opposite sides of a line, this exacerbates society's association of Black skin with "the iconic ghetto." The ghetto and the idea that all Blacks come from it, he argues, "justify the normative sensibility of the white space" that excludes Blacks or requires an explanation when they are present.[3]

Anderson observed a west Philadelphia neighborhood becoming whiter and less economically diverse as it gentrified. In his framing, "white space" is necessarily richer than Black space, and people engaged in exclusion get their ideas about Blackness from real or imagined notions of what transpires in high-poverty Black neighborhoods.[4] It is *affluent* white space that is most practiced in the art of excluding Blacks and hoarding opportunity from *all people* who live elsewhere. Wealthy neighborhoods and the people who live in them are at the top of an American caste system at the intersection of geography, race, and class. Anderson's intuitions about the role of physical lines of division are apt. Exclusive and exclusionary white space could not exist without a constructed ghetto that concentrates poverty elsewhere.

So it is with Rittenhouse Square. The Philadelphia visitors' bureau describes it as "the heart of Center City's most expensive and exclusive neighborhood." Center City covers the original boundaries of the city, before it was merged with Philadelphia County. Any visitor familiar with the ways of modern American segregation would read this profile of the Rittenhouse neighborhood and expect to enter a bastion of upper-class whiteness: "With a bevy of high-rise residences filled with top-end luxury apartments, and some of the best fine dining experiences in the city, residents can marvel at their options, while also enjoying the luxury retail shopping in the area, all of which help surrounds [sic] the handsome tree-filled park."[5]

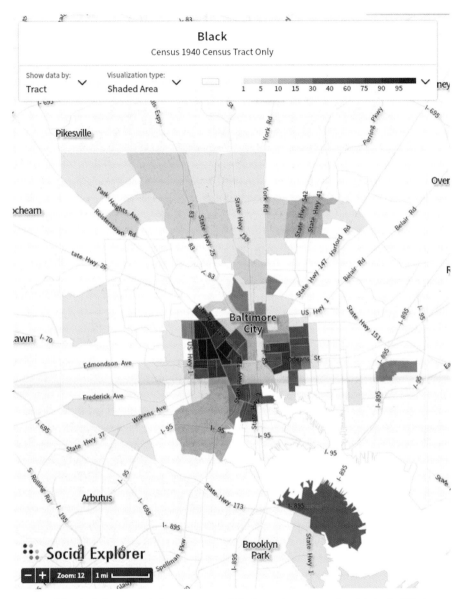

Map 1.1. The shaded areas track the percentage of Black people, segregated mainly in the "Black Butterfly."

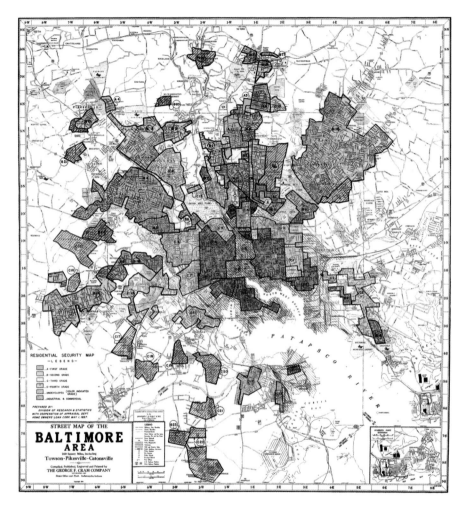

Map. 1.2. HOLC map. Redlined areas coincide with Black neighborhoods.

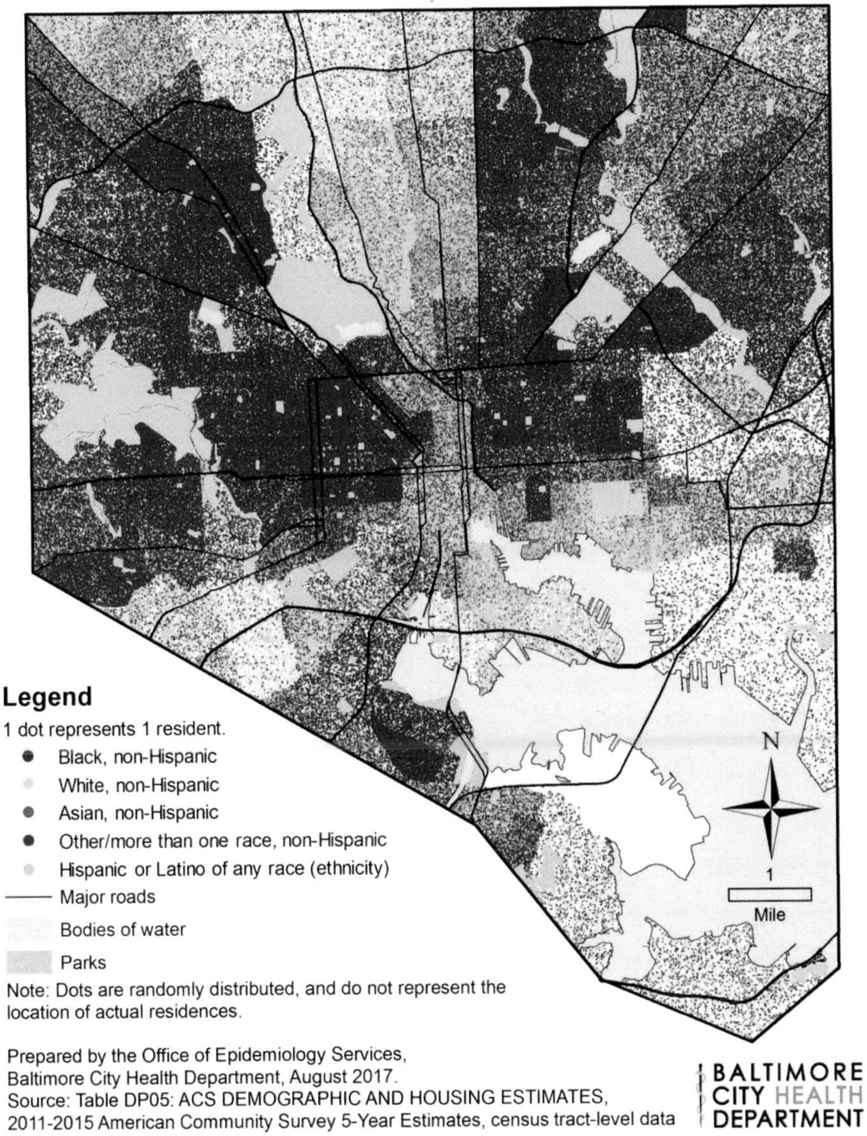

Legend

1 dot represents 1 resident.

- ● Black, non-Hispanic
- ○ White, non-Hispanic
- ● Asian, non-Hispanic
- ● Other/more than one race, non-Hispanic
- ○ Hispanic or Latino of any race (ethnicity)
- —— Major roads
-   Bodies of water
-   Parks

Note: Dots are randomly distributed, and do not represent the location of actual residences.

N

1

Mile

Prepared by the Office of Epidemiology Services, Baltimore City Health Department, August 2017.
Source: Table DP05: ACS DEMOGRAPHIC AND HOUSING ESTIMATES, 2011-2015 American Community Survey 5-Year Estimates, census tract-level data

BALTIMORE
CITY HEALTH
DEPARTMENT

Map 1.3. Geographic Distribution of Residents by Race and Ethnicity, Baltimore City, 2011–2015

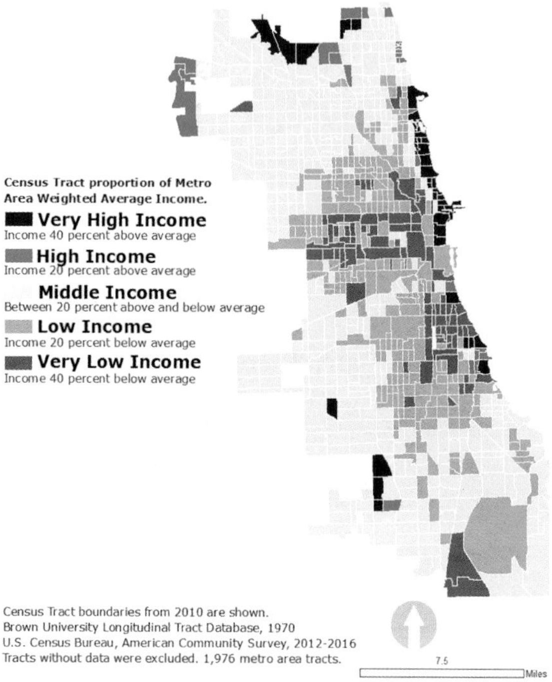

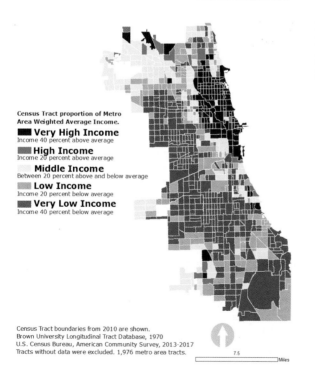

Map 3.1. Average Individual Income, 1970. City of Chicago, Relative to Seven County Metro Area.

Census Tract proportion of Metro Area Weighted Average Income.

Very High Income
Income 40 percent above average

High Income
Income 20 percent above average

Middle Income
Between 20 percent above and below average

Low Income
Income 20 percent below average

Very Low Income
Income 40 percent below average

Census Tract boundaries from 2010 are shown.
Brown University Longitudinal Tract Database, 1970
U.S. Census Bureau, American Community Survey, 2012-2016
Tracts without data were excluded. 1,976 metro area tracts.

7.5 | Miles

Map 3.2. Average Individual Income, 2017. City of Chicago, Relative to Seven County Metro Area.

Census Tract proportion of Metro Area Weighted Average Income.

Very High Income
Income 40 percent above average

High Income
Income 20 percent above average

Middle Income
Between 20 percent above and below average

Low Income
Income 20 percent below average

Very Low Income
Income 40 percent below average

Census Tract boundaries from 2010 are shown.
Brown University Longitudinal Tract Database, 1970
U.S. Census Bureau, American Community Survey, 2013-2017
Tracts without data were excluded. 1,976 metro area tracts.

7.5 | Miles

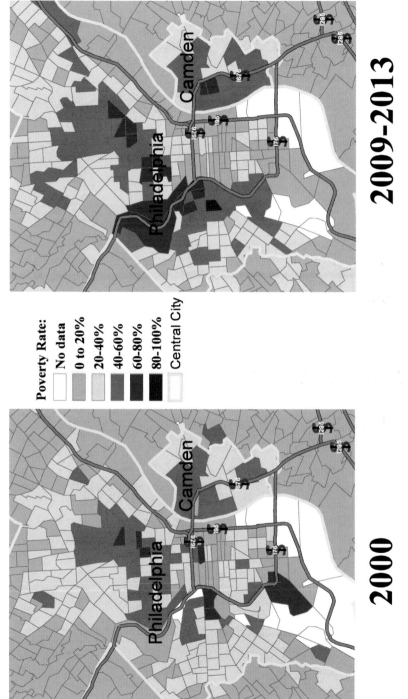

Map 5.1. US Census 2000 and ACS 2009–2013 Map Compilation of Philadelphia

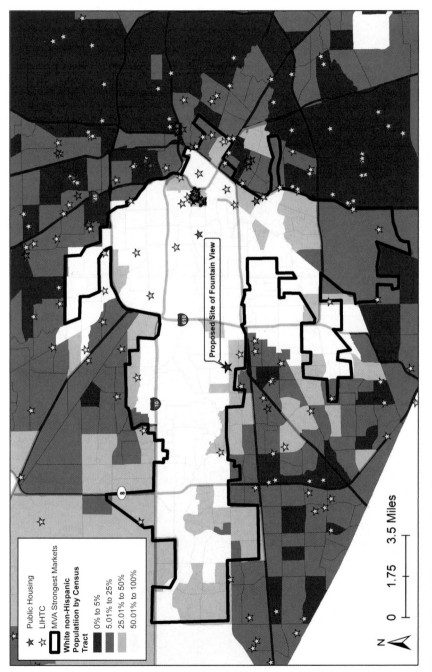

Map 5.2. Subsizided Housing in Harris County

Legend:

★ Public Housing
☆ LIHTC
☐ MVA Strongest Markets

White non-Hispanic Population by Census Tract
- 0% to 5%
- 5.01% to 25%
- 25.01% to 50%
- 50.01% to 100%

Proposed Site of Fountain View

N

0   1.75   3.5 Miles

STATE OF CONNECTICUT

This map displays the spatial pattern of distribution of opportunity by census tract based on Education, Economic & Mobility, and Housing & Neighborhood indicators, overlaid with non-White population.

Map 6.1. Comprehensive Opportunity with Non-White Population Overlay

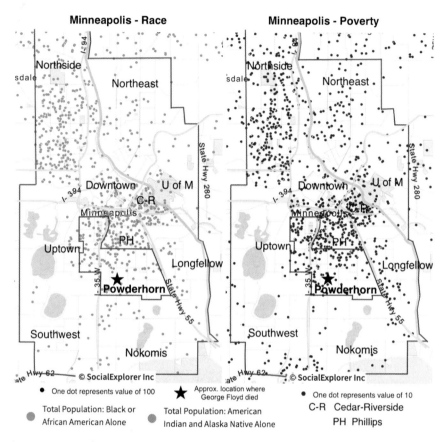

Minneapolis - Race

Minneapolis - Poverty

- One dot represents value of 100
- ★ Approx. location where George Floyd died
- ● Total Population: Black or African American Alone
- ● Total Population: American Indian and Alaska Native Alone
- One dot represents value of 10
- C-R Cedar-Riverside
- PH Phillips

Map 8.1. Minneapolis–Race, Minneapolis–Poverty

Rittenhouse Square and other nearby very white spaces are part of the old Seventh Ward that W. E. B. Du Bois chronicled in *The Philadelphia Negro*, though Black Americans are now a tiny minority. True to Anderson's instincts, the neighborhood surrounding Rittenhouse Square, and Center City generally, have become more affluent since 2000 even as many other neighborhoods in Philadelphia and adjacent Camden, New Jersey, became much poorer. Maps tell the story better than words. Paul Jargowsky describes an "architecture of segregation" in which the number of people living in concentrated poverty climbed by 91 percent in the first decade and a half of the new millennium. He produced side-by-side color-coded maps of this change in several metropolitan areas, the first map a snapshot of economic segregation in 2000, the second showing segregation patterns by about 2013. They illustrate the dramatic expansion of poor space and bulwarking of affluent space in favored suburbs and newly desirable city centers.[6]

Jargowsky's side-by-side maps of Philadelphia appear as Map 5.1 in the insert. Rittenhouse Square is located in the lower left quadrant of affluent Center City, which straddles I-676 and is bounded to the west and east by rivers and interstate highways. The maps show that between 2000 and 2013 concentrated poverty was virtually eliminated from Center City as it exploded elsewhere.[7]

Philadelphia is just one example. I viewed Jargowsky's maps of thirty-two sample regions, from Akron, Ohio, to Washington, DC, and the overwhelming pattern was one of intensifying poverty-free areas separated from expanding poverty-concentrated areas, often with a street or highway demarcating the boundary between the two. The maps depict startling geographic shifts that occurred in less than fifteen years.

Pittsburgh, Pennsylvania, experienced a revival in the 2000s, driven in part by its more than sixty robotics and self-driving-car startup companies and tech firms, like Uber and Google. In Jargowsky's companion maps of this city at the confluence of three rivers, with hundreds of bridges that cross them, virtually all the poverty areas that were once scattered in 2000 were eliminated from the southern and western parts of the city, below and west of interstates, by

2013. And poor folks became extremely concentrated in the east, in and around the Hill District of playwright August Wilson's boyhood, a hilly area perched above downtown and sequestered by two rivers.

Wilson, in his ten-play cycle, touches on the plunder and pain descendants in the Hill District endured in each decade of the twentieth century, as well as their joy and genius. His mystical character and sage, Aunt Ester, lived at 1839 Wylie Avenue and at over three hundred years old was symbolic ancestor to all descendants of slavery. In real life, Wylie Avenue was once dense with nightclubs where jazz giants like Earl Hines, Art Blakey, Billy Eckstine, and Mary Lou Williams held forth. As a child, Wilson lived at 1727 Bedford Avenue, in two rooms above and behind a storefront. It has been restored as a landmark and community arts center. Across the street was Bedford Dwellings, the city's oldest public-housing complex, which has been redeveloped into mixed-income housing. With vision, this corridor of historic Black segregation, not far from white space, could redevelop inclusively and preserve rather than displace the Black American culture that Wilson chronicled.[8]

The Hill District was one place in Pittsburgh that great migrants were conscribed to. It, too, received HOLC's D rating, marking a gem of creativity red and "hazardous." Negroes there were also removed by urban renewal. Wilson wrote about it in his play *Two Trains Running*. Set in 1969, a year after riots, the owner and inhabitants of a soul food café are forced to contend with impending condemnation by the city and external forces weighing down on them. Instead of contesting removal, the owner, Memphis, fights for just compensation.

Jargowsky also mapped Houston. West Houston was scrubbed of any concentrated poverty while Ward Five in the east, bounded by two interstates, became intensely poor. Ward Five had been and continues to be very Black and poor, surrounded by Houstonians who speak 145 languages. Concentrated poverty also spread to the Houston suburbs as the western half of the city center became the place for affluent movers. In Dallas, poverty concentrated in the southeast quadrant inside the beltway; north Dallas above I-30 is its affluent opposite, though a fair housing organization, the Inclusive Communities Project, has made inroads in locating some low-income people in high-opportunity areas.[9]

Areas coded red for greater than 40 percent poverty overwhelmed some of the cities that Jargowsky mapped. The hearts of cities like Cleveland, Detroit, Fresno, Gary, Milwaukee, Rochester, East St. Louis, and Syracuse hemorrhaged deep red as concentrated poverty expanded in all directions. Other researchers document similar patterns. Across fifty-one cities, one study found nearly three times as many high-poverty areas in 2010 than in 1970. In the wake of the civil rights movement, precious few "ghettoes" were transformed. Instead, many more majority-Black high-poverty areas were added.[10]

Of course, individual cities vary and there are a range of types of people and neighborhoods that inhabit them. Geographer Elizabeth Delmelle, in a comprehensive study of neighborhood change between 1990 and 2010 in America's fifty largest cities, found that neighborhoods of concentrated Black poverty remained the most persistent type, followed by those of concentrated white and Asian affluence. These neighborhoods at polar extremes increased in spatial concentration while more moderate-income multiethnic neighborhoods became more fragmented, showing more possibilities for racial and economic mixture.[11]

Stark lines shape local politics. The Philadelphia city council deadlocked over a proposal to *require* developers in Center City, University City (home to the University of Pennsylvania and other educational institutions), and other dense areas to include affordable units in their new residential buildings—a policy known as mandatory inclusionary zoning. Instead a watered-down bill was passed giving developers who wanted to build taller buildings the choice whether, in exchange for more density, to build affordable housing on-site or to make payments to the city's affordable housing trust fund.[12] Segregation precipitates a zero-sum politics with distinct winners and losers. Society tends to overvalue white space and the needs of the people who live there and devalue Black neighborhoods and their residents' concerns. It is the concentration of affluence, intentionally separated from neighborhoods where concentrated poverty persists or expands, that fuels the divided American City.[13]

GEOGRAPHY BEGETS CASTE

In pre-civil-rights America, we had a caste system based mainly on race in which those who could claim whiteness were accorded social and legal privileges of citizenship and those who could not, especially Black Americans, were denied. Isabel Wilkerson, in her best-selling book *Caste: The Origins of Our Discontents*, describes caste as a system of power relations in which ancestry or immutable traits are used to construct a rigid social hierarchy premised on the alleged supremacy of one group and the presumed inferiority of other groups. She powerfully illuminates the endurance of social caste in the United States and India. I agree with her that caste is "the infrastructure of our divisions."[14] Here I illuminate the centrality of geography to American caste, its mechanisms for distributing benefits and burdens and shaping racial perceptions about who is deserving. As sociologist Robert Sampson demonstrates in his important book *Great American City: Chicago and the Enduring Neighborhood Effect*, there is a spatial logic to inequality and "differentiation by neighborhood is not only everywhere to be seen . . . it has durable properties—with cultural and social mechanisms of reproduction" that affect the allocation of social advantage and disadvantage and of resources.[15] Patrick Sharkey also underscores that because of rigid segregation and severe disinvestment in poor Black neighborhoods, place—where one lives—is a crucial mechanism for producing racial inequality.[16]

I begin with the concentration of affluence. Segregation by income is most extreme for those in the ninetieth or higher percentile of the income scale. The affluent are the least exposed to poverty and their segregation increases with the size of the metropolis they live in.[17] In large cities, regular folk can easily call out neighborhoods occupied by rich people: Georgetown in Washington, DC, the Gold Coast in Chicago, the Upper East Side in Manhattan, Buckhead in Atlanta, and Pacific Heights in San Francisco, to name a few. Wherever affluence is concentrated, the neighborhood is usually very white. Nationally, whites and Asians are less likely to be exposed to poverty and more likely to live in middle-class settings than Black and Latinx people. The majority of whites and Asians live in neighborhoods with a poverty rate below 14 percent.[18]

My theory of American caste is tied to how geography reifies power and opportunity for those in a few rich neighborhoods and contributes to powerlessness and permanence of poverty for descendants. The segregation of affluence facilitates opportunity hoarding, whereby the most affluent neighborhoods enjoy the best public services, environmental quality, and private, public, and natural amenities, while *all* other communities are left with fewer, poorer-quality resources.[19] Segregated affluence occurs not only within cities but increasingly between them, as entire localities have become preserves of the wealthy. Segregation of the highly educated has increased even faster than that of the affluent. In the 2000s, only seventeen counties in America had a population in which more than half are college educated. College graduates living in America's most highly educated metro areas are more residentially isolated than Black Americans.[20]

In any given American metropolis, most people know where the poor are concentrated, especially the hoods that people with choices avoid. At the highest and lowest ends of the real estate spectrum, the role of geography in constructing American caste is fairly transparent, if not an article of faith. Widespread segregation enables insulation from people we fear. It also facilitates a tarnished but persistent myth of an American Dream that increasingly belongs only to those who can buy their way into poverty-free havens.[21]

Residents of high-opportunity neighborhoods rise on the benefits of exceptional schools and social networks. Favored places confer intangibles—the habits of success you observe and emulate, the people and ideas you are exposed to, the books you are motivated to read, the selective schools and jobs you learn about. At the other end of the spectrum, neighborhoods with high poverty, limited employment, underperforming schools, distressed housing, and violent crime depress life outcomes. I discuss these harsh effects of the hood in chapter 7. Here I address the consequences of concentrated affluence. Using the phraseology of social scientist Charles Tilly and others, I argue that segregation facilitates three phenomena that contribute to American residential caste: social distancing, boundary maintenance, and opportunity hoarding.[22]

BOUNDARY MAINTENANCE

Individual choices, particularly avoidance of Black areas, contribute to boundary maintenance. When it comes to choosing where to live, many non-Black people are wary of living in close proximity to Black Americans, and whites are the wariest of all. Whites tend to prefer majority-white neighborhoods that are less than 20 percent Black and often resist moving to spaces with more than a smattering of nonwhite people.[23] While most whites accept integration in principle, many still express strong preferences to remain socially distant from nonwhites, particularly Black Americans.[24]

Beyond individual preferences, collective action and state-sanctioned policies play a critical role. The affluent maintain boundaries through exclusionary or restrictive zoning or simply using their political power to oppose development that they don't want. Author Richard Reeves calls it "inverse ghettoization"—local rules, regulations, or NIMBYism that badly distort real estate markets.[25] Exclusive suburbs created and maintained their exclusivity through a phalanx of zoning requirements that ensured that only expensive and expansive single-family homes on large lots were built along with only the most desirable, environmentally pristine, tax-revenue producing uses of land. No or few apartments, much less low-income or affordable ones, were allowed.[26] Recent research indicates that suburban white enclaves still actively segregate through restrictive zoning and anti-Black prejudice.[27]

Within cities, habits of segregation begun in the twentieth century continue into the twenty-first, though the policies and practices that sustain segregation may be less visible and the boundaries of affluent white space may shift. What happens or doesn't happen on the ground in neighborhoods reflects who has power to influence decision makers. A mandatory inclusionary zoning ordinance may be tabled, as happened in Philadelphia.

Map 5.2, in the insert, identifies each public housing project in Houston, Texas, with a red star and shows that virtually no public housing is located in the majority-white spaces of the city. Most other major cities in Texas mirror this pattern. In the Lone Star State, housing developments that receive subsidies from the federal Low-

Income Housing Tax Credit (LIHTC) program overwhelmingly are located in poor nonwhite areas. Not surprisingly, given their concentrations of poor families of color, Texas cities and the state generally rate very low on social mobility for poor children.[28] Texas may be more effective at insulating white space from low-income housing because the state enables neighborhood groups to block LIHTC projects it disagrees with.[29] But nationally, only about 17 percent of LIHTC projects are built in high-opportunity neighborhoods with high-performing schools, low crime, and easy access to jobs.[30]

These patterns persist even in cities led by Black mayors. Lee Brown, an African American, served as mayor of Houston for three terms, from 1998 to 2004. Sylvester Turner, elected in 2015 on his third try, is Houston's second African American mayor. Upon taking the helm, he inherited a segregated city created by a long history of intention. By its own admission, in an analysis submitted to HUD and approved by the mayor and city council in 2015, the city of Houston *concentrated more than 71 percent of all government-subsidized housing in only five of its 88 neighborhoods, all of which were very poor and nonwhite.*[31]

In the twentieth century, Houston, like Dallas, Phoenix, and other southwestern cities, followed the national playbook of "slum clearance" and intentionally segregated public housing to confine Negroes and Mexican Americans.[32] The Houston Housing Authority (HHA), under pressure from HUD during the Obama years, finally attempted to desegregate its public housing when it proposed its first ever project in a predominantly white, high-opportunity area. The proposed Fountain View housing complex was going to be mixed-income and architecturally consistent with surrounding housing in a west Houston neighborhood near the tony Galleria shopping mall. An architect's rendering presented an attractive complex that looked like other market-rate housing in the area. At a public hearing on the project, an HHA official presented the agency's sorry history of intentional segregation and cited recent research documenting the much-improved social mobility for poor children of living in middle-class settings. But the very white crowd was unmoved, as were elected officials.[33]

The US congressman, city councilman, and school board member who represented the 87-percent white census tract where Fountain View was to be located all spoke against it. "The research—that's not the issue," said the then US congressman, John Culberson, in response to the HHA's presentation. He pledged to sponsor a bill in Congress to make federal housing policy "race neutral." Despite a documented history of decades of racial discrimination by state actors, he wanted to wrest from government the ability to consider race in locating publicly subsidized housing, although targeting areas made whiter through discrimination was necessary to remedy that discrimination.[34]

Mayor Turner, born in 1954, the year *Brown v. Board of Education* was decided, grew up in a large unincorporated Black community that was later annexed by Houston. He prevented the Fountain View project from going forward by refusing to bring it to the city council for a vote to approve needed LIHTC subsidies, citing "costs and other concerns" for the proposed $53 million development. A month later, HUD opened a civil rights investigation.

In its report, HUD concluded that "the city maintains a system for approving LIHTC projects that [are] dependent on whether there is opposition from the residents of the neighborhood" and does so "against a well-documented backdrop of racially motivated opposition to affordable housing and a history of segregation." According to Obama's HUD, Mayor Turner's professed concern about cost was mere pretext because the federal LIHTC funds did not come from city coffers. HUD concluded that the mayor had caved to "racially motivated local opposition." The report catalogued a litany of coded racial statements made by residents and officials opposing the project, including "bringing them here will bring down this area" and "people come in here and they steal the tires off our Suburbans."[35]

But the opposition won. The project was scuttled. It was part of a pattern at the time of neighborhood opposition often successfully blocking proposed affordable housing. As in *Plessy v. Ferguson,* as with Jim Crow, all that mattered was what those with the power to exclude wanted, despite a constitutional mandate of equality and civil rights laws that Mayor Turner's generation of Black youth agitated for. Mayor Turner reached an agreement with Trump's HUD in 2018 to end the civil rights investigation. Turner and the city acknowledged the need for affordable housing everywhere and committed to "a site selection policy prioritizing high opportunity areas."[36]

Houston is not an outlier, merely an example of how and why states reify affluent white space. Even in Washington, DC, which has an ostensibly mandatory inclusionary zoning ordinance, virtually all of the inclusionary units that are built under the law are located east of Rock Creek Park. Affluent, very white Ward Three to the west has received less than 1 percent of the affordable units recently built under the law. Extremely low-income families, those making less than $30,000, are not benefiting from the program at all.[37] Some low-income housing advocates may defend this result, arguing that more affordable housing can be built in less expensive areas and that Black neighborhood activists want preservation and investment in affordable housing stock where they live.[38] Advocates of *fair* housing, myself included, argue that government should not encourage or institutionalize residential stratification.[39] Bastions of exclusion, once created, encourage people who benefit from them to justify and protect what they have and reap more than their fair share of public resources.

Another example of boundary maintenance in the District are two public elementary schools within one mile of each other near Capitol Hill. One, Brent Elementary, is 61 percent white and 9 percent economically disadvantaged (the school district's term for poor). Payne Elementary is 70 percent Black and 100 percent economically disadvantaged.[40] Imagine the resistance that would ensue if the DC schools chancellor attempted to redraw attendance zones to better integrate both schools or to ensure that Payne is not overwhelmed by poverty. A school superintendent in Minnesota lost her job when she tried to move boundary lines to keep a school from becoming racially isolated.[41] Imagine also the resistance that would ensue if, instead, the DC schools chancellor decided to reassign the most experienced teachers in the school system to the most impoverished schools, or to dramatically reduce the student-to-teacher ratios only for the poorest schools—among the few evidence-based reforms that improve achievement in very high-poverty schools.[42] Neither reforms are likely to happen because of the entrenched expectations and influence of those advantaged by boundaries.

Divides borne of decades of anti-Black policies—restrictive covenants, redlining, urban renewal, segregated public housing, community-destroying interstate highways—persist like ancient ruins. A Black part of town is separated from an idealized white area, a pattern that occurs in communities small and large.[43] Railroad tracks, highways, rivers—barriers made by God and man—persist as walls of exclusion. Interstate 49 in Shreveport, Louisiana, runs north to south, still dividing the Black west side from the white east. In Kansas City, Missouri, north-south running Troost Avenue became the "Troost Wall," only in this city, where young Charlie Parker immersed himself in jazz and nightlife, Blacks are confined to the east. Main Street in Buffalo, New York, and Highway 41 in Milwaukee, Wisconsin, produce similarly stark Blacks-to-the-east and whites-to-the-west patterns.[44]

The most well-known divides traverse cities for miles. Infamously, Delmar Boulevard runs from east to west across St. Louis, Missouri. North of Delmar lies an overwhelmingly Black neighborhood pockmarked by boarded-up, vacant houses. Fewer than 10 percent of the residents have college degrees. Retail is scarce, though there are liquor stores and small family-owned markets. South of Delmar, mansions stand and impress. This neighborhood is very white, and about 70 percent of residents have graduated from college. They enjoy a density of retail and dining options. A white mother interviewed by the BBC for a short documentary about the contrast worried about the worldview her child will develop as they traversed "the Gucci grocery store" and the "ghetto grocery store."[45] Similarly, 8 Mile Road on the north boundary of Detroit divides predominantly white space from lower-income Black space. Prior to the COVID-19 pandemic, city and suburban neighborhoods were changing in both the Detroit and St. Louis metro regions. White professionals were moving into the urban core, and middle- and upper-income Blacks were moving to the suburbs in both regions. It remains to be seen how patterns will settle, but pronounced divides remain.

Often a divide spans mere blocks. A neighborhood north of the Georgetown Law campus in Washington, DC, where I teach, was rebirthed as NOMA, for North of Massachusetts Avenue. Varying classes and races confront each other along Florida and New York

Avenues. One census tract is 65 percent white, with a median income of $109,000. It is adjacent to a tract that is 63 percent Black, with a $17,303 median, meaning half of the folks here make less than this meager wage.[46] A formerly notorious housing project in the vicinity, Sursum Corda, has been torn down, slated to be replaced with a mixed-income development. Luxury condominium buildings are being constructed nearby. If promises are kept, and the city's inclusionary zoning ordinance is enforced, original residents of Sursum Corda will return to live among higher-income people and serve as an example to the rest of the city of residential inclusion.[47]

On a day I walked through NOMA in 2019, a Black-owned barber shop, Popular Cuts, held on, a sign in its front window still urging people to vote for Obama. Around the corner, along K Street, were design-chic places that cater to people making six figures—a fancy nail salon, coffee shop, juice bar, and bike store. This is Census Tract 47.01. It was about one-fifth white, 70 percent Black, and clearly transitioning. It is divided by I-395; the Black and poor side to the east feels very different than the white and upper-income blocks to the west.

On the Black side are sturdy but weathered townhouses, most not yet touched by the remodeling wave sweeping the city. Red or brown brick has not yet been painted a soothing shade of gray. House numbers are marked in old English fonts, not art deco. Ordinary black and brown front doors have not yet been replaced with modern, primary-colored ones. Serviceable vertical black iron railings frame front entries instead of horizontal stainless ones that scream remodeled-cool. In this un-redeveloped corner of NOMA, I see plain, struggling Blackness, interrupted by the occasional vacant, boarded property.

My Black American eyes see beauty and dignity in these residents' struggle. There are few businesses here and very few public trash cans. The occasional ones I see are overflowing. Less than a mile away, on the gentrifying majority-white west side of the same census tract, there is a well-tended public trash can nearly every twenty feet. No dog walker there will have to carry poop for long. How is it that such a stark disparity in trash collection—a public service—exists within the same census tract? Derek Hyra, another urban sociologist, conducted a case study in the Shaw/U Street neighborhood of

Washington, DC, and concluded that the gentrification caused not only cultural displacement but also decreased political power among long-term residents.[48] Segregation and boundary maintenance contribute to separate and unequal distribution of resources.

OPPORTUNITY HOARDING

What happens in a society in which income and wealth are increasingly concentrated in certain neighborhoods? Douglas Massey reasons that where social boundaries conform to geographic ones, the processes of social stratification that come naturally to human beings become much more efficient and effective: "If out-group members are spatially segregated from in-group members, then the latter are put in good position to use their social power to create institutions and practices that channel resources away from the places where out-group members live." The same power, he writes, can be used to "direct resources systemically toward in-group areas." Massey, invoking Charles Tilley's phraseology, calls this opportunity hoarding and argues that segregation exacerbates it.[49]

Segregation puts affluent, high-opportunity places in direct competition with lower-opportunity communities for finite public and private resources. Affluent neighborhoods often receive more than their fair share of resources at the expense of, and often subsidized by, everyone else. Those who advocate to bring resources to already-advantaged places contribute to disinvestment and decline elsewhere though they are not likely to perceive or acknowledge this connection.[50]

Non-rich Americans of all colors and political persuasions should care about the segregation of affluence, not only because opportunity hoarding and unequal public and private investment results but because it limits possibilities for their own social mobility. Those excluded from the best schools, amenities, and networks that lead to great jobs and selective higher education are more likely to be stuck in the socioeconomic class they were born into or to fall lower on the income scale. Rising geographic separation of the affluent appears to contribute to rising inequality.[51] They rose together in the late twentieth century. As those with the power to set wages for others became ever more residentially isolated from people who need their paychecks, CEO-to-worker pay increased 875 percent between 1978 and 2012, and by 2017, CEOs were paid 361 times more than the average worker.[52]

Segregation of affluence strikes at the heart of American shibboleths. Rather than facilitating robust upward mobility, it protects the wealthiest from competition from everyone else.[53] In 2010, only 42 percent of all Americans lived in a middle-class neighborhood, down from 65 percent in 1970.[54] This is due to the rising segregation of affluence and of poverty. With economic sorting, there are fewer middle-class neighborhoods, and those that persist are at risk of declining and becoming poorer as affluent people, and their tax base, concentrate elsewhere.

An example: Once-aspirational residential suburbs of Philadelphia struggle to pay for schools and to replace old water and sewer lines that violate environmental mandates. Low-income voucher holders moved to struggling suburbs as poor people were priced out of Philadelphia. As poor people moved in, middle-class and wealthy people fled, a pattern of suburbanization of poverty that occurred in many metropolitan areas. As one town councilman in struggling Norristown, Pennsylvania, said of its predicament, in the *National Catholic Reporter,* "We've lost that sense as Americans that we can all still live together and that's part of what's made the inequality in this country so crass and gross. People don't want to be around each other anymore."[55]

The risk for a nation in which elites increasingly live apart from everyone else is that the resources and tax base to pay for programs and institutions that ordinary people need will continue to erode. Worse, those who live in concentrated poverty are likely to be trapped there. In an America that segregates wealth and opportunity from the poor, neither city, suburb, nor rural hamlet will be an engine of upward mobility for poor folk.[56]

Those who live in affluent areas may resist this analysis, offended that it somehow denies their hard work. Individuals toil mightily to get into or stay in the winner column. My argument is that (1) it is much easier to win while riding the "up" escalator; and (2) the policies and habits that facilitate a ride up for a relative few also force many others to take the "down" escalator.[57] I have presented my theory of the distributional effects of concentrated affluence. Here is more evidence from specific contexts to support it.

SERVICES, PUBLIC GOODS, INFRASTRUCTURE, AND DEVELOPMENT

Paul Jargowsky correctly asserts that the expansion of high-poverty hoods—and impliedly, its opposite, the concentration of affluence— is the result of intentional public policy choices. He argues that our nation's investment in affluent, exclusionary suburbs and exurbs, beginning in the 1970s, was excessive and far beyond what was needed to meet metropolitan population growth. As older, underutilized communities languished or declined in that era, regions paid for new infrastructure in exclusionary new suburbs.[58] The federal government rained down more than half a trillion dollars on states to subsidize the cost of roads leading out to an ever-expanding suburban frontier. Much as the federal government pursued foundational policies that assisted locals in constructing and maintaining poor Black space, highways and redlined FHA mortgage insurance were foundational federal investments in suburbanizing white space.[59] Academics, myself included, have bemoaned the tyranny of suburban-favored quarters that are subsidized by the people they exclude. People of all colors and classes who live elsewhere helped pay for the roads, sewers, and other golden infrastructure that made these low-poverty, resource-rich places possible.[60]

This pattern of overinvestment in exclusionary predominantly white space and disinvestment or neglect elsewhere is replicated within cities across the country. Jessica Trounstine, in her important book *Segregation by Design*, argues that segregation, developed and maintained over a century, institutionalized the preferences of white property owners, protecting their property values and giving exclusive access to high-quality public amenities. She amassed empirical evidence to support her theory that segregation creates a city politics that reproduces inequality—a racial and economic hierarchy of favored and disfavored residents. After local governments deployed land use, slum clearance, and other policies to tightly compact Black Americans, they denied them adequate sewers, roads, garbage collection, and/or public health services. Trounstine argues that this nefarious role of segregation in city politics continues to this day. She asserts that wealthy whites still try to segregate themselves, and local governments still acquiesce in their desires, invest more in their neighborhoods, and disinvest elsewhere.[61]

For example, Trounstine examined detailed ward-level data from Baltimore, Boston, Chicago, and Philadelphia, and found that sewer extensions were much less likely to be built in neighborhoods with large numbers of Black renters, and this inequality persists. She analyzed all American cities and found that more segregated cities had more racial inequality in water and sewer access. Meanwhile, unequal service provisions informed white folks' judgments about poor and minority people. Disinvestment in Black neighborhoods contributed to conscious and unconscious biases about the effect of nonwhites on property values and quality of public goods. Segregation begat disinvestment. Disinvestment begat whites' biased attitudes, which in turn contributed to segregation. Trounstine also found that segregated cities, often gripped by race and class divisions, tend to spend less on public goods like roads, policing, parks, and sewers.[62] Underinvestment facilitated by segregation and political division harms all residents in a segregated city. Sewers overflow more frequently in segregated places.[63]

History repeats. Researchers argue that business elites bend local government to their will, ensuring the luxury residential and commercial development that they want gets built, regardless of competing community and housing needs. In the first two decades of the new millennium, public and private investment rained down on favored parts of central cities.[64]

Across the country, cities supported innovation districts, tech and startup incubators that could enhance or transform a local economy. They wooed millennials and talent for whom global or coastal cities became too expensive. No city claimed that constructing white space buffered from Black space was its aim, though centrifugal social forces and a phalanx of public and private policies can do just that. Neighborhoods on an upward trajectory, like those of the White L in Baltimore, were shaped in part by avoidance of Black and Latinx people. Areas targeted for development—often downtown, near a university, a hospital, or another key institution—often became whiter than the rest of the city.[65] Segregation made it easy for developers and individuals to select these favored areas, especially in northern and midwestern cities to which great migrants flocked.

City planner and writer Alan Mallach discovered this pattern in his analysis across all census tracts in older postindustrial cities that experienced revitalization in the first two decades of the twenty-first century. In Baltimore, four people lived in a neighborhood that was declining for each person who lived in a reviving or gentrifying area. In the Black neighborhoods of Baltimore, Cleveland, Newark, Pittsburgh, and beyond, the number of jobs and businesses were falling. Even some middle-class Black neighborhoods became poor. Conditions in the hood grew worse, even as the overall economy may have improved. Descendants were trapped in poverty—sustained, multigenerational poverty. The growing polarization of highly segregated cities is along this fault line between neighborhoods of concentrated abundance and concentrated need.[66]

Chicago's largest and most populous neighborhood, Austin, is overwhelmingly Black. About 40 percent of its residents earn less than $25,000 annually. It was savaged by foreclosures after the financial crisis yet excluded from many of the city's key neighborhood development programs.[67] An Urban Institute study released in 2019 found that majority-white neighborhoods in Chicago received about three times more public and private investment than majority-Black neighborhoods.[68] Private actors tend to invest more in affluent white space.[69] Supermarkets, for example, are common in white neighborhoods, and they offer healthier and cheaper food than the small grocery or convenience stores much more likely to be found in poor Black neighborhoods. Researchers have linked this neighborhood disparity to disparities in obesity between Blacks and whites.[70]

For descendants on the South and West Sides of Chicago, watching booming downtown development while the city shuttered school after school in their neighborhoods added to the insult. Chicago Public Schools (CPS) closed seventy schools over eight years by 2012. Then, in 2013, Mayor Rahm Emanuel closed fifty additional public elementary schools—the largest one-time mass school closure in the country. The Great Cities Institute at the University of Illinois at Chicago found that race was a significant determinant of closure. Schools with large numbers of Black students had a higher probability of closure than other schools with comparable test scores, locations, and utilization rates.[71] Majority-Black zip codes had disproportionately high closings while closings in zip codes that were about one-third Black or less were disproportionately low.[72] As school infrastructure in Black hoods evaporated, the city invested in new options elsewhere. An investigative report by a local public radio station in 2016 revealed that new school building expansions since the 2013 closures were "overwhelmingly granted" to specialized schools that serve relatively low percentages of low-income and Black students.[73]

Other cities mirror this pattern of disinvestment in the infrastructure of opportunity for Black neighborhoods. In Cleveland, Detroit, New Orleans, Philadelphia, Baltimore, and New York City, leaders in the name of "reform" closed schools en masse in poor Black and brown neighborhoods. In Baltimore, the Black Butterfly endured half of the school closures in the city; schools in affluent white communities in north Baltimore were spared.[74]

Mallach argues that cities misallocate resources. They confer billions in tax abatements or direct investment in sports stadiums (largely to entertain suburbanites), convention centers, and marquee commercial projects supported by developers or influential business leaders rather than in far cheaper services that can transform marginal neighborhoods or individual lives. He suggests cities should invest in programs and infrastructure that eliminate the hurdles to opportunity for low-income and underemployed adults, like specialized training for the many jobs that do not require a college degree and public transit that makes commutes to job-rich places affordable and sustainable.[75]

The story of Baltimore and the Red Line that was not built, and the diversion of funds to white areas, illustrates a common racial dimension to this trend of disinvestment from transit. Similar stories could be told about other metro areas with large numbers of descendants. More than 70 percent of public transit agencies in the United States have recently cut service or raised fares, with a disproportionate impact on the poor.[76] Poor folks need public transit more than others, but in many cities, the poorest neighborhoods have the worst access to it.[77]

Even with programs designed to help areas in need, affluent white spaces appear to be first in line. An NPR investigation of federal disaster relief spending found that it tends to exacerbate wealth inequalities. The rich get richer and the poor get poorer after a hurricane, flood, or other natural disaster because wealthy homeowners with savings are better able to meet rigid risk requirements for disaster relief. Sociologists confirm that white neighborhoods benefit disproportionately from FEMA spending; after disasters, Black residents tend to lose wealth and white residents gain wealth.[78] Like HOLC's redlining in the 1930s, FEMA's risk standards become destiny for Black neighborhoods. Black people already savaged by predatory lenders and foreclosures during the Great Recession, drained of equity and homeownership, and reduced to renting have a very hard time recovering both from natural and man-made disasters.

The wealthy also benefited from the Trump administration's Opportunity Zones program. Lucrative tax incentives, in theory, would be invested in "low-income communities," selected by state governors. Governors were given discretion to pick a limited number of qualifying census tracts from their states, including nonpoor areas adjacent to poor areas.

The program, included in President's Trump's signature 2017 tax legislation, was itself arguably an exercise in exacerbating inequality. The tax incentives for Opportunity Zones were extraordinarily generous, completely eliminating any taxation of capital gains for long-term investments. They precipitated a marketing bonanza by Wall Street, and critics painted the program as a flawed giveaway for projects likely to have happened anyway, without controls to ensure that poor communities and residents actually benefited.[79] Once again, a small cadre of capitalists grew richer exploiting "the ghetto," here an idea stretched to include adjacent white areas. In Louisville, Kentucky, rapidly gentrifying areas like Nulu, Butchertown, and Portland that had already received major capital investment were named Opportunity Zones, along with the central business district, while seven of the city's eighteen poorest tracts were left out of the program.[80] In 2020, presidential candidate Joe Biden and congressional

Democrats proposed reforming the program to create more jobs and investment for low-income communities and prevent abuses.

Private actors also favor whiteness and disfavor Blackness. Redlining and denial of traditional credit to Black Americans continues. The Center for Investigative Reporting sponsored a year-long study, published in 2018, that analyzed thirty-one million records revealed by the Home Mortgage Disclosure Act. Even after controlling for applicants' income, loan amounts, and neighborhood, the center found racial disparities in mortgage lending—a disturbing pattern of denials of Black and Latinx applicants for traditional mortgages where white applicants with similar qualifications would be accepted. This modern-day redlining, persisted in sixty-one metro areas, from Atlanta to Detroit, Philadelphia to San Antonio, and beyond.[81]

Philadelphia, the City of Brotherly Love, where Black Americans and abolitionists once pursued their dreams for happiness and freedom, was among the worst sites for lending discrimination. According to the Center for Investigative Reporting study, banks focused on serving whites in white areas. Despite fair credit laws, they placed nearly three-quarters of their branches in majority-white neighborhoods, and whites received ten times more conventional mortgages than Black and Latinx applicants in 2015 and 2016. The greater the number of Black or Latinx people in a neighborhood, the more likely a loan application would be denied, even accounting for income and other factors.[82]

Again, as a recent Federal Reserve study suggests and other research has shown, the redlining practices that the federal government set in motion in the 1930s persist today in the same neighborhoods originally marked as hazardous.[83] Borrowers from these neighborhoods are more likely to be denied traditional credit and preyed on with subprime products, showing that despite a century of resistance, anti-Black geographic patterns of exclusion and exploitation are remarkably stable and institutionalized.[84] Predatory installment contracts, the very same usurious products peddled to redlined descendants from the 1930s to the 1960s, have returned. Large financial firms, backed by private equity investors, swarmed like vultures to pick through the carrion of the 2008 foreclosure crisis. They could purchase a foreclosed home at auction, say, for $5,000, and sell it immediately with no repairs through a land contract for $30,000. The land contract is designed to produce failure by the buyer, who believes she is acquiring a home but in fact accumulates no equity unless and until the final installment is made. Under the contract's usurious terms, the vulture investor intentionally churns the property, swiftly evicting the installment buyer and moving to the next target. Black and Latinx people in marginal neighborhoods were disproportionate targets for this plunder. Their dollars, earned through "essential" work, which should have gained them equity, instead were transferred to financial titans.[85] This is the latest iteration of what author and academic Keeanga-Yamahtta Taylor calls "predatory inclusion" in her critical book *Race for Profit*. Rather than transforming credit practices and creating real inclusion in housing markets after the passage of fair housing and credit laws, the same institutional players that shaped residential segregation simply found new ways to extract profit in Black neighborhoods.[86]

Cities, too, engage in financial predation. I discuss later the use of predatory policing of descendants to raise revenues. Less known are disparate practices in property taxation. A recent national study by the Center for Municipal Finance found that cities are taxing owners of low-valued properties at higher rates than they should and taxing owners of high-valued properties at lower rates than they should.[87] For this and other systemic practices, legal scholar Bernadette Atuahene identifies localities including Ferguson, Missouri; New Orleans; Washington, DC; and Detroit as "predatory cities."[88]

The processes I have described are what systemic racism looks like. Understanding it requires neighborhood analysis comparing how the denizens of white space and Black and brown hoods are treated by public and private actors. Political and market processes favor wealthy white areas, and their advantages have effectively been institutionalized or locked in.[89] Those who live elsewhere, particularly in the hood, are not favored and can be preyed on. The game of opportunity, indeed, is rigged. This inconvenient truth is very evident in the way America has chosen to finance public education.

CHAPTER 6

MORE OPPORTUNITY HOARDING

Separate and Unequal Schools

Communities that maintain boundaries reap tremendous rewards for their children. In 2016, overwhelmingly white school districts received $23 billion more in state and local funding than majority-nonwhite districts that serve about the same numbers of children.[1] Reflect on that. The same number of children, and the whitest set, receives $23 billion more. A kindergartener, still innocent of the ways of her country, when presented with this word problem would scream "That's not fair!" As George Orwell satirized in *Animal Farm*, despite the shared revolutionary value, "All animals are equal," the pigs became superior tyrants, though intellectually honest ones. In the end they openly amended the farm's communal principle with, "but some animals are more equal than others."[2]

This great disparity is caused by inequality in property tax wealth and the widespread practice of relying heavily on property taxes to finance public education. Differences in local tax bases, in turn, result from the architecture of segregation that America intentionally created. It does not have to be this way. A report by the Organization for Economic Co-operation and Development notes that US public education systems reinforce the disadvantages of segregation, while other OECD countries mitigate these disadvantages. OECD countries with high-performing education systems put their most talented teachers and extra resources in disadvantaged schools and finance education at the state rather than the local level.[3] The vast majority of US states do the exact opposite.[4]

States try and often fail to make up the difference between what poor districts can spend to educate children compared to affluent districts. According to the Education Law Center's most recent annual report card on state school finance, the majority of states "have unfair funding systems with 'flat' or 'regressive' funding distribution patterns that ignore the need for additional funding in high-poverty districts." Only eleven states had "progressive" funding systems that adequately funded poor districts, down from a high of twenty-two in 2008.[5] In the wake of the Great Recession, poor school districts lost ground. Brutal cuts in school budgets because of the COVID-19 pandemic are likely to have harsh impacts on poor districts and deepen these structural inequities.[6]

Every state in the nation has a constitution that guarantees public education. Lawyers and activists invoke these state education clauses, and while legal theories have changed over decades, segregation of affluence and of need leads to endless battles over how to pay for schools that actually meet state-mandated school performance goals. In many states, court-ordered school finance reforms did increase funding for poor school districts. And more funding, invested wisely in higher teacher salaries and smaller class sizes, has been shown to improve student outcomes for poor children.[7] But school finance reforms are always subject to political challenge and easily perceived in zero-sum terms by affluent and middle-class taxpayers. The outcome of most state legislative debates tends to reflect the desires of organized, affluent areas.[8]

New York's state constitution guarantees a "sound basic education" to the children of this empire. New York also has the most segregated school system in the country, according to the Civil Rights Project of UCLA.[9] Local sources supply 55 percent of funding for public schools in New York, state aid provides an additional 40 percent, and federal grants contribute the last 5 percent. As a result of a lawsuit brought by the Campaign for Fiscal Equity in 2006, the state created a Foundation Aid funding formula designed to reflect the actual cost of providing a "sound basic education" in a given district.

A court-appointed special master consulted with experts on inputs, outputs, and regional differences to develop a formula that was supposed to reflect the higher costs of educating children in concentrated poverty.

The Schenectady City School District, one of the poorest in New York, is one of those districts. It was supposed to have 100 percent of Foundation Aid in order to meet the constitutional mandate for educating the children it serves. In 2014, it was receiving 54 percent of Foundation Aid. It filed a civil rights complaint with the US Department of Education's Office for Civil Rights (OCR), alleging that thirty-seven majority nonwhite school districts received less than their constitutionally promised Foundation Aid and that the whiter a school district, the more likely it was to receive all, or close to all, its promised Foundation Aid.[10] The Middletown City School District filed a similar complaint.[11]

Like the descendants of Baltimore after Governor Hogan canceled the Red Line and reallocated resources to white areas, Schenectady's complainants alleged a Title VI violation under the Civil Rights Act of 1964. They noted that the median school district in the state was funded at 82 percent of constitutionally mandated Foundation Aid, and the majority of districts at or above this level of funding were majority-white districts. Such "white" districts had only a 5 percent chance of being funded at 60 percent or less of what the Foundation Aid formula said was due. Again, the Schenectady district, 66 percent nonwhite and 74 percent poor, then received only 54 percent of the Foundation Aid to which it was entitled.[12]

As a result of its low funding, high need, and state budget freezes and shortfalls, Schenectady had to make painful decisions, including cutting instructional support staff and guidance counselors; eliminating some pre-K programs, electives, and advanced placement courses; and increasing class sizes and student-to-teacher ratios. Schenectady students had to endure shortages of textbooks, library and technology resources, physical education, and extracurricular offerings. The District struggled to educate students with special education needs or students who were English-language learners.[13] Schenectady and similarly situated poor cities were faced with the conundrum of raising property taxes to pay for critical education needs, which suppressed property values and made it hard to attract economic development, rendering struggling communities even more disadvantaged.[14]

The leaders, teachers, parents, and children of Schenectady claimed that New York systematically underfunded school districts with high percentages of nonwhite students and systematically fully funded very white school districts. It was a dual system of education, separate and unequal. The Obama administration's OCR took a year to decide to open an investigation based on these allegations of racial disparity and did not conclude the investigation before Obama left office.[15]

Schenectady's funding had crept up to about 64 percent of Foundation Aid by the time I interviewed its school superintendent in 2019. Laurence T. Spring, the superintendent who filed the complaint and has since resigned, told me that he believed OCR put pressure on New York State to raise his district's funding so that OCR could eventually claim the case was moot and it would not have to opine on a claim of systemic racism.[16] Fully funding all poor districts of color would require sacrifices from those advantaged by the status quo. In this case, neither the state nor the federal government seemed prepared to demand much of advantaged people, regardless of what antidiscrimination law required. In 2020, the New York Advisory Committee to the US Civil Rights Commission issued a report alleging that the Empire State continues to underfund high-need school districts and that this amounts to racial discrimination.[17]

By April 2020, as the COVID-19 pandemic was surging across New York State, the Trump administration's OCR closed Schenectady's complaint without making any findings. It noted that a similar complaint had been filed in New York state court by different plaintiffs under state education law and that some Schenectady school parents had joined that lawsuit. OCR said it was closing the federal claim under its official policy of not pursuing federal investigations when similar state claims are pending, though it admitted in its closure letter that the state complaint "*does not specifically address allegations of race or national origin discrimination.*"[18] OCR had six years to investigate and respond to a basic, evidence-backed claim that white school districts received more funds than nonwhite ones. Frustrated Schenectady parents, waiting in vain for relief, joined a state lawsuit, which was used as an excuse to squelch a complaint that asked the federal government to address pro-white systemic racism. Just as justice was denied to Baltimoreans in the Red Line complaint, the national government once again evaded reckoning with supremacy.

According to an analysis by the nonprofit Education Trust, New York State has one of the country's least equitable funding systems. It underfunds districts that serve poor and minority children even though the state spends more per pupil for public education than any other state in the country.[19] Political compromises forged in the state legislature suggest why. One, known as "save harmless," required that no district in New York would receive less state aid than it had the year before. This meant that legislators would have to add to the pot of state aid in order to give poor districts more; it could never reduce state aid to any district in order to give more to a poorer district. Governor Andrew Cuomo contends that most of state education aid goes to the poorer school districts but that the poorest schools within those districts are not sufficiently targeted. He has sought an equity-funding formula to ensure that the neediest schools receive the bulk of state education aid.[20]

Another compromise successfully demanded by Republican state senators from Long Island was that if any additional aid was distributed in their region, as required by the Foundation Aid formula, their school districts would receive a share of it, regardless of whether their districts actually needed it under the formula. They dubbed it the "shares agreement."[21]

As one sharp critic put it, "Instead of targeting additional aid to the few truly needy districts, all are given more."[22] As this book was going to print, Governor Cuomo and state legislators announced a budget agreement that would raise taxes on the wealthy and, over a three-year phase-in period, fully fund Foundation Aid for poor districts. The two-decade Campaign for Fiscal Equity continues. Other states have struggled with the same conundrum. Even when faced with court orders to remedy inequality or inadequacy in funding for poor districts under state constitutions, some states in the name of "reform" actually left poor school districts worse off by effecting a net reduction in their funding.[23]

Opportunity hoarding also occurs *within* school districts. A study found that, in New York City, the poorest public schools receive 12 percent *less* in funding than the wealthiest ones. In Buffalo, the poorest schools received 26 percent less.[24] Both Buffalo and New York City school districts are extremely segregated.

New York City mayor Bill de Blasio tried and failed to institute reforms to guarantee entrance for the highest achievers from every middle school to the most sought-after and well-resourced high schools—a strategy that would have mitigated the disadvantages of applying from a segregated, high-poverty neighborhood or school. In a school system that is 70 percent Black and Latinx, only 10 percent of Black and brown children attend New York's premier public high schools.[25] New York City and other school systems reserve prestigious public goods, funded by all taxpayers, for those that can ace a single high-stakes test that rewards expensive test preparation and being in the know about selective opportunities and how to access them.[26]

Advocates in Connecticut tried a different strategy to tackle school funding inequality. A racially diverse coalition filed a complaint in Connecticut, one of the richest states in the country, on behalf of children of all colors in poor school districts. Black, Latinx, mixed-race, white, English-language learners, and children with special needs were among the plaintiffs; all of them attended schools with high concentrations of at-risk students. They argued that under the Connecticut constitution they had a right to a suitable and substantially equal educational opportunity. The adult plaintiffs in the lawsuit had formed the Connecticut Coalition for Justice in Educational Funding. They had done their homework, gathered allies among parents, students, teachers, unions, and citizens and wielded data about less fortunate school districts: Bridgeport, Danbury, Windham, East Granby, East Hartford, Plainfield, Norwich, New Britain, New London, and Stamford.[27]

Ordinary whites joined this fight to ask for what Homer Plessy had asked for in 1896—true equality. Yet the plea wasn't to attend affluent schools but to have what affluent schools had. In Greenwich and Darien, the complaint alleged, schoolchildren "have easy access to guidance counselors, school psychologists, personal laptops, and up-to-date textbooks," while kids in concentrated poverty do not. In a system heavily dependent on local property taxes, Greenwich spends six thousand dollars more per pupil annually than Bridgeport. Connecticut youth in poor districts "have fewer guidance counselors, tutors, and psychologists, lower-paid teachers, more dilapidated facilities and bigger class sizes than wealthier districts," the complaint asserted.[28]

The coalition cataloged shortfalls endured by children of all colors, most of whom were not Black, in its complaint. One example of a descendant child was Olivia Jenkins, a fourteen-year-old African American at East Hartford High School. The majority of her classmates were nonwhite and poor; 9 percent were deemed gifted. Despite having many students who did not perform well on standardized tests, East Hartford High had no remedial programs or tutoring so students at this school were much less likely than their affluent counterparts to complete essential courses. For every computer, there were 6.9 students, compared to a state average of 3.3. And only 29 percent of those computers were moderate- or high-powered, compared to a state school average of 77 percent.

Other schools named in the complaint had similar problems. Some elementary schools lacked pre-K because of inadequate state funding. Other schools fell far below state averages in printed materials in their libraries. The litany of deficits that the coalition identified in their complaint contravened the Connecticut state school board's own published statements about what constitutes an adequate education. The coalition challenged a system of finance that produced gross inequality, of inputs and of outcomes. It presented a history of struggle in the state legislature to appropriate and maintain funding that would make up for low property tax wealth in poor school districts. The plaintiff children, forced to attend poorly resourced, underperforming schools of concentrated need, were condemned to an educational underclass, the complaint argued.[29]

After a decade of litigating, the Connecticut Coalition for Justice in Educational Funding did not prevail. The trial judge ordered the state to develop sweeping educational reforms and challenged the rationality of a school finance system that "allows rich towns to raid money desperately needed by poor towns [and] makes a mockery of

the state's constitutional duty to provide adequate educational opportunities to all students."[30] The Connecticut Supreme Court disagreed. It acknowledged that the plaintiffs' case revealed inequities
in "an imperfect public educational system" but concluded that the
court was limited to determining whether the state had met its constitutional mandate to provide "a minimally adequate education"
and ruled that it had. The Court said it was up to the legislature to
address education policy.[31] Neither the courts nor the legislature in
Connecticut would rectify a system that favors advantaged places.

This result is worse than the Supreme Court's holding in *Plessy v.
Ferguson* because that case at least acknowledged racial separation
was state policy and required formal equality in publicly provided services.[32] The Connecticut Supreme Court, like the pigs in *Animal Farm,*
was content to dispense with the pretense that the community's social contract—the state constitution—required equality. The so-called
Constitution State, descended from the Fundamental Orders of 1639,
an early written constitution for self-rule, seems to have broken its
original aspiration to "unite ourselves to walk and lie peaceably and
lovingly together."[33] The Puritans who migrated from England and
massacred Pequots to take their lands for the Connecticut Colony
were not free of sin. Connecticut had more enslaved Africans than
any other state in New England before slavery was gradually abolished there. Like everywhere else in America, the original sin of white
supremacy manifests in a modern system of residential caste that
guarantees that some people are in fact more equal than others.

Although the coalition did not raise the issue in its lawsuit, racial segregation in Connecticut, too, is the result of decades of intentional state and federal policy. And nonwhite people bear the brunt
of it. As Map 6.1 in the insert shows, they are concentrated in the
lowest-opportunity areas of the state.

The Connecticut Fair Housing Center, which fights housing discrimination for its clients for free, used the proceeds from some of
its court victories to commission this visual analysis by the Kirwan
Institute for the Study of Race and Equity at Ohio State University.
One neon dot equals five hundred nonwhite people. Pale areas are
low opportunity, the darkest areas are the highest-opportunity bastions. Under the visionary leadership of john a. powell, law professor

and opportunity champion, researchers compiled data on ten indicators for every census tract in the state. The indicators tracked opportunity and neighborhood conditions, including school standardized
test scores and college completion, rates of unemployment, poverty,
homeownership, receipt of public assistance, and commute times to
job centers. Compiling all of this data, researchers were able to cat-
egorize every census tract, from very low to very high opportunity.[34]

Bridgeport, East Hartford, Norwich, New Britain, and New London, among the named districts in the coalition's school funding case,
appear on the map as low or very low opportunity and very nonwhite.
Clearly, the structure of opportunity in Connecticut is racialized: 81
percent of Black Americans and 79 percent of Latinx lived in areas
with the least opportunity, places where nearly 60 percent of all subsidized family housing stood and over half of recent mortgage foreclosures in the state occurred. Kirwan Institute researchers compared
their opportunity map to historic HOLC redline maps of Connecticut
cities. They found that only 3 percent of areas that received an A rating from HOLC were very low opportunity but nearly 100 percent of
areas rated D were.[35] Again, past racism became current destiny.

This map and analysis are a snapshot of American caste in 2009,
a timeframe overlapping with the coalition's court case. The footprint of concentrated advantage and disadvantage likely shifted in
the ensuing decade but an architecture of segregation remains. On
close examination of the map, though, you can find a few very-high-
opportunity areas that included numbers of nonwhite people. West
Hartford is one of these unicorns. Its website speaks volumes about
its ethos:

> The Town of West Hartford is dynamic and diverse, offering the best
> of the urban and suburban experience. We are an inclusive and en-
> gaged community with caring and responsible leadership. Our res-
> idents are enriched by excellent public schools, outstanding public
> safety, vibrant public spaces, and programs and services for all ages.[36]

Public—a potent word repeated three times in this mission statement—from a town that wants its diverse citizens to rise together.
Phil Tegeler, a civil rights lawyer and an architect of the *Sheff v.*

O'Neill lawsuit that successfully challenged school and housing segregation in Hartford, is a longtime resident of West Hartford. Historically, this suburb with the longest border to majority-minority
Hartford, was a white-flight suburb. According to Tegeler, West Hartford evolved and decided to celebrate and support its diversity with
investments in poorer areas of the city and in magnet and public
schools, where more than thirty languages are spoken.[37]

As the map shows, while not all Black and brown people in Connecticut were excluded from high-opportunity areas, most were.
Very white rural areas of low opportunity on the map show that not
all white people were advantaged. Connecticut's persistent architecture of racial segregation benefits those in affluent white space and
harms others. The Connecticut Supreme Court and legislature appear to have thrown up their hands.[38]

The Education Law Center's annual report card on school finance
suggests a similar acquiescence by the *majority* of states. Maryland
was one them. The Education Trust recently found that schools in
the city of Baltimore and Prince George's County are the most poorly
funded in the state, compared to their needs.[39] These jurisdictions
also happen to be very Black compared to other parts of the state.
The American Civil Liberties Union (ACLU) and LDF recently filed
a lawsuit on behalf of the Baltimore City Public Schools over insuffi-
cient funding, the fifth such appeal to the courts under the Maryland
state constitution's education clause. The state entered into a consent
decree to provide more funding and revamped governance of Baltimore's school system after a 1994 court ruling. In part because of
this case, the state legislature passed a law in 2002 establishing a formula for distributing state education aid. In its recent suit, the ACLU
and LDF argued that Maryland stopped adjusting the formula for
inflation after 2008 and Baltimore's school funding is dramatically
less than needed to provide its children with constitutionally adequate education.[40]

More than half of Black American students in Maryland attend
chronically underfunded schools, compared to only 8 percent of
white children. The complaint surveyed disparate conditions Black
children endured: fewer and less experienced teachers, winters without heat, summers without air conditioning, concentrated poverty

and racial isolation requiring more—teachers, counselors, and other recourses—but met with less, and an alleged spending shortfall of $290 million to $353 million annually. As I write in early 2021, the case is pending, and this and other battles for fairness in funding of public education continue throughout the nation.[41]

Even where per-pupil school funding has been equalized or states invest more in high-poverty schools, other forces produce unequal educational experiences. Segregation greatly influences teacher quality. Very-white, poverty-free schools tend to attract the best teachers. OCR, the federal education department office that investigated Schenectady's complaint, has released data showing that students of color and low-income students are less likely to have access to rigorous coursework and experienced teachers than their white and wealthy counterparts.[42]

One study of Washington State found, across every measure of teacher quality, that great teachers were inequitably distributed. Students receiving free and reduced lunch, racial minorities, and students with low academic performance were much less likely than their advantaged peers to be taught by a quality teacher.[43] After the Charlotte-Mecklenburg school district in North Carolina ended its long-standing school integration policy and stopped busing students, those schools to which Black students were repatriated experienced a decrease in several measures of teacher quality.[44] Senior and experienced teachers are more likely to command higher salaries and choose to work in schools in wealthier neighborhoods while teachers in high-poverty schools are more likely to teach subjects they are not certified to teach and receive lower salaries.[45]

High-quality teachers also tend to be hoarded in Texas. A 2009 study found that, compared to white students, Black students attend schools with less experienced teachers and that this inequity significantly affected a widening academic-performance gap.[46] This is a story about political power and how resources are allocated; the fairy tale often told of Black-white achievement gaps is a convenient myth about Black people not being motivated to learn. Again, OECD countries with high-performing education systems place their most talented teachers in disadvantaged schools.[47] In America, no one says out loud, "Let's give poor Black and brown kids the least experienced teachers." But that is closer to the truth of American caste than the false shibboleth of the land of opportunity.

DEFYING BROWN

Segregation is the fundamental subtext for all school finance and school quality debates. Public schools are more racially segregated than they have been at any point in the last fifty years. Most Black and Latinx public school students attend majority-minority schools. Nearly 40 percent of Black students attend schools that have been described as apartheid schools, with more than 90 percent students of color.[48]

Boundary maintenance is as apparent as opportunity hoarding in public education. Sometimes affluent and apartheid schools are shockingly close to each other. According to a recent analysis on school boundaries, one in five public school students "live[s] virtually across the street from a significantly whiter and richer school district" and for every student enrolled in affluent bastions, three neighboring students "are left behind in lower-funded schools serving far more nonwhite students."[49]

A Black American lawyer tells me about moving his child from J. O. Wilson Elementary in northeast Washington, DC, a school nearly 90 percent Black with low test scores, to a "lottery school" blocks away that was about 70 percent white. Both schools were public, but the "white" one could be accessed only by negotiating and winning a lottery process. It was much better resourced, with more consistency and less turnover among teachers, the lawyer said. As a parent whose children bypassed our neighborhood elementary school for a "lottery" slot to well-resourced, racially diverse public charter schools in DC, I understand his choice and the extremes. Our family was able to avoid sending our Black sons either to overwhelmingly white schools or to apartheid, impoverished schools. We were lucky, literally winning the school lottery on the third try, landing at the Washington Yu-Ying Elementary School, which afforded my sons an excellent international baccalaureate immersion education in Mandarin. No one would call this fabulous school in which white children were a minority "white space." But among public neighborhood and charter schools in the District, extremes of very white and very Black, advantaged and hyper-poor, continue. Whether intentional or acquiesced in, it is still segregation. An old idea has been made new and respectable in its colorblind pretensions and willful ignorance to systems that exclude. An unspoken and unspeakable subtext is that some children are valued more than others, effectively told that they are less worthy of public investment than others. It is an American horror we do not own up to.

About 80 percent of all students in the United States attend a public school, and most of them are assigned based on where they live.[50] Racial disparities in per-pupil spending persist in states with regressive approaches to school funding, because people of color are more likely to live in high-poverty school districts with lower tax revenues.[51] The Department of Education projects that the white student population in public high schools will decrease in this decade as the Black, Latinx, and Asian/Pacific Islander populations grow apace.[52] As public schools become poorer and more colored, and more whites and affluent people retreat to private or home schools, these tensions are likely to worsen.

When the Supreme Court decided *Brown v. Board of Education of Topeka* in 1954, it overruled the formal fiction of *Plessy v. Ferguson* that separate could be equal. The *Brown* case should also be understood as finally overruling *Dred Scott* and attempting to bring Black Americans into equal personhood and citizenship.[53] In the unanimous *Brown* opinion, Chief Justice Warren wrote about the common public school as an institution critical to rendering American youth successful citizens:

> Education is perhaps the most important function of state and local governments . . . It is the very foundation of good citizenship . . . it is doubtful that any child may reasonably be expected to succeed in life if he is denied the opportunity of an education. Such an opportunity, where the state has undertaken to provide it, is a right which must be made available to all on equal terms.[54]

Warren did not address inequality of resources between white and then-Negro schools, focusing instead on the intangible messages that state sponsored segregation sent to Black children. Warren also did not address the message that segregation and white supremacy sent to white children, although the NAACP did raise this issue in its brief.[55] Whatever Black children thought of Jim Crow segregation in 1954, and the evidence was mixed regarding their alleged feelings of inferiority, segregation had material consequences. Racially identifiable schools were unequal then, as they are now. The Supreme Court in ensuing years effectively sanctioned separate and unequal schooling, particularly with *Milliken v. Bradley*, the 1974 case that exempted white suburbs surrounding Detroit from participating in cross-boundary school integration with the city, and hence exempted white suburbs everywhere. *Milliken,* decided only six years after the Court had finally begun to enforce *Brown* with alacrity, presaged its demise.

There are myriad ways in which opportunity is hoarded in public education. Beyond inequitable public funding, affluent parents raise funds privately to pay for additional resources. For their own children, they would not stand for schools that look like prisons, twenty-five-year-old textbooks, leaking or wasp-infested ceilings, useless and outdated technology, crowded classrooms, and exhausted teachers who pay for supplies with their own limited paychecks. These are among the conditions thousands of teachers across the country shared with the *New York Times* in 2018.[56]

Affluent schools differ markedly in the type of education they offer. Though students in advantaged schools suffer the stresses of an arms race to selective higher education, they are engaged to think critically and have the possibility of stimulating, liberal inquiry. Descendant children receive soul-crushing drills to meet standardized tests, privatized "reforms" designed by and profiting outsiders, school-to-prison policing, and school closures that punish whole communities for being poor.[57]

There are alternatives to an America divided against itself, investing less in the education of its fastest growing populations, preparing white youth less for the realities of living in a diverse country. Louisville, Kentucky, evolved from a place that once promoted segregation to one that resists it. For decades in the twentieth century, the city was hypersegregated. Like every other place that constructed ghettos, Louisville used zoning, redlining, urban renewal, highways, and other tactics to contain Black people. Then-mayor Charles Farnsley admitted Louisville's urban renewal plan was designed to "drive the Negro back from the central area" so that "downtown did not become a black belt."[58]

In the 1970s, more than 90 percent of the students in Louisville schools were Black, and approximately 95 percent of students in Jefferson County's suburban district were white.[59] The region's taste for integration had to be acquired. White mothers were the mass of massive resistance to school integration throughout the nation.[60] When a court ordered Louisville schools to desegregate in 1970, white parents protested against busing. The Kentucky National Guard had to be called in. In time, with actual experience participating in integrated schools, leaders and parents grew to appreciate the benefits of a unified city-county school system in which there were no failing, apartheid schools to run from.

After court-ordered school desegregation was lifted, Louisville's unified school district maintained a race-conscious school assignment and busing plan because it wanted schools to stay integrated. In 2007, the Supreme Court declared voluntary school integration plans in Louisville and Seattle, Washington, unconstitutional because they considered the race of individual students. But Justice Anthony Kennedy, who wrote the critical opinion in the case, *Parents Involved in Community Schools v. Seattle School District No. 1*, declared that all school districts have a compelling interest in promoting school diversity and avoiding racial isolation. Kennedy suggested race-conscious alternatives like drawing school attendance zones to mitigate residential segregation in order to achieve school integration.[61]

Louisville worked with school integration expert Gary Orfield to adopt a new plan that mixes students based on their neighborhood characteristics. Among multiple neighborhood factors considered are race, household income, and parents' education. The school district exempted racially balanced neighborhoods from busing, creating incentives for parents to choose residential integration. And students can apply for sought-after magnet and specialty programs like language immersion.[62] Researchers found that levels of housing segregation fell precipitously in Louisville Metro as parents knew that school assignments did not depend on where students lived.[63] In 2010, metropolitan Louisville was no longer hypersegregated. Black-white dissimilarity—the percentage of Blacks who would have to move to be evenly distributed—declined from very high to moderate over four decades. Successful and enduring school integration explains this transition.[64]

In 2003, the city of Louisville combined its government with surrounding Jefferson County. This shared destiny of tax base and resources is called Louisville Metro, a consolidation that reduced white flight and stabilized property values in the urban core.[65] Louisville Metro is still shaped by past racism, but it has begun to work at residential integration. The Metropolitan Housing Coalition successfully pressured government to correct and amend its laws. Louisville enacted a local fair housing law that covers virtually all rental properties, including those exempted by federal law. It is considering banning discrimination by source of income, which protects low-income voucher holders. Louisville also amended its zoning code to incentivize developers to build multifamily and affordable housing in formerly sacrosanct single-family zones. For now, Louisville does not have a mandatory inclusionary zoning law, and like many cities, does not have enough affordable housing, but advocates continue to fight for inclusion.

Louisville has adopted an online interactive project, titled Redlining Louisville, which maps past HOLC redlining and current neighborhood data. It is a digital reckoning of sorts. Mayor Greg Fischer said the project was meant to acknowledge "unnecessary hurdles . . . placed in front of some residents [and] spark a community conversation that results in removing those hurdles."[66] A municipal agency makes the tool available to the public through its website. It conducted a year-long series of community dialogues to spread knowledge about how and why west end Black neighborhoods became separate and unequal.[67]

In 2019, Louisville Metro published its first formal housing-needs assessment, examining the full range of types of housing needed to provide diverse residents with fair, affordable options and access to economic mobility within each neighborhood. The assessment identifies policies and development strategies to meet assessed need, and

Louisville Metro has committed to revisiting this assessment every five years.[68] Louisville is far from perfect. Demands for justice for Breonna Taylor, killed by Louisville police on March 13, 2020, and for transformation and accountability of policing in the city continue. In late May 2020, white women moved forward when a Black Lives Matter leader asked them to use their bodies to stand between the police and Black protestors. They formed a line, locked arms, and the photo of these white allies went viral.[69] It was a moment that suggested possibilities for mutual liberation from the dogmas and structures of supremacy.

Louisville Metro's economy soared as segregation levels fell.[70] Whether separatists like it or not, they are tied to others. Economies ignore boundaries. Metropolitan regions that are less segregated do better economically as a whole than those still fragmented by fear.[71]

Other communities got started much earlier than Louisville in attacking the segregationist order: Shaker Heights, Ohio. Oak Park, Illinois. The Shepherd Park neighborhood of Washington, DC. They are among the local unicorns that intentionally pursued residential integration in the 1960s. Perhaps visionary residents recognized that the damage from segregation would be mutual. Or they affirmed their "I-am-not-a-racist" identity by acting to prevent systemic racism in housing markets.

Places with a sizeable middle class that integrate rather than exclude poor families have higher rates of upward mobility for poor children: DuPage, Illinois. Bergen, New Jersey. Bucks, Pennsylvania. Fairfax, Virginia. King, Washington State. Montgomery, Maryland. These are among the top counties in the country for social mobility. Every year a child lived in these places would raise her earnings as an adult. At the opposite end of the spectrum, places with stark residential segregation, including Baltimore and Milwaukee, penalize children who live there, detracting from their life chances and adult earnings. Counties with higher rates of social mobility tended to be less segregated, with lower income inequality, better schools, less violent crime, and more two-parent households.[72] In the 2018 book *Moving Toward Integration*, three housing scholars documented that for the 10 percent of Blacks who live in urban metro areas with only moderate segregation, their outcomes on indicators like employment, education, and life span are much closer to that of whites than in highly segregated places that correlate with stark racial inequality.[73]

Some localities become "equality innovators," as legal scholar Robin Lenhardt calls them.[74] They raise minimum wages to enable human beings to live as such. They ban boxes that limit job prospects for returning citizens. They mandate inclusionary housing. They enact and enforce human rights and antidiscrimination protections along multiple dimensions. Transforming systems from exclusionary to inclusive, from racist to anti-racist, requires coalition and hard, never-ending work. And seeing and naming the systems that harm descendants is the first step to racial reckoning.

CHAPTER 7

NEIGHBORHOOD EFFECTS

*What the Hood and America
Demand of Descendants*

I met Lakia Barnett on an overcast September morning in 2018. A client of a legal clinic at Georgetown Law, where I teach, she agreed to tell me the story of her family's search for housing and stability in the DC metro area. Lakia was a married, Black, mother of three in her thirties. She didn't own a car, so I agreed to pick her up and take her to lunch at a restaurant of her choosing for the interview, a respite for two mothers while our kids were in school. The Barnett family lived in Southeast DC, east of the Anacostia River in Ward Eight, the city's poorest ward.

The drive from the law school, near halls of Congress and courts superior and Supreme, to Lakia's home took about fourteen minutes. I drove the interstate past Southwest DC, remade by urban renewal and gentrification, and MLK Boulevard. Lakia's block in Garfield Heights, minutes from the Maryland border, seemed sturdy and unremarkable. I parked in front of a modest, brick row house. A chain-link fence enclosed a small front yard that offered little room for child's play.

I entered the gate and knocked on the door, and Lakia emerged, engaged in an urgent conversation on her cellphone. She nodded, followed me to my car, and continued talking, rattling instructions to a volunteer for a production that she and other women were putting on. They were staging monologues to tell their stories of pain and triumph and inspire others; it was Lakia's brainchild and new mission. With long extensions that she twisted as she talked, Lakia sounded more like an entertainment producer than a HUD voucher holder who had recently moved from a homeless shelter.

She escaped by luck, pluck, and fierce advocacy on her behalf from a Georgetown Law student and faculty advisor. Lakia had known stability. In 2013, she and her husband had been living in the same apartment for seven years, in a working-class Black neighborhood in Temple Hills, Maryland, until hell came to them. Simultaneously, they were both laid off and soon fell behind on rent. Then they were robbed. Masked men invaded in the early afternoon, perhaps not expecting an unemployed parent at home with young kids. Lakia recalled staring at the gun in her face as she pleaded with the invaders not to harm her children. The Barnetts were the seventh family in the area to be robbed. The invaders stole all their valuables and the rent money they had accumulated. "Everything else after that was just a tornado," she said. "We filed a police report. They didn't find [the robbers] and I don't think the police really cared. They may have even suspected us." The sheriff came to evict them with no notice. "They told us to get out immediately," she said.

Broke, they moved in with Lakia's mother in Northeast DC after which the mother herself was soon evicted. The Barnetts spent the next two years moving, from family to friends to hotels, wherever they could stay until they wore out their welcome or ran out of money. Lakia and her husband, who prefers to remain anonymous, tried hard to find jobs. "No one would hire us," Lakia said of this period. "We had high school diplomas but no clear skills." Lakia had worked with children at a YMCA until that program was shuttered and she was laid off. Her husband had been a concierge at an apartment building.

Lakia described herself as "very hands-on with my children." She could not afford childcare and could only work during school hours. She managed to get hired as a dietary aide at a hospital, delivering trays of food to patients. After about a year, she was fired abruptly by a supervisor who would not accommodate her request for time off to deal with her mother's emergency hospitalization and yet another eviction. "I was not allowed to have any error in my life," she said of her supervisor.

The Barnetts lived on Temporary Assistance to Needy Families (TANF), family donations, and informal work her husband found. Lakia's friends, shocked when she announced she was expecting a third child, encouraged her to abort. They had two sons and after she gave birth to a girl, her husband told her, "I *knew* this was my girl because everybody wanted us to get rid of her." They were a devoted, Christian family that held on to each other through turbulence.

A week after her daughter was born, Lakia relented and went to an intake center for DC homeless shelters. They lived in a squalid hotel on New York Avenue in Northeast DC for nine months. "It was terrible," she said. A wet ceiling dripped on her asthmatic son. His eyes swelled, and her other son developed issues with his stomach. There were fights among residents, and prostitutes hailed customers across the street from the hotel.

This was Lakia's first experience living in concentrated poverty. She felt that about half the residents were people like herself, who were "trying hard to do things right," she said. The other half had succumbed to hopelessness. "A lot of people there had lost a sense of life," Lakia said of residents who took or sold drugs or engaged in other destructive behavior. "You have to understand," she elaborated, "some people do things because they don't see any other way to survive."

Lakia tried to make the best of the hotel-shelter. She organized a dance group for young girls who lived there and found herself ministering to residents. She became an advocate for women in the shelter, particularly those who had been abused domestically or sexually. She is still haunted by the day she watched as an infant was taken from a mother, purportedly because of the deeds of a violent boyfriend.

The Barnetts moved to DC General after Lakia complained about health risks to her children. This large shelter on the premises of a former hospital, which has since closed, "felt like a prison," she said. The security guards and some staff were "nasty" and treated residents like they were "the lowest," she stated. "A lot of people have been misunderstood because they are homeless. They have feelings, ambition, goals but they didn't know how to execute" to achieve them. At the shelter, she said, "there was no room to see the individual, to find out what passions or vision they had to make themselves better." The attitude of the staff was "just go take anything" for a job, even though working at a McDonald's, she said, might not be a sustainable path. "No one would know from my being homeless that I could publish two books, host my own radio show, or start a [theater] movement" for women, she said proudly of her journey.[1]

The decaying DC General homeless shelter was infested by rats, and bugs that bit children. A baby died there. An eight-year-old, Relisha Rudd, was taken from the building by a janitor in 2014 and was never found. An investigation revealed more than a dozen claims of shelter employees sexually abusing tenants.[2] Mayor Muriel Bowser closed the shelter in 2018, replacing it with six smaller facilities scattered throughout the city, including one erected in affluent Ward Three, over the objections of some locals. While living at DC General, Lakia learned to tap the resources and networks of service providers, particularly an onsite legal clinic.

Georgetown's Health Justice Alliance set out to improve outcomes for poor families by addressing multiple social determinants of their health, including stable housing and quality education. A Georgetown Law student helped Lakia advocate for her children. Both sons have dyslexia and other disabilities. The student-lawyer helped Lakia negotiate the DC school lottery. In DC's segregated school system, a "great" school meant a whiter school than Lakia was used to. The elementary school her sons had attended had a way of "dropping the ball," she said. Through the lottery, they accessed better options. Her younger son, Jermel, was placed at School Within A School Elementary, its child-centered teaching philosophy inspired by the Reggio Emilia schools of Italy, which Lakia described as "really great." The school had more of a "mixture" of students and more "structure" than where he had been, she said.

Lakia's advocate helped her acquire an Individualized Education Program (IEP) for both her sons. The federal government grants about $12 billion annually to states and localities to pay for services for the 10 percent of American children with special needs. Federal law gives children with special needs procedural protections like the IEP, in which the state acknowledges a child's disability and commits in writing annually to the services it will provide to help the child meet stated educational goals. Affluent families are more likely to know about the program and invoke the federal right to sue school districts to enforce their individual rights.[3] With IEP status, Lakia's sons received tailored services and transportation to school on a small yellow bus dedicated to special-needs children. This, and the caring adult aide who rode the bus to look out for children, felt like a godsend. With Georgetown's help, Lakia also applied for and received assistance under the federal Supplemental Security Income (SSI) program for Jermel, who has a hearing disability and developmental issues that the IEP process helped identify. Lakia said that because of her family's size and her son's SSI status, she also received another miracle, a HUD-funded housing choice voucher.

The District of Columbia's waiting list for this voucher program stretches to nearly forty thousand people. Lakia was informed that she had only six months to sign a lease to use the voucher before it would expire. She launched into action, searching on Craigslist and other applications on her cellphone. In the District, unlike most states, a local law prevents discrimination by source of income in real estate transactions.[4] Using the voucher was "funny" Lakia said, in the quizzical sense, "Some would try to charge us double once they heard you had a voucher."

She persevered and discovered an affordable place for rent a few blocks from million-dollar homes on Capitol Hill. The owner told her the unit would be ready in a few weeks and she was open to taking the voucher. Lakia promised her children they would be in a home by Christmas. She cried with anguish when the landlord withdrew, complaining about the paperwork associated with the program, and stopped communicating with her. Another landlord for a listing she liked told her baldly that they did not accept vouchers. Another told her that they had a minimum-income requirement. All of these responses were potential violations of local fair-housing law.

A Georgetown Law student filed a complaint on Lakia's behalf against two landlords through the DC Office of Human Rights, then pursued mediation. Lakia told her story to the mediator with plaintive power and received a damage settlement for discrimination. Meanwhile, the expiration date for signing a lease with the voucher was approaching. Georgetown requested an extension based on the repeated discrimination she encountered. The local housing authority refused. Instead it did something that Georgetown Law faculty advisor Yael Cannon tells me she had never seen it do for any voucher holder. They assigned a team of people to help Lakia, gave her a list of rental vacancies with landlords who accepted vouchers, and had someone to drive her to see them. All of the listings were east of the Anacostia River in very poor neighborhoods.

The home that the Barnetts moved to was "the most decent property" they were shown, Lakia said. Despite the sturdiness of their block, she says they live "ten minutes by foot from places where people get shot." She also says that the neighborhood's Garfield Elementary School "is not great" and that she would not send her children there. All of the children at Garfield are economically disadvantaged. To its credit, the school has used Title I federal funding to provide a comprehensive, year-round program of learning, raising student achievement on standardized tests by about 50 percent in re-

Lakia Barnett

cent years. But less than half of Garfield students are meeting or exceeding standardized expectations. At the time of our interview, the school was ranked a color-coded red "priority," the lowest, in state-monitored categories of school performance known as ESEA.[5] Lakia feels that her sons' disabilities have been a blessing, a source of leverage to get services and access to quality apart from where they live. She dreams of one day returning to suburban Maryland, to a more pastoral space.

The Barnetts' housing search mirrors that of low-income families studied in Seattle. Raj Chetty and a team of researchers sought to understand why it is that low-income families tend to end up in low-income hoods. All of the participants in this randomized experiment had housing vouchers like the one that Lakia obtained. Some families received personalized counseling and assistance in searching for homes, and others in a control group were left to their own devices. The experiment debunked the myth that poor people live in poor areas merely out of preference. Researchers, reviewing extensive quantitative and qualitative data, concluded that difficulty in overcoming barriers in accessing housing in high-opportunity spaces was a central driver of residential segregation. More than half of low-income voucher holders that received highly personalized housing search assistance moved to high-opportunity areas compare to only 14 percent of those in the control group. Chetty and his colleagues concluded that the barriers to income integration for these families were most effectively removed by high-touch personal interventions to support individual families.[6]

The nation's legendary housing mobility programs, run by experienced nonprofits in Chicago, Dallas, and Baltimore, provide precisely this kind of personalized services to enable poor folk to have real choices about where to live.[7] It is what Lakia sought for her family and received from Georgetown's Health Justice Alliance—a humanized approach that responded to her family's specific challenges and enabled them to stabilize. But Lakia's family was denied their choice to live in a high-opportunity hood. The ideology of choice or freedom, like the American Dream, is largely denied to descendants. Those who live in affluent space and believe they have earned everything they have, including the right to exclude, participate in this false, limited ideology of freedom for an advantaged few. It helps explain the seeming permanence of racism and its structures. Those who benefit from the architecture of segregation can justify living on high ground by pathologizing low-income people who try to cross the moat.

Garfield Heights, where the Barnetts landed, is overwhelmingly Black. A child born between 1978 and 1983 at Lakia's current address was not likely to rise above her birth circumstances as an adult. Researchers at the US Census Bureau and Harvard and Brown Universities developed the Opportunity Atlas, mapping adult outcomes for every census tract in the country for the children born as the nation transitioned from presidents Carter to Reagan. The Atlas's measured adult outcomes for children born in Garfield Heights were a median household income of $21,000 and a very high incarceration rate of 6.2 percent, more than 1 in 20 adults.[8]

The Barnetts live in the zip code 20020. The first rental, promised and then denied to them, was on Capitol Hill in Lincoln Park, which straddles the 20002 and 20003 zip codes. Lincoln Park surrounds a sprawling park of the same name, where Union soldiers were hospitalized during the Civil War. For now, a controversial sculpture of Abraham Lincoln emancipating a last, kneeling fugitive slave stands at the east end of this expanse, planned by Pierre L'Enfant in his original design for the city. At the opposite west end stands a bronze sculpture of Black American educator-activist Mary McLeod Bethune. She hands her legacy to two Black children, and her words echo at the sculpture's base: "I leave you love. I leave you hope. I leave you the challenge of developing confidence in one another."

When Bethune's likeness was installed, many residents in the surrounding neighborhood were Black. Today, Lincoln Park, due east of the US Capitol, is an affluent, majority-white neighborhood. In an

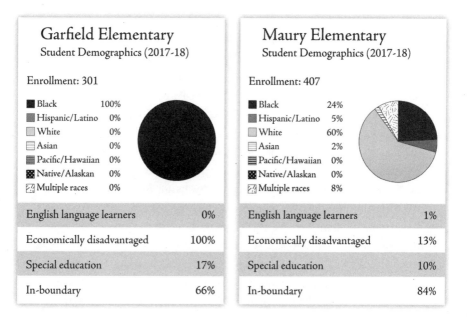

Garfield Elementary
Student Demographics (2017-18)

Enrollment: 301

■ Black	100%
■ Hispanic/Latino	0%
□ White	0%
▤ Asian	0%
▥ Pacific/Hawaiian	0%
▦ Native/Alaskan	0%
▨ Multiple races	0%

English language learners	0%
Economically disadvantaged	100%
Special education	17%
In-boundary	66%

Maury Elementary
Student Demographics (2017-18)

Enrollment: 407

■ Black	24%
■ Hispanic/Latino	5%
□ White	60%
▤ Asian	2%
▥ Pacific/Hawaiian	0%
▦ Native/Alaskan	0%
▨ Multiple races	8%

English language learners	1%
Economically disadvantaged	13%
Special education	10%
In-boundary	84%

online search in 2019, the cheapest property for sale in Lincoln Park was a one-bedroom, 805-square-foot condo for $415,000, with an estimated mortgage of $1,700 per month, the price for a singleton to live in a neighborhood with an excellent elementary school. Maury Elementary in Lincoln Park has a GreatSchools.org rating of nine out of ten for its students' "above average" performance on standardized tests and yearly academic improvement. It also received effusive five-star ratings from many satisfied parents.[9] The school performs well above the District average in standardized tests.[10] Racially and economically Maury Elementary is worlds apart from Garfield Elementary, the neighborhood school that the Barnett family was able to bypass only with the determined assistance of Georgetown Law students.

THE EFFECTS OF CONCENTRATED POVERTY

Only about 30 percent of Black and Latinx families reside in middle-class neighborhoods where less than half of the people are poor. Meanwhile, more than 60 percent of white and Asian families live in environs where most of their neighbors are not poor. The majority of whites and Asians live in neighborhoods with a poverty rate below 14 percent. As urban sociologist John Logan put it, "It is especially true for African Americans and Hispanics that their neighborhoods are often served by the worst-performing schools, suffer the highest crime rates, and have the least valuable housing stock in the metropolis."[11]

Five decades of social science research demonstrate what common sense tells us. Neighborhoods with high poverty, limited employment, underperforming schools, distressed housing, and violent crime depress life outcomes. They create a closed loop of systemic disadvantage such that failure is common and success aberrational. Even the most motivated child may not be able to overcome unsafe streets, family dysfunction, a lack of mentors and networks that lead to jobs and internships, or the general miasma of depression that can pervade high-poverty places.

One study found that a high-poverty neighborhood virtually guarantees downward mobility.[12] Living in a severely disadvantaged neighborhood impedes the development of verbal cognitive ability in children, correlates to a loss of a year of learning for Black students, and lowers high school graduation rates by as much as 20 percent.[13] Disadvantaged neighborhoods have been found to raise stress and levels of depression, independent of the impact of an individual's personal stressors like poverty, joblessness, or family crises.[14]

Children in poor neighborhoods are especially vulnerable because they deal with a confluence of multiple, chronic stressors.[15] As Douglas Massey summarized, the "spatial concentration of disadvantage . . . predicts a plethora of . . . maladies, including high rates of violence, crime, infant mortality, and homicide and low levels of life expectancy, public trust, interpersonal connection and political efficacy."[16] Black neighborhoods are also much more likely than others to contain or be close to toxic environmental hazards like trash incinerators and waste dumps.[17] Poor Black and Latinx neighborhoods have high rates of pollution relative to other places.[18] Formerly redlined hoods are now five degrees hotter in summer, on average, than areas once favored for conventional mortgages. Black and brown hoods lack trees and parks that cool bodies and the air. In some cities, the difference in summer temperature between the hood and favored space rises to twelve degrees, while a one-degree increase in heat increases the risk of death by 2.5 percent.[19]

Living in the hood is life-shortening. Recent research suggests that Black Americans are uniquely exposed to neighborhood stress that shortens telomeres—the repetitive nucleotic sequences at the ends of chromosomes that protect genetic material from deterioration. The normal process of telomere shortening that comes with aging is accelerated by environmental stress. This phenomenon subjects Black Americans to greater risk of disease and death throughout their lifetimes. Prolonged exposure to the cumulative deprivations of segregated neighborhoods increases risk of hypertension, cardiovascular disease, diabetes, and other disease. It has also been shown to undermine memory, mental health, and cognitive functioning.[20]

In Baltimore, for example, life expectancy in poor Black neighborhoods lags that in wealthier white environs by twenty years. In the Clifton-Berea neighborhood, where *The Wire* was filmed, residents can expect to live to age sixty-seven, the same as in Rwanda and about the same as in other poor Black neighborhoods in Philadelphia,

Chicago, and beyond. Among the causes for health disparities in Baltimore, as identified by an *Atlantic* reporter, were increased exposure to trauma, lead poisoning and allergens of poor-quality housing, fast-food "swamps," and healthy-food deserts.[21] Large supermarkets stock more healthy foods at lower prices than grocery and convenience stores, yet predominantly Black census tracts have the fewest supermarkets among all census tracts.[22]

Numerous studies correlate high lead exposure with impoverished Black neighborhoods. There is no safe level for exposure to lead, which has been linked to irreversibly reduced IQ and increased infant mortality, anxiety and depression, hypertension, impulsivity and attention deficit disorder, aggression, delinquency, crime, and homicide. Average blood lead levels are highest in poor communities of color; the primary sources are aged water pipes, gasoline exhaust, smelting plants, and chipping paint.[23]

The water crisis in Flint, Michigan, a hypersegregated, majority-Black city, underscores how concentrated Black poverty can lead to toxic inequality. Concentrated Blackness, once created, stands apart. It becomes easier for those in power to make distinctions, to treat people geographically confined differently than decision makers might treat their own family, neighbors, or perceived in-group.

Flint, like other communities in Michigan, enjoyed clean water from a Great Lake, via the Detroit water system. Upon his election, Republican governor Rick Snyder sought and signed legislation expanding powers of emergency managers. He invoked this law to supplant democratically elected local officials, mainly in majority-Black cities.[24] Snyder declared a financial emergency and appointed emergency managers in Flint. It appears that they, in turn, made the decision to draw water from the polluted Flint River to cut costs.[25] Emergency managers also decided not to treat the polluted water with an anticorrosive, creating a man-made crisis. The pipes corroded, leached lead, and poisoned children and families. A General Motors plant stopped using Flint's water because it was too corrosive for car parts. Yet state officials insisted for over a year that the water was safe to drink, despite knowing about an outbreak of Legionnaires' disease that killed a dozen people and undisclosed tests of a Flint resident's water that showed extraordinarily high lead levels.[26]

The crisis hit hardest in Flint's poorest and "Blackest" wards. Again, no amount of lead exposure is considered safe. Yet elevated blood lead levels for young children in Wards Five, Six, and Seven of Flint rose from 4 percent before the crisis to 10 percent after, levels that should shock the conscience and are unheard of for children in affluent white space. In Genesee County municipalities outside of Flint, the incidence of elevated blood lead levels was just 0.7 percent before the crisis and 1.2 percent after. Peter Muennig, a professor of public health at Columbia University, estimates that elevated blood lead levels found in over eight thousand Flint children will result in about $400 million in social costs. A task force commissioned by Governor Snyder concluded that the long-term damage of lead exposure "will necessitate sustained investments in education, public and mental health, juvenile justice, and nutrition needs over the next 10 to 20 years."[27] But the distributional politics of segregation does not augur well for such investments being made or sustained.

The Michigan Civil Rights Commission concluded that a long history of intentionally created racial segregation created the conditions for this racially disparate crisis. It asserted that race was a factor, though it did not find that the individual actors in this drama were intentionally racist. A lack of power and influence by locals, a segregated landscape, and a racialized structure of public policy all amounted to systemic racism.[28]

Malignant neglect or prioritizing money over Black health may explain why Black children in the poorest neighborhoods have had some of the highest-recorded blood-lead levels. Exposure is worse where children spend long hours indoors to avoid neighborhood violence. In Baltimore, in the 1990s, even after the adoption of stricter regulations, private landlords and the city's underresourced public agencies neglected properties in segregated neighborhoods. During that time, Baltimore did not bring a single enforcement action against a landlord, leaving chipped lead paint and dust to be ingested by young bodies. A lead poisoning rate fifteen times the national average has since been lowered dramatically by a crackdown on landlords in Baltimore.[29]

A caring government can make a pronounced difference in the lives of vulnerable citizens. An uncaring one can do permanent damage. Families of color may lack resources to mitigate toxins in their homes and neighborhoods, yet the Trump administration's Environmental Protection Agency proposed steep cuts to testing for lead exposure.[30] Similarly, even as descendant families in high-poverty hoods suffer greater exposure to polluted air and higher rates of asthma, the Trump administration stopped enforcing clean air regulations.[31]

Neglect can be bipartisan. In overwhelmingly Democratic and ostensibly progressive Washington, DC, the opioid epidemic received an anemic response from Mayor Bowser's administration, critics argued, because the many older Black Americans dying of overdoses were concentrated in marginalized Black neighborhoods.[32] Meanwhile, in 2020, during a pandemic that fell disproportionately on Black lives, the disparity in life expectancy between the richest and poorest neighborhoods of the District of Columbia was twenty-seven years.[33]

This is what it means to be a descendant. Aunt Hagar's children are exposed to concentrated disadvantage and have little or no power to influence public policies that cause or reify their disadvantage. Black Americans, regardless of their socioeconomic status, experience radically more neighborhood disadvantage than others, which, in turn, is the critical mechanism for transmitting and reproducing Black poverty over lives and generations.[34]

REJECTING NARRATIVES OF BLAME AND PATHOLOGY

At this point, some readers are rehearsing well-worn counternarratives that blame descendants for their plight. One can choose not to commit crimes, not to have children you can't raise, not to get high. One can study hard, be an involved parent, reject "thug life," cooperate with the police, so the arguments go. Such lectures rarely acknowledge the singular segregation that poor Black people are subjected to or the ways in which the state often makes matters worse through punitive, anti-Black public policies and disinvestment. Worse, the righteous critics of descendants in concentrated poverty often engage in racism. Somehow whites who exhibit social pathology get to be individuals, but a Black person who does represents an entire race.[35]

Meanwhile, nonpoor people typically avoid concentrated disadvantage because they can. Affluent parents pay handsomely to insulate their children from poverty and every conceivable disadvantage. Some parents cheat and bribe to buy their child a place at a selective college rather than trusting their offspring to chart their own destiny.[36] It is awfully rich to blame people who can't avoid concentrated poverty for the worse outcomes such environments engender. Such blame assumes that descendants have similar opportunities for social mobility when in fact the state has constructed *and maintained* a separate and unequal reality for them.

There are many reasons to resist pathologizing descendants in poor neighborhoods. The first is objective evidence that outcomes for poor Black families can change when they are allowed to move from concentrated poverty to higher ground. The *Gatreaux* court order that enabled residents of public housing to move to higher-income neighborhoods was replicated in a federal demonstration program known as Moving to Opportunity. Recent research demonstrated that children whose families moved when they were young, under age thirteen, significantly improved college attendance and earnings compared to a control group that stayed in a high-poverty environment. When they became adults, their annual incomes were 31 percent higher than those of non-movers. The youth who moved were also likely to live in better neighborhoods as adults.[37] Other researchers found that moving to a low-poverty area "greatly improved the mental health, physical health, and subjective well-being of adults as well as family safety."[38]

Admittedly, the Moving to Opportunity experiment did not change *economic* outcomes for older children or adults, as was the case for adult *Gautreaux* movers.[39] A person long exposed to concentrated poverty and its disadvantages will have a harder time making their way economically than those less exposed. That young children experience greater rewards from moving underscores that environment matters. When Montgomery County, Maryland, enabled Black and Latinx residents of public housing to move to a middle-class neighborhood and attend middle-class school, the children did much better academically than counterparts left behind in high-poverty schools who were given extra resources.[40]

Likewise, a recent longitudinal study by researchers for the Federal Reserve Bank of Philadelphia found that long-term residents and children who are able to stay in gentrifying neighborhoods benefit as opportunity moves to them and poverty declines. They suggested policies to promote affordable housing in high-demand urban areas and mitigate displacement.[41] In other words, governments should be promoting policies that stabilize and include.

A congeries of intangibles comprises opportunity or the lack thereof. Researchers have developed an aggregate measure of neighborhood assets and stressors that they call the Child Opportunity Index, based on nineteen indicators relevant to child development. Not surprisingly, based on these indicators, neighborhoods rate very differently, from very low to very high opportunity. And Black and Latinx children are much more likely to live in the lowest-opportunity neighborhoods than are white children.

Forty percent of Black children and 32 percent of Latinx children live in the one-fifth of neighborhoods that rank lowest in opportunity, compared to only 9 percent of white children. Nearly 60 percent of *poor* Black children live in the lowest-opportunity settings. Inequities in neighborhood opportunity are most pronounced in metropolitan areas with high levels of segregation.[42]

According to the developers of the Child Opportunity Index, "Segregated schools are perhaps the most powerful pathways through which segregated neighborhoods affect children."[43] This implicates another reason for rejecting narratives of blame. Society tells descendant children to get an education and pull themselves up but often relegates them to grossly inferior schools.

Schools with large numbers of Black and brown students often have more novice teachers, more teachers with less academic preparation and no teacher certification, higher teacher turnover, larger class sizes, and higher poverty levels in the student body.[44] Decades of social science demonstrate that high poverty in a school creates educational challenges.[45] More than 60 percent of Black and Latinx children attend high-poverty schools where more than half the population is poor. The typical white or Asian child in public school attends a school where most of the children live above the poverty line.[46]

Segregation shapes future educational outcomes, as does integration, when it is achieved. Long-term studies of Black students found better outcomes for those who attended integrated schools: higher achievement and attendance at more selective colleges, higher incomes, better jobs, lower incarceration, and superior long-term health. Desegregation reduced violent crime by young Black men by as much as one-third.[47] Other children benefit from, and are not harmed by, school integration. Children of all races and incomes who attend integrated schools improve their critical thinking skills, are less apt to accept stereotypes as truth, lead more integrated lives as adults, and are more civically engaged. Racial minorities in integrated schools also achieve at higher levels, with no detriment to the learning of white students.[48] We let pervasive stereotypes and fear obscure such truths.

In addition to segregating poor Black and brown kids into separate and unequal schools, several states take a carceral, punitive approach to kids trapped in concentrated disadvantage. With the introduction of zero-tolerance policies in the 1990s, inner-city schools became places where minor infractions that might be overlooked in a middle-class school were policed as crimes that sent children into the criminal justice system.[49] Regarding the narrative of blame, whatever violent crime or disruptive social behavior a small minority of descendants in high-poverty neighborhoods commit, the response of the state has been overly punitive and racially disparate, making matters worse, not better. As Patrick Sharkey has argued, since the 1960s, "the dominant approach to dealing with the challenges of urban poverty and violent crime has been to disinvest in low-income communities and to invest in the police and the criminal justice system—a strategy of abandonment and punishment."[50]

Common sense tells us that concentrated poverty and social isolation will lead to social ills. It happens in poor Black space.[51] It happens in poor white space.[52] But poor whites, statistically are more likely to live in middle-class surroundings than concentrated poverty. Poor Blacks are typecast as dangerous and unworthy of such inclusion.

Again, environment matters. An analysis of the resegregation of Charlotte-Mecklenburg, North Carolina, schools found that poor Black males were 15 percent more likely to be arrested for a crime if they were assigned to a school with 60 percent students of color than a school with 40 percent students of color. Its authors speculated that placing high numbers of those most vulnerable to crime together raised the probability of negative peer influences.[53]

We should expect some people to succumb to a deprived, dangerous environment. In *Great American City: Chicago and the Enduring Neighborhood Effect,* Robert Sampson demonstrated that concentrated disadvantage powerfully affects individual outcomes and rates of behavior across neighborhoods, a phenomenon he called "neighborhood effect." Not every individual succumbs to the undertow of the hood but among the neighborhood effects of concentrated disadvantage are joblessness, poverty, single-parent families, violence, incarceration, and reduced collective efficacy.[54]

The narrative of pathology blames the people who lost the neighborhood lottery for these neighborhood effects and masks a legacy of intentional state discrimination in creating ghettos. American government has thrown billions at segregating and caging poor Black people and those who pathologize them expect them to be superhuman and leap over the many structural barriers and negative conditions placed in their way. We shall have overcome when descendants are not required to be superheroes to escape the hood, when they are treated as just *human.* Ordinary people ride the bus rather than spread their arms to fly. To succeed, they need that bus to arrive on time and a realistic route to prosperity.

The narrative of pathology paints too broadly. Most violent crime is committed in "hot spots" by "a tiny group of people who are linked together in a tight network of victims and offenders."[55] In Boston, for example, young gang members in high-risk neighborhoods comprise only 3 percent of the youth population of those neighborhoods and only 1 percent of the city's total youth population, but 60 percent of youth homicides involving guns or knives are attributable to gangs.[56] The vast majority of young Black men and descendants do not commit violent crime, though far too many Americans righteously and falsely assert that they do.

Researchers have sought to understand why it is that some poor Black neighborhoods are worse than others in terms of violent crime. That poor hoods vary suggests, again, that descendants are not inherently violent. Social scientists have established a relationship between poor Black neighborhoods and violent crime, but recent research suggests that cities can disrupt that connection. Black elected officials, civilian review boards of police departments, and a liberal voter base are among the factors that moderate the relationship between Black neighborhoods and violence. Black segregation does not automatically predict neighborhood violence. Examining a representative sample of census tracts from large US cities and violent crime data, researchers concluded that increased percentage Blackness in a neighborhood correlated with increased violence "only in cities with limited black political opportunities."[57] This study also found that in cities with high levels of grassroots advocacy and protest on behalf of communities of color, including riots, the positive association between percentage Black and violence was disrupted.[58]

Yes, violence occurs even in Black neighborhoods of cities with Black political incorporation and grassroots advocacy. When the tiny minority shoots and kills, descendants bleed, mothers cry in anguish, communities suffer the consequences of living with violence. But studies about the variability in violence across neighborhoods and cities suggest something about power relations between the state and poor Black neighborhoods and the lens through which descendants are seen. Seeing descendants as citizens worthy of political incorporation and engagement, as potential assets with the ability, if empowered, to reduce violence and improve conditions in their neighborhoods, could produce different, more positive neighborhood effects. That would require rejecting persistent cultural stereotypes and investing more in inclusion and the civic infrastructure of poor Black neighborhoods.[59]

Lakia Barnett received a housing choice voucher but lost the neighborhood lottery. Black boys fare best in neighborhoods with low poverty, high rates of father presence among Blacks, and low levels of racial bias among whites.[60] In my own life, my husband and I—Black American professionals with resources and six college and advanced degrees between us—carefully chose such a neighborhood in which to raise our twin sons. We were confident that our culturally dexterous neighbors in Shepherd Park would not feel threatened by Black teenagers horsing around and that they would call us rather than the police in any unexplained situation.[61] As I labored on this book, we moved to integrated Crestwood to live in my husband's lovingly restored childhood home. Some comments on the Crest-wood neighborhood listserv made us less sanguine, but we are heartened by the many yard signs attesting that Black Lives Matter and the ordinary kindnesses neighbors bestow on each other. Less than 5 percent of Black children grow up in optimal environments rich with Black fathers and low in poverty and anti-Black prejudice.[62] One can try to blame Black people for the absence of Black fathers, a story that leaves out the role of deindustrialization and mass incarceration in reducing the pool of marriageable Black men.[63] One could also examine why the Barnetts and other descendant families could not find housing, or acceptance, in affluent neighborhoods like Lincoln Park.

CHAPTER 8

SURVEILLANCE

Black Lives Matter

Rayshard Brooks.

George Floyd. Ahmaud Arbery. Breonna Taylor.

Atatiana Jefferson.

Philando Castile. Alton Sterling. Sandra Bland.
Freddie Gray. Walter Scott.

Akai Gurley. Laquan McDonald.

Tamir Rice. Michael Brown. Eric Garner.

Trayvon Martin. Rekia Boyd.

Oscar Grant.

These are some of the names we say, those of Black people who were loved by their families and should not have died senselessly. There are many more names we have forgotten or never heard. Police are more than twice as likely to kill a Black person than a white person.[1] Hate criminals kill Black Americans at higher rates than any other racial group in the United States.[2] There is another story to engage you, yet again, with an ancient problem of American caste. Fortunately, this tale does not end in murder.

Darryl Atwell drove a silver Toyota Prius, though his buddies ribbed him for it. It was not the peacock car that a cardiothoracic anesthesiologist and son of Howard University might have chosen to reward himself or to impress women. Atwell preferred to spend his money on art. For him, collecting was an act of cultural preservation. He lent works to museums, showing African Americans as "productive people doing everyday things," he told me. On an October evening in 2018, two police officers who stopped Atwell in Washington, DC, may have seen him differently.

He had been visiting his friend Ellington Robinson, an artist who regularly fed the souls and stomachs of a hip Black crowd. Atwell, a teetotaler, didn't need anything more to feel good. On a Saturday evening at Robinson's house, the talk could turn from art to politics to basketball. Atwell could spend time with the art on his friend's walls or just eat and listen to the music and a cross section of Black strivers, solving the world's problems through banter. The occasion for that evening may have been a send-off party for someone moving from the DC diaspora to the African continent from which all Blackness sprang. Atwell looked at his watch and remembered he had promised to visit his friend Rosalyn, who lived downtown. "Atwell, where are you going, we're just getting started," Robinson had said. These soirees regularly extended past midnight. Atwell felt pulled by the fun but also his other social commitment. He promised to return and left with every intention of doing so.

Atwell drove south on Sherman Avenue. Ahead, a parked car blocked the right lane. He accelerated, passed a car on his left, then moved into the left lane. He did not notice a police car behind him. "Are you in a hurry to get somewhere?" a Black officer asked after stopping him. A Latino officer stood slightly back, observing, his hands tucked inside a bulletproof vest, a stance of superior rank, literal or assumed, Atwell could not tell. He answered the inquiry, explaining to the officers that he was headed to see a friend but was not in any rush. The Black officer asked Atwell for his identification. His proof of insurance and car registration were in the glove compartment, and as he contemplated reaching for them, he thought of Philando Castile, a man who was killed trying to do the same thing while also reporting his lawfully carried firearm.

"Officers, I am going into the glove compartment to get my registration and insurance," Atwell said. He had no idea why he had been pulled over, and his tone betrayed irritation. He insisted that the officers acknowledge what he said before he moved. The Latino officer, hands still in his vest, said, "Well, you see where my hands are." Atwell repeated his assertion, asking them to acknowledge his statement, and the Latino officer repeated his. On the third try, Atwell said he did not care where the officer's hands were, he wanted to be sure the officer knew why he was reaching into the glove compartment. From Atwell's perspective, he was trying to comply with authority and live another day. The Latino officer became agitated with the dark-skinned Black man before him who spoke as if he thought of himself as somebody. In Atwell's view, it did not matter that both officers were men of color. The police operate under their own codes, he thought. Atwell handed over his identification and waited as they retreated, presumably to run a data search. Ten minutes passed, too long to be a routine license check, he thought.

Upon returning, the Black officer ordered Atwell to exit his vehicle. Atwell asked why, and the officer said in order to relay what he had done wrong. "I don't have to get out of the car for you to explain what I did," Atwell resisted, still mystified as to why he had been stopped. He did not view his brief acceleration and lane change as exceptional. The Black officer repeated his order with more power, "Get out of the car." Atwell complied, expecting a lecture. "You are under arrest for reckless driving," the Black officer said evenly.

"I was shocked and livid," Atwell told me during an interview in March 2020. They cuffed Atwell's hands behind his back; "crazy tight, it hurt my wrists," he said. A white policewoman arrived and was assigned the role of putting Atwell in the back of a police car. Athletic and 6 feet, 1½ inches tall, he tried to position his long legs in the confined space between the barricade and the back seat. He could not sit normally with his legs in front of him. "Just get in the car," the female officer said, exasperated, and belted him in. As the police drove him to jail, he thought of Freddie Gray, his body contorted, legs turned forty-five degrees from his torso, and arms cuffed behind his back, knowing how damaging an impact from a car accident could be in this position.

I asked Atwell if he ever told the police he was a medical doctor. He said it did not occur to him, that he had never used his profession to curry favor. His friends jokingly call him "Letter-of-the-Law

Larry." Atwell had tried to do everything right in his life. He was born in the US to Trinidadian immigrant parents. His mother, especially, had instilled in him pride, dignity, and a fierce work ethic. As a child, he was an honor student who skipped grades. He graduated from St. John's College High School at age sixteen, sixth in his class, and attended Howard for both college and medical school. That even he was being grabbed by this system underscored to him its pervasive injustice.

"I think they arrested me to show me a lesson [for speaking up for myself]," he told me. He had never been arrested before; he didn't even have an unpaid parking ticket. At most, he thought the officers might give him a citation. Instead, they took him to a police station, where he was searched, fingerprinted, and booked. After asking multiple times, Atwell was allowed to call his brother, who is a lawyer. There was nothing to do but wait to be released, his brother explained. The system was processing him and others; he would be released that day unless they found an outstanding warrant for his arrest, his brother told him. Atwell sat alone in a holding cell from about 7 p.m. until 1:30 a.m., caught in the bureaucratic motion of the carceral state. On release, the same officers who arrested him returned his personal items. Atwell stared angrily at the Black officer, who looked away. Atwell wanted to hold the brother accountable, wanted him to feel some guilt for participating in this farce, but the Black man in blue displayed no remorse. Atwell detected a smirk and smug satisfaction from the Latino officer. Disgusted, he walked blocks to the arrest scene to collect his car.

"I felt so dehumanized, degraded and defeated," Atwell told me. "I thought of all the people who have gone through this . . . from fugitive slaves onward," he said of famous and ordinary Black Americans we learn about who have endured capture. "This whole system that is meant to make money . . . and assert authority and dominion over others. And it is meant to humiliate you. Those officers, I could see it in their face. I don't honestly think all police are bad, but they forever tainted how I feel about [the police]."

This is Dr. Darryl Atwell's telling of his story. I did not attempt to discern the officers' version of events, and ultimately the prosecutor chose not to pursue the case. That added to Atwell's anger about the arrest. It was totally unwarranted in his view and his distress about police treatment was cumulative. "In my experience, I've had no good experience with police officers," Atwell said.

He shared some of his personal police history with me. While completing his two-year cardiothoracic fellowship at Duke University in Durham, North Carolina, in the mid-1990s, he experienced ongoing discrimination, that is, "driving while Black." After the third or fourth time that local law enforcement stopped him, he mentioned this experience in passing to the head of his program, who volunteered to speak to the police department on his behalf. "It was random stuff," Atwell said. Once he was stopped for driving "too slowly." Another time he was stopped, he was told, for driving "suspiciously." He never received a ticket for these stops.

The stops seemed more frequent in Cleveland, Ohio, where Atwell worked for eight years at Cleveland Clinic. Upon moving there, he immediately noticed the stark segregation of the city. The clinic, one of the highest-ranking research hospitals in the United States, was located "right in the hood," as Atwell put it, in an economically depressed area on the East Side of downtown Cleveland. The East Side is overwhelmingly Black. Atwell chose to live there, five minutes from Cleveland Clinic. Later he bought a house in the integrated, eastern suburb of Shaker Heights because he was advised that its property values would be more stable than in depressed eastern Cleveland.

The West Side was very white, including ethnic Slavs and Poles. "Cats from Cleveland did not go to Little Italy," Atwell said of his Black brethren who tended not to venture beyond the East Side. As a man who went where he wanted, Atwell often felt like an explorer.

In his recollection, he was stopped about six times in eight years. The most harrowing, he said, was a stop on the West Side. He recalled driving to a restaurant or club and had just crossed into the west. This time, a white policeman claimed that Atwell had driven on the wrong side of the road, improbably, against oncoming traffic.

"You get sick of it," Atwell said of the memory, "being accosted about something you know you didn't do." He handed over his driver's license, with his Cleveland Clinic medical ID inadvertently stuck to it. Atwell asked the officer several times to return his work ID and the officer ignored him. Fed up, Atwell taunted the man: "Give it back to me; you will never need a doctor's ID because you will never be a doctor. After this is over, I am going to be a doctor, and you will be out here, on the streets, being a cop." He admits he was trying to belittle him, something ordinarily he would never do. In the moment, mean words were Atwell's bid for dignity. To his credit, the police officer did not escalate hostilities, though he continued to pursue the stop wherever it might take him. The officer tried to search the car, pointing a flashlight in and pulling on the door handle. "No, you may not search my car," Atwell asserted.

The officer ordered him to exit his vehicle, in those days, a light blue Mercedes CLK 320. Soon five white police officers surrounded him. Atwell became the center of a too-familiar American scene for the voyeurs who drove by. A Black man, hands placed on the hood of his car, legs spread, police exploring his body with their hands, searching for weapons that were not there. Did they enjoy it?

In this instance, Atwell says he felt like trash. They had complete dominion over him, and he felt his life was in peril. The story reminded me of a similar one told to me by one of my law students—another Black male who said he had been stopped nineteen times and, in the worst episode, sat crying on the hood of a police car, handcuffed, certain he was going to die. Philando Castile was stopped more than forty-six times by police before an officer shot him to death; only six of the stops were for offenses an officer could have observed before pulling him over.[3]

This time, Atwell received only a citation, which he challenged in court. The police did not show up, and the judge dropped the charge, but not without a parting accusation: "Be careful which side of the road you drive on in the future," meaning the judge presumed the police report was true. This, too, angered Atwell, who had prepared a soliloquy but held his tongue and bolted from the courtroom.

Atwell returned to Washington in 2006, and while he endured fewer traffic stops in the formerly Chocolate City, they were never pleasant. He did not understand the automatic antagonism he seemed to encounter in his interactions with police. He recalled being detained in 2017 for not signaling before turning at a stop sign. He had come to a full stop. The intersection was clear. He forgot to signal. "Have you ever been locked up?" was the officer's first belligerent question, he recalled. "I'm not going to answer that question," Atwell replied, again, a sarcastic assertion of dignity. "Oh, you want to make things difficult, I can do that," the officer escalated. It was four o'clock in the afternoon. Atwell recalled wondering, "Don't the police have better things to do, crimes to solve . . . why start out with such hostility?"

Atwell was so upset by this interaction that he pursued a mediation. In the District of Columbia, a citizen complainant has the option of sitting down with an officer and a mediator to discuss what happened as a form of restorative justice. Atwell asked the officer why he began a traffic stop with a question about whether he had a criminal record. "If I was a 16-year-old-girl, would you have asked me that question?" he interrogated. "There are a lot of bad people," the officer declared, claiming he used that opener to protect himself. Atwell challenged him: If he did have a criminal record, he could easily lie about it. Why assume that *he* was bad? Under the prodding of the mediator, Atwell says the officer acknowledged that his approach was inflammatory. The mediation left Atwell only partially satisfied. He felt it had been worth the effort to get one cop to rethink his interactions with Black citizens. And yet it was only a year later, that another cop escalated a traffic stop, arrested, and humiliated him on Sherman Avenue.

"Would it be fair of me to say all police officers are bad?" he wondered aloud as we concluded our interview. "If Black people based [their opinions of all whites on] their experience with some whites," he reasoned, "we would say all whites are bad and should be avoided. But we don't do that." He applauded Black Americans for affording others what is often denied to themselves. "Black people are not given the benefit of the doubt even when it [accords with] rational evidence," he argued, proceeding to give examples of his experience as a Black doctor in a white coat. "Whose jacket are you wearing?" he was once asked of the doctor's coat he wore with his name embroidered on it. "Who is the doctor on this case?" "Are you a tech?" He described episodes where people, usually whites, reached to explain away what should have been obvious: the Black man before them was a doctor and the person in superior position to decide

Darryl Atwell

what would happen under the circumstances. White people about to undergo surgery, after being introduced to Atwell, the doctor who was going to administer anesthesia, would often ask incredulously, "Where did you go to school?"[4]

Black folk, men especially, are often viewed through a lens of suspicion and can experience what sociologist Elijah Anderson calls "nigger moments" as they go about their business. A learned association of Blackness with criminality, Anderson asserts, is incubated in the iconic "ghetto."[5] In a study of Chicago neighborhoods, sociologists Robert Sampson and Stephen Raudenbush found that perceptions of neighborhood disorder, like race itself, were socially constructed and rose with levels of concentrated poverty and percentages of Black and Latinx residents.[6] Ideas constructed to justify creating and maintaining the hood can attach to Black skin, wherever the Black person is encountered.[7]

Black women also suffer disproportionately the burdens of aggressive policing. Sandra Bland was stopped for changing lanes without signaling, ordered to put out her cigarette, arrested when she refused, and found hanging dead in her jail cell three days later. Atatiana Jefferson was killed in her home about 2:30 a.m. by a Fort

Worth cop during what was supposed to be a check on her welfare;
he saw a Black person in the window and shot instantly.[8] Breonna
Taylor was shot and killed when police invaded her home in the middle of the night.[9] These women and untold others are members of a
grim eternal Black sisterhood.

Elijah Anderson's insight illuminates another sinister aspect of
American residential caste. The hood, once constructed, facilitates
not only unequal distribution of resources, opportunity hoarding in
affluent white space, and ideas about Blackness, it also contributes
to a different style of policing of Black people and an overinvestment
by the state in law enforcement and incarceration. And it contributes
to systemic private surveillance of Black Americans by self-appointed
citizen patrollers, often with the encouragement of the state.

POLICING THE HOOD AND DESCENDANTS

A study commissioned by the ACLU of Washington, DC, aligns with
Anderson's theory. Researchers invoked a freedom of information
statute to access Metropolitan Police Department arrest records for
the years 2013–17. They found that Black people were arrested at
ten times the rate of whites and that such racially disproportionate
arrests occurred in 90 percent of all the city's census tracts. Whether
in very white space, very Black space, or multiracial spaces in between, Black bodies were more likely to be arrested.[10]

For example, Black Americans, who then comprised 47 percent
of the city's population, accounted for 76 percent of arrests for noise
complaints. They accounted for 99 percent of those arrested for
gambling. Among the other categories of relatively minor nonviolent offenses for which Blacks were disproportionately apprehended
or cited: possession of an open container of alcohol, consuming marijuana in public (in a city where private consumption is now legal),
and driving without a permit. Nearly four-fifths of the ten-thousand-
odd souls arrested for not carrying a permit while driving were Black.
And yet the police officers who stopped Black drivers could not have
known beforehand that they were missing a permit. This sharp disparity led researchers to speculate that Black people were being
stopped more often for behavior for which others might receive a

pass and that these stops helped drive Black arrest rates higher.[11] As I discussed when debunking ghetto myths, and wearily repeat here, Black people do not commit violent, much less nonviolent, crime at dramatically higher rates than whites and certainly not ten times the rate of whites.[12]

The Supreme Court has enabled differential policing in Black neighborhoods with its Fourth Amendment jurisprudence. The Court has held that if police observe someone in a "high crime area" and can articulate an additional factor arousing their suspicion, this meets the "reasonable suspicion" standard necessary to render a stop of that person constitutional.[13] It is a no-win situation for residents of poor Black hoods. Police stop and search more frequently in majority-Black areas, leading to higher rates of arrest. A hood becomes a "high crime area," raising probabilities of even more stops and death at the hands of police.

In recent years, police killed about one thousand people annually in the United States, a number that far exceeds per capita police killings in most developed countries.[14] Researchers have found a correlation between racial segregation and police killings. Police are more likely to use violent force in a majority-Black neighborhood than in majority-white space, especially if the neighborhood is poor. And police interactions are more likely to be fatal in the hood. Segregation enables police to use a style of policing that would not be tolerated in white space, and segregation helps explain why it is that Black people, especially men, are much more likely than white folk to be killed by the police.[15]

In the wake of the 1992 Los Angeles riots, which were spurred by the acquittal of police officers who beat Rodney King for a reported fifteen minutes, Congress passed a law giving the federal Department of Justice (DOJ) authority to investigate police departments for patterns or practices of unconstitutional policing and seek consent decrees to redress them. About forty of the country's roughly eighteen thousand police departments have entered consent decrees or other settlement agreements for pattern or practice violations.[16] The Obama administration's DOJ investigated police departments and negotiated nineteen consent decrees or similar directives. Each consent decree included proposed reforms and required law enforcement agencies to take remedial measures, without any admission of guilt. The DOJ's investigative reports on errant police departments illuminated an often-predatory relationship between police and descendants in the hood, though the Trump administration disavowed this work.

In Baltimore, between 2010 and 2014, the DOJ reported that police conducted over one hundred thousand stops in the Western and Central Districts. The least populated police districts in the city, comprising only 12 percent of Baltimore's population, endured 44 percent of all stops recorded citywide. Poor hoods in East and West Baltimore were disproportionately targeted. Descendants told the DOJ about repeated encounters with the police, in the street and on sidewalks. One said he had been stopped thirty-four times. Several hundred residents said they had been stopped at least ten times. Some were stopped multiple times in the same week without being charged for any crime.[17]

Cops lawed and ordered, telling descendants to clear corners where they congregated and talked. One officer directed youth to disperse because "it looks bad." The DOJ concluded that these frequent dispersal orders lacked any legal basis and that they were not effective in fighting crime. Overall, the Baltimore Police Department's pedestrian stops uncovered slight criminal activity and the rate of finding criminal activity when Black Americans were stopped and searched was lower still.[18]

The DOJ's investigation of the Chicago Police Department examined a legendary police tactic called the "jump out." Plainclothes officers in unmarked vehicles would jump out of their cars and advance on young men, sometimes with guns drawn. At night, not surprisingly, individuals often fled, not waiting around to find out that the aggressors were in fact police officers. The inevitable chase led police to shoot innocent people running in at least two circumstances.[19] The CPD deployed tactical gang or narcotics units that do not answer service calls but conduct stops and look for reasons to arrest people. The DOJ talked to Black citizens in targeted neighborhoods about their relations with the police. One youth said he felt like he lived in "an open-air prison." Another said, "They patrol our streets like they are the dog catchers and we are the dogs." One officer admitted to the DOJ that "kids" on the North Side of Chicago who get caught with marijuana receive a citation while those on the South Side would get arrested.[20]

Boys in the hood were presumed to be thugs—that is, presumed guilty—while others were presumed innocent. Some officers used words in their interactions with young Black men that attested to this differential attitude. In its report, the DOJ wrote:

> Black youth told us that they are routinely called "nigger," "animal," or "pieces of shit" by CPD officers. . . . Such statements were confirmed by CPD officers. One officer we interviewed told us that he personally has heard co-workers and supervisors refer to black individuals as monkeys, animals, savages, and "pieces of shit." . . .
>
> Our investigation found that there was a recurring portrayal by some CPD officers of the residents of challenged neighborhoods—who are mostly black—as animals or subhuman. One CPD member told us that the officers in his district come to work every day "like it's a safari."[21]

Jump outs were not exclusive to Chicago. In his unflinching book *Chokehold: Policing Black Men*, Paul Butler describes how the tactic was deployed in poor Black neighborhoods in Washington, DC, especially those experiencing an influx of white residents. It didn't matter that many of the police chasing young Black men were also Black men. They were frontline soldiers who did the job assigned to them, which in gentrifying neighborhoods, Butler asserted, was catering to whites' desires and fears.[22]

In 1994, the New York Police Department adopted "zero-tolerance policing" of minor quality-of-life offenses. Two academics had theorized in a magazine article entitled "Broken Windows" that physical and social disorder created the perception that no one cared about a particular neighborhood, therefore inviting more serious crime.[23] In ensuing decades, New York's zero-tolerance policy entrenched a practice of aggressive order-maintenance policing in certain neighborhoods. "Broken windows" policing broke lives as the number of encounters between police and citizens multiplied exponentially, producing stops, summonses, arrests, and occasionally death, sometimes for trivial offenses.[24] Eric Garner, the large Black man and father of six who said he could not breathe as multiple officers tackled him, had allegedly been selling "loosies," or untaxed single cigarettes. He died for the "crime" of trying to make some extra money to support his family, in a gentrifying neighborhood in which police had been tasked with stopping such cultural side hustles.[25]

At its height, New York City's zero-tolerance program ensnared one-fifth of the Black population of the city. One study estimated that a Black male age eighteen to nineteen had an 80 percent probability of being stopped. And yet a successful class-action constitutional challenge to stop-and-frisk, *Floyd v. City of New York*, revealed that police rarely recovered any evidence of crime, and nearly 90 percent of these stops did not result in arrest.[26]

Whatever the intentions behind the broken-windows theory, analyses of zero-tolerance policing in New York City at its height show how segregation facilitates differential policing. The NYPD could not police minor infractions everywhere, so specific neighborhoods and populations were targeted. Suddenly, a young man standing on the sidewalk with his bike became a target. He and others like him could no longer move about as if they were free; behavior that most people would consider ordinary was criminalized and led sometimes to an arrest. Even when charges were dropped, the arrest record could lead to a kind of civil death. Descendants living in targeted hoods quickly learned how difficult it was to succeed and thrive.[27] Meanwhile, true physical disorder in those neighborhoods—litter, abandoned vehicles, and actually broken windows—were not being remedied.

While New York's zero-tolerance program was abandoned under Mayor de Blasio, separate and unequal policing continued. In 2018, the *New York Times* conducted an investigation of arrests for petty marijuana use and found the NYPD almost always made arrests at higher rates in areas with more Black citizens. In Queens, for example, majority-Black Queens Village experienced an arrest rate ten times that of Forest Hills, which has only a tiny Black population, even though the rate of complaints about marijuana use was the same for each precinct. Across very segregated New York City, the police arrested Black people for low-level marijuana violations at eight times the rate of whites over the three years that the *Times* investigated.[28]

Where segregation endures, anti-Black policing habits do not seem to die. New York City was the nation's hotspot in fighting the COVID-19 pandemic in the early spring of 2020. COVID deaths soared within Black communities, but punitive policing continued. The Brooklyn district attorney released data on arrests made in the borough for violations of social distancing rules between mid-March and early May. Police arrested thirty-five Blacks, four Hispanics, and one white. One-third of these arrests occurred in the predominantly Black neighborhood of Brownsville. No arrests were made in whiter Park Slope. Elsewhere, in videos in which whites could be seen flouting social distancing in parks in lower Manhattan, police handed them masks. Mayor de Blasio initially defended the NYPD, distinguishing their actions from the zero-tolerance era. A crescendo of complaints was generated by a video of officers tackling and arresting Kaleemah Rozier after stopping her for not wearing her mask properly; de Blasio pledged to reset police involvement with social distancing, focusing them on dispersing large crowds rather than issuing summonses.[29]

Breaching social-distancing rules was not a crime, but routine behavior was criminalized in instances of arrest. Only Black people, it seems, were targeted for systemic policing. They constituted 88 percent of those arrested in this sample from Brooklyn, a borough that was only a third Black.[30]

George Floyd's slow execution brought 20/20 focus on racist policing in the United States. Less clear in that radical moment was the role of segregation in his death. Map 8.1 in the insert marks the spot where Floyd died in south Minneapolis with a black star. He departed this earth near the intersection of Thirty-Eighth Street and Chicago Avenue, in racially mixed Powderhorn, not far from dividing lines to white space. One green dot on the map equals one hundred Black people. One red dot equals ten poor people. Like every other segregated city, Minneapolis's stark segregation was constructed with great intention—a history of racially restrictive covenants, redlining, urban renewal, and exclusion similar to that of other cities.[31] This produced segregation helps explain why the Twin Cities region has one of the highest standards of living in the country *and* among the nation's highest rates of racial inequality—on dimensions like income, wealth, employment, life expectancy, and educational attainment.[32] Racial disparities were also endemic in policing. The Minneapolis Police Department was perennially accused of racist misconduct. Police in Minneapolis and the region killed Black men: Jamar Clark in 2015. Philando Castile in 2016. Thurman Blevins in 2018. Mario Benjamin in 2019. George Floyd in 2020. Protest and ineffective "reforms" were familiar rituals even before George Floyd died. Criminologist Philip M. Stinson told the *New York Times* that the data on the department's use of force since 2015 suggested police in Minneapolis "routinely beat the hell out of black men."[33]

Powderhorn is due south of some of the "Blackest" and poorest neighborhoods on the southside, and it is buffered by an interstate from the very white, affluent Southwest neighborhood. My research assistant lived in Southwest and in Powderhorn at different stages of his life. He tells me that police in Powderhorn tended to be "hunters" and that in Southwest they acted as "protectors," if they were seen at all. His anecdote accords with social science about differential policing between Black and white neighborhoods.[34]

According to recent data, Minneapolis police used force against Black people at seven times the rate of whites. The *New York Times* published a map that encoded the spots where force was used since 2015; the map showed a pockmarked density of purple circles in the very same hoods dense with Black folk and poverty. Police wielded guns, chemical irritants, Tasers, chokeholds, body-pins, fists, and other brute force in the hood. Meanwhile, the white working-class Northeast quadrant, across the Mississippi River from very Black areas, were spared such intense use of force, as was the affluent white Southwest.[35]

Powderhorn is not a poor Black neighborhood, though at the time Floyd was killed it was majority nonwhite and gentrifying. Researchers have found connections between gentrification and heightened order-maintenance policing.[36] Anti-Black policing habits incubated in the hood in Minneapolis apparently were brought to Powderhorn, though in the *Times* map not with the same density of violent encounters.[37]

Like so many other white police officers, Derek Chauvin did not live in the neighborhoods he hunted. He resided in a suburb of St.

Paul that was over 80 percent white and owned a second home in Florida, where he was registered to vote, in a suburb that was 85 percent white.[38] George Floyd, son of the historically Black and proud Third Ward of Houston, grew up living in Cuney Homes public housing. The world views and possibilities of both men surely were shaped by their very different environments.

What explains separate and unequal policing, the dramatically different style of policing in Black and white neighborhoods? Academics have theories. One argues that policing in Black neighborhoods is thinly disguised suppression, "a direct instrument of racial and ethnic control."[39] Others similarly, though less bluntly, associate excessive, violent policing in the hood with broad, errant perceptions of threatening racial minorities.[40] Paul Butler argues that police, political leaders, and even ordinary people are afraid of Black men. The system is working precisely as it was designed to do, he reasons: Treat Black men as violent threats and thugs that need to be forcefully restrained.[41]

Others theorize that policing in the hood is *spatial* containment; the ghetto itself, with attendant massive police surveillance, is an institution of invasive social control.[42] Sociologist Loïc Wacquant argued the iconic ghetto and the American prison are in a "deadly symbiosis," asserting that the criminal justice system utilizes the "crime-and-punishment" paradigm as a front to cover for its more invidious goal: the controlling and containment of poor Black Americans.[43]

James Baldwin had a similar view of the hood's subordinating purposes. "This innocent country set you down in a ghetto in which, in fact, it intended that you should perish," he wrote to his nephew in *The Fire Next Time*. "[F]or the heart of the matter is here, and the root of my dispute with this country."[44] The prophetic writer, born and raised in Harlem before expatriating to France, knew the ways of ghetto policing. In 1960, Baldwin noted that for Harlemites the police "represent the force of the white world, and that world's real intentions are, simply, for that world's criminal profit and ease, to keep the black man corralled up here, in his place."[45]

As to the "world's criminal profit and ease," aggressive policing reaps revenues, and serious costs, for the localities that deploy it. Beyond containment, another function of anti-Black policing is economic plunder. In 2014 alone, New York City received nearly $32 million from fees, fines, and surcharges paid to the criminal courts by people facing misdemeanors, summonses, or other low-level violations. Researchers estimated that, over two decades of zero-tolerance policing, the city's take from this program exceeded a half billion dollars. They concluded that most of these revenues were "extracted from relatively poor segments of the population, who live in heavily policed neighborhoods."[46]

Policing as revenue raising became infamous after police officer Darren Wilson shot and killed eighteen-year-old Michael Brown in Ferguson, Missouri, in 2014. The Black Lives Matter movement ignited. National and international press covered the story. Wilson was not indicted. But the Obama Department of Justice investigated Ferguson police practices and issued a scathing report, concluding that the city regularly violated the constitutional rights of Black citizens in order to help fund itself.[47]

Whether in small suburbs like Ferguson, or a metropolis like New York City, the burdens of policing for so-called public-order crimes fell disproportionately on descendants. And the legal proceedings that ensued after a traffic stop, say for a vehicle defect or drinking an open container in public, could metastasize to enduring financial burdens, criminal stigma, loss of jobs, or housing.[48] In places engaged in revenue-raising public-order policing, the state invested heavily in the bureaucratic regime needed to process and manage so many cases. With bureaucratic expansion, criminal justice became less about solving crime and transparently tied to cash flow.[49] Another example: The District of Columbia issued $1 billion in traffic and parking citations from 2017 to 2019, according to the American Automobile Association.[50] While the AAA did not suggest any racial disparities surrounding these fines, the DC-ACLU's evidence of harsh racial disparity in traffic arrests suggest that these financial burdens, too, fell disproportionately.[51] Scholars have connected the dots, theorizing that policing and other predation by cities of Black people in their neighborhoods is a result not only of racially discriminatory design but economic incentives.[52] With the budget shortfalls of the COVID-19 pandemic, there is a serious risk this predatory economic relationship between cities and Black neighborhoods will continue.[53]

Though aggressive policing produces revenues for local governments, it harms taxpayers as well as Black citizens. A UCLA law professor looked at payouts by large cities to victims of police misconduct over five years and found they totaled nearly three-quarters of a *trillion* dollars.[54] Perhaps the only beneficiaries of systemic, anti-Black policing are owners and shareholders of corporations that profit from mass incarceration. In Chicago alone, there are 851 city blocks in which taxpayers spend more than $1 million per block to incarcerate residents who used to live there. Those blocks are concentrated in the West and South Sides, in the hoods that Chicago built to contain descendants.[55]

Children are also swept into the carceral state. As with segregated neighborhoods, segregated schools facilitate an entirely different relationship between police and young citizens. One legal scholar found that a school's percentage of minority students and of poverty is a strong predictor of the use of strict security measures, even after controlling for actual levels of school crime and disorder and neighborhood crime.[56]

The euphemism "school resource officer" is misplaced. So-called "SROs," a full- and part-time force of over fifty thousand in American public schools, are most likely to be deployed where there are large populations of Black or Latinx students. A December 2016 White House analysis concluded that rising numbers of SROs in Black and brown schools were not matched with a similar increase in school counselors.[57]

In New York City, in 2017, 5,200 full-time police officers patrolled public schools while the schools employed only about 3,000 guidance counselors. The ACLU charged that students of color were arrested and detained for trivial offenses. SROs normalized policing in educational environments, particularly in Black and brown hoods; they approached students not as assets to be supported and developed but as potential criminals.[58] Examples abound. A school police officer in Dolton, Illinois, confronted fifteen-year-old Marshawn Pitts in a hallway about a dress-code violation, failing to tuck in his shirt. After Pitts walked away, the officer slammed him against lockers, beat him, and broke his nose. In Columbia, South Carolina, an officer flipped a Black female student named Shakara from her desk and assaulted her; the viral video caused an outcry.[59] Thankfully, in the revolutionary spring of 2020, some school districts began to take police out of schools.[60]

Policing, like segregation, remains a dominant factor in Black American life. One organization asked descendants about their reality and desired solutions, mounting a survey of thirty thousand Black people in America. An overwhelming majority of respondents said that excessive use of force by police and police killings were a problem in Black communities. A large majority concluded that gun violence was also problem. Respondents agreed that police departments need to be held accountable and government must support alternatives to aggressive policing and mass incarceration to make Black communities safer.[61] The good news in the wake of George Floyd's killing was that a decisive majority of Americans also came to believe the police were likely to use excessive force against Black people, up from only 33 percent in the year 2014.[62] With this altered consciousness and new political reality, the long-term work of transforming policing and investing in noncarceral approaches to public safety began.

PRIVATE SURVEILLANCE AND SUPREMACY

On a spring day in 2018, a golf course owner in York County, Pennsylvania, called 911 twice, asking police to remove five Black women who were, in his view, golfing too slowly. CNN cataloged this and twenty-six other sad stories it ran that year of Black people being surveilled for living their lives. Among these stories was Sheila Stubbs, a veteran county supervisor campaigning for a seat in the Wisconsin State Assembly. As she canvassed for votes on the white west side of Madison, someone called the police, thinking she was a drug dealer. In a picture of her canvassing earlier in the year, she wore a badge identifying herself as a candidate, armed only with a clipboard, long pink-lacquered fingernails, and a winning smile.[63]

Barbecuing by a lake in Oakland. Entering one's own gourmet lemonade business in San Francisco. A registered guest at a hotel in Portland, Oregon, taking a call from his mama in the lobby. A child mowing lawns for candy money in a Cleveland, Ohio, suburb. As with bird-watcher Christian Cooper being targeted in Central Park by Amy Cooper, these and other acts of "living while Black" caused a nondexterous person to call the police.[64]

The nondexterous person could be called Freddy, whether male, female, or nonbinary. Freddy feels more comfortable calling the police than accepting a Black person going about their business. The Black person is not free in these moments, not free to be Black and do things that white people usually do unmolested. The Black person carries this awareness of being watched, particularly by white people, everywhere she goes. Freddy is not free either—of socially constructed assumptions and a sense of entitlement to demand that the state enforce a certain social order. A common theme in stories of Black surveillance is boundary maintenance, both racial and geographic. Freddy acts on the idea that Black people don't belong in certain places. As Elijah Anderson argues in a salient article "The White Space," "In the absence of routine social contact between blacks and whites, stereotypes can rule perceptions, creating a situation that estranges blacks."[65]

As with slavery, as with Jim Crow, law and social practice continue to conscript non-Blacks into monitoring and policing Black bodies. The worst of these social practices is violent vigilantism. Ahmaud Arbery was jogging in the brilliant light of a Georgia Sunday. The apparent mistake this twenty-five-year-old, dark-skinned man made was to run in a majority-white neighborhood and enter a home under construction.

Ahmaud Arbery lived in a diverse though traditionally Black neighborhood called Fancy Bluff, across a four-lane highway from Satilla Shores, a very white river-front subdivision with a mixture of working- and middle-class residents.[66] Both neighborhoods were located in a majority-Black city, Brunswick, on the Georgia coast. Satilla Shores had Spanish moss and a few nondexterous and probably racist residents.

Arbery jogged nearly daily. He was familiar to his neighbors in Fancy Bluff and waved at them.[67] But in Satilla Shores, modern-day paddy rollers, a white father and son, armed and dangerous, judged this young Black man running to be a burglar. One man called 911 alarmed, "There's a black male running down the street." Another resident called to report a Black man walking through an open construction site and then, also, "running down the street." The dispatcher asked what he was doing wrong; the caller did not answer the question.[68]

Gregory McMichael, a former police detective, had been decertified as a law enforcement officer for repeated failure to attend mandatory use-of-force and firearms trainings.[69] He appointed himself and his son, Travis McMichael, as patrollers. They chased Arbery in a pickup truck. A third white man, William Bryan, a neighbor of the McMichaels', pursued in a second vehicle. Together, they hounded Arbery, and Travis McMichael shot and killed him. One prosecutor claimed that the McMichaels had acted lawfully under Georgia's citizen arrest and self-defense statutes, seeing exoneration in a video where many across the nation saw murder.[70]

This is what living in white space can do to some people. Those used to being dominant, or unused to seeing dark bodies around, become suspicious of Black people doing utterly ordinary things. Jogging in daylight, being lost and asking for directions, listening to hip-hop while parked at a convenience store while a friend shops, or walking to his father's house from an errand to buy Skittles are but a few circumstances in which white or non-Black individuals perceived a threat and shot to kill a young Black man.[71]

Ahmaud. Trayvon. Emmett Till. Prominent Black victims of vigilantes remain for a while in our collective memory as others are forgotten and new ones inevitably emerge. Old-time lynch mobs may have acted on different stereotypes than do modern-day vigilantes, but with the lens of "thug" now applied by so many, Blackness itself is still a provocation.

Arbery's killers were charged and prosecuted; their acts deemed extralegal. But the state of Georgia enabled such behavior through permissive laws that make it easy to obtain a gun, and encourage rather than discourage using it. Georgia, like nearly three-quarters of US states, has a "stand your ground" law.[72] The Georgia law eliminates any duty to retreat and entitles gun owners to use force when they "reasonably believe" it is necessary to defend themselves or others against death or great bodily injury or to prevent the commission of a "forcible felony" like armed robbery.[73] Nationally, this legal architecture privileges white vigilantism against Black bodies. Where a shooter is white and the victim Black, a shooting is ten times more likely to be justified under a stand-your-ground statute than if the shooter is Black and the victim white.[74] Georgia also has a statute that dates to the Civil War that empowers citizens to arrest fellow citizens they observe committing a crime if law enforcement is not present.[75] As of early 2021, a bipartisan effort to reform the law was mounting though many advocates had demanded outright repeal, and a 2020 a bill to repeal did not gain traction.[76] Again, old habits borne of supremacy do not die naturally.

Pre-civil-rights America acquiesced in lynching, never managing to pass an antilynching bill through Congress when Black bodies were actively being hanged, impaled, and burned in the most medieval manner.[77] Nothing could be done about it, such was the strength of Southern supremacists in Congress and of sexual-predator mythology. In 2020, the effort in Congress to pass long-overdue legislation was stymied when Republican senator Rand Paul demanded a narrower definition of what constitutes a federally criminal lynching in the Emmett Till Antilynching Act. And yet, America largely tolerates angry white men asserting their gun rights.

Other laws quietly enable surveillance of Black folk to protect white space. Sundown towns of old have a twenty-first century tool to exclude. An estimated two thousand localities in forty-eight states have adopted "crime-free housing" ordinances that make landlords responsible for the actions or nonactions of their tenants. Legal scholar Deborah Archer surveyed these laws, showing how they perpetuate housing segregation using race-neutral tools and insidious racial habits of law-enforcement and private actors. These ordinances explode the range of activities that can cause an eviction, and they are applied disproportionately to Black tenants.[78]

Faribault, Minnesota, a small city fifty miles south of the Twin Cities, adopted one of the harshest ordinances in the country. It requires landlords to obtain a license and threatens them with revocation if they do not actively evict any tenants who violate the ordinance's crime-free standards or otherwise cause a public nuisance. The landlord must conduct a background check on all prospective adult tenants and may consider arrests or even just contact with the police as a basis for denying a lease. The ordinance prohibits disorderly conduct by tenants or their guests and gives Faribault police the power to order an eviction without an arrest or conviction of any crime.[79]

Such ordinances are often adopted following an influx of racial diversity. The Black population of Faribault, almost entirely Somali immigrants and refugees, exploded in the first decade of the twenty-first-century—the number of Black households rose 542 percent. Most Black residents of downtown Faribault were renters. Longtime residents complained about increases in crime and drugs, though police records did not support these claims. In fact, the overall crime rate did not increase dramatically in this period. The Faribault police chief admitted that friction and complaints were a result of cultural differences in how varied residents used public space.[80]

Racial animus, a desire to control Blacks entering previously white space, fueled the passage of the Faribault ordinance. Certain properties likely to be owned by whites were exempted. A single-family homeowner who rented to a relative did not have to be concerned with that relative's history of contact with law enforcement. Similar exemptions applied in other crime-free ordinances across the country. Archer concluded that these laws were a system of racial control that "will intensify scrutiny and increase adverse police interactions," for Black and brown people "turning everyday interactions into sources of anxiety, trauma, and indignity."[81] They also heighten the risk of homelessness for struggling descendants. The vicious circle continues. Archer concluded that by "spatially concentrating people with criminal convictions or other criminal legal system contacts into fewer communities, crime-free ordinances risk stigmatizing those communities, further perpetuating the negative impacts of racial segregation."[82]

Nuisance laws, in particular, are a source of anti-Black surveillance. They offer opportunities for someone who doesn't like something they see going on in the neighborhood to call the state and complain. One study of nuisance citations in Milwaukee found that properties located in integrating Black neighborhoods had the highest likelihood of receiving a citation. Researchers who interviewed police officers about their motivations in giving citations theorized

police may have been particularly attentive to disorder in transitioning neighborhoods or may have received a disproportionate number
of citizen complaints there, or both.[83]

Peoria is one of more than one hundred cities in the state of Illinois that have adopted chronic nuisance ordinances. These laws
target landlords whose tenants are repeatedly cited for disturbances
as mundane as noise and housing code violations to drug possession
and violent crime. But only two incidents in a year could render a
property an "aggravated chronic nuisance" and force an eviction.
A 2017 lawsuit charged that more than 70 percent of nuisance citations in Peoria were in Black neighborhoods, even though Blacks
made up only 27 percent of the population. Worse, the city deployed
military-style armored vehicles that its police department nicknamed
armadillos for their "intentionally ugly and obnoxious" appear-
ance. The armadillos were outfitted with ten infrared video cameras,
pointing outward and designed to let "repeat troublemakers" know
the police were watching them.[84] The lawsuit alleged these nuisance
abatement vehicles were deployed at the request of politicians and
well-connected local residents and were placed almost exclusively in
areas with significant Black populations.[85] In 2020, Peoria entered
into a settlement of the lawsuit and committed to amend its nuisance
ordinance and police practices to give targeted citizens more protection. Black Peorians will learn, eventually, whether these reforms are
meaningful, though chronic nuisance ordinances persist nationally.

Ironies abound. When a descendant tries to seek protection from
the state, calling 911, say, to control a violent partner, in places with
chronic nuisance ordinances, she can be evicted if she calls two or
three times.[86] Descendants cannot win. They are surveilled, overpo-
liced, and underprotected.

The state and private patrollers also apply a lens of suspicion to
residents of public housing. "One strike and you're out," Bill Clinton announced in 1996, ushering in a new era of meanness and strict
enforcement toward public housing tenants.[87] The one-strike policy allowed public housing agencies (PHAs) to terminate a tenant's
lease for criminal activity even if the tenant had no knowledge of
the activity; the Supreme Court upheld this "vicarious liability." A
mother could be evicted for the clandestine actions of a son that she

could not have prevented. The one-strike policy was a progenitor of crime-free housing ordinances applied to private rental properties across the land.[88]

As with redlining of old, the federal government led the way in teaching new habits of predation applied disproportionately to Black people. HUD also authorized local public housing agencies to ban nonresidents allegedly connected with criminal activity from entering a specified property and arrest them for trespassing. The vague criteria and the use of police to enforce these banishment lists restricted public housing tenants in their ability to invite friends, family, or guests, often with little or no explanation. In some cases, nonresidents were banned for the "offense" of just standing on the property.[89]

The Obama administration sought a different direction. In addition to calling on all localities to affirmatively promote fair housing, in 2015, it advised local public housing agencies to stop using one-strike policies for minor violations. And it reminded PHAs of their "obligation to safeguard the due process rights of applicants and tenants."[90] Congresswoman Alexandria Ocasio-Cortez and Senator Kamala Harris introduced bills in the 116th Congress that would have repealed this one-strike rule, but the bills were never voted on.

Technology has made third-party surveillance of Black bodies even more efficient and pervasive. Ostensibly liberal San Francisco launched a mobile app, Open311, in 2013. It enabled residents to report perceived public disorder like loitering, trash, and vandalism, by taking a picture and uploading it, with their location. The 311 line was established in 2007 for nonemergency calls about quality-of-life conditions, which included noncriminal human behavior like congregating, sleeping, eating, or drinking in public spaces. After the mobile app was introduced, calls to 311 spiked, especially in gentrifying communities of color. Private spies invited aggressive policing, criminalization of ordinary behavior, and harm to longtime residents.[91] Researchers found that San Francisco officers targeted minorities in gentrifying neighborhoods for order-maintenance policing and that relatively affluent white in-migrants played a role in this process.[92] Young longtime Black and brown residents ended up beaten or killed by the police in hoods and barrios where whites were moving in.[93]

In any gentrifying neighborhood cultural friction is common and in-migrants may view longtime residents and their cultural and behavioral norms as criminal. Applying this lens and calling the police can actually criminalize what had been normal and dramatically shift cultural norms.[94] In rapidly gentrifying hoods in New York City, researchers found a pattern of white in-migrants making 311 complaints about Black and Latinx folk because they commonly misinterpreted social and cultural behaviors as disorderly.[95] This explains how 105-year-old Ramon Hernandez, who had played dominoes on his Harlem block sidewalk unmolested for four decades, became a target. According to research by *BuzzFeed*, in the two years that whites started moving in, the spot where Hernandez and another domino player regularly set up a card table appeared to be the source of over a thousand 311 calls. Someone kept calling, so the police kept coming.[96]

On neighborhood listservs and other social media applications like Amazon's Neighbors or NextDoor, gentrifiers speak for themselves about their suspicions of longtime residents. The *East Bay Express,* a local newspaper, reported that white in-migrants in the Mission neighborhood and nearby Oakland were using community watch-group platforms to target African Americans and Latinx *gente* for "being near bus stops, standing in 'shadows,' making U-turns, and hanging around outside coffee shops."[97]

Technology exacerbates anti-Black bias. One study looked at comments made over the course of a year on a listserv for a majority-white neighborhood. It overlapped with the first year of Obama's presidency and suggested, as descendants well knew, that America was not post-racial. Black men overwhelmingly were the subject of suspicious persons posts, and in the majority of comments about them, the poster reported they had called the police, despite describing actions that in many cases were perfectly legal. A "very polite young man" also identified as Black, knocking on the door asking to borrow a cellphone charger became the subject of a suspicious person report, while a white "yard man" going door-to-door looking for work was vouched for and no police were called, even though he was alleged to have engaged in burglaries. Those saying they called the police about Black men were validated by others, and this practice seemed to be normalized, amplifying fear of Black men and putting them, more than any other group, in direct contact with police.[98]

Neighborhood listservs seem quaint compared to the new infrastructure of surveillance created by doorbells with video cameras. Amazon, in particular, has encouraged a vast customer base to buy its video doorbell product Ring and upload videos of suspicious persons to its free social media crime reporting app, Neighbors. To date, Amazon reportedly has entered into partnerships with over two thousand police and fire departments, which encourage customers to share videos with the police.[99] Together, Ring, Neighbors, and their users create a collective ecosystem of paranoia and fear, and a familiar, life-threatening mantra of "call the police," applied mainly to people of color. Every dark body captured on camera is a potential porch pirate, and even the delivery person doing his or her job gets reported for not being sufficiently gentle with packages. Amazon applied for a patent for its facial recognition software, Rekognition, and may add that software to its Ring product.[100]

And yet the federal government's own laboratory, the National Institute of Standards and Technology, found that facial recognition software, increasingly deployed by police departments and localities across the country is seriously inept in detecting nonwhite faces. Black Americans were one hundred times more likely to be misidentified than white men.[101] A dark-skinned Black woman, Joy Buolamwini, used her MIT doctoral research to reveal some intersectional truth: facial recognition software tended to be most inaccurate in misidentifying dark-skinned Black women.[102]

Enough. In 2020, the cry of #BlackLivesMatter went mainstream, the source of beautiful signs and public art painted on American streets. Wokeness—or the desire to achieve it—spread like brushfire, and all institutions seemed to be looking within to consider their own systemic racism. But there is so much to abolish, replace, and repair. Systems of surveillance, hoarding, segregation, inequality, and plunder. Will America atone for its original sins and *current* damage to descendants in ways that actually transform Black lives?

CHAPTER 9

ABOLITION AND REPAIR

First came love. DeVone Boggan is a blue-eyed Black man with a gruff voice who regularly sports a houndstooth trilby. Boggan, then a youth-development consultant, had never worked on violence prevention, though he was a sharp analyst. He saw gun-toting youth in the hoods of Richmond, California, as "babies growing up in a war zone," he told CNN.[1] In 2007, Richmond was one of the most violent cities in the country. Its homicide rate of forty-six per one hundred thousand was eight times the national average. Chicago, with its reputation for gang violence, had a rate of sixteen per one hundred thousand. The math also revealed something else.

Richmond's police department concluded that 70 percent of the gun violence in the city was caused by only twenty-eight people. Boggan said a police officer might call some of these young men "'serial killer' . . . because of what they're suspected of doing."[2] He saw them as human beings capable of transformation. Key Richmond leaders were willing to take a chance on Boggan's idea of focusing not on "hot spots" but on the relatively few "hot people" who were pulling triggers or very likely to shoot. He proposed identifying those who law enforcement considered the most lethal in the city but had avoided prosecution and showering them with positive support rather than the threat of incarceration. His empathy led him to develop a program that healed rather than damaged. As I write this in the revolutionary summer of 2020, only three separate incidents of gun-related fatalities have occurred in Richmond this year, two of which appear to involve domestic violence rather than gang activity. The third was a drive-by shooting in April, with one victim.[3]

The program illuminates larger lessons about what abolition and repair might look like in historically isolated and preyed-on Black neighborhoods. Before presenting details and independent evaluation of its contributions to Richmond's dramatic violence reduction, I share the classic, Black American origins of Boggan's humanity. Where did this lens that was so critical to innovation come from? I wanted to know, so I contacted and interviewed him.

Boggan, too, is a descendant—of great migrants who left agrarian Greenville, Alabama, for Albion, Michigan. The Albion Malleable Iron Company hired Black southerners to fill the labor voids created by World Wars I and II. Boggan's paternal grandfather, Daniel Boggan Sr., was a frugal farmer who owned land in Greenville but was lured north in 1942 when a cousin recruited him to work for Malleable. In Albion, a hamlet one hundred miles west of Detroit, Daniel Sr. became an ironworker. He held on to the farm in Greenville and also bought and worked a small farm in Albion that helped feed his family and others. He and his wife, Rofie Jean, raised nine children, including Boggan's father, Daniel Jr.

Boggan's grandparents were community pillars who, as he explained, "saw themselves as responsible for reproducing the best of themselves [and the race]." "They were always feeding, housing, and teaching people," he said, marveling that their formal education ended with junior high school. The next generation included Boggan's father and six uncles, one of whom became a Rhodes scholar. They modeled a striving manhood for Boggan and continued the family tradition of uplifting others. But it took a while for Boggan to understand and embrace this legacy.

When Boggan was nine years old he was shattered to accidentally discover that his biological mother was white and that the only mother he had ever known, his father's Black American wife, Mary Curtis, was his adoptive mother. This family secret and his Black parents' bitter divorce distressed young Boggan. Worse for him, his father moved away. As Boggan was coming of age, his father, Daniel Jr., was pioneering through a series of government management jobs across the country—from Jackson and Flint, Michigan, to Portland, Oregon to San Diego County to Essex County, New Jersey. Ultimately, Daniel Boggan Jr. became city manager for Berkeley, California.

As a young teen, Boggan lived with Mary, a registered nurse, and two younger brothers in the Coronado Gardens housing cooperative on the Black, west side of Lansing, Michigan. Boggan uses several adjectives to describe his teenage self: confused, mad, angry, undisciplined, and obnoxious. Boggan confesses that while he never engaged in gang activity or became a hard-core criminal, he did sell marijuana joints for extra income and hung in the streets. Two Black male mentors reached and changed him. The first was a volunteer at the Lansing Boys and Girls Club. Andre Williams was a senior at Michigan State, and Boggan said of him, "He just started talking to me and got through my shield. . . . He was different from any other adult. He was there. He reached out. He made me feel good about myself."

In that period, Boggan was estranged from his father and a constant challenge to his mother, Mary. He recalled one time when he "got into it with Mom" and she "popped me on the head with a cast iron skillet" while Andre was present. Andre left but returned two days later. The critical message to Boggan, who had tried to scare his mentor away, was "he was not leaving," he was going to be there, even through tough times, even when Boggan deserved punishment, though not violence, from exhausted Mary.

Clyde Ethington, Boggan's tenth-grade history teacher, was the first Black male teacher Boggan had ever had. Ethington made it clear he thought Boggan was smart, college material and held him accountable, daily, for doing the work required of an aspiring collegian. Every previous parent-teacher conference in his life had been "bad," Boggan said, with the teacher pointing out his deficits. At his first conference with Ethington and his mom, Boggan explained, Ethington was able to take all of his student's negative energy and "wrap it in a package as a positive." It was the first parent-teacher conference that made Boggan's mother smile.

Boggan's academic life shifted, and he began to lean into his studies. Still, Mary sent him to live with his father. "My mom said that I had become uncontrollable and 'incorrigible,'" he said. "Essentially, at sixteen, I thought that I was grown," Boggan concluded. He went on to graduate from the University of California at Berkeley and then earned a law degree attending evening classes at Golden Gate University.

Boggan reconciled with and admired his father and replicated, in his own way, Daniel Jr.'s engagement with making cities better. He has a positive relationship with his mother, Mary, and, among the "fiery women" in his life, he remains particularly influenced by his blunt maternal grandmother, Essie Curtis, another community icon in Albion. After completing his education, Boggan tried to give other youth similar opportunities for transformation. For more than a decade, he worked as a consultant and advocate for youth mentoring and development programs.

The city of Richmond was desperate for change when his idea and proposal was accepted and ratified by the city council. The Office of Neighborhood Safety (ONS) was born and Richmond's city manager recruited Boggan to serve as its first director. ONS was created with a $611,000 general fund commitment from the city; Boggan raised approximately $600,000 from private sources.

Boggan insisted that ONS operate completely independent of law enforcement. He hired "neighborhood change agents," a new employee classification within Richmond city government. They conducted what Boggan calls "street outreach" in the neighborhoods most beset by shootings, to anticipate and mediate conflict, and disrupt retaliatory cycles of gun violence. The change agents would talk to all sides in any "beef" to defuse the situation and get them to stand down. The change agents also acted as informal mentors to the young people they encountered in these neighborhoods and as case managers to those formally tied to an ONS program. Having a felony record and intimate knowledge of the codes of the street were effective prerequisites in a job that required building trust with hardened individuals and traumatized communities. These outreach workers would hunt, surveil, and target those potentially most violent young actors, not to frisk or arrest them, but to love them madly.

Joseph McCoy, an ONS outreach coordinator, told NPR, "We do something real simple that folks just don't realize how, how powerful it is. . . . We come from a sincere place that we love each and every last one of the people we touch and we try to touch as many people as possible."⁴ As Richard Wright wrote in *12 Million Black Voices*, a poetic account of the lives of rural- and ghetto-poor descendants during the Great Depression, "Our scale of values differs from that of the world from which we have been excluded . . . and our love is not its love."⁵

The outreach workers identified their targets, developed trust, and brought them to ONS to make a pitch. If the young man—and they all happened to be men—agreed to refrain from "hunting," as the workers put it, stay in contact daily, and avoid trouble as much as possible, he would participate in an eighteen-month Peacemaker Fellowship. The fellowship offered 24/7 support from an assigned case manager and an individually tailored LifeMAP (Management Action Plan) that identified what obstacles the target faced, what he needed, and what he would do to overcome them, and specific goals like getting a GED or a driver's license. Peacemaker Fellows also received cognitive behavioral therapy, help navigating social services, substance abuse treatment if needed, connection to job training, internships, and jobs, and the chance to travel, from across town to South Africa. Most innovatively, if they met goals from their LifeMAP, addressed conflict in healthier ways, and promoted community peace, they could also receive a monthly stipend of as much as $1,000 for nine months. Donations from partners like the Kaiser Foundation paid for the stipends.⁶ Almost every target decided to become a Peacemaker Fellow, though some took repeated attempts to convince.

Boggan's theory of change was simple: give these young men the kind of constant, unconditional love and support that most well-resourced parents give their children. Boggan also had a critical insight, perhaps borne of his own youthful digressions. Though these young men, who had engaged in thuggish behavior, were probably among the most violence-prone Richmondites, that very experience made them potentially the most powerful change agents in the city. If they developed a desire to live and disentangled themselves from the codes of the street, they could influence others around them and the next generation. That is, they could begin to change the codes by which boys in the hood were living. "The stipend is a gesture of saying you are valuable, your expertise is valuable, your contribution to this work of creating a healthier city is valuable," Boggan told radio station KQED in 2016.[7]

Paying potential criminals to promote peace created controversy and attracted critics, including a Black American who served on the Richmond city council, Courtland "Corky" Boozé. According to *Mother Jones* magazine, Boozé wanted ONS and Boggan brought "to their knees" and demanded proof of the program's impact.[8] Boggan frequently found himself explaining and defending ONS's comprehensive approach and his theory of change. Once when he was about to begin a media interview, one of his outreach coordinators suggested he don a hat that he usually wore on the weekends. Grandmother Essie had given it to him. It belonged to his maternal grandfather, Tom Curtis, whom Boggan described as "a light-shining Black man," and also a great migrant—from Bradenton, Florida, to Albion, Michigan. Boggan had inherited Curtis's collection of hats and the trilby symbolized the grandfather's dignity and strength. Boggan wears them as he advocates for new generations of descendants.

Anecdotal and empirical evidence did validate the impact of ONS and the Peacemaker Fellows. The Peacemaker Fellowship began in 2010, and by 2017, gun assaults and homicides had fallen by 66 percent in Richmond.[9] Boggan believed that ONS and its fellows had to have played a role. "When you actually focus on the very people involved in gun violence, I think you can't argue that they're not

DeVone Boggan

contributing to the safer environment happening in this city," he told CNN. But he also credited the contributions of "police work and an improved economy."[10]

A peer-reviewed independent study facilitated by the School of Public Health at UC Berkeley found that the Peacemaker Fellowship program was associated with a 55 percent annual reduction in gun-related deaths. Researchers also concluded that, with less shooting, the fellowship program may have contributed to a 16 percent annual increase in violence by other methods.[11] When I raised this surprising possibility with Boggan, he demurred: "I can tell you that Peacemaker Fellows didn't start killing or harming . . . by other means [like] knives and fighting."

Researchers at the University of Southern California's Price School of Public Policy conducted an independent cost-benefit analysis of the Peacemaker Fellowship. They conservatively estimated that the nominal cost of the program produced outsized benefits, in their words, "a net present value (NPV)" of over $535 million to the city of Richmond from the first five years of the program.[12] According to an independent evaluation conducted on the Sacramento Peacemaker Fellowship Program, modeled on Richmond's, for every dollar invested Sacramento received eighteen to forty-one dollars in benefits due to costs avoided through violence reduction.[13] Perhaps the men who have graduated from Richmond's Peacemaker Fellowship constitute the most profound evidence of success. By 2019, of the 127 fellows who had gone through the program in Richmond, 122 were still alive, the vast majority of which were no longer gun-violence suspects.[14] As sons and brothers, and often fathers to someone, still present and different from how they used to be, individually and collectively, they have helped to stop a spiral and begin a more virtuous cycle.

Boggan left ONS and founded Advance Peace, an organization dedicated to helping other cities replicate its systems change model. To date, more than twenty cities across the country have opened offices of violence prevention similar to ONS. In California, the cities of Sacramento and Stockton have created peacemaker fellowships, and both cities have begun to see reductions in gun-related homicides.[15] Other cities have shown similar bravery and are seriously considering starting peacemaker fellowships. In Richmond, ONS and its Peacemaker Fellowship continue, run by Sam Vaughn, a veteran ONS street outreach worker.

As I concluded my interview with Boggan, I asked him whether he observed multiplier effects in Richmond neighborhoods from which the original Peacemaker Fellows sprang. He told me that while these very poor neighborhoods felt safer, economic development had not reached them, though gentrification was happening elsewhere in the city. When he was directing ONS, it appeared to him that the main "instruments" operating in the fellows' hoods were the police and ONS.[16]

There are larger lessons to be gleaned from Richmond's experience. Repair began with the people who would pull the trigger. Young Black males are much more likely than others to be a victim of gun violence. It makes sense to apply a tourniquet where it will most stop the bleeding. Peacemaker Fellows stopped shooting and began promoting peace in themselves and influencing others. Boggan's strategy of focusing on hot people rather than hotspots made this intervention *much* cheaper than targeting entire neighborhoods with aggressive policing. Richmond was not a rich city, but it could afford this *transformative* experiment. In fact, the city was so blood-soaked and overcome that it couldn't afford not to try Boggan's idea. The hoods of Richmond have not been fully remade; there is still much work to do in creating and connecting descendants to opportunity. But a better, more humane relationship between the city and these neighborhoods began by applying a lens of love to the most feared descendants, seeing them as assets and investing directly in them. Now all descendants breathe freer of police and gang predation in their hoods, and all Richmondites enjoy a much less violent city.

Our nation is now in a position similar to the dilemma Richmond faced. We are at a crossroads and a time of choosing which political vision and which public policies to conquer intersecting crises of COVID-19, climate change, and racial injustice. There was an alarming spike in homicides in Black neighborhoods over the summer of 2020, much larger than the ritual rise and fall of the season, though crime overall remained at generational lows. Murder rates were stable in white neighborhoods but rose precipitously in Black ones. Criminologists theorized on the whys, while community folk on the predominantly Black East Side of Kansas City pointed to a new sense of despair in a year of pandemic and prominent police killings of Black people. A reverend in Kansas City who, like Boggan, ran a program to provide social support to those most prone to violence, told the *New York Times* that "many of his clients [feel] hopelessly trapped in a system in which they will never thrive."[17]

The pandemic and conflict between uprising citizens and militarized forces threatened to overwhelm some places. Deaths rose in Baltimore, from the virus and an uptick in gun-related homicides.[18] Similar patterns emerged in the District of Columbia, Chicago, Milwaukee, and other cities thick with descendants.[19] Once again, communities that have been most vulnerable and abused in America's racial caste system shoulder a disproportionate burden of the country's social and economic crises—a role they were designed to play.

A silver lining of the pandemic was that the mutuality of American suffering was utterly transparent. A virus that exploited every human and societal vulnerability thrived in a separate and unequal nation. More investment in Black and brown neighborhoods in healthcare, testing, and tracing and prior development of amenities that determine health would have lessened the spread of and deaths from the pandemic. Meanwhile, Baltimore tried a novel, privately funded experiment of flying surveillance planes from the sky, in a desperate gamble that this would somehow stop gun violence on the ground.[20]

The pandemic shred government budgets, and pain abounds. I argue that a tourniquet should be applied where the bleeding gushes, where policy innovation will be most effective in starting a virtuous cycle for local and national healing, and where the moral argument for state intervention is strongest.

THE CASE FOR ABOLITION AND REPAIR

I begin by revisiting the key insights I have presented in this book. For centuries, America has been locked in a vicious cycle of creating and reifying anti-Black institutions that do harm to descendants and to the whole. One anti-Black caste system—chattel slavery—was replaced by another, and then another, down through the generations, to the modern-day institution of the hood and residential caste. Each anti-Black institution was constructed because of a pervasive ideology of white supremacy. Anti-Black mythologizing was the main tool for dividing and conquering, for creating solid white political majorities. Myths about descendants propelled laws and policies that conferred wealth on whites, plundered Black bodies and communities, and conscripted non-Blacks into othering and surveilling Black people. Our system of residential caste is ingenious in its ability to hide the truth of how and why we subordinate some and lift up others.

The hood persists through classic processes of anti-Black caste: boundary maintenance, opportunity hoarding, and stereotype-driven surveillance. Today, government at all levels overinvests in affluent white space and disinvests in Blackness, with the exception of excessive spending on policing and incarceration. Segregation is at the heart of structural racism in America. In theory, the US Constitution and civil rights laws demand equal protection and treatment of Black Americans. In practice, American law and public policies have encouraged rather than discouraged segregation. Horizontal competition between communities of abundance and communities of need sets up a budgetary politics in which affluent spaces and people usually win. Politicians and non-descendants of all colors have participated in ghetto myths to justify containing descendants in high-poverty environs, or prisons, and to justify shrinking government, except the military and law enforcement. Fortunately, a revolutionary awakening has begun to disrupt this tired politics. A growing, multiracial coalition believes that Black Lives Matter. But the structures and policies that undermine Black lives, and divide the American house against itself, endure.

Segregation and its mechanics of racialized favor and disfavor undermine opportunity for everyone. The American system of residential caste works only for the few who can buy their way into gold-standard neighborhoods that enjoy the best of everything. Everyone participates in this racialized system of opportunity for the few. The American way means trying to get into "good" neighborhoods and schools and avoid "bad" ones. Movers know, though they may not say it out loud, that what is really going on is avoidance of poor Black people in large numbers. Extreme segregation persists in metropolitan areas where large numbers of great migrants landed. The processes of residential caste and structural racism also operate, though perhaps less visibly, in less overtly segregated places.

Poverty-free havens and poverty-dense hoods would not exist if the state had not designed, constructed, and maintained this physical racial order. Intentional state action to create and maintain the racialized order included government-encouraged racially restrictive covenants, exclusionary zoning, Negro-cleansing "urban renewal," intentionally segregated public housing, an interstate highway program laid to create racial barriers, endemic redlining, and intentionally disinvesting in basic services for Black neighborhoods. Individuals making choices about where to live may not recognize or acknowledge how much the state, through investment and disinvestment, shapes racial patterns and perceptions.

Residents of affluent white space hoard and receive more than their fair share of public and private treasure. They and the state also engage in boundary maintenance. Policing, surveillance, exclusionary zoning, and predatory nuisance laws protect affluent white interests and keep descendants at bay. Hoary stereotypes apply to descendants wherever they are. An insidious, unhealthy relationship persists between the state and descendants trapped in concentrated poverty. An unhealthy relationship also persists between people in the hood and those who fear and dehumanize them.

People with no intimate knowledge of Blackness get their ideas about Black people through stereotypes about the hood. This divides regions and causes many to retreat or secede from shared public institutions. It undermines the social contract. The more racially divided a region is, the more inequality, the lower social mobility for poor children, and the weaker regional economy it tends to have. Given the outsize role of ghetto mythology in American politics, extreme segregation of advantage and disadvantage divides the nation and undermines our ability to pursue humane policies that promote the common good. Add to the harms of anti-Black residential caste the enduring forces of unregulated capitalism, technological disruption, COVID-19, and conspiracy-fueled domestic terrorism, and a nation once a beacon to the world could fall like ancient Rome.

Healing a nation that began with, and still suffers from, white supremacy requires *abolition* of the processes of residential caste *and repair* in poor Black neighborhoods. To use the word "abolition" is to acknowledge that we should seek enduring transformation and not modest ephemeral reform. If the processes of caste described in this book are not abolished, we, like earlier generations of Americans, will be leaving to future generations the undone work of reconstruction and of reckoning with our nation's original sin. Here I write of abolition of anti-Black processes on the continuum from slavery. The other original sin of Indigenous genocide and ecocide must also be reckoned with, with Indigenous nations and their assertions of sovereignty leading the way.[21] Once again, in focusing on the anti-Black system of residential caste that ensnares us all, I am not denying that other groups suffer from oppression borne of white supremacy and other false ideologies. And I say to fellow agitators, authors, and advocates, write your books, tell your stories, and gather power so that we all might one day be emancipated.

The first abolition was impoverished. Enslaved people were freed, but they were not free. Instead of receiving reparation for the taking of their labor and the damage of slavery's violence, rape, denial of education and of personhood, the emancipated were forced into follow-on institutions of Black subordination. Most of all the emancipated were denied the agency of property ownership—the proverbial forty acres and the freedom to till their own land and be left alone by white people.[22]

Abolition requires both the destruction of anti-Black institutions and the creation of new, humane structures of opportunity. In her 2003 book *Are Prisons Obsolete?*, the activist-philosopher-author Angela Davis advocated for the collective building up of a "constellation of alternatives" to carceral systems.[23] The city of Richmond began that kind of reconstruction in creating the ONS and Peacemaker Fellowships. In her 2005 book *Abolition Democracy*, Davis expanded on the meaning of the phrase that W. E. B. Du Bois coined in his groundbreaking work *Black Reconstruction in America*. In *Abolition Democracy,* Davis wrote that abolition "is not only, or not even primarily, about abolition as a negative process of tearing down, but it is also about building up." Davis emphasized what Du Bois had argued in *Black Reconstruction,* "that in order to fully abolish the oppressive conditions produced by slavery, new democratic institutions would have to be created."[24]

Similarly, Ruth Wilson Gilmore, geographer, scholar, and prison abolitionist, writes of "carceral geographies"—mainly the prison industrial complex, and its phalanx of extractive practices—and calls for "abolition geographies" to negate them. "Abolition geography starts from the homely premise that freedom is a place," she writes. The hood, as I have described in this book, is an enclosure, a place with an operating logic of confinement, surveillance, disinvestment, and dislocation from opportunity—processes intentionally created through federal and local policy. Thus, while abolition requires dismantling these anti-Black processes, it also requires the creation of new relationships to place and land, to resources, and to one another. As Gilmore writes, "making something into something else . . . is what negation is" and what abolition and repair, or reconstruction, requires. Her "abolition geography," like Du Bois's and Davis's "abolition democracy," is a way of "political organizing, and of being in the world [of] trying every little thing" to change and free ourselves of the old order and establish a new social order in the places where we live.[25]

Applying this understanding to the subject of this book, abolition requires dismantling and reversing *current* anti-Black processes of residential caste—investment and "greenlining" of Black neighborhoods rather than disinvestment and economic predation; inclusion rather than boundary maintenance; equitable public funding rather than overinvestment and hoarding for high-opportunity places; humanization and care rather than surveillance and stereotyping. After a century of redlining, urban "Negro Removal," intentionally concentrating poor Black Americans in segregated housing, disinvestment, foreclosures, and predation, without an insistent effort to stop this legacy of plunder, the modern descendants of slavery in iconic hoods cannot thrive. The state is obligated to repair what supremacy still breaks, that is, what the state put in motion and continues to reify. As we rebuild from the ravages of COVID-19, if we return to the norms of residential caste, the vicious cycle continues. With scarcity, there is a serious risk that the state will continue to overinvest in elites and prey on Black people for fees and revenue.

My theory of repair is that those most traumatized by the processes of residential caste most deserve care and the chance to be change agents in their own liberation. That is what freedom means. I argue for prioritizing poor Black neighborhoods because they are at the center of American anti-Black residential caste. America exploits neighborhood difference and that is a key mechanism for redistributing wealth and resources to elites and for anti-Black plunder. A neighborhood analysis is critical both for understanding these processes *and for disrupting them.* The hood is where repair of the relationship with the state is most needed, both morally and as a matter of fiscal common sense. As with the transforming scenario of Richmond and its Peacemaker Fellows, focusing on the folk who are potentially the most powerful change agents directly confronts the stereotypes and fear on which residential caste is built. Only by focusing on that deep wound can healing begin.

An example and some review of ground I have covered: It is immoral and does not make fiscal sense to spend more than $1 million per inner-city block to incarcerate residents for nonviolent drug offenses. In Chicago in the late 2000s, there were 121 such "million-dollar blocks" for nonviolent drug offenses; other large cities had similar patterns of expenditure that tracked concentrated Black poverty.[26] Again, Black people do not use drugs at higher rates than whites. Such concentrated punitive spending is likely the result of aggressive policing in poor Black neighborhoods. This punitive investment paid dividends only to companies that profit from incarceration. It is not premised on seeing nonviolent drug offenders as potential assets who could contribute to society if they could overcome addiction. Punitive approaches merely take the drug user out of the community, causing harm to children who need parents and others who love and rely on that person. Punitive approaches harm the individual and all of the people on the block the user was torn from. It is a senseless waste of money that invests in a downward spiral.

Government spends mightily in the hood for policies and practices that harm. With 851 "million-dollar blocks" in Chicago for incarceration from *all kinds* of crime, the state spent nearly a billion dollars on mass incarceration from very poor, historically segregated city blocks over a four-year period.[27] The real issue is whether we value descendants enough to overcome the politics and vested interests of the status quo. The dominant political narrative determines policy choices. Anti-Black, tough-on-crime politics begat destructive policies that continue to damage. So yes, money should be redirected from incarceration and policing to investments in historically defunded hoods for strategies that show promise of healing.

Researchers at the University of Chicago Crime Lab and the University of Pennsylvania found that a program that gave Black teens in high-violence neighborhoods a summer job and an adult mentor reduced arrests for violent crime by 43 percent.[28] A wealthy Texas couple who pride themselves on "transformative" results-oriented philanthropy paid for the $3.7 million airplane surveillance demonstration in Baltimore, which ended with questionable results.[29] They and others might direct their treasure to a proven community organization that can offer jobs and mentors to the city's most vulnerable teens.

So the last should be first, and the first last, Jesus declared according to Matthew's Gospel. Descendants in the hood are hurting. Like Richmond's Peacemaker Fellows, they also have strengths. Like Lakia Barnett, the powerhouse I featured in chapter 7, descendants have expert knowledge about myriad obstacles that they must overcome. A novel idea is to ask them what they most need to prosper and listen carefully to the answers. Policymakers who live elsewhere might be surprised at the common-sense brilliance of their insights.

If you are not willing to ask descendants what they need to be free, you are not really interested in their freedom and may be perhaps too invested in your own status and advantage. Seeing descendants as human assets and potential change agents is the first step to necessary emotional reconciliation. With revolutionary imagination and constant grassroots organizing, we can begin to create new institutions and practices based on first principles of stopping damaging investment in downward spirals and beginning upward cycles of reconciliation and repair. A new abolition democracy, driven by neighborhood analysis, would get at all of the intersecting systems that create racial inequality. Organizing also transforms the private

struggles of individuals into a joyful movement to create new communities that work for and empower descendants, and all people.

AN ETHIC OF LOVE

In a powerful essay, author-activist bell hooks explored the potential
and necessity of love in human rights work. She argues that without
"an ethic of love shaping the direction of our political vision and our
radical aspirations, we are often seduced, in one way or the other,
into continued allegiance to systems of domination."[30] To use the
word "love" in a movement for racial justice is to demand a radically
new, empathetic seeing of folk who are persistently dehumanized.
That is what is required and, as hooks argues, the individual who
chooses to apply a lens of love to oneself and others immediately begins their liberation from cultures of domination. Applying love as
the ethical foundation for politics, hooks argues, will best position us
to transform. A lens of love introduces a critical eye that resists the
ethic and language of domination and seeks truth about how systems
of domination work. "Awareness," she concludes, "is central to the
process of love as the practice of freedom."[31]

I walk my integrated neighborhood of Crestwood and am encouraged by the posters telling me that Black Lives Matter. Some
neighbors also display a familiar rainbow sign, proclaiming belief
in love, science, and kindness. They hunger for something better
and more humane than American caste. I take them at their chosen
words. However, I say to all who profess that Black Lives Matter,
be prepared to be uncomfortable and proactive in seeking transformation. It will require more of you than a sign. But in agitating for
transformation, you will also gain.

In her essay, hooks clarified the operational role of love in creating the Beloved Community that Martin Luther King Jr., John Lewis,
and others have championed. By working in community with others
to build something new, premised on ethical values of love and equal
humanity, the advantaged person who chooses this work gets to experience joy in the struggle.[32] Acting on the truth of our profound inter-
dependence, or what legal scholar David Troutt stresses as mutuality,
is other-regarding but also self-interested—a better way for humans

to share a town, city, metropolis, or planet.[33] Other-regarding *agape* love is the only sustainable basis for political communities. A country premised on supremacy and a hierarchy in which descendants are at the bottom—what we have had in America for centuries—is exhausting and not sustainable because it is premised on and engenders violence.

While we must prioritize poor Black neighborhoods, broader systems work is never finished in America. Among the undone tasks of reconstruction, we need to restore civil rights, particularly voting rights, and end gerrymandering. We can and should promote residential and school integration. We can and should transform our immigration system and fulfill our promise to undocumented Dreamers. Corporations and all public and private institutions should continue to work at being anti-racist. This, and so much systems work, is needed to repair what is broken in America.

Regarding abolition and repair of residential caste, there are concrete steps the federal government could take to dismantle and repair structural racism. In a divided country, local governments have even more room to innovate on racial justice. Abolition of the old order has to start somewhere. Structural forces, isolation, and hoarding harm poor rural descendants, and they, too, deserve repair.[34] Here I focus on cities because I believe they are our best hope for a brave new politics that could disrupt the habits of residential caste. Since the Black Lives Matter movement ignited in 2015, many cities have been forced to reckon with systems that surveil and plunder in Black neighborhoods. The people drawn to cities large and small, myriad in their colors and desires, are apt to be open to difference, offering a chance to build something new, a society that includes and works for everyone.

I suggest three critical pillars to guide state action: (1) change the relationship of the state with descendants from punitive to caring, (2) see descendants as potential assets and empower them to be change agents, and (3) invest resources and transfer assets to support descendants and respected community institutions in the process of repair. Here is the crux: dismantling unjust budgetary habits and reducing systemic racism will require sacrifices from white communities that have disproportionately benefited from anti-Black policies for decades. After a revolutionary moment where 96 percent of Americans have acknowledged that Black Americans face discrimination, are we finally ready to readjust our spending priorities?[35]

A critical point bears repeating. Applying a humane lens to descendants frees policymakers to innovate and focus on evidence-based strategies that might be cheaper and certainly more effective than punitive policies borne of racial dogma. At the local level, details of what to cut and where to reallocate should be forged by multiracial coalitions that are constantly gathering political power, led by indigenous Black voices with expert knowledge of what their neighborhoods need. In this way, the processes of abolition and repair will also repair democracy. Beyond repairing the state's relationship with high-poverty Black neighborhoods and the people who live there, transformative strategies might begin to repair our broken race relations. As street violence is reduced and descendants humanized, nondescendants might avoid and surveil Black people less. Perhaps they would support investments in public institutions and participate in them more. Out of the ashes of the COVID pandemic and a five-decade cultural war about the hood, a reinvigorated public sphere and social contract might emerge.

Among the new processes that might be instantiated would be a regular neighborhood analysis that looks critically at all of the money being spent by the state across neighborhoods and a constant evaluation of *racial equity*. There are pieces of this dream. Seattle, Minneapolis, and a few other cities formally require a racial equity analysis in budgeting.[36] In 2018, Baltimore adopted a law requiring city agencies to assess existing and proposed policies "for disparate outcomes based on race, gender, or income" and to proactively develop policies and investments to prevent and redress those disparities. A first in the country, Baltimore also amended its city charter—by a ballot referendum that nearly 80 percent of voters approved—to establish a permanent Equity Assistance Fund to attack structural racism and advance racial equity in housing, education, and capital expenditures.[37]

In Milwaukee, Black citizens were outraged to learn that nearly half of the city's annual budget went to its police department. In the summer of 2019, the African American Roundtable and other community groups launched the Liberate MKE campaign, which surveyed 1,100 residents across the city about how to allocate their tax dollars. Citizens identified three priorities: violence prevention not tied to policing, affordable housing, and jobs for youth. They wanted participatory practices that empowered residents to influence city budgets. Other recommendations arising from the survey included increasing pay for city internships and representation from historically underrepresented neighborhoods in those internships *and* a universal basic income (UBI) program. Liberate MKE proposed eliminating sixty police officer positions by not filling retirement vacancies to free up savings and setting an overall goal of moving $25 million from policing to community safety and health programs.[38] The COVID-19 pandemic and George Floyd's death added momentum to their demands. The campaign succeeded in procuring an initial reallocation of $900,000 from policing to priorities citizens had identified. The city council also authorized a UBI pilot.[39]

Before our revolutionary season of 2020, I thought replacing the anti-Black lens with one of care and concern for descendants was improbable. Now, I perceive a hunger for healing. According to the *New York Times*, an estimated fifteen million to twenty-six million people protested peacefully for Black lives in some 2,500 localities—perhaps the largest movement in US history.[40] New empathy can spur audacious thinking.

Among the revolutionary possibilities for repair, initiate peacemaker fellowships in other violence-torn neighborhoods. And while America may not be ready to support a universal basic income for all who need it, ascendant coalitions that do control governments could try a UBI pilot in neighborhoods where the state intentionally created ghettos. Stockton, California, initiated an eighteen-month pilot UBI program in 2018 in which it transferred $500 monthly to 125 people without conditions. Preliminary evaluations were positive. Recipients of the stipend reported feeling less anxious, spending more time with their family and using the money on things like groceries, utility bills, and credit card debt. In 2020, the mayor of Stockton, Michael D. Tubbs, announced a six-month extension of the program, through January 2021, paid for by a philanthropist interested in making UBI a national priority.[41] Evidence from UBI programs in other countries suggests that they can increase happiness, health, school attendance, and trust in social institutions and reduce crime.[42] Mayor Tubbs founded a network, Mayors for a Guaranteed Income, with more than twenty-five mayors from across the country to advance this policy idea—once advocated by Thomas Paine, Milton Friedman, Richard Nixon, Martin Luther King Jr., and the Black Panther Party—that is gaining traction.[43]

Call it restitution, if you will, though I do not offer UBI in poor Black neighborhoods as a substitute for any larger program of reparations for slavery or state exclusion of Black Americans from its wealth-building programs.[44] Law professor Katherine Franke argues for collective land ownership strategies in lieu of individual reparations for the legacy of slavery.[45] Richard Rothstein, author of *The Color of Law*, advocates for policies that offer access to civic commodities like housing and education to redress systemic housing discrimination against Black Americans.[46] Public health researcher Lawrence Brown proposes reparation and investment in Black neighborhoods subjected to historic trauma due to state policies.[47] Similarly, I am arguing for repair of the harms of ghetto construction and continued, *present* state-sponsored residential caste. Try a UBI program in traumatized hoods, not only because it is morally right but also because it could work. As a descendant myself who sends remittance payments to a struggling relative, I can attest to the transformational power of $500 a month in stabilizing a life and enabling my loved one to rebuild.

Abolition and repair should go beyond participatory politics to transfer or share resources with historically defunded communities, to build them up and give descendants some agency in how their communities develop and flourish. Forty acres for each newly freed individual was beyond the political will of the United States in 1865, but today, housing activists are demanding collective ownership strategies to solve homelessness and the crisis of affordable housing. In Philadelphia, as the pandemic raged, fifty unhoused families, headed mainly by Black women, moved into vacant homes owned by the local housing authority, a protest borne of desperate need. After a months-long standoff, the housing authority ultimately agreed to transfer the homes to a community land trust and allow the families to stay.[48] Seattle recently transferred city-owned property to Black-lead community organizations that provide much needed services in the historically redlined and rapidly gentrifying Central District. One recipient, the Africatown Community Land Trust, was formed to preserve Black cultural heritage and provide affordable housing through acquisition and stewardship of land. Seattle conferred a $1 million grant to improve the transferred property. The city also allocated $100 million to its Equitable Communities Initiative to invest in communities impacted by systemic racism.[49] Other cities like New York are trying similar collective ownership innovations to combat displacement of communities of color.[50]

Perhaps follow the lead of Lawrence, Massachusetts, which made bus lines from its poorest neighborhoods free. Other cities that have offered free bus lines include Olympia, Washington; Kansas City, Missouri; and Boston.[51] Invest in well-resourced, culturally competent education, with greatly reduced class sizes, in high-poverty neighborhood schools. And allow descendants in concentrated poverty to be first in line in any lottery for accessing great integrated schools and neighborhoods. Invest in parks and neighborhood centers that offer recreation and human services in poor Black neighborhoods. Descendants should also have no-cost access to community college, GED programs, relevant job training, and connection to actual jobs and healthcare, including mental health and drug treatment if they need it. Free services for the freedom and liberation of descendants, who have been intentionally trapped by the state in hypersegregated poor neighborhoods.

An education example: NBA legend LeBron James supported a new school for children in Akron, Ohio. The Chosen Ones for this school were students who had performed between the 10th and 25th percentile on standardized tests in second grade. At the "I Promise School," children who might have been labeled "worst" are celebrated daily. They and their parents are supported with extras. James's family foundation donated about $600,000 to enable this public school to hire more teachers, reduce class sizes, and provide after-school programming and tutors. His foundation also covers the cost of a family resource center located at school where parents can access GED instruction, work counseling, health, and legal services. It also stocks a room with food, clothing, and supplies where parents can enter and take what they need. In its first year, I Promise students made extraordinary gains on standardized tests—90 percent of them scored in the 99th percentile for improvement, meeting and exceeding individual goals in math and reading.[52] A transformed education politics would mean that we would not have to rely on celebrities or foundations to mitigate school inequality. Taxpayers and school districts would provide extra support and care in all high-poverty schools, even as we fight to prevent any school from being overwhelmed by poverty.

These are just a few of the possibilities. Once descendants are asked what they and their communities need to prosper, they should play a role in charting community transformation. The answers will vary with the community. In Baltimore, the citizen advisory committees that toiled on plans for development around their proposed station for the Red Line would likely argue that the Red Line should be built as planned and that descendants from their neighborhoods should receive priority for the jobs it creates. They might also argue for fully funding and exceeding the proposals of the Kirwan Commission for Baltimore's apartheid schools.

The movement for Black Lives and other Black-led organizations have proposed policies and demanded transformation and repair.[53] Some succeeded, like Milwaukee, in procuring reallocations in 2020. Austin and Los Angeles cut $150 million from their police department's budgets. New York City reallocated $1 billion from policing to mental health, homelessness, and educational services. San Francisco reallocated $120 million to invest in the city's Black residents.[54] This movement caught up to intellectuals who had called for abolition of incarceration and militarized police departments.[55] It is a continuation of four centuries of resistance, for abolition of anti-Black institutions. New generations, less tired, more radical, have taken up the mantle. No justice, no peace, indeed.

We need to dismantle systems of private policing of Black folk. Some advocate penalizing racially discriminatory use of 911 calls; New York State recently adopted such a law.[56] Among many transformative new policies, repair would mean that when a descendant calls 911 for help, they actually receive care and protection, not surveillance, harm, or the threat of eviction or death. Transformation will have occurred when an officer sees a young man running and the officer knows his name and says, "Have a nice run, Jamal," or if he is a stranger in distress, "Young man, what is wrong? May I help you?"

That said, the true culprit in creating residential caste is the federal government—a near-century-old legacy. National government has also been captured and gridlocked by the dogmas and gerrymandered structures of the caste system it sponsored. But multihued citizens mobilize and run for office. Demographic change and accelerating political engagement by women, particularly Black women, and communities of color do not augur well for politicians still mired in white-identity politics. A tipping point, now or soon, could restore our national political institutions to promoting the common good.

An unshackled Congress could also abolish anti-Black policies and processes it set in motion and repair continuing damage to descendants. Scholars and advocates have argued that because federal, redlined, mortgage-insurance programs invested hundreds of billions (in present dollars) in pro-white wealth-building, new investments should be allocated now to Black communities. Legal scholar Rachel Godsil called for an immediate $60 billion investment in communities hit hardest by COVID-19, financed by repealing tax breaks for large corporations that were included in the first federal COVID relief package.[57] Others, like Senator Cory Booker, focus on targeted investment in redlined communities, including baby bonds for newborn descendants.[58]

Bolder still, Congress could atone for the federal legacy of promoting segregation by enacting a law that bans exclusionary zoning—local laws that privilege single-family homes and exclude denser, affordable housing. Congress could condition federal infrastructure or other spending on measurable local progress in creating affordable housing in high-opportunity areas. Congress could adopt spending formulas that guarantee that areas of persistent poverty receive their fair share of federal resources. And it could eliminate the $23 billion gap in what America spends on white versus nonwhite school districts by nearly tripling existing funding for the Title I program for high-poverty schools.

The five decades of ghetto mythologizing that I described in this book will have been fully disrupted when the president of the United

States uses the office's pulpit to speak honestly and transparently about the federal government's legacy of pro-white and anti-Black racism, helping these ideas for repair become mainstream. President Biden has moved in this direction. In his inaugural address, he acknowledged America's long dance between its founding ideal of universal human equality and supremacist ideology. "A cry for racial justice some four hundred years in the making moves us. The dream of justice for all will be deferred no longer," he said. For the first time in an inaugural address, a US president said the words "white supremacy" and that we must confront and defeat extremism and domestic terrorism.[59]

Hours later, on the same day, Biden began to govern, issuing a flurry of executive orders. Among them, he rescinded the Trump administration's harmful ban on diversity and sensitivity training for federal agencies and contractors. He abolished Trump's 1776 Commission that attempted to shape American education by denying the role of white supremacy in American history. And he signed an executive order to promote racial equity. The White House's Domestic Policy Council—led by the formidable former UN ambassador Susan E. Rice—was tasked with steering all federal agencies to root out "systemic racism" and embed fairness in all its decision-making processes and programs.

The equity order directs federal agencies to assess, report on, and plan for removing systemic barriers to opportunities "for people of color and other underserved groups." It calls on the federal government, where legally permissible, to "allocate resources to address the historic failure to invest sufficiently, justly, and equally in underserved communities" and tasks the director of the Office of Management and Budget to work with agencies to make that happen. Critically, the order creates a data working group to study best methods for measuring progress.[60] Only by collecting data and paying attention to where federal dollars are spent can the US government disrupt the racial redlining it institutionalized.

In a speech promoting this ambitious, government-wide racial equity agenda, Biden confronted directly the central message of dog-whistling, the myth "that America is a zero-sum game . . . [that] 'If you get ahead, I fall behind' . . . [or worse] 'If I hold you down, I lift myself up.'" Invoking economic studies and common sense, Biden declared that our nation is "morally deprived because of systemic racism" but also "less prosperous . . . less successful . . . less secure."[61] The equity order noted that closing racial gaps in wages and access to credit and higher education would add $5 trillion to the American economy over the next five years.[62]

The Biden administration must also restore and enforce the Obama-era rule to affirmatively further fair housing, along with other fair housing, fair lending, and anti-racist policies that the Trump administration gutted. It should continue and expand the Department of Justice's role in investigating police departments for systemic civil rights violations. The federal government should aggressively enforce existing and restored civil rights protections and issue new guidelines that promote inclusion and equity.

Whatever proposals for repair that win consensus, they could be paid for in part by repealing recent excessive tax breaks for wealthy individuals and corporations and cutting excessive investments in segregation and punitive strategies that exacerbate racial inequality. All levels of government have a moral obligation to stop investing in segregation, to stop doubling down on practices born of a long, sinister, racist past. The federal government, too, should invest in new institutions and policies that support a virtuous cycle of inclusion, humanization, and repair. All levels of government should actively promote not only anti-racism but integration. And ascending coalitions must continue to organize, win elections, and hold government accountable for this work.

I end with a personal note to the people for whom I wrote this book. As an elder once told a room full of Black alumni of my undergraduate alma mater: *Love is our wealth.* Whatever the state and non-descendants do to and think of us, we must love ourselves and lift each other up, particularly our brothers and sisters who are being crushed under the weight of supremacist institutions.

ACKNOWLEDGMENTS

The seed of this book was planted with an invitation to give the Francis Biddle Memorial Lecture at Harvard Law School in 2018. Thank you to Tomiko Brown-Nagin and John Manning for extending the opportunity to speak at my alma mater, which forced me to think ambitiously about what I might say that would be worthy of the occasion. That lecture formed the basis of the proposal for this book, which I submitted to Beacon Press.

Thank you to my editor, Joanna Green, for having great faith in the idea and helping me clarify that I was writing not only about concentrated poverty but also its opposite, affluent space, and the entire system of residential caste. Thank you to the wonderful team at Beacon Press for the passionate work you did at every stage of production and promotion for this book. You have backed me through three books and helped me grow as a writer. I am eternally grateful.

Thank you to the scholars, writers, journalists, civil rights lawyers, and advocates who have grappled with the age-old problem of American caste and its many manifestations. I could not have written this book without your magnificent work. In presenting my own theory, I tried to offer something of an intellectual and social history, particularly of the contributions of Black scholars to this struggle. Your truth-telling matters.

Georgetown Law has been my employer for a quarter century now. I could not have written this or prior books without being part of this community that works at racial justice. I am particularly grateful to our dean, Bill Treanor, and associate dean Paul Ohm, who provided me with financial support and a research leave to write this book.

My faculty colleagues Sheila Foster and Robin Lenhardt read the entire manuscript and gave me substantive comments throughout. You both raised the bar as I was struggling to the finish and greatly improved the final draft. I appreciate your friendship and support.

Thanks so much to the scholars and advocates who read and gave me vital feedback on particular chapters: Heather Abraham, Bill Buzbee, Peter Byrne, Yael Cannon, Julie Cohen, Michael Diamond, Jane Ehrenfeld, James Forman Jr., Megan Haberle, Sophie House, Sherrilyn Ifill, Adam Levitin, Hilary Malson, Naomi Mezey, Ajmel Quereshi, Mike Seidman, Bob Stumberg, Phil Tegeler, David Troutt, and Robin West, along with many participants in the Georgetown Law Faculty Scholarship Workshop. All of you contributed in very important ways that made the book better.

Thank you to Heather Abraham and the student-attorneys she supervised at the Georgetown Law Civil Rights Clinic—Jenna Casolo, Tunu Wadutumi, and Valencia Richardson—who filed and pursued freedom of information requests with the Maryland and federal departments of transportation, regarding the Baltimore Red Line, the Title VI complaint that was closed without formal findings. Thanks to my colleague Aderson Francois, for agreeing to have the clinic take on this project, which took a year. My research assistant, Oge Maduike, and I waded through the documents that the Maryland Department of Transportation disclosed to the clinic. Collectively we unearthed devastating truth that I tell in the book.

Thank you to my research and technical assistant, Tia Hockenberry, who also filed a successful FOIA request about the Schenectady School District's Title VI complaint and did yeoman's work in seeking permissions for images and maps used in the book.

Thank you to my colleague Yael Cannon for introducing me to her friend and client Lakia Barnett and giving me the idea of featuring Lakia in a chapter to underscore the constraints that descendants face in seeking opportunity.

Thank you to the people who gave me time and interviews for this book: Earl Andrews, Darryl Atwell, Lakia Barnett, DeVone Boggan, Yael Cannon, Rev. Linda Davis, Samuel Jordan, Jason Kise,

Elwyn C. Lee, Laurence Spring, and Phil Tegeler. I am particularly grateful to those who allowed me to feature your stories in depth, endured my follow-up questions, and permitted me to include images of you in the book. Special thanks to Mr. Andrews for the cold day we spent riding buses and rail in Baltimore, which brought home what it is like trying to get somewhere in that slow, fragmented "system." I am also very grateful to Dr. Lee, who took me on a half-day tour of the Third Ward of Houston, and to Rev. Davis and a long-time resident-leader of Cuney Homes who preferred to remain anonymous, who both spoke to me, enabling me to better understand the struggles and strengths of descendants.

My research assistants worked tirelessly on this project and I am profoundly grateful to them: Jason Kise, Oge Maduike, Ivanley Noisette, Juliette Singarella, Tanesha Williams, and Lynn Zhang. Time and again you found sources to support my argument and helped advance my thinking. Jason Kise was particularly helpful in using data and tools from Social Explorer to produce some maps that appear in the book and in sharing his personal experience living in varied neighborhoods, which illuminated practices of opportunity hoarding and surveillance.

Andrea Muto was my library liaison for years and my partner, especially, in archival research. Special thanks to Andrea, Thanh Nguyen, and the wonderful staff of the Georgetown Law Library for extensive research and cite-checking support, much of it undertaken by the following student research assistants who improved specific chapters: Joey Cahill, Austin Donahue, Gabriela Figueras, Zhengyan Gu, Julie Kidder, Laixin Li, Melissa Moran, Jordan Pino, Ramya Reddy, and William Spruance.

Thank you to my students over the years in my writing seminar on segregation. I learned a lot from your research papers. In particular, I relied on sources or events brought to my attention by Victoria Brown, Tiauna Mathieu, Sarah Miller, Makenna Osborn, Tamera Overton, Noemi Schor, Rachel Smith, and Christiann Tavitas.

Thank you to the individuals and organizations that pioneered color-coded race and opportunity mapping, and those that gave me permission to feature maps in this book. I so appreciate John Relman for hosting a panel at his law offices on the power of race-coded maps to mobilize people and juries to understand and help dismantle residential caste. That event and Relman's personal testimony powerfully influenced my thinking about how I would use maps and organize my argument about the cumulative processes of residential caste in this book. Thank you to Paul Jargowsky for producing your Architecture of Segregation map series, which also greatly influenced me, and for taking the time to explain the data and research animating your work on concentrated poverty.

My assistant Ashley Freeman was a great aide and ally. Thanks also to the entire faculty support staff at Georgetown for your cheerful assistance.

Thanks to the sister-writers who provided support, encouragement, inspiration, or just a laugh about the madness that is book writing, as I toiled: Amy Alexander, Julie Cohen, Annette Gordon-Reed, Natalie Hopkinson, Diane McWhorter, Michele Norris, Dolen Perkins-Valdez, and Darlene Taylor. Amy Alexander introduced me to her "vis ed guy," who in turn introduced me to John David Coppola, who magically improved the visual quality of images used in the book.

Thank you to *Politico Magazine* for giving me the opportunity to write a series of pieces that previewed themes of this book. The feedback from *Politico* editors and readers was very helpful in honing my thoughts.

Thank you to my friends and family for enduring another book. The sister network sustained me, as did my earth-angel cousins, Elizabeth Cashin McMillen and Dorothy Reed. Heartfelt thanks to my pastor, Rev. Dr. Darryl Roberts, for your uplifting sermons, particularly in a year of pandemic, that reminded me always to lean on God.

Finally, to my husband, Marque, and sons, Langston and Logan, thank you for your love, support, and patience. I could not have done this without you.

NOTES

PROLOGUE

1. Thomas Jefferson, *Notes on the State of Virginia* (London, 1787), 229, 240.
2. Thomas R. Dew, "Review of the Debate in the Virginia Legislature," in *Slavery Defended: The Views of the Old South*, ed. Eric L. McKitrick, 20, 31 (Englewood Cliffs, NJ: Prentice-Hall, 1963), 30, 31.
3. John C. Calhoun, "Speech on the Reception of Abolition Petitions, Delivered in the Senate, February 6th, 1837," in *The Works of John C. Calhoun*, ed. Richard K. Cralle (New York: D. Appleton & Co., 1853), 2:630; incompletely reported in Cong. Globe, 24th Cong., 2d Sess. 157–59 (1837).
4. Henry Cleveland, *Alexander H. Stephens in Public and Private: With Letters and Speeches, Before, During, and Since the War* (Philadelphia, 1866), 723.
5. J. H. Van Evrie, *Negros and Negro "Slavery": The First an Inferior Race; The Latter Its Normal Condition* (New York, 1861), 188. Van Evrie was a doctor and editor of the *Weekly Day Book* and author of several books defending slavery.
6. S. Rep. No. 42–41, pt. 2, at 318 (1871), quoted in Martha Hodes, *White Women, Black Men: Illicit Sex in the 19th-Century South* (New Haven, CT: Yale University Press, 1997), 169.
7. S. Rep. No. 42–41, pt. 11, at 76 (1872), quoted in Hodes, *White Women*, 169.
8. William L. Katz, *Eyewitness: The Negro in American History* (New York: Pitman Publishing, 1967), 389–90.
9. "Showing Glendive in MT," The Homepage of James W. Loewen, accessed August 8, 2018, https://sundown.tougaloo.edu/sundowntownsshow.php ?id=1687. Glendive is in Montana. Its anti-Black sentiments and apparent actions to violently oust Negroes were widely shared. See James Loewen, *Sundown Towns* (New York: Simon & Schuster, 2005), cited in Richard Rothstein, *The Color of Law: A Forgotten History of How Our Government Segregated America* (New York: Liveright Publishing, 2017), 42, 262.
10. John Hancock, "The New Deal and American Planning: The 1930s," in *Two Centuries of American Planning*, ed. Daniel Schaffer (Baltimore: Johns

Hopkins University Press, 1988), 201 (quoting a memo about zoning written by Bettman and other members of the American City Planning Institute in collaboration with President Franklin D. Roosevelt's National Land Use Planning Committee).

11. St. Clair Drake and Horace Cayton, *Black Metropolis: A Study of Negro Life in a Northern City* (New York: Harper and Row, 1962), 1:188.

12. Richard Nixon, "What Has Happened to America?," *Reader's Digest*, October 1967, 50.

13. "Words Fail; Miami Cops Get Tough with Negro Thugs," *Standard-Speaker*, December 27, 1967, https://www.newspapers.com/clip/52372056/walter-everett-headley-1905–1968.

14. "'Welfare Queen' Becomes Issue in Reagan Campaign," *New York Times*, February 15, 1976, https://www.nytimes.com/1976/02/15/archives/welfare-queen-becomes-issue-in-reagan-campaign-hitting-a-nerve-now.html (noting that this "item in Mr. Reagan's repertoire is one of several that seem to be at odds with the facts").

15. Presidential Statement on Signing Legislation Rejecting U.S. Sentencing Commission Recommendations, 31 Weekly Comp. Pres. Doc. 1961, 1962 (October 30, 1995). At the time, the sentencing disparity between crack and powder cocaine was one hundred to one.

16. William J. Bennett, John J. DiIulio, and John P. Walters, *Body Count: Moral Poverty . . . and How to Win America's War Against Crime and Drugs* (New York: Simon & Schuster, 1996), 26 (wrongly predicting a wave of violence by "superpredators"). Instead a dramatic reduction in violent crime ensued, see Elizabeth Becker, "As Ex-Theorist on Young 'Superpredators,' Bush Aide Has Regrets," *New York Times*, February 9, 2001, https://www.nytimes.com/2001/02/09/us/as-ex-theorist-on-young-superpredators-bush-aide-has-regrets.html.

17. Mia de Graaf, "Bill Maher Controversially Describes Murdered Teenager Michael Brown as 'Thug Who Didn't Deserve to Be Shot,'" *Daily Mail*, October 27, 2014, http://www.dailymail.co.uk/news/article-2809048/Bill-Maher-controversially-describes-murdered-teenager-Michael-Brown-thug-didn-t-deserve-shot.html.

18. Aaron Blake, "The First Trump-Clinton Presidential Debate Transcript, Annotated," *Washington Post*, September 26, 2016, https://www.washingtonpost.com/news/the-fix/wp/2016/09/26/the-first-trump-clinton-presidential-debate-transcript-annotated/?noredirect=on&utm_term=.1e206d08268c.

19. Donald J. Trump (@realdonaldtrump), Twitter, May 29, 2020, 12:53 a.m., https://twitter.com/realDonaldTrump/status/1266231100780744704.

INTRODUCTION

1. Sarah Maslin Nir, "White Woman Is Fired After Calling Police on Black Man in Central Park," *New York Times*, May 26, 2020, https://www.nytimes.com/2020/05/26/nyregion/amy-cooper-dog-central-park.html.

2. Sarah Maslin Nir, "The Bird Watcher, That Incident and His Feelings on the Woman's Fate," *New York Times*, May 27, 2020, https://www.nytimes.com/2020/05/27/nyregion/amy-cooper-christian-central-park-video.html.

3. Jonah E. Bromwich, "Amy Cooper, Who Falsely Accused Black Bird-Watcher, Has Charge Dismissed," *New York Times*, February 16, 2021, https://www.nytimes.com/2021/02/16/nyregion/amy-cooper-charges-dismissed.html.

4. Hannah Natanson, "The White House Put Up a Wall. The People 'Made It Beautiful,'" *Washington Post*, June 10, 2020, https://www.washingtonpost.com/local/the-white-house-put-up-a-wall-the-people-made-it-beautiful/2020/06/10/aa28d364-aa9f-11ea-9063-e69bd6520940_story.html.

5. Defense Exhibit 2 at 15–16, State v. Lane, No. 27-CR-20–12951 (Minn. 4th Dist. Ct. July 7, 2020), https://mncourts.gov/mncourtsgov/media/High-Profile-Cases/27-CR-20–12951-TKL/Exhibit207072020.pdf (transcript of Thomas Lane body worn camera).

6. Defense Exhibit 2 at 15–16, State v. Lane, 13.

7. See Sheryll Cashin, *Loving: Interracial Intimacy and the Threat to White Supremacy* (Boston: Beacon Press, 2017), 169–89.

8. Elijah Anderson, "The Iconic Ghetto," *Annals of the American Academy of Political and Social Science* 642, no. 1 (July 2012): 8–24.

9. Richard V. Reeves, *Dream Hoarders: How the American Middle Class Is Leaving Everyone Else in the Dust, Why That Is a Problem, and What to Do About It* (Washington, DC: Brookings Institution Press, 2018), 19–38; Sheryll Cashin, *Place, Not Race: A New Vision of Opportunity in America* (Boston: Beacon Press, 2014), 19–40; Douglas S. Massey, *Categorically Unequal: The American Stratification System* (New York: Russell Sage Foundation, 2007). See also Jonathan Spader et al., "Fostering Inclusion in American Neighborhoods," in *A Shared Future: Fostering Communities of Inclusion in an Era of Inequality*, ed. Christopher Herbert et al. (Cambridge, MA: Joint Center for Housing Studies of Harvard University, 2018).

10. Jacob S. Rugh, Len Albright, and Douglas S. Massey, "Race, Space, and Cumulative Disadvantage: A Case Study of the Subprime Lending Collapse," *Social Problems* 62, no. 2 (May 2015): 186–218; Ylan Q. Mui, "Ex-Loan Officer Claims Wells Fargo Targeted Black Communities for Shoddy Loan," *Washington Post*, June 12, 2012, https://www.washingtonpost.com/business/economy/former-wells-fargo-loan-officer-testifies-in-baltimore-mortgage-lawsuit/2012/06/12/gJQA6EGtXV_story.html?utm_term=.a5c6098216d7.

11. Adam J. Levitin, "How to Start Closing the Racial Wealth Gap," *American Prospect*, June 17, 2020, https://prospect.org/economy/how-to-start-closing-the-racial-wealth-gap.

12. Elizabeth Kneebone and Natalie Holmes, "U.S. Concentrated Poverty in the Wake of the Great Recession," *Brookings*, March 31, 2016, https://www.brookings.edu/research/u-s-concentrated-poverty-in-the-wake-of-the-great-recession.

CHAPTER 1: BALTIMORE

1. Lawrence Brown, "Two Baltimores: The White L vs. the Black Butterfly," *Baltimore Sun*, June 28, 2016, https://www.baltimoresun.com/citypaper/bcpnews-two-baltimores-the-white-l-vs-the-black-butterfly-20160628

-htmlstory.html. See also Lawrence T. Brown, *The Black Butterfly: The Harmful Politics of Race and Space in America* (Baltimore: Johns Hopkins University Press, 2021).

2. Antero Pietila, *Not in My Neighborhood: How Bigotry Shaped a Great American City* (Chicago: Rowan and Littlefield, 2010), 9, 14, 25, 32.

3. Pietila, *Not in My Neighborhood*, 8, 19–20.

4. Christopher Silver, "The Racial Origins of Zoning in American Cities," in *Urban Planning and the African American Community: In the Shadows*, ed. June Manning Thomas and Marsha Ritzdorf (Thousand Oaks, CA: Sage Publications, 1997), 27.

5. "Baltimore Tries Drastic Plan of Race Segregation," *New York Times*, December 25, 1910, https://timesmachine.nytimes.com/timesmachine/1910/12/25/105900067.html.

6. W. Ashbie Hawkins, "An Alarming Condition," *Afro-American*, August 20, 1892. In 1907, the *Afro-American* raised capital by selling stock exclusively to Black stockowners, including Hawkins and employees of the paper. This emancipated the paper from white influence, allowing it to crusade against racial segregation and voter disfranchisement and to cultivate a militant Black readership. Hayward Farrar, *The Baltimore Afro-American: 1892–1950* (Westport, CT: Greenwood Press, 1998), 5–6.

7. Julia P. H. Coleman to NAACP, May 26, 1918; W. Ashbie Hawkins to NAACP, February 22, 1919, NAACP Administrative File, Subject File, Discrimination, Transportation, Julia Coleman, 1918–19, Reproduced from the Collections of the Manuscript Division, Library of Congress; Farrar, *The Baltimore Afro-American*, 33; Larry S. Gibson, *The Young Thurgood: The Making of a Supreme Court Justice* (New York: Prometheus Books, 2012), 136.

8. Pietila, *Not in My Neighborhood*, 16, 23, 31, 74; Dennis A. Doster, "'This Independent Fight We Are Making Is Local': The Election of 1920 and Electoral Politics in Black Baltimore," *Journal of Urban History* 44, no. 2 (March 2018): 134–52, doi.org/10.1177/0096144217746163.

9. W. Ashbie Hawkins, "We Have Disproved Every Charge," *Afro-American*, October 29, 1920; Doster, "'This Independent Fight We Are Making Is Local.'"

10. Hawkins, "We Have Disproved Every Charge."

11. Elizabeth Evitts Dickinson, "Rowland Park: One of America's First Garden Suburbs, and Built for Whites Only," *Johns Hopkins Magazine* (Fall 2014), https://hub.jhu.edu/magazine/2014/fall/roland-park-papers-archives.

12. Pietila, *Not in My Neighborhood*, 35, 49.

13. Pietila, *Not in My Neighborhood*, 61–70. See also Robert K. Nelson et al., "Baltimore, MD, Mapping Inequality," *American Panorama*, https://dsl.richmond.edu/panorama/redlining/#loc=12/39.2994/-76.6166&opacity=0.82&city=baltimore-md&adview=full; Courtland Milloy, "In Freddie Gray's Neighborhood, There Are Signs Things Are Getting Better," *Washington Post*, August 30, 2016, https://www.washingtonpost.com/local/in-freddie-grays-neighborhood-there-are-signs-things-are-getting-better/2016/08/30/61efaf34-6ece-11e6-8365-b19e428a975e_story.html; Michael Anft,

"Three Years After His Death, Freddie Gray's Neighborhood Faces a New Loss," *Medium*, April 19, 2018, https://www.citylab.com/equity/2018/04/three-years-after-his-death-freddie-grays-neighborhood-faces-a-new-loss/558434.

14. Pietila, *Not in My Neighborhood*, 70, 72.

15. "Segregation a Boon to Real Estate Sharps," *Afro-American*, January 23, 1915.

16. Pietila, *Not in My Neighborhood*, 95–104.

17. Pietila, 159, 171.

18. Pietila, 146, 154.

19. Alec MacGillis, "The Third Rail: In Baltimore, Public Investment—and Disinvestment—in Transportation Have Figured Greatly in the Persistence of Racial and Economic Inequality," *Places Journal*, March 2016, https://placesjournal.org/article/the-third-rail.

20. Pietila, *Not in My Neighborhood*, 204.

21. Pietila, *Not in My Neighborhood*, 219; "Harlem Park," Baltimore Heritage, accessed September 17, 2020, https://baltimoreheritage.org/history/harlem-park; Complaint at 13–14, Balt. Reg'l Initiative Developing Genuine Equal, Inc. v. Maryland (2015).

22. Raymond A. Mohl, "Race and Space in the Modern City: Interstate-95 and the Black Community in Miami," *in Urban Policy in Twentieth-Century America*, ed. Arnold R. Hirsch and Raymond A. Mohl (New Brunswick, NJ: Rutgers University Press, 1993), 102, 134–36; "Sweet Auburn Historic District," National Park Service, https://www.nps.gov/nr/travel/atlanta/aub.htm.

23. Pietila, *Not in My Neighborhood*, 95. "Red Line Community Compact: Defining the Success of Baltimore's Red Line Transit Project," Go Baltimore Redline, 2008, 8; Complaint, Baltimore Regional Initiative Developing Genuine Equality v. Maryland, 13–15; John Miller, "Roads to Nowhere: How Infrastructure Built on American Inequality," *Guardian*, February 21, 2018, https://www.theguardian.com/cities/2018/feb/21/roads-nowhere-infrastructure-american-inequality.

24. Pietila, *Not in My Neighborhood*, 95–104, 219, 244. A recent study conducted by the Federal Reserve Bank of Chicago demonstrated a decline in Fair Housing Act mortgage insurance and in private lending in C- and D-rated communities after the creation of Baltimore's HOLC map. It further found that HOLC maps had a lasting impact on the communities they described, including Baltimore. The authors write, "Maps led to reduced credit access and higher borrowing costs which, in turn, contributed to disinvestment in poor urban American neighborhoods with long-run repercussions. . . . Being on the lower graded side of D-C boundaries led to rising racial segregation from 1930 until about 1970 or 1980 before starting to decline thereafter . . . Nevertheless, racial segregation along both the C-B and D-C borders remains in 2010, almost three quarters of a century later. Moreover . . . the maps had sizeable effects on homeownership rates, house values and rents." Daniel Aaronson et al., "The Effects of HOLC's 'Redlining' Maps," *Federal Reserve Bank of Chicago* (2019): 1, 36.

25. Renewing Inequality, https://dsl.richmond.edu/panorama/renewal/#view=0
/0/1&viz=cartogram&city=baltimoreMD&loc=13/39.3020/-76.6170.

26. Pietila, *Not in My Neighborhood*, 214, 229–33.

27. William A. Galston, "Pittsburgh's Revival Lesson for Baltimore," *Wall Street Journal*, May 6, 2015, https://www.wsj.com/articles/pittsburghs-rev ival-lesson-for-baltimore-1430867776.

28. Thompson v. HUD, 1 No. MJG-95–309 (D. Md. 1995); Anft, "Three Years After His Death, Freddie Gray's Neighborhood Faces a New Loss"; Laurie Braham, "Foes Killing House Plan Funds," *Chicago Tribune*, December 15, 1994, https://www.chicagotribune.com/news/ct-xpm-1994–12–15 –9412150065-story.html; Michael A. Fletcher, "Mikulski, Champion of Liberal Causes, Led Fight to Kill MTO," *Baltimore Sun*, September 25, 1994, http://articles.baltimoresun.com/1994–09–25/news/1994268041 _1_mikulski-mto-housing-in-baltimore.

29. Ron Cassie, "Back to the Future," *Baltimore*, April 2018, https://www .baltimoremagazine.com/2018/4/20/thirty-years-ago-kurt-schmoke-openly -advocating-for-decriminalization-of-marijuana.

30. Cassie, "Back to the Future."

31. Michael S. Rosenwald and Michael A. Fletcher, "Why Couldn't $130 Million Transform One of Baltimore's Poorest Places?," *Washington Post*, May 2, 2015, https://www.washingtonpost.com/local/why-couldnt-130-million -transform-one-of-baltimores-poorest-places/2015/05/02/0467ab06-f034 –11e4-a55f-38924fca94f9_story.html?utm_term=.551acoa5cooe.

32. MacGillis, "The Third Rail."

33. "Community Health Assessment," Baltimore City Health Department, September 20, 2017, 7–9, 10, https://health.baltimorecity.gov/sites/default /files/health/attachments/Baltimore%20City%20CHA%20-%20Final %209.20.17.pdf.

34. Complaint, *Baltimore Regional Initiative Developing Genuine Equality v. Maryland*, 3.

35. Complaint, *Baltimore Regional Initiative Developing Genuine Equality v. Maryland*, 3.

36. Complaint, *Baltimore Regional Initiative Developing Genuine Equality v. Maryland*, 11–12.

37. Lawrence Brown, "Baltimore's White L Crime Panic & Post-Uprising Policies," *Medium*, November 15, 2017, https://medium.com/@BmoreDoc /baltimores-white-l-crime-panic-post-uprising-policies-794f21f1ffbd.

38. MacGillis, "The Third Rail."

39. WBAL-TV II Baltimore, "Video: Baltimore's Struggle to Get to Work," posted May 11, 2017, YouTube video, 3:30, https://www.youtube.com /watch?time_continue=122&v=9lDtuOyFNVk; Complaint, *Baltimore Regional Initiative Developing Genuine Equality v. Maryland*; Sarah Kline, "Weighing Maryland's Economic Future: Assessing the Benefits from the Red and Purple Lines," *Transportation for America*, May 2015, 8, https:// t4america.org/wp-content/uploads/2015/05/Maryland-Transit-Report.pdf; Interview with Samuel Jordan, November 1, 2018, notes on file with the author.

40. Pietila, *Not in My Neighborhood*, 249; Complaint, *Baltimore Regional Initiative Developing Genuine Equality v. Maryland*, 3–4, 9; MacGillis, "The Third Rail."

41. "Red Line Community Compact."

42. Complaint, *Baltimore Regional Initiative Developing Genuine Equality v. Maryland*, 14; MacGillis, "The Third Rail."

43. Patrick Sharkey, *Stuck in Place: Urban Neighborhoods and the End of Progress Toward Racial Equality* (Chicago: University of Chicago Press, 2013), 120; Robert J. Sampson, "'Broken Windows' and the Meanings of Disorder" and "The Theory of Collective Efficacy," in *Great American City: Chicago and the Enduring Neighboring Effect* (Chicago: University of Chicago Press, 2012), 2139-3112, Kindle.

44. Complaint, *Baltimore Regional Initiative Developing Genuine Equality v. Maryland*, 6–8; "Red Line Community Compact"; MacGillis, "The Third Rail."

45. In a third debate with opponent Democrat Anthony Brown, Governor Hogan "all but said he'd kill the Red Line and the Purple Line and dump transportation cash into roads [and] played to his strength among rural voters . . ." See Barry Rascovar, "Some Glimmers of Clarity on Issues," Maryland Reporter.com, October 19, 2014, http://marylandreporter.com /2014/10/19/there-you-go-again-how-brown-and-hogan-did-in-the-last -debate; MacGillis, "The Third Rail."

46. "Purple Line: About the Project, Overview," Maryland Transit Administration, https://www.purplelinemd.com/about-the-project/overview.

47. Michael Laris, "Maryland Governor Lists Transportation Priorities, Meets with Top Trump Administration Officials," *Washington Post*, March 22, 2017, https://www.washingtonpost.com/local/trafficandcommuting/maryland -governor-lists-transportation-priorities-meets-top-trump-administration -officials/2017/03/22/f86e20f6–0f2a-11e7–9d5a-a83e627dc120_story.html ?utm_term=.fea08d489298.

48. Andrew Metcalf, "Report: Purple Line Among 50 Infrastructure Projects Deemed Priorities by Trump Team," *Bethesda Magazine*, January 25, 2017, https://bethesdamagazine.com/bethesda-beat/transportation/report-purple -line-among-50-infrastructure-projects-deemed-priorities-by-trump-team.

49. Martin Di Caro, "What Does Larry Hogan's Election Mean for the Purple Line?," WAMU, November 6, 2014, https://wamu.org/story/14/11/06 /would_larry_hogan_really_kill_the_purple_line_in_maryland.

50. Robert McCartney et al., "Maryland Gov. Larry Hogan Says Purple Line Will Move Forward," *Washington Post*, June 25, 2015, https://www .washingtonpost.com/local/2015/06/25/a255fe8c-1b4d-11e5–93b7 –5eddc056ad8a_story.html?utm_term=.7fecb02fa2af.

51. Complaint, *Baltimore Regional Initiative Developing Genuine Equality v. Maryland*, 7; "Red Line Community Compact," 3–5; MacGillis, "The Third Rail."

52. Complaint, *Baltimore Regional Initiative Developing Genuine Equality v. Maryland*, 7.

53. "Maryland," *CNN Politics*, December 21, 2018, https://www.cnn.com /election/2018/results/maryland/governor.

54. Anft, "Three Years After His Death, Freddie Gray's Neighborhood Faces a New Loss."

55. Christina Sterbenz, "A 'Big Question' Surrounds the Arrest of Freddie Gray, Which Sparked Riots Across Baltimore," *Business Insider*, April 30, 2015, https://www.businessinsider.com/did-police-have-a-right-to-stop -freddie-gray-2015-4; MacGillis, "The Third Rail."

56. "Timeline: Freddie Gray's Arrest, Death, and the Aftermath," *Baltimore Sun*, April 12, 2015, http://data.baltimoresun.com/news/freddie-gray; https://www.bbc.com/news/world-us-canada-32546204.

57. Joel Gunter, "Baltimore Police Death: How Did Freddie Gray Die?" *BBC News*, May 1, 2015, https://www.bbc.com/news/world-us-canada-32546204; Natalie Sherman et al., "Freddie Gray Dies a Week After Being Injured During Arrest," *Baltimore Sun*, April 19, 2015, https://www.baltimoresun .com/news/crime/bs-md-freddie-gray-20150419-story.html.

58. MacGillis, "The Third Rail."

59. Yvonne Wenger, "Unrest Will Cost City $20 Million, Officials Estimate," *Baltimore Sun*, May 26, 2015, https://www.baltimoresun.com/maryland /baltimore-city/bs-md-ci-unrest-cost-20150526-story.html.

60. "The Problem with 'Thugs,'" *Baltimore Sun*, April 29, 2015, https://www .baltimoresun.com/opinion/editorial/bs-ed-thugs-freddie-gray-20150429 -story,amp.html; German Lopez, "The Baltimore Protests over Freddie Gray's Death, Explained," *Vox*, August 18, 2016, https://www.vox.com /2016/7/27/18089352/freddie-gray-baltimore-riots-police-violence.

61. Ahiza Garcia, "Mayor Backtracks: 'We Don't Have Thugs in Baltimore,'" *Talking Points Memo*, April 28, 2015, https://talkingpointsmemo.com /livewire/thugs-baltimore-mayor-stephanie-rawlings-blake.

62. David Jackson, "Obama Stands by the Term 'Thugs,' White House Says," *USA Today*, April 29, 2015, https://www.usatoday.com/story/theoval/2015 /04/29/obama-white-house-baltimore-stephanie-rawlings-blake/26585143.

63. "Gov. Hogan Declares State of Emergency, Activates National Guard," *CBS Baltimore*, April 27, 2015, https://baltimore.cbslocal.com/2015/04/27 /gov-hogan-puts-maryland-national-guard-on-notice.

64. "The Problem with 'Thugs.'"

65. "The Problem with 'Thugs.'"

66. Luke Broadwater and Michael Dresser, "In West Baltimore, Frustration over Red Line's Demise," *Baltimore Sun*, June 16, 2015, https://www .baltimoresun.com/news/maryland/education/bs-md-ci-red-line-loss -20150626-story.html.

67. "Red Line Community Compact," 5; "Re: Cancellation of Baltimore Red Line Project—Administrative Complaint," Baltimore Transit Equity Coalition, http://www.moretransitequity.com/wp-content/uploads/2016/06 /titleVI_complaint_121915.pdf.

68. Sheryll Cashin, "How Larry Hogan Kept Blacks in Baltimore Segregated and Poor," *Politico*, July 18, 2020, https://www.politico.com/news/magazine /2020/07/18/how-larry-hogan-kept-black-baltimore-segregated-and-poor -367930.

69. Sarah Larimer, "'Kids Are Freezing': Amid Bitter Cold, Baltimore Schools, Students Struggle," *Washington Post*, January 5, 2018, https://www .washingtonpost.com/local/education/kids-are-freezing-amid-bitter-cold -baltimore-schools-students-struggle/2018/01/05/8c213eec-f183-11e7 -b390-a36dc3fa2842_story.html; Talia Richman, "Leaky Roofs, Lead in the Water, Fire Risk: Baltimore Schools Face Nearly $3 Million in Maintenance Backlog," *Baltimore Sun*, September 27, 2018, https:// www.baltimoresun.com/education/bs-md-ci-facilties-costs-20180914 -story.html.

70. "Governor Hogan Rolls Back Tolls Statewide—Saving Marylanders $54 Million a Year," Office of Governor Larry Hogan, https://governor.maryland .gov/2015/05/07/governor-hogan-rolls-back-tolls-statewide-saving -marylanders-54-million-a-year; Colin Campbell, "MTA to Raise Transit Fares for Buses, Subway, Light Rail, Mobility Shuttles in June," *Baltimore Sun*, https://www.baltimoresun.com/maryland/baltimore-city/bs-md -mta-bus-fare-increase-20190514-story.html.

71. "Red Line Community Compact," 4, 9–10; Lillian Reed, "Baltimore Police Video Shows Takedown of Man," *Baltimore Sun*, June 15, 2019, 1, 9, http://digitaledition.baltimoresun.com/html5/desktop/production/default .aspx?pubid=99644e1a-52da-4fe3-8f78-a84e4fe4d386; Michael Dresser, "Hogan Shifts Money to Roads, but Not Everyone's a Winner," *Baltimore Sun*, July 18, 2015, https://www.baltimoresun.com/maryland/bs-md-hogan -highways-20150718-story.html; Dan Rodricks, "Larry Hogan's $61.5 Million 'Nowhere' Highway Project Gets Underway in Western Maryland," *Baltimore Sun*, December 14, 2018, https://www.baltimoresun.com/bs-md -rodricks-sunday-column-1216-story.html.

72. Eric Cortellessa, "Who Does Maryland's Governor Really Work For?" *Washington Monthly*, March 2020, https://washingtonmonthly.com /magazine/january-february-march-2020/who-does-marylands-governor -really-work-for/.

73. Complaint, *Baltimore Regional Initiative Developing Genuine Equality v. Maryland*, 24–33.

74. Complaint, *Baltimore Regional Initiative Developing Genuine Equality v. Maryland*, 8.

75. Stefanie DeLuca and Peter Rosenblatt, "Walking Away from the Wire: Mobility and Neighborhood Opportunity in Baltimore," 27 Housing Policy Debate 519, 527 (2017), https://www.tandfonline.com/doi/full/10.1080 /10511482.2017.1282884.

76. Kline, "Weighing Maryland's Economic Future," 4.

77. Complaint, *Baltimore Regional Initiative Developing Genuine Equality v. Maryland*, 2, 9–10.

78. Complaint, *Baltimore Regional Initiative Developing Genuine Equality v. Maryland*, 14; "Red Line Community Compact," 8–10.

79. Complaint, *Baltimore Regional Initiative Developing Genuine Equality v. Maryland*, 10; "Asthma," Baltimore City Health Department, https://health .baltimorecity.gov/node/454; "Trouble in the Air: Millions of Americans Breath Polluted Air," Environment Maryland, https://environmentmaryland

.org/sites/environment/files/reports/Trouble%20in%20the%20Air%
20vMD.pdf.

80. Letter from Charles E. James Sr., director, Departmental Office of Civil
Rights, to Pete K. Kahn, Maryland Secretary, Department of Transportation, July 13, 2017, on file with the author.

81. Cashin, "How Larry Hogan Kept Blacks in Baltimore Segregated and Poor."

82. Interview with Samuel Jordan, November 1, 2018, notes on file with the author.

83. "BaltimoreLink: Reliably Less Than Promised," *Baltimore Sun*, July 6,
2018, https://www.baltimoresun.com/opinion/editorial/bs-ed-0709
-baltimore-transit-20180706-story.html.

84. Katherine Shaver, "New Bus System Revives Anger, Frustration over Lost
Light-Rail in Baltimore," *Washington Post*, July 15, 2017, https://www
.washingtonpost.com/local/trafficandcommuting/new-bus-system-revives
-anger-frustration-over-lost-light-rail-in-baltimore/2017/07/15/0a11b22a
-61a4-11e7-8adc-fea80e32bf47_story.html?utm_term=.d3f2cae4aa3c.

85. Richard Gilpin, July 17, 2013, 10:41a.m., "Comment on," Shaver, "New
Bus System"; trejean, July 16, 2017, 10:57 a.m., "Comment on," Shaver,
"New Bus System"; Suburb Lifer, July 17, 2017, 1:56 p.m. "Comment on,"
Shaver, "New Bus System."

86. Eugene L. Meyer, "The Road Less Traveled," *Bethesda Magazine*, September 30, 2013, https://bethesdamagazine.com/Bethesda-Magazine/September
-October-2013/The-Intercounty-Connector.

87. Andrew Zaleski, "A $9 Billion Highway That Promises to Pay for Itself,"
Bloomberg CityLab, September 26, 2017, https://www.citylab.com
/transportation/2017/09/a-9-billion-highway-that-promises-to-pay-for
-itself/541119.

88. Brown, *The Black Butterfly*, 111–14; Brown, "Two Baltimores"; Audrey G.
McFarlane and Randall K. Johnson, "Cities, Inclusion and Exactions,"
Iowa Law Review 102 (2017): 2145.

89. Baynard Woods and Brandon Soderberg, "In Baltimore, Police Officers Are
the Bad Guys with Guns," *New York Times*, May 14, 2019, https://www
.nytimes.com/2019/05/14/opinion/police-guns-baltimore.html.

90. James Forman Jr., *Locking Up Our Own: Crime and Punishment in Black
America* (New York: Farrar, Straus and Giroux, 2017); Rebecca Leber,
"Liberal Policies Didn't Fail Baltimore. Here's What Did," *New Republic*,
May 1, 2015, https://newrepublic.com/article/121685/liberal-policies-arent
-whats-wrong-baltimore.

91. Prison Policy Initiative, *The Right Investment? Corrections and Spending in
Baltimore City* (February 2015), https://www.prisonpolicy.org/origin/md
/report.html.

92. Prison Policy Initiative, *The Right Investment?*

93. Richard Rothstein, "From Ferguson to Baltimore: The Fruits of Government-
Sponsored Segregation," *Working Economics Blog*, April 29, 2015, https://
www.epi.org/blog/from-ferguson-to-baltimore-the-fruits-of
-government-sponsored-segregation.

94. Luke Broadwater and Talia Richman, "Are City Services Worse in Black
Baltimore Neighborhoods? Racial Equity Bill Would Require Answers,"

Baltimore Sun, August 1, 2018, https://www.baltimoresun.com/news
/maryland/baltimore-city/bs-md-ci-racial-equity-charter-20180731-story
.html.

95. See Urban Institute, *"The Black Butterfly": Racial Segregation and Investment Patterns in Baltimore* (February 5, 2019), https://apps.urban.org
/features/baltimore-investment-flows; Lawrence T. Brown, *The Black Butterfly*.

CHAPTER 2: WHITE SUPREMACY BEGAT "THE GHETTO"

1. Sheryll Cashin, *The Agitator's Daughter: A Memoir of Four Generations
of One Extraordinary African American Family* (New York: PublicAffairs,
2008), 30; see also W. E. B. Du Bois, *The Philadelphia Negro* (Pennsylvania: University of Pennsylvania, 1899).

2. Cashin, *The Agitator's Daughter*.

3. Cashin, *The Agitator's Daughter*, 29–36; Andy Waskie, "Biography of Octavius V. Catto: 'Forgotten Black Hero of Philadelphia,'" https://general
meadesociety.org/octavius-catto-biography, accessed August 17, 2019.

4. Cashin, *The Agitator's Daughter*, 37.

5. Du Bois, *The Philadelphia Negro*, 37.

6. Du Bois, *The Philadelphia Negro*, 37.

7. Du Bois, *The Philadelphia Negro*, 37.; W. E. B. Du Bois, *The Souls of Black
Folk* (1903) (New York: Modern Library, 1996).

8. See generally, Stewart E. Tolnay and E. M. Beck, *A Festival of Violence: An
Analysis of Southern Lynchings, 1882–1930* (Urbana: Board of Trustees
of the University of Illinois, 1995); see also *The Rape of Recy Taylor*, dir.
Nancy Buirski (New York: Transform Films, 2018), a documentary of six
white boys who gang-raped a Black mother.

9. Mitchell Duneier, *Ghetto: The Invention of a Place, the History of an Idea*
(New York: Farrar, Straus and Giroux, 2016), xii.

10. C. Van Woodward, *The Strange Career of Jim Crow* (New York: Oxford
University Press, 1955), noting that segregationist attitudes in the South
hardened after the 1890s.

11. John E. Vacha, "The Best Barber in America," *Time*, January/February
2000.

12. Vacha, "The Best Barber in America."

13. Kenneth L. Kusmer, *A Ghetto Takes Shape: Black Cleveland, 1870–1930*
(Urbana: University of Illinois Press, 1976), 42–46.

14. Kusmer, *A Ghetto Takes Shape*, 171.

15. Kusmer, 47–48.

16. Vacha, "The Best Barber in America."

17. Langston Hughes, *The Big Sea: An Autobiography* (1940) (New York: Hill
and Wang, 1993), 27.

18. Kusmer, *A Ghetto Takes Shape*, 167.

19. Kusmer, 167–69.

20. DeNeen L. Brown, "'They Was Killing Black People': A Century-Old Race
Massacre Still Haunts Tulsa," *Washington Post*, September 28, 2018,
https://www.washingtonpost.com/news/local/wp/2018/09/28/feature/they
-was-killing-black-people.

21. Tim Madigan, *The Burning: Massacre, Destruction, and the Tulsa Race Riot of 1921* (New York: St. Martin's Press, 2001), 215–16.

22. Abby Zimet, "The More Things Change: Tulsa's Race Massacre That History Books Turned into a Race 'Riot,'" *Common Dreams*, June 8, 2008, https://www.commondreams.org/further/2018/06/08/more-things-change -tulsas-race-massacre-history-books-turned-race-riot.

23. Victor Luckerson, "Black Wall Street: The African American Haven That Burned and Then Rose from the Ashes," *National Affairs*, June 28, 2018, https://www.theringer.com/2018/6/28/17511818/black-wall-street-oklahoma -greenwood-destruction-tulsa.

24. Special to the Times, "Tulsa in Remorse to Rebuild Homes; Dead Now Put at 30," *New York Times*, June 3, 2021, A1.

25. Richard Rothstein, *The Color of Law: A Forgotten History of How Our Government Segregated America* (New York: Liveright Publishing, 2017), 43.

26. Melvyn Stokes, D. W. Griffith's The Birth of a Nation: *A History of "The Most Controversial Picture of All Time"* (New York: Oxford University Press, 2007), 111; John Hope Franklin, "Birth of a Nation: Propaganda as History," *Massachusetts Review* 20, no. 3 (1979): 417–34; John Milton Cooper, *Woodrow Wilson* (New York: Alfred Knopf, 2011), 204–6; Kusmer, *A Ghetto Takes Shape*, 174; Vacha, "The Best Barber in America."

27. Kusmer, *A Ghetto Takes Shape*, 176; Aubrey Solomon, *The Fox Film Corporation: 1915–1935* (Jefferson, NC: McFarland, 2011), 15, 228.

28. Cameron McWhirter, *Red Summer: The Summer of 1919 and the Awakening of Black America* (New York: Macmillan, 2011).

29. Vacha, "The Best Barber in America."

30. Vacha, "The Best Barber in America."

31. Kusmer, *A Ghetto Takes Shape*, 48–51, 171–72.

32. Cashin, *Loving*, 8–9.

33. See St. Clair Drake, *Churches and Voluntary Associations Among Negroes in Chicago* (Chicago: WPA, 1940); St. Clair Drake and Horace R. Cayton, *Black Metropolis; A Study of Negro Life in a Northern City* (Chicago: University of Chicago Press, 1993), Kindle; Kenneth B. Clark, *The Dark Ghetto: Dilemmas of Social Power* (Middletown, CT: Wesleyan University Press, 1989) ; Kenneth Clark and Jeannette Hopkins, *A Relevant War Against Poverty: A Study of Community Action Programs and Observable Social Change* (New York: Harper Collins, 1969); William Julius Wilson, *Power, Racism, and Privilege* (London: Macmillan, 1973); William Julius Wilson, *The Truly Disadvantaged: The Inner City, the Underclass, and Public Policy* (Chicago: University of Chicago Press, 1987); William Julius Wilson and Richard Taub, *There Goes the Neighborhood: Racial, Ethnic, and Class Tensions in Four Chicago Neighborhoods and Their Meaning in America* (New York: Vintage Books, 2006); Elijah Anderson, *Streetwise: Race, Class, and Change in an Urban Community* (Chicago: University of Chicago Press, 1990); Elijah Anderson, *Code of the Street: Decency, Violence, and the Moral Life of the Inner City* (New York: W. W. Norton, 2000).

34. Drake and Cayton, *Black Metropolis*, 4230–32, 4244–45.

35. Drake and Cayton, *Black Metropolis*, 4420, 4424, 4427.
36. Drake and Cayton, *Black Metropolis*, 4228.
37. Drake and Cayton, *Black Metropolis*, 268.
38. Drake and Cayton, *Black Metropolis*, 383.
39. Duneier, *Ghetto*, 59–60 (quoting and citing Gunnar Myrdal, *An American Dilemma: The Negro Problem and Modern Democracy* (New York: Harper & Row, 1962).
40. Duneier, *Ghetto*, 67 (quoting and citing Drake and Cayton, *Black Metropolis*).
41. See, for example, Rothstein, *The Color of Law*; Sheryll Cashin, *The Failures of Integration: How Race and Class Are Undermining the American Dream* (New York: PublicAffairs, 2004); Douglas S. Massey and Nancy A. Denton, *American Apartheid: Segregation and the Making of the Underclass* (Cambridge, MA: Harvard University Press, 1993); Kenneth T. Jackson, *Crabgrass Frontier: The Suburbanization of the United States* (New York: Oxford University Press, 1985).
42. Cashin, *The Failures of Integration*; Aaronson et al., "The Effects of HOLC's 'Redlining' Maps."
43. Rothstein, *The Color of Law*; Cashin, *The Failures of Integration*.
44. Ta-Nehisi Coates, "The Case for Reparations," *Atlantic*, June 2014, https://www.theatlantic.com/magazine/archive/2014/06/the-case-for-reparations/361631.
45. Arnold R. Hirsch, *Making the Second Ghetto: Race and Housing in Chicago, 1940–1960* (Chicago: University of Chicago Press, 1998), 41–42, 80, quoting Drake and Cayton.
46. Hirsch, *Making the Second Ghetto*, xiii, xiv, 14–15.
47. Cashin, *The Failures of Integration*; Rothstein, *The Color of Law*.
48. All of these assertions about Pruitt-Igoe are depicted in the documentary *The Pruitt-Igoe Myth*, 2011. "The Pruitt-Igoe Myth," YouTube video, posted by "Chandra Ward Stefanik," September 27, 2015, https://www.youtube.com/watch?v=xKgZM8y3hso.
49. Massey and Denton, *American Apartheid*; Douglas S. Massey and Jonathan Tannen, "A Research Note on Trends in Black Hypersegregation," *Demography* 52 (2015): 1028–29.
50. Massey and Denton, *American Apartheid*, 77.
51. Cashin, *The Agitator's Daughter*, 127–53, 155–60.
52. "Poverty Rate by Race/Ethnicity 2017," Henry J. Kaiser Family Foundation, https://www.kff.org/other/state-indicator/poverty-rate-by-raceethnicity.
53. Sheryll Cashin, "Reparations for Slavery Aren't Enough. Official Racism Lasted Much Longer," *Washington Post*, June 21, 2019, https://www.washingtonpost.com/outlook/reparations-for-slavery-arent-enough-official-racism-lasted-much-longer/2019/06/21/2c0ecbe8-9397-11e9-aadb-74e6b2b46f6a_story.html.
54. See Mary E. Pattillo, *Black Picket Fences: Privilege and Peril Among the Black Middle Class* (Chicago: University of Chicago Press, 1999).

CHAPTER 3: SEGREGATION NOW

1. Richard Rothstein, "Why Los Angeles Is Still a Segregated City After All These Years," *Los Angeles Times*, August 20, 2017, http://www.latimes.com /opinion/op-ed/la-oe-rothstein-segregated-housing-20170820-story.html.
2. National Advisory Commission on Civil Disorders, *The Kerner Report*, ed. Sean Wilentz (Princeton, NJ: Princeton University Press, 2016), Kindle ed., 119, 216, 225, 234, 1042, 1046.
3. National Advisory Commission on Civil Disorders, *The Kerner Report*, 148, 151, 525, 952, 1122.
4. National Advisory Commission on Civil Disorders, *The Kerner Report*, 2.
5. Leonard S. Rubinowitz and Imani Perry, "Crimes Without Punishment: White Neighbors' Resistance to Black Entry," *Journal of Criminal Law and Criminology* 92, nos. 1/2 (Autumn 2001–Winter 2002): 353, https://scholarlycommons.law.northwestern.edu/jclc/vol92/iss2/3.
6. Frank James, "Martin Luther King Jr. in Chicago," *Chicago Tribune*, January 3, 2008, http://www.chicagotribune.com/news/nationworld/politics/chi-chicagodays-martinlutherking-story-story.html.
7. "Chicago Campaign," Martin Luther King, Jr. Research and Education Institute at Stanford University, https://kinginstitute.stanford.edu/encyclopedia/chicago-campaign, accessed September 30, 2019 ("King believed that turning . . . attention to the North made sense: 'In the South, we always had segregationists to help make issues clear. . . . Indeed, after riots in Watts, Los Angeles, in August 1965, it seemed crucial to demonstrate how nonviolent methods could address the complex economic exploitation of African Americans in the North."); Abdallah Fayyad, "The Unfulfilled Promise of Fair Housing," *Atlantic*, March 31, 2018, https://www.theatlantic.com/politics/archive/2018/03/the-unfulfilled-promise-of-fair-housing/557009/, King viewing slums as "a system of internal colonialism not unlike the exploitation of the Congo by Belgium."
8. National Advisory Commission on Civil Disorders et al., *The Kerner Report*, 1094.
9. Clark, *Dark Ghetto*, 4, quoting "Man, age about 33."
10. Ibram X. Kendi, *Stamped from the Beginning: The Definitive History of Racist Ideas in America* (New York: Hachette Book Groups, 2017), 405.
11. Elizabeth Hinton, *From the War on Poverty to the War on Crime: The Making of Mass Incarceration in America* (Cambridge, MA: Harvard University Press, 2016).
12. *Report of the National Advisory Commission on Civil Disorders* (Washington, DC: Kerner Commission, 1968), 580.
13. Fair Housing Act, 42 U.S.C. § 3608(d) (1968); Otero v. New York City Hous. Auth., 484 F.2d 1122, 1140 (2d Cir. 1973).
14. Nikole Hannah-Jones, "Living Apart: How the Government Betrayed a Landmark Civil Rights Law," ProPublica, June 25, 2015, https://www.propublica.org/article/living-apart-how-the-government-betrayed-a-landmark-civil-rights-law.
15. Hannah-Jones, "Living Apart."

16. Douglas S. Massey, "The Legacy of the 1968 Fair Housing Act," *Sociological Forum* 30, no. S1 (2015): 571, 577, doi:10.1111/socf.12178.

17. Hannah-Jones, "Living Apart."

18. Molly Moorhead, "Mitt Romney Says 47 Percent of Americans Pay No Income Tax," PolitiFact, September 18, 2012, https://www.politifact.com/truth-o-meter/statements/2012/sep/18/mitt-romney/romney-says-47-p ercent-americans-pay-no-income-tax.

19. Mitt Romney (@MittRomney), "Black Lives Matter" Twitter, June 7, 2020, 6:30 p.m. https://twitter.com/MittRomney/status/1269758561720156160.

20. Hannah-Jones, "Living Apart"; "Ben Carson vs. the Fair Housing Act," editorial, *New York Times*, May 13, 2018, https://www.nytimes.com/2018/05/13/opinion/ben-carson-hud-fair-housing-act.html; Fred McGhee, "The Most Important Housing Law Passed in 1968 Wasn't the Fair Housing Act," Shelterforce, September 5, 2018, https://shelterforce.org/2018/09/05/the-most-important-housing-law-passed-in-1968-wasnt-the-fair-housing-act.

21. McGhee, "The Most Important Housing Law Passed in 1968"; Corianne Payton Scally, Amanda Gold, and Nicole DuBois, *The Low-Income Housing Tax Credit: How It Works and Who It Serves* (Urban Institute, July 2018), vi, https://www.urban.org/sites/default/files/publication/98758/lithc _how_it_works_and_who_it_serves_final_2.pdf; Ingrid G. Ellen, Keren M. Horn, and Katherine M. O'Regan, "Poverty Concentration and the Low Income Housing Tax Credit: Effects of Siting and Tenant Composition," *Journal of Housing Economics* 34 (2016): 50, http://dx.doi.org/10.1016/j.jhe.2016.08.001.

22. Kirk McClure, Alex F. Schwartz, and Lydia B. Taghavi, "Housing Choice Voucher Location Patterns a Decade Later," *Housing Policy Debate* 25 (2015): 228, Table 6, http://dx.doi.org/10.1080/10511482.2014.921223.

23. Thompson v. US Dept. of Housing & Urban Dev., 348 F. Supp. 2d 398, 408 (D. Md. 2005).

24. *Fifty Years of "The People v. HUD": A HUD 50th Anniversary Timeline of Significant Civil Rights Lawsuits And HUD Fair Housing Advances* (Washington, DC: Poverty & Race Research Action Council, 2018). See also Florence Wagman Roisman, "Long Overdue: Desegregation Litigation and Next Steps to End Discrimination and Segregation in the Public Housing and Section 8 Existing Housing Programs," *Cityscape* 4, no. 3 (1999).

25. Alex Polikoff, *Waiting for Gautreaux: A Story of Segregation, Housing, and the Black Ghetto* (Evanston, IL: Northwestern University Press, 2006), 52, 65; "The Gautreaux Lawsuit," Business and Professional People for the Public Interest, https://www.bpichicago.org/programs/housing-community-development/public-housing/gautreaux-lawsuit, accessed October 8, 2018; Barack Obama, *Dreams from My Father: A Story of Race and Inheritance* (New York: Three Rivers Press, 2004), 164–86.

26. See James Rosenbaum et al., "The Urban Crisis; The Kerner Commission Report Revisited: Can the Kerner Commission's Housing Strategy Improve Employment, Education, and Social Integration for Low-Income Blacks?," *University of North Carolina Law Review* 71 (1993): 1530–31.

27. Polikoff, *Waiting for Gautreaux.*

28. Polikoff, *Waiting for Gautreaux.* See *Fifty Years of "The People v. HUD."*

29. Rachel Kaufman, "Housing Advocates Sue HUD over Fair Housing Rule Suspension," Lawyers' Committee for Civil Rights Under Law, May 9, 2018, https://lawyerscommittee.org/housing-advocates-sue-hud-over-fair-housing-rule-suspension. The Trump administration in 2017 suspended a key Obama policy that would help low-income people move: the Small Area Fair Market Rents program would have increased the amount of money the government would pay for voucher holders to rent homes in high-opportunity areas. See Alana Semuels, "Trump Administration Puts on Hold an Obama-Era Desegregation Effort," *Atlantic*, August 30, 2017, https://www.theatlantic.com/business/archive/2017/08/trump-hud/538386. The Trump administration has also intended to roll back regulations that bar discrimination on the basis of "disparate impact," especially regulations that prevent discrimination in housing. See Adam Serwer, "Trump Is Making It Easier to Get Away with Discrimination," *Atlantic*, January 4, 2019, https://www.theatlantic.com/ideas/archive/2019/01/disparate-impact/579466. See also Emma Brown, "Trump's Education Department Nixes Obama-era Grant Program for School Diversity," *Washington Post*, March 29, 2017, https://www.washingtonpost.com/news/education/wp/2017/03/29/trumps-education-department-nixes-obama-era-grant-program-for-school-diversity.

30. Donald Trump (@realDonaldTrump), Twitter, July 29, 2020, 12:19 p.m., https://twitter.com/realDonaldTrump/status/1288509568578777088.

31. Matthew Yglesias, "Trump's Tweets About Saving the 'Suburban Lifestyle Dream,' Explained," *Vox*, August 3, 2020, https://www.vox.com/2020/8/3/21347565/suburban-lifestyle-dream-trump-tweets-fair-housing.

32. Jonathan Mahler and Steve Eder, "'No Vacancies' for Blacks: How Donald Trump Got His Start, and Was First Accused of Bias," *New York Times*, August 27, 2016, https://www.nytimes.com/2016/08/28/us/politics/donald-trump-housing-race.html.

33. Liam Dillon and Taryn Luna, "California Bill to Dramatically Increase Home Building Fails for the Third Year in a Row," *Los Angeles Times*, January 30, 2020, https://www.latimes.com/california/story/2020-01-29/high-profile-california-housing-bill-to-allow-mid-rise-apartments-near-transit-falls-short.

34. Maria Krysan and Kyle Crowder, *Cycle of Segregation: Social Processes and Residual Stratification* (New York: Russell Sage Foundation, 2017), 78.

35. Wilson, *The Truly Disadvantaged.*

36. Douglas S. Massey and Jacob S. Rugh, "Segregation in Post-Civil Rights America: Stalled Integration or End of the Segregated Century?," *Du Bois Review* 11, no. 2 (2014): 211, doi:10.1017/S1742058X13000180; Spader et al., "Fostering Inclusion in American Neighborhoods."

37. Douglas S. Massey, "Still the Linchpin: Segregation and Stratification in the USA," *Race and Social Problems* 12:1–12 (2020), 2, https://doi.org/10.1007/s12552-019-09280-1.

38. Roxanne Dunbar-Ortiz, *An Indigenous Peoples' History of the United States* (Boston: Beacon Press, 2014); Johnson v. M'Intosh, 21 U.S. 543, 543 L. Ed. 681 (1823). US law has not rejected the law of discovery and its racist underlying assumption that Christian Europeans "discovered" land that was already occupied or that Congress has a plenary right to abrogate treaty obligations to the Indigenous nations. See Juan Perea et al., eds., *Race and Races: Cases and Resources for a Diverse America* (St. Paul, MN: West Academic Publishing, 2007), 184–85.

39. For example, Canada, like the United States, derives its jurisprudence from British common law. Through its constitution and Supreme Court, Canada has created significant legal protections for Indigenous peoples that cannot be overturned by its legislature or popular will. In the Constitution Act of 1982, Canada explicitly recognized treaty and other rights to land and land use held by its first people that cannot be abrogated by politics. See Perea et al., *Race and Races*, 262–63. An Australian high court also decided in 1992 to reconsider fundamental assumptions for colonial dominion and restore certain rights to native people. See Mabo v. Queensland, 107 ALR 1, 1992 WL 1290806 (1992).

40. Richard H. Sander, Yana A. Kucheva, and Jonathan M. Zasloff, *Moving Toward Integration: The Past and Future of Fair Housing* (Cambridge, MA: Harvard University Press, 2018), 10; Douglas Massey and Nancy Denton, "Hypersegregation in U.S. Metropolitan Areas: Black and Hispanic Segregation Along Five Dimensions," *Demography* 26, no. 3 (1989): 373–91; Patrick Sharkey, "Spatial Segmentation and the Black Middle Class," *American Journal of Sociology* 119, no. 4 (January 2014): 921, doi:10.1086/674561.

41. Douglas S. Massey et al., "Black Immigrants and Black Natives Attending Selective Colleges and Universities in the United States," *American Journal of Education* 113, no. 2 (2007): 246.

42. "Why Are the Twin Cities So Segregated," Institute on Metropolitan Opportunity at University of Minnesota Law School, February 2015, https://www.minnpost.com/wp-content/uploads/sites/default/files/attachments/WhyAretheTwinCitiesSoSegregated22615.pdf, showing how the poverty housing industry and the poverty education complex, two growing industry pressure groups within the Twin Cities political scene have worked with local, regional, and state government to preserve the segregated status quo, and in the process have undermined school integration. See also Spader et al., "Fostering Inclusion in American Neighborhoods," and chapter 5 of this book.

43. Massey, "The Legacy of the 1968 Fair Housing Act," 578.

44. Massey and Denton, *American Apartheid*.

45. Massey and Tannen, "A Research Note on Trends in Black Hypersegregation," 1031–32.

46. See chapter 8 on anti-Black surveillance.

47. Cashin, *The Failures of Integration*, 127–66; Abby Goodnough, "Harvard Professor Jailed; Officer Is Accused of Bias," *New York Times*, July 20,

2009, https://www.nytimes.com/2009/07/21/us/21gates.html; Deanna Paul, "Police Handcuffed a Black Man Who Was Moving into His Own Home. Now He Wants Them Fired," *Washington Post*, March 22, 2019, https://www.washingtonpost.com/nation/2019/03/22/police-handcuffed-black -man-who-was-moving-into-his-own-home-now-he-wants-them-fired. See also chapter 8 of this book on anti-Black surveillance.

48. Sharkey, "Spatial Segmentation and the Black Middle Class," 929.
49. Pattillo, *Black Picket Fences*. See also Sharkey, "Spatial Segmentation and the Black Middle Class."
50. Sharkey, "Spatial Segmentation and the Black Middle Class," 921.
51. Sharkey, "Spatial Segmentation and the Black Middle Class," 927.
52. Sharkey, 930, 935–38. See also Karyn Lacy, *Blue-Chip Black: Race, Class, and Status in the New Black Middle Class* (Berkeley: University of California Press, 2007).
53. See Paul Jargowsky, "Stunning Progress, Hidden Problems: The Dramatic Decline of Concentrated Poverty in the 1990s," *Brookings*, May 1, 2003, https://www.brookings.edu/research/stunning-progress-hidden-problems-th e-dramatic-decline-of-concentrated-poverty-in-the-1990s; William Julius Wilson, "Another Look at the Truly Disadvantaged," *Political Science Quarterly* 106, no. 4 (Winter 1991–92): 642–43.
54. Paul A. Jargowsky, *Concentration of Poverty in the New Millennium: Changes in the Prevalence, Composition, and Location of High-Poverty Neighborhoods* (Washington, DC: Century Foundation/Rutgers Center for Urban Research and Education, 2013).
55. US Census Bureau, "Race, Hispanic or Latino by Race, Poverty Status in for Children Under 18, Poverty Status in for Population Age 18 to 64, and Poverty Status in for Population Age 65 and Over, 2012–2016." Prepared by Social Explorer, accessed July 4, 2018.
56. "Who Can Live in Chicago?," Nathalie P. Voorhees Center for Neighborhood and Community Improvement, https://voorheescenter.wordpress .com/2018/06/06/who-can-live-in-chicago-part-i, accessed September 23, 2020
57. Kimberly Jones, "How Can We Win," YouTube video, 6:21, June 1, 2020, https://www.youtube.com/watch?v=sb9_qGOa9Go.
58. Jargowsky, *Concentration of Poverty in the New Millennium*.
59. Massey and Rugh, "Segregation in Post-Civil Rights America," 205.

CHAPTER 4: GHETTO MYTHS THEY TOLD A NATION

1. Josh Levin, *The Queen: The Forgotten Life Behind an American Myth* (New York: Hachette Book Group, 2019).
2. Josh Levin, "The Welfare Queen," *Slate*, December 19, 2013, http://www.slate.com/articles/news_and_politics/history/2013/12/linda_taylor _welfare_queen_ronald_reagan_made_her_a_notorious_american_villain .html.
3. Levin, *The Queen*, 142; Josh Levin, "The Myth Was $150,000 in Fraud. The Real Story Is More Interesting," *New York Times*, May 17, 2019,

https://www.nytimes.com/2019/05/17/opinion/sunday/welfare-queen-myth
-reagan.html.

4. Levin, *The Queen*, 115; Levin, "The Welfare Queen."

5. Ian Haney López, *Dog Whistle Politics: How Coded Racial Appeals Have Reinvented Racism & Wrecked the Middle Class* (New York: Oxford University Press, 2014), 57. See Lee Atwater's quote describing Reagan's tactic of using racially charged language to incite white voters.

6. Ta-Nehisi Coates, "On Race-Hustling," *Atlantic*, October 3, 2012, https://www.theatlantic.com/politics/archive/2012/10/on-race-hustling/263210.

7. Haney López, *Dog Whistle Politics*, 57; Coates, "On Race-Hustling."

8. Haney López, *Dog Whistle Politics*, 57.

9. Jason DeParle, *American Dream: Three Women, Ten Kids, and a Nation's Drive to End Welfare* (New York: Penguin Books, 2004), chapter 5.

10. See generally DeParle, *American Dream*.

11. Haney López, *Dog Whistle Politics*, 59.

12. John B. Judis and Ruy Teixeira, *The Emerging Democratic Majority* (New York: Simon & Schuster, 2004), 22–23.

13. Haney López, *Dog Whistle Politics*, 67–68.

14. Levin, "The Welfare Queen."

15. George E. Peterson et al., *The Reagan Block Grants: What Have We Learned?* (Washington, DC: Urban Institute Press, 1986), 1; Timothy Conlan, *New Federalism: Intergovernmental Reform from Nixon to Reagan* (Washington, DC: Brookings Institution Press, 1988), 178.

16. Brockell, "She Was Stereotyped as the 'Welfare Queen.'"

17. Haney López, *Dog Whistle Politics*, 66.

18. Cashin, *Place, Not Race*, 7–9.

19. Massey and Denton, *American Apartheid*; Cashin, *The Failures of Integration*, 320.

20. Massey and Denton, *American Apartheid*; Cashin, *The Failures of Integration*, 320.

21. Loïc Wacquant, *Urban Outcasts: A Comparative Sociology of Advanced Marginality* (Cambridge, UK: Polity Press, 2008), 44; Michael B. Katz, *The Undeserving Poor: From the War on Poverty to the War on Welfare* (New York: Pantheon Books, 1989).

22. David Stoesz, "The Fall of the Industrial City: The Reagan Legacy for Urban Policy," *Journal of Sociology and Social Welfare* 19, no. 1 (1992): 149–67, 153.

23. Thomas Byrne Edsall and Mary D. Edsall, *Chain Reaction: The Impact of Race, Rights, and Taxes on American Politics* (New York: Norton, 1992), 148, quoting *Washington Post*, January 29, 1976.

24. Michelle Alexander, *The New Jim Crow: Mass Incarceration in the Age of Colorblindness* (New York: New Press, 2012), 49.

25. Alexander, *The New Jim Crow*, 53.

26. See, e.g., Forman, *Locking Up Our Own*; John Pfaff, *Locked In: The True Causes of Mass Incarceration—and How to Achieve Real Reform* (New York: Basic Books, 2017).

27. Paul Butler, *Chokehold: Policing Black Men* (New York: New Press, 2017), 69–73.

28. Elise Viebeck, "How an Early Biden Crime Bill Created the Sentencing Disparity for Crack and Cocaine Trafficking," *Washington Post*, July 28, 2019, https://www.washingtonpost.com/politics/how-an-early-biden-crime-bill-created-the-sentencing-disparity-for-crack-and-cocaine-trafficking/2019/07/28/5cbb4c98–9dcf-11e9–85d6–5211733f92c7_story.html.

29. Loïc Wacquant, "Deadly Symbiosis: When Ghetto and Prison Meet and Mesh," *Punishment & Society* 3, no. 1 (2001): 95–133, 95.

30. "Mass Incarceration," American Civil Liberties Union, 2020, https://www.aclu.org/issues/smart-justice/mass-incarceration.

31. Alexander, *The New Jim Crow*, 53, 142.

32. Laura I. Appleman, "The Treatment-Industrial Complex: Alternative Corrections, Private Prison Companies, and Criminal Justice Debt," *Harvard Civil Rights-Civil Liberties Law Review* 55 (2020): 40–47, https://harvardcrcl.org/wp-content/uploads/sites/10/2020/09/Appleman.pdf; Tim Requarth, "How Private Equity Is Turning Public Prisons into Big Profits," *Nation*, April 30, 2019, https://www.thenation.com/article/archive/prison-privatization-private-equity-hig; see also Jacob Whiton, "In Too Many American Communities, Mass Incarceration Has Become a Jobs Program," *Brookings*, June 18, 2020, https://www.brookings.edu/blog/the-avenue/2020/06/18/in-too-many-american-communities-mass-incarceration-has-become-a-jobs-program; Kara Gotsch and Vinay Basti, "Capitalizing on Mass Incarceration: U.S. Growth in Private Prisons," Sentencing Project, August 2, 2018, https://www.sentencingproject.org/publications/capitalizing-on-mass-incarceration-u-s-growth-in-private-prisons; Brigette Sarabi and Edwin Bender, *The Prison Payoff: The Role of Politics and Private Prisons in the Incarceration Boom* (Western Prison Project, 2000), https://www.prisonpolicy.org/scans/Prison_Payoff_Report_WPP_2000.pdf.

33. Bryan Stevenson, "Opinion: This Is the Conversation About Race We Need to Have Now," Ideas.Ted.com, August 17, 2017, https://ideas.ted.com/opinion-this-is-the-conversation-about-race-that-we-need-to-have-now.

34. Peter Edelman, *Not a Crime to Be Poor: The Criminalization of Poverty in America* (New York: New Press, 2017).

35. Kendi, *Stamped from the Beginning*, 391–502.

36. Felicia Pratto, Jim Sidanius, and Shana Levin, "Social Dominance Theory and the Dynamics of Intergroup Relations: Taking Stock and Looking Forward," *European Review of Social Psychology* 17 (2006): 271–320.

37. Elsewhere, I have surveyed Jefferson's specious arguments regarding the alleged inferiority of Africans to whites and Indigenous people, his implied justifications for slavery, and his economic dependency on the institution; see Cashin, *Loving*, 55–58, citing Thomas Jefferson, *Notes on the State of Virginia*, in *Thomas Jefferson, Writings* (New York: Library of America, 1984), 264–67.

38. Alexey Zhavoronkov and Alexey Salikov, "The Concept of Race in Kant Lectures on Anthropology," *International Journal of Philosophy* 7 (2018): 275–92.

39. Immanuel Kant, "Of the Different Human Races," 1775.
40. Jefferson, *Notes on the State of Virginia*, 212.
41. See Kendi, *Stamped from the Beginning*; Henry Louis Gates Jr., *Stony the Road: Reconstruction, White Supremacy, and the Rise of Jim Crow* (New York: Penguin Press, 2017).
42. Wacquant, *Urban Outcasts*, 91.
43. Wacquant, *Urban Outcasts*, 48.
44. Wacquant, *Urban Outcasts*.
45. Daniel Moynihan, *The Negro Family: The Case for National Action* (Office of Policy Planning and Research, US Department of Labor, March 1965).
46. See, e.g., William Ryan, *Blaming the Victim* (New York: Random House, 1971).
47. Charles Murray, *Losing Ground: American Social Policy, 1950–1980* (New York: Basic Books, 1984); Charles Murray and Richard J. Herrnstein, *The Bell Curve: Intelligence and Class Structure in American Life* (New York: First Free Press, 1994); Charles Murray, "Drug Free-Zones," *Current* 36 (1990): 19–24.
48. "Charles Murray," Southern Poverty Law Center, https://www.splcenter.org/fighting-hate/extremist-files/individual/charles-murray.
49. Nicole Hemmer, "'Scientific Racism' Is on the Rise on the Right. But It's Been Lurking There for Years," *Vox*, March 28, 2017, https://www.vox.com/the-big-idea/2017/3/28/15078400/scientific-racism-murray-alt-right-black-muslim-culture-trump; Jacquelyne Johnson Jackson, "The Bell Curve: What's All the Fuss About?" *The Black Scholar* 25, no. 1 (1995): 11–20, 17; Jeb Bush, interview with Richard Lowry, National Review Ideas Summit, C-SPAN, April 30, 2015, https://www.c-span.org/video/?325690-1/national-review-institute-2015-ideas-summit; Robert Pear, "Q&A: Charles Murray; Of Babies and Stick," *New York Times*, April 11, 1986, 11; Juan Williams, "Author's Attacks on 'Great Society' Shift Social Debate," *Washington Post*, May 28, 1985, https://www.washingtonpost.com/archive/politics/1985/05/28/authors-attacks-on-great-society-shift-social-debate/584fa524-f516-4209-8c0b-35b689ce8aaf; Charles Murray, "Losing Ground Two Years Later," *Cato Journal* 6, no. 1 (1986): 19–28, Law-georgetown-csm.symplicity.com/students/app/document-library/content/e9b2224b4a167e697f0453ff7e9c4c55.
50. Gates Jr., *Stony the Road*; see also my discussion in chapter 1 regarding Black enclaves in Baltimore in which W. E. B. Du Bois and other elites resided.
51. William Julius Wilson, *More Than Just Race: Being Black and Poor in the Inner City* (New York: W. W. Norton, 2009); Orlando Patterson and Ethan Fosse, *The Cultural Matrix: Understanding Black Youth* (Cambridge, MA: Harvard University Press, 2015).
52. Randall Kennedy, "The State, Criminal Law, and Racial Discrimination: A Comment," *Harvard Law Review* 107 (1994): 1255–68; Justice Clarence Thomas, Dissenting Opinion, Chicago v. Morales, 527 U.S. 41 (1999).
53. Paul Butler, "Racially Based Jury Nullification: Black Power in the Criminal Justice System," *Yale Law Review* 105 (1995): 677–725.
54. See generally Cora Daniels, *Ghettonation: Dispatches from America's Culture War* (New York: Broadway Books, 2007).

55. See Forman, *Locking Up Our Own: Crime and Punishment in Black America.*

56. Beth Schwartzapfel and Bill Keller, "Willie Horton Revisited," Marshall Project, June 13, 2015, https://www.themarshallproject.org/2015/05/13 /willie-horton-revisited.

57. Schwartzapfel and Bill Keller, "Willie Horton Revisited"; Roger Simon, "The GOP and Willie Horton: Together Again," *Politico*, May 19, 2015, https://www.politico.com/story/2015/05/jeb-bush-willie-horton-118061.

58. Richard Craig, *Polls, Expectations, and Elections: TV News Making in U.S. Presidential Campaigns* (Lanham, MD: Lexington Books, 2015), 66.

59. Peter Barker, "Bush Made Willie Horton an Issue in 1988, and the Racial Scars Are Still Fresh," *New York Times*, December 3, 2018, https://www .nytimes.com/2018/12/03/us/politics/bush-willie-horton.html.

60. Matthew R. Pembleton, "George H. W. Bush's Biggest Failure? The War on Drugs." *Washington Post*, December 6, 2018, https://www.washingtonpost .com/outlook/2018/12/06/george-hw-bushs-biggest-failure-war-drugs; Tracy Thompson, "D.C. Student Is Given 10 Years in Drug Case," *Washington Post*, November 1, 1990, https://www.washingtonpost.com/archive/local /1990/11/01/dc-student-is-given-10-years-in-drug-case/2384c4eb-8871 -4d28-a4f0-a3919335c311.

61. Alexander, *The New Jim Crow*, 55.

62. Monte Piliawsky wrote of the move as one of many tactics in the Clinton campaign that was "a subtly orchestrated exercise in Realpolitik that bordered on covert racism." Monte Piliawksy, "Racism or Realpolitik? The Clinton Administration and African-Americans," *Black Scholar* 24, no. 2 (1994): 2–10, 6; many Blacks saw it as simple pandering. Niall Stanage, "The Clintons and Race: A Timeline," *Hill*, June 23, 2015, https://thehill .com/homenews/campaign/245914-the-clintons-and-race-a-timeline. Christopher Hitchens reflected on this moment as a maneuver in Clinton's own "southern strategy." Christopher Hitchens, *No One Left to Lie To: The Triangulations of William Jefferson Clinton* (London: Verso: 1999), 24.

63. Schwartzapfel and Keller, "Willie Horton Revisited."

64. Michelle Alexander, "Why Hillary Clinton Doesn't Deserve the Black Vote," *Nation*, February 10, 2016, https://www.thenation.com/article/hillary -clinton-does-not-deserve-black-peoples-votes.

65. David A. Super, "The Cruelty of Trump's Poverty Policy," *New York Times*, July 24, 2019, https://www.nytimes.com/2019/07/24/opinion/trump -poverty-policy.html.

66. Charles Derber and Yale R. Magrass, *Capitalism: Should You Buy It? An Invitation to Political Economy* (New York: Routledge, 2016), 219.

67. Super, "The Cruelty of Trump's Poverty Policy."

68. Toni Morrison, "Comment," Talk of the Town, *New Yorker*, September 28, 1998, https://www.newyorker.com/magazine/1998/10/05/comment-6543.

69. "(1993) William J. Clinton, 'The Freedom to Die,'" *Black Past*, March 12, 2012, https://www.blackpast.org/african-american-history/1993-william-j -clinton-freedom-die.

70. Farah Stockman, "On Crime Bill and the Clintons, Young Blacks Clash with Parents," *New York Times*, April 18, 2016, https://www.nytimes .com/2016/04/18/us/politics/hillary-bill-clinton-crime-bill.html.

71. "(1993) William J. Clinton, 'The Freedom to Die.'"

72. Presidential Statement on Signing Legislation Rejecting U.S. Sentencing Commission Recommendations, 31 Weekly Comp. Pres. Doc. 1961 (October 30, 1995).

73. Heidi Gillstrom, "Clinton's 'Superpredators' Comment Most Damaging by Either Candidate," *Hill*, September 30, 2016, https://thehill.com/blogs /pundits-blog/crime/298693-hillary-clintons-superpredators-still-the-most -damaging-insult-by.

74. Michelle Mark, "Where Hillary Clinton Stands on Criminal Justice," *Business Insider*, October 8, 2016, https://www.businessinsider.com/where -hillary-clinton-stands-on-criminal-justice-2016–10.

75. William J. Bennett, John D. DiIulio Jr., and John P. Walters, *Body Count: Moral Poverty—and How to Win America's War Against Crime and Drugs* (New York: Simon & Schuster, 1996).

76. Elizabeth Becker, "As Ex-Theorist on Young 'Superpredators,' Bush Aide Has Regrets," *New York Times*, February 9, 2001, https://www.nytimes .com/2001/02/09/us/as-ex-theorist-on-young-superpredators-bush-aide -has-regrets.html.

77. "Solutions: American Leaders Speak Out on Criminal Justice," Brennan Center for Justice, April 27, 2015, https://www.brennancenter.org/our-work /policy-solutions/solutions-american-leaders-speak-out-criminal-justice.

78. Alexander, *The New Jim Crow*, 17.

79. Alexander, *The New Jim Crow*, 139.

80. Obama, *Dreams from My Father*.

81. Julie Bosman, "Obama Sharply Assails Absent Black Fathers," *New York Times*, June 16, 2008, https://www.nytimes.com/2008/06/16/us/politics /15cnd-obama.html; "Why Jesse's Testy: Obama's 'Tough Love' for Black Community," *New York*, July 10, 2008, https://nymag.com/intelligencer /2008/07/why_jesses_testy_obamas_tough.html; Vanessa Williams, "To Critics, Obama's Scolding Tone with Black Audiences Is Getting Old," *Washington Post*, May 20, 2013, https://www.washingtonpost.com/lifestyle /style/to-critics-obamas-scolding-tone-with-black-audiences-is-getting-old /2013/05/20/4b267352-c191–11e2-bfdb-3886a561c1ff_story.html; Derecka Purnell, "Why Does Obama Scold Black Boys?," *New York Times*, February 23, 2019, https://www.nytimes.com/2019/02/23/opinion/my-brothers -keeper-obama.html.

82. BET Staff, "Obama Delivers Some Tough Love," BET, March 3, 2008, https://www.bet.com/news/news/2008/03/03/newsarticlepoliticsbarack obamatexasspeech.html.

83. Bosman, "Obama Sharply Assails Absent Black Fathers."

84. Michael Eric Dyson, *Is Bill Cosby Right? Or Has the Black Middle Class Lost Its Mind?* (New York: Basic Books, 2005).

85. Michael Eric Dyson, "Obama's Rebuke of Absentee Black Fathers," *Time*, June 19, 2008, http://content.time.com/time/subscriber/article/0,33009,1816485,00.html.

86. Jo Jones and William D. Mosher, "Fathers' Involvement with Their Children: United States, 2006–2010," *National Health Statistics Reports* 71 (2013).

87. Williams, "To Critics, Obama's Scolding Tone with Black Audiences Is Getting Old."

88. Frank James, "Obama Explains Black America to White America," NPR, July 19, 2013, https://www.npr.org/sections/itsallpolitics/2013/07/19/203706929/obama-explains-black-america-to-white-america; Huma Khan and Michelle McPhee, "Obama Defends Criticism of Cambridge Police in Arrest of Gates," ABC News, July 23, 2009, https://abcnews.go.com/Politics/story?id=8153681&page=1.

89. John Gramlich and Kristen Bialik, "Obama Used Clemency Power More Often than Any President Since Truman," Pew Research Center, January 20, 2017, https://www.pewresearch.org/fact-tank/2017/01/20/obama-used-more-clemency-power.

90. "Smart on Crime: Reforming the Criminal Justice System for the 21st Century," Department of Justice, August 2013, 3–4, https://www.justice.gov/sites/default/files/ag/legacy/2013/08/12/smart-on-crime.pdf.

91. Michael D. Shear et al., "How Trump Reshaped the Presidency in over 11,000 Tweets," *New York Times*, November 2, 2019, https://www.nytimes.com/interactive/2019/11/02/us/politics/trump-twitter-presidency.html.

92. Vanessa Romo, "El Paso Walmart Shooting Suspect Pleads Not Guilty," NPR, October 19, 2016, https://www.npr.org/2019/10/10/769013051/el-paso-walmart-shooting-suspect-pleads-not-guilty.

93. Eileen Sullivan, "Trump Again Accuses American Jews of Disloyalty," *New York Times*, August 21, 2019, https://www.nytimes.com/2019/08/21/us/politics/trump-jews-disloyalty.html.

94. Josh Dawsey, "Trump Derides Protections for Immigrants from 'Shithole' Countries," *Washington Post*, January 12, 2018, https://www.washingtonpost.com/politics/trump-attacks-protections-for-immigrants-from-shithole-countries-in-oval-office-meeting/2018/01/11/bfc0725c-f711-11e7-91af-31ac729add94_story.html#comments-wrapper.

95. Olivia B. Waxman, "President Trump Played a Key Role in the Central Park Five Case. Here's the Real History Behind *When They See Us*," *Time*, May 31, 2019, https://time.com/5597843/central-park-five-trump-history.

96. "Donald Trump," PolitiFact, https://www.politifact.com/personalities/donald-trump.

97. Aaron Rupar, "Trump Still Refuses to Admit He Was Wrong About the Central Park 5," *Vox*, June 18, 2019, https://www.vox.com/policy-and-politics/2019/6/18/18684217/trump-central-park-5-netflix.

98. Rosie Gray, "Trump Defends White-Nationalist Protesters: 'Some Very Fine People on Both Sides,'" *Atlantic*, August 15, 2017.

99. Victoria M. Massie, "Donald Trump's 'Inner City' Has Nothing to Do with Where Black People Live," *Vox*, October 20, 2016, https://www.vox .com/identities/2016/9/28/13074046/trump-presidential-debate-inner-city.

100. Kelly Swanson, "Trump Tells Cops They Should Rough People Up More During Arrests," *Vox*, July 28, 2017, https://www.vox.com/policy-and -politics/2017/7/28/16059536/trump-cops-speech-gang-violence-long-island.

101. Jonathan Swan, "Trump to Protestors: All Lives Matter," *Hill*, February 29, 2016, https://thehill.com/blogs/ballot-box/presidential-races/271159 -trump-to-protesters-all-lives-matter.

102. Shear et al., "How Trump Reshaped the Presidency in over 11,000 Tweets."

103. Charles M. Blow, "The Rot You Smell Is a Racist POTUS," *New York Times*, July 28, 2019, https://www.nytimes.com/2019/07/28/opinion /trump-racist-baltimore.html.

104. Arthur Delaney and Ariel Edwards-Levy, "Americans Are Mistaken About Who Gets Welfare," *Huffington Post*, February 5, 2018, https://www .huffpost.com/entry/americans-welfare-perceptions-survey_n_5a7880cde4 b0d3df1d13f60b.

105. Super, "The Cruelty of Trump's Poverty Policy."

106. Peter Wade, "Trump's New Budget Goes After Social Safety Net Programs," *Rolling Stone*, February 9, 2020, https://www.rollingstone.com /politics/politics-news/trump-budget-cuts-social-safety-net-programs -949898.

107. Donald Trump, "Remarks by President Trump at 2019 Prison Reform Summit and FIRST STEP Act Celebration," speech, White House, April 1, 2019, https://www.whitehouse.gov/briefings-statements/remarks-president -trump-2019-prison-reform-summit-first-step-act-celebration.

108. German Lopez, "The Controversial 1994 Crime Law That Joe Biden Helped Write, Explained," *Vox*, September 29, 2020, https://www.vox .com/policy-and-politics/2019/6/20/18677998/joe-biden-1994-crime-bill -law-mass-incarceration.

109. Jerry Kang, "Trojan Horse of Race," *Harvard Law Review* 118, no. 5 (2005): 1489–1593; see also Jerry Kang and Kristen Lane, "Seeing Through Colorblindness: Implicit Bias and the Law," *UCLA Law Review* 58, no. 2 (2010): 465–519; Darren Lenard Hutchinson, "'Continually Reminded of Their Inferior Position': Social Dominance, Implicit Bias, Criminality, and Race," *Washington University Journal of Law Policy* 46 (2014).

110. Lanier Frush Holt, "Writing the Wrong: Can Counter-Stereotypes Offset Negative Media Messages About African Americans," *Journalism and Mass Communication Quarterly* 90, no. 1 (2013): 108–25.

111. Patrick Sharkey, *Uneasy Peace: The Great Crime Decline, The Renewal of City Life, and the Next War on Violence* (New York: W. W. Norton, 2018), 5–6.

112. "Crime Data Explorer," FBI, https://crime-data-explorer.fr.cloud.gov /explorer/national/united-states/crime/2007/2017.

113. Laura Strickler, Julia Ainsley, and Ken Dilanian, "'We Have a Problem': Federal Agencies Scramble to Fight Domestic Terror with Limited Resources," *NBC News*, August 5, 2019, https://www.nbcnews.com/politics /national-security/we-have-problem-federal-agencies-scramble-fight -domestic-terror-limited-n1039441; Nicole Einbinder, "The Trump Administration Has Actually Cut Government Resources to Fight White Supremacy and Domestic Terror," *Business Insider*, August 6, 2019, https:// www.businessinsider.com/trump-cut-resources-fight-white-supremacy -domestic-terrorism-2019-8.

114. See "Race and Hispanic Origins of Victims and Offenders, 2012–2015," Bureau of Justice Statistics, 2017, https://www.bjs.gov/index.cfm?ty =pbdetail&iid=6106, finding that "during 2012–15, half (51%) of violent victimizations were intraracial; that is, both victims and offenders were the same race or both were of Hispanic origin" and that "in the majority of violent victimizations, white victims' offenders were white (57%) and black victims' offenders were black (63%)"; "Violent Victimization Committed by Strangers, 1993–2010," Bureau of Justice Statistics, 2012, https://www.bjs.gov/content/pub/pdf/vvcs9310.pdf, finding that "violent victimizations committed by strangers accounted for about 38 percent of all nonfatal violence in 2010," and that "from 1993–2008 . . . among homicides . . . between 73% and 79% were committed by offenders known to the victims."

115. "Characteristics and Financial Circumstances of TANF Recipients, Fiscal Year 2017," Office of Family Assistance, US Department of Health & Human Services, 2018, Tables 10, 19, 33, https://www.acf.hhs.gov/sites /default/files/ofa/fy17_characteristics.pdf. Of the remaining recipients, 1.2% were American Indian or Alaska Native; 2.1% were Asian American; 0.7% were Native Hawaiian or Pacific Islander; and 2.2% were multiracial.

116. "Characteristics and Financial Circumstances of TANF Recipients, Fiscal Year 2011," Office of Family Assistance, US Department of Health & Human Services, 2012, Tables 8, 21, 35, https://www.acf.hhs.gov/sites/default /files/ofa/appendix_fy2011_final_amend.pdf; "Characteristics and Financial Circumstances of TANF Recipients, Fiscal Year 2012," Office of Family Assistance, US Department of Health & Human Services, 2013, Tables 8, 21, 35, https://www.acf.hhs.gov/sites/default/files/ofa/tanf_characteristics_fy _2012.pdf; "Characteristics and Financial Circumstances of TANF Recipients, Fiscal Year 2014," Office of Family Assistance, US Department of Health & Human Services, 2015, Tables 10, 19, 33, https://www.acf.hhs .gov/sites/default/files/ofa/tanf_characteristics_fy2014.pdf; "Characteristics and Financial Circumstances of TANF Recipients, Fiscal Year 2015," Office of Family Assistance, US Department of Health & Human Services, 2016, Tables 10, 19, 33, https://www.acf.hhs.gov/sites/default/files/ofa /characteristics_and_financial_circumstances_of_tanf_recipients.pdf; "Characteristics and Financial Circumstances of TANF Recipients, Fiscal Year 2016," Office of Family Assistance, US Department of Health &

Human Services, 2017, Tables 10, 19, 33, https://www.acf.hhs.gov/sites
/default/files/ofa/fy16_characteristics.pdf.

117. "Characteristics of Supplemental Nutrition Assistance Program Households: Fiscal Year 2010," US Department of Agriculture, 2013, Table A.23,
https://fns-prod.azureedge.net/sites/default/files/2010Characteristics.pdf;
"Characteristics of Supplemental Nutrition Assistance Program Households: Fiscal Year 2011" US Department of Agriculture, 2013, Table
A.23, https://fns-prod.azureedge.net/sites/default/files/2011Characteristics
.pdf; "Characteristics of Supplemental Nutrition Assistance Program
Households: Fiscal Year 2012" US Department of Agriculture, 2014, Table
A.23, https://fns-prod.azureedge.net/sites/default/files/2012Characteristics
.pdf; "Characteristics of Supplemental Nutrition Assistance Program
Households: Fiscal Year 2013" US Department of Agriculture, 2014, Table
A.23, https://fns-prod.azureedge.net/sites/default/files/ops/Characteristics
2013.pdf; "Characteristics of Supplemental Nutrition Assistance Program
Households: Fiscal Year 2014" US Department of Agriculture, 2015, Table
A.23, https://fns-prod.azureedge.net/sites/default/files/ops/Characteristics
2014.pdf; "Characteristics of Supplemental Nutrition Assistance Program
Households: Fiscal Year 2015" US Department of Agriculture, 2016, Table
A.23, https://fns-prod.azureedge.net/sites/default/files/ops/Characteristics
2015.pdf; "Characteristics of Supplemental Nutrition Assistance Program
Households: Fiscal Year 2016" US Department of Agriculture, 2017, Ta-
ble 3.5, https://fns-prod.azureedge.net/sites/default/files/ops/Characteristics
2016.pdf; "Characteristics of Supplemental Nutrition Assistance Program
Households: Fiscal Year 2017" US Department of Agriculture, 2019, Table 3.5, https://fns-prod.azureedge.net/sites/default/files/resource-files
/Characteristics2017.pdf.

118. Tim Wise, "Black Kids Aren't 'Illegitimate,' Your Data Comprehension
Is: Racist Lies About Out-of-Wedlock Birthrates," *Medium*, February 12,
2018, https://medium.com/@timjwise/black-kids-arent-illegitimate-your
-data-comprehension-is-racist-lies-about-out-of-wedlock-836fa501b869.

119. See Cashin, *Loving*, 10.

120. Cashin, *Loving*, chapter 8; Katie Toth, "'Ghetto Parties' Common On
College Campuses," WSHU Public Radio, March 1, 2016, https://www
.wshu.org/post/ghetto-parties-common-college-campuses#stream/0; Kristen Decarr, "'Ghetto-Themed' Party Offends at CT's Fairfield University,"
Education News, March 3, 2016.

121. Juliana Menasce Horowitz, Anna Brown, and Kiana Cox, *Race in America 2019* (Pew Research Center, April 9, 2019), https://www.pewsocial
trends.org/2019/04/09/race-in-america-2019.

122. Horowitz et al., *Race in America 2019*.

123. Horowitz et al., *Race in America 2019*; Erin Cooley, Jazmin Brown-
Iannuzzi, and D'Jonita Cottrell, "Liberals Perceive More Racism Than
Conservatives When Police Shoot Black Men—But, Reading About White
Privilege Increases Perceived Racism, and Shifts Attributions of Guilt, Re-
gardless of Political Ideology," *Journal of Experimental Social Psychology*
85 (2019): 1–9, doi:10.1016/j.jesp.2019.103885.

124. Steven A. Tuch and Michael Hughes. "Whites' Racial Policy Attitudes in the Twenty-First Century: The Continuing Significance of Racial Resentment," in *Race, Racial Attitudes, and Stratification Beliefs: Evolving Directions for Research and Policy*, ed. Matthew O. Hunt and George Wilson, 134–52 (Thousand Oaks, CA: Sage Publications, 2011).

CHAPTER 5: OPPORTUNITY HOARDING

 1. Melissa DePino (@missydepino), Twitter, April 12, 2018, 5:12 p.m., https://twitter.com/missydepino/status/984539713016094721?lang=en.
 2. Elijah Anderson, "The White Space," *Sociology of Race and Ethnicity* 1, no. 1 (2015); Elise C. Boddie, "Racial Territoriality," *UCLA Law Review* 58: 401–462 (2010), 407 (noting that "a primary vehicle for racial discrimination against people of color historically has been exclusion from white space").
 3. Anderson, "The White Space," 10, 19.
 4. Anderson, "The White Space," 18–19.
 5. "Attraction: Rittenhouse Square," Visit Philadelphia, https://www.visit philly.com/things-to-do/attractions/rittenhouse-square-park.
 6. Paul Jargowsky, "Architecture of Segregation," Century Foundation, August 7, 2015, https://tcf.org/content/report/architecture-of-segregation.
 7. Jargowsky, "Architecture of Segregation."
 8. John L. Dorman, "August Wilson's Pittsburgh," *New York Times*, August 15, 2017, https://www.nytimes.com/2017/08/15/travel/august-wilsons -pittsburgh.html; Christine H. O'Toole, "Hill Streets," *The Magazine of the Heinz Endowments* 2 (2018): 36, https://www.heinz.org/UserFiles /Library/2018_Issue_2-complete.pdf.
 9. "Stories of Housing Mobility In Dallas," Mobility Works, January 2015, https://www.housingmobility.org/stories-housing-mobility-clients-dallas.
10. Alan Mallach, *The Divided City: Poverty and Prosperity in Urban America* (Washington, DC: Island Press, 2018), 88, Kindle, citing Joe Cortright and Dillon Mahmoudi, "Lost in Place: Why the Persistence and Spread of Concentrated Poverty—Not Gentrification—Is Our Biggest Urban Challenge," *City Observatory*, December 2014, http://cityobservatory.org/wp -content/uploads/2014/12/LostinPlace_12.4.pdf.
11. Elizabeth C. Delmelle, "The Increasing Sociospatial Fragmentation of Urban America," *Urban Science* 3, no. 9 (2019), https://doi.org/10.3390 /urbansci3010009. See also Richard Florida, "Urban Neighborhoods, Once Distinct by Race and Class, Are Blurring," *Bloomberg CityLab*, February 9, 2019, https://www.citylab.com/life/2019/02/city-race-class -neighborhood-white-black-rich-segregate/583039.
12. "Philadelphia City Council Passes Landmark $100 Million Affordable Housing Package," Philadelphia City Council, October 4, 2018, http:// phlcouncil.com/philadelphia-city-council-passes-landmark-100-million -affordable-housing-package.
13. Mallach, *The Divided City*, 113, 96, 118; Joe Cortright, "Is St. Louis Gentrifying," *City Observatory*, August 14, 2018, http://cityobservatory .org/is-st-louis-gentrifying; Cortright and Mahmoudi, "Lost in Place: Why

the Persistence and Spread of Concentrated Poverty—Not Gentrification—Is Our Biggest Urban Challenge"; Richard Florida, "The Complicated Link Between Gentrification and Displacement," *Bloomberg CityLab*, September 8, 2015, https://www.citylab.com/equity/2015/09/the-complicated-link -between-gentrification-and-displacement/404161.

14. Isabel Wilkerson, *Caste: The Origins of Our Discontents* (New York: Random House, 2020), 58, Kindle.

15. Sampson, *Great American City*, 302.

16. Sharkey, *Stuck in Place*, 5.

17. Spader et al., "Fostering Inclusion in American Neighborhoods," 29–30, 37.

18. Sheryll D. Cashin, "Integration as a Means of Restoring Democracy and Opportunity," in Herbert et al., *A Shared Future*, 68.

19. Cashin, "Integration as a Means of Restoring Democracy and Opportunity."

20. Thurston Domina, "Brain Drain and Brain Gain: Rising Educational Segregation in the United States, 1940–2000," *City and Community* 5, no. 4 (2006): 394.

21. For polling evidence of the values animating the persistent belief in the American Dream, see, e.g., Samantha Smith, "Most Think the 'American Dream' Is Within Reach for Them," Pew Research Center, October 31, 2017, http://www.pewresearch.org/fact-tank/2017/10/31/most-think-the -american-dream-is-within-reach-for-them.

22. See Charles Tilly and Arnold S. Feldman, "The Interaction of Social and Physical Space," *American Sociological Review* 25 (1960): 877–84; Charles Tilly, *Durable Inequality* (Berkeley: University of California Press, 1998). Subsequent studies cite *Durable Inequality* in analyzing the stubborn persistence of categorical differences and the boundary maintenance such persistence entails. See, for example, Paul Hanselman and Jeremy E. Fiel, "School Opportunity Hoarding? Racial Segregation and Access to High Growth Schools," *Social Forces* 95, no. 3 (March 2017): 1098, doi: 10.1093/sf/sow088, applying Tilly's framework and discussing boundary maintenance, social distancing, and opportunity hoarding as distinct concepts.

23. Justin Steil and Reed Jordan, "Household Neighborhood Decisionmaking and Segregation," in Herbert et al., *A Shared Future*, 114–24.

24. Lawrence D. Bobo et al., "The Real Record on Racial Attitudes," in *Social Trends in American Life: Findings from the General Social Survey Since 1972*, ed. Peter V. Marsden (Princeton, NJ: Princeton University Press, 2012), 38–93.

25. Reeves, *Dream Hoarders*, 104.

26. Cashin, *The Failures of Integration*.

27. Massey and Rugh, "Segregation in Post-Civil Rights America," 205–32.

28. In fact, Texas ranked on par with Cameroon, Ecuador, and Peru on common measures of income inequality and low on social mobility. See Thomas Brown et al., "Intergenerational Mobility Project: A Snapshot of Social Mobility in Texas," Hobby School of Public Affairs at University of Hous-

ton White Paper Series, June 2017, http://www.uh.edu/hobby/cpp/white
-paper-series/hspa-white-paper-series_no-12.pdf.

29. See Kriston Capps, "Another Front in the Texas War to Preserve Segregated
Housing," *Bloomberg CityLab*, February 15, 2017, https://www.citylab
.com/equity/2017/02/texas-legislation-gives-neighborhoods-right-to-veto
-low-income-housing/516723, noting that "since 2001, Texas law has given
state legislators unprecedented power over the competitive application process for LIHTC projects in their districts" and that "one opposing letter has
the potential to defeat an application."

30. Mallach, *The Divided City*, 188, citing University of Kansas professor Kirk
McClure quoted in Laura Sullivan, "Affordable Housing Program Costs
More, Shelters Fewer," NPR, May 9, 2017, https://www.wvtf.org/post
/affordable-housing-program-costs-more-shelters-less#stream/0.

31. This admission appeared in Houston's "Analysis of Impediments to Fair Housing Choice," submitted to HUD in 2015 as part of the process for compliance
with the Fair Housing Act. See Neal Rackleff, "2015 Analysis of Impediments
to Fair Housing Choice," City of Houston Housing and Community Development, August 2015, https://houstontx.gov/housing/plans-reports/impediments/
AI%20Final%208.18.2015%20reduced%20size.pdf.

32. Robert Fairbanks, *War on the Slums in the Southwest: Public Housing and
Slum Clearance in Texas, Arizona, and New Mexico, 1935–1965* (Philadelphia: Temple University Press, 2014).

33. "Video: Anger over Proposed Public Housing in High Opportunity Houston
Neighborhood," Texas Housers, March 14, 2016, https://texas
housers.net/2016/03/14/video-anger-over-proposed-public-housing-in-high
-opportunity-houston-neighborhood. Culberson, a nine-term Republican
incumbent, was defeated by a moderate Democrat, Lizzie Pannill Fletcher,
in 2018.

34. "Video: Anger over Proposed Public Housing."

35. John Henneberger, "Houston, It's Time to Stop Accommodating Segregation," *Shelterforce*, February 7, 2017, https://shelterforce.org/2017/02/07
/houston-its-time-to-stop-accommodating-segregation.

36. Alvaro "Al" Ortiz, "Turner Announces Agreement Resolving HUD's Investigation That Found Improprieties on Procedures for Low Income Housing
Projects," Houston Public Media, March 9, 2018, https://www.houston
publicmedia.org/articles/news/2018/03/09/272519/turner-announces
-agreement-resolving-huds-investigation-that-found-improprieties-on
-procedures-for-low-income-housing-projects.

37. Andrew Giambrone, "Map: Nearly All of D.C.'s New Affordable Housing
Is Being Developed East of Rock Creek Park," DC Curbed, September 11,
2018, https://dc.curbed.com/2018/9/11/17846984/map-affordable-housing
-rock-creek-park-dcfpi.

38. Comments made by Robert Stumburg and Michael Diamond, two profes-
sors at Georgetown Law at the author's June 4, 2019, faculty talk.

39. Cashin, "Integration as a Means of Restoring Democracy and Opportunity;" Massey, *Categorically Unequal*.

40. Brent Elementary School, District of Columbia Public Schools, https://
    profiles.dcps.dc.gov/Brent+Elementary+School, accessed October 12, 2020;
    Payne Elementary School, District of Columbia Public Schools, https://
    profiles.dcps.dc.gov/Payne+Elementary+School, accessed October 12, 2020.
41. Greg Toppo and Paul Overberg, "Diversity in the Classroom: Sides Square
    Off in Minnesota," *USA Today*, March 18, 2015, https://www.usatoday
    .com/story/news/nation/2014/11/25/minnesota-school-race-diversity
    /18919391. See also "A Plan to Diversify New York's Segregated Schools,"
    editorial, *New York Times*, September 2, 2019, https://www.nytimes.com
    /2019/09/02/opinion/nyc-schools.html (city officials saying they are strongly
    encouraging school districts across the city to adopt integration plans).
42. William J. Mathis, "The Effectiveness of Class Size Reduction," National Ed-
    ucation Policy Center at University of Colorado Boulder, June 2016, https://
    nepc.colorado.edu/sites/default/files/publications/Mathis%20RBOPM-9%
    20Class%20Size.pdf.
43. "Segregated in the Heartland," *Governing*, January 23, 2019, https://www
    .governing.com/topics/public-justice-safety/gov-segregation-series.html.
44. Emily Badger and Darla Cameron, "How Railroads, Highways and Other
    Man-made Lines Racially Divide America's Cities," *Washington Post*, July
    16, 2015, https://www.washingtonpost.com/news/wonk/wp/2015/07/16
    /how-railroads-highways-and-other-man-made-lines-racially-divide
    -americas-cities/?utm_term=.8dabc8fb73b7.
45. "Crossing a St. Louis Street That Divides Communities," Vimeo, Septem-
    ber 25, 2012, https://vimeo.com/50172283; see also Melody Goodman,
    "White Fear Creates White Spaces and Exacerbates Health Disparities,"
    Institute for Public Health at Washington University School of Medicine,
    February 16, 2016, https://publichealth.wustl.edu/white-fear-creates-white
    -spaces-and-exacerbates-health-disparities/ (including a visual of the Del-
    mar Divide with demographic data of the two areas separated by the Del-
    mar Boulevard).
46. As of 2016, Census Tract 106 was 65 percent white with a median income
    of $109,000. It is immediately adjacent to Census Tract 88.03 which was
    63 percent Black with a median income of $17,303. See American Commu-
    nity Survey (2016).
47. Jon Banister, "Zoning Commission Approves Updated Plans for 1,100-Unit
    Sursum Corda Project," *Bisnow*, October 23, 2019, https://www.bisnow
    .com/washington-dc/news/multifamily/zoning-commission-approves-updated
    -plans-for-1100-unit-sursum-corda-project-101441.
48. Derek Hyra, "The Back-to-the-City Movement: Neighborhood Redevelop-
    ment and Processes of Political and Cultural Displacement," *Urban Studies*
    52, no. 10 (2015): 1753–73.
49. Massey, *Categorically Unequal*, 19.
50. Mallach, *The Divided City*, 142, noting "the complex relationship between
    gentrification and decline [elsewhere], and the fact that the overarching
    question of power transcends and subsumes both."
51. Sean F. Reardon and Kendra Bischoff, "Income Inequality and Income Seg-
    regation," *American Journal of Sociology* 116, no. 4 (2011): 1092–1155.

52. Natalie Sabadish and Lawrence Mishel, "CEO Pay in 2012 Was Extraordinarily High Relative to Typical Workers and Other High Earners," Issue Brief #367, Economic Policy Institute, June 26, 2013, https://files.epi.org /2013/ceo-pay-2012-extraordinarily-high.pdf; Diana Hembree, "CEO Pay Skyrockets to 361 Times That of the Average Worker," Forbes, May 22, 2018, https://www.forbes.com/sites/dianahembree/2018/05/22/ceo-pay -skyrockets-to-361-times-that-of-the-average-worker/#25b77268776d.

53. Others have made similar arguments. See, e.g., Reeves, Dream Hoarders, 104–8, quoting economists.

54. Reardon and Bischoff, "Income Inequality and Income Segregation."

55. Vinnie Rotondaro, "Once-Aspirational Philadelphia Suburbs Struggle with Poverty," National Catholic Reporter, March 25, 2015, https://www.ncr online.org/news/parish/once-aspirational-philadelphia-suburbs-struggle -poverty.

56. Mallach, The Divided City, 170, 205, 288.

57. Cashin, Place, Not Race, 24.

58. Jargowsky, "Architecture of Segregation."

59. Cashin, The Failures of Integration, 110–17, 355n66.

60. Cashin, The Failures of Integration; Cashin, "Localism, Self-Interest and the Tyranny of the Favored," Georgetown University Law Center, Business, Economics, and Regulatory Law Working Paper No. 194751 (December 1999), http://dx.doi.org/10.2139/ssrn.194751; Myron Orfield, Metropolitics: A Regional Agenda for Community and Stability (Washington, DC: Brookings Institution Press, 1997).

61. Jessica Trounstine, Segregation by Design: Local Politics and Inequality in American Cities (Cambridge, UK: Cambridge University Press, 2018), 253, 446, 491, 616, Kindle.

62. Troustine, Segregation by Design, 650, 675.

63. Trounstine, Segregation by Design, 678.

64. Andrea Gibbons, City of Segregation: 100 Years of Struggle for Housing in Los Angeles (New York: Verso, 2018); Mallach, The Divided City.

65. Mallach, The Divided City, 111, 211–12.

66. Mallach, The Divided City, 234.

67. David Jackson, "Chicago Development Programs Bypass Austin," Chicago Tribune, September 28, 2013, https://www.chicagotribune.com/news/ct -xpm-2013-09-28-ct-met-austin-development-history-20130929-story.html.

68. Brett Theodos et al., "Neighborhood Disparities in Investment Flows in Chicago," Urban Institute, May 2019, https://www.urban.org/sites/default /files/publication/100261/neighborhood_disparities_in_investment_flows _in_chicago_1.pdf.

69. Cashin, The Failures of Integration, 117–23.

70. Kelly M. Bower et al., "The Intersection of Neighborhood Racial Segregation, Poverty, and Urbanicity and Its Impact on Food Store Availability in the United States," Preventive Medicine 58 (2014): 33–39, doi:10.1016/j .ypmed.2013.10.010.

71. Rachel Weber et al., Why These Schools? Explaining School Closures in Chicago, 2000–2013 (Chicago: Great Cities Institute, University of Illinois

at Chicago, November 2016), 21, https://greatcities.uic.edu/wp-content
/uploads/2017/01/School-Closure.pdf.

72. Randall K. Johnson, "Where Schools Close in Chicago," *Albany Government Law Review* 7 (2014): 508, 518.

73. Pavlyn Jankov and Carol Caref, "Segregation and Inequality in Chicago Public Schools, Transformed and Intensified Under Corporate Education Reform," *Education Policy Analysis Archives* 25 (2017): 2, 19.

74. Jessica Shiller, "The Disposability of Baltimore's Black Communities: A Participatory Action Research Project on the Impact of School Closings," *Urban Review* 50, no. 1 (2017): 23–44.

75. Mallach, *The Divided City*, 124, 205, 223, 234, 240–44.

76. Mary Hui, "What City Bus Systems Can Tell Us About Race, Poverty and Us," *Washington Post*, September 7, 2017, https://www.washingtonpost
.com/local/social-issues/what-city-bus-systems-can-tell-us-about-race-poverty
-and-who-we-are/2017/09/07/6531d26a-9260-11e7-8754-d478688d23b4
_story.html.

77. Gillian B. White, "Our Struggling Public Transportation System Is Failing America's Poor," *Atlantic*, May 16, 2015, https://www.theatlantic.com
/business/archive/2015/05/stranded-how-americas-failing-public
-transportation-increases-inequality/393419.

78. Rebecca Benincasa and Robert Benincasa, "How Federal Disaster Money Favors the Rich," NPR, March 5, 2019, https://www.npr.org/2019/03/05
/688786177/how-federal-disaster-money-favors-the-rich; Junia Howell and James R. Elliott, "As Disaster Costs Rise, So Does Inequality," *Socius: Sociological Research for a Dynamic World* 4 (2018), https://doi.org/10.1177
/2378023118816795.

79. Jeff Ernsthausen and Justin Elliott, "One Trump Tax Cut Was Meant to Help the Poor. A Billionaire Ended Up Winning Big," ProPublica, June 19, 2019, https://www.propublica.org/article/trump-inc-podcast-one-trump
-tax-cut-meant-to-help-the-poor-a-billionaire-ended-up-winning-big. See also Adam Looney, "Will Opportunity Zones Help Distressed Residents or Be a Tax Cut for Gentrification?," *Brookings*, February 26, 2018, https://
www.brookings.edu/blog/up-front/2018/02/26/will-opportunity-zones-help
-distressed-residents-or-be-a-tax-cut-for-gentrification, noting that this tax "subsidy [is] based on capital appreciation, not on employment or local services, and includes no provisions intended to retain local residents or promote inclusive housing" and because the subsidy's value depends on "rising property values, rising rents, and higher business profitability" it could end up being a subsidy for displacement and gentrification.

80. Timothy Weaver, "Tax Law's 'Opportunity Zones' Won't Create Opportunities for the People Who Need It Most," *The Conversation*, May 15, 2018, http://theconversation.com/tax-laws-opportunity-zones-wont-create
-opportunities-for-the-people-who-need-it-most-94955.

81. Aaron Glantz and Emmanuel Martinez, "For People of Color, Bans Are Shutting the Door to Homeownership," *Reveal*, February 15, 2018, https://
www.revealnews.org/article/for-people-of-color-banks-are-shutting-the-door
-to-homeownership.

82. Glantz and Martinez, "For People of Color, Bans Are Shutting the Door to Homeownership."

83. Aaronson et al., "The Effects of HOLC's 'Redlining' Maps"; Jacob Faber, "Contemporary Echoes of Segregationist Policy: Spatial Marking and the Persistence of Inequality," *Urban Studies* (2020), https://doi.org/10.1177/0042098020947341.

84. Faber, "Contemporary Echoes of Segregationist Policy."

85. Jeremiah Battle Jr., Sarah Mancini, Margot Saunders, and Odette Williamson, *Toxic Transactions: How Land Installment Contracts Once Again Threaten Communities of Color* (National Consumer Law Center, July 2016), https://www.nclc.org/images/pdf/pr-reports/report-land-contracts.pdf.

86. See Keeanga-Yamahtta Taylor, *Race for Profit: How Banks and the Real Estate Industry Undermined Black Homeownership* (Chapel Hill: University of North Carolina Press, 2019).

87. "Property Taxes and Equity," Harris Public Policy, University of Chicago, https://harris.uchicago.edu/research-impact/centers-institutes/center-municipal-finance/research-projects/property-tax, accessed February 1, 2021.

88. Bernadette Atuahene, "Predatory Cities," *California Law Review* 108, no. 1 (February 2020): 107, https://doi.org/10.15779/Z38NS0KZ30.

89. Legal scholar Daria Roitmayr makes a similar though broader claim that racial inequality reproduces itself automatically from generation to generation, a "lock-in" effect of racial monopoly power, though I offer a geographic analysis that complicates this picture and illuminates the dominance of wealthy white enclaves. See Daria Roithmayr, *Reproducing Racism: How Everyday Choices Lock In White Advantage* (New York: New York University Press, 2014).

CHAPTER 6: MORE OPPORTUNITY HOARDING

1. "Nonwhite School Districts Get $23 Billion Less Than White Districts Despite Serving the Same Number of Students," *EdBuild*, https://edbuild.org/content/23-billion, accessed February 1, 2021.

2. George Orwell, *Animal Farm* (Orlando: Harcourt Brace, 1990), 118.

3. Andreas Schleicher, ed., *Preparing Teachers and Developing School Leaders for the 21st Century: Lessons from Around the World* (Paris: Organisation for Economic Co-Operation and Development, 2012), www.oecd.org/site/eduistp2012/49850576.pdf.

4. Bruce D. Baker, Danielle Farrie, and David Sciarra, "Is School Funding Fair? A National Report Card," iv–v, http://www.edlawcenter.org/assets/files/pdfs/publications/Is_School_Funding_Fair_7th_Editi.pdf.

5. Baker et al., "Is School Funding Fair? A National Report Card," iv.

6. Mary McKillip, "Tracking State School Aid Cuts in the Pandemic," Education Law Center, August 25, 2020, https://edlawcenter.org/news/archives/school-funding-national/tracking-state-school-aid-cuts-in-the-pandemic.html.

7. Baker et al., "Is School Funding Fair?," 1. "States that invest in the resources that matter—low pupil-to-teacher ratios, especially for high poverty

districts, and competitive wages—tend to have higher academic outcomes among children from low-income families and smaller income-based achievement gaps."

8. Cashin, *The Failures of Integration*, 268.

9. Interview with Laurence Spring, March 11, 2019, notes on file with the author; see also John Kucsera and Gary Orfield, *New York State's Extreme School Segregation: Inequality, Inaction and a Damaged Future* (Civil Rights Project, March 2014), https://civilrightsproject.ucla.edu/research /k-12-education/integration-and-diversity/ny-norflet-report-placeholder /Kucsera-New-York-Extreme-Segregation-2014.pdf.

10. Laurence T. Spring, "Schenectady City District Complaint Under the Civil Rights Act of 1964 and the Equal Educational Opportunities Act of 1974," http://www.schenectady.k12.ny.us/UserFiles/Servers/Server_412252/Image /Advocacy/USDeptofED_OCR_Complaint.pdf, 13–16.

11. Mary Lou Lang, "Feds to Investigate Alleged Discrimination in Aid to NY Schools," *Washington Free Beacon*, December 5, 2014, https://freebeacon .com/issues/feds-to-investigate-alleged-discrimination-in-aid-to-ny-schools.

12. Spring, "Schenectady City District Complaint."

13. Spring, "Schenectady City District Complaint," 2.

14. Interview with Laurence Spring, March 11, 2019, notes on file with the author.

15. Interview with Laurence Spring, March 11, 2019.

16. Interview with Laurence Spring, March 11, 2019.

17. New York Advisory Committee to the US Commission on Civil Rights, *Education Equity in New York: A Forgotten Dream* (US Commission on Civil Rights, February 10, 2020), usccr.gov, 106–23, https://www.usccr.gov/pubs /2020/02–10-Education-Equity-in-New%20York.pdf.

18. Letter from Timothy C. J. Blanchard, director, New York Office of US Dept. of Education Office of Civil Rights to MaryElle Elia, commissioner, New York State Education Department, April 17, 2020, obtained by Freedom of Information Act Request and on file with the author, emphasis added.

19. Ivy Morgan and Ary Amerikaner, *Funding Gaps: An Analysis of School Funding Equity Across the US and Within Each State* (Education Trust, February 2018), https://edtrust.org/wp-content/uploads/2014/09/Funding GapReport_2018_FINAL.pdf; "Spending Per Pupil Increased for Sixth Consecutive Year," US Census Bureau, May 11, 2020, https://www.census .gov/newsroom/press-releases/2020/school-system-finances.html.

20. Joseph Spector, "Why School Funding in New York Is Still a Major Fight," *Democrat & Chronicle*, March 22, 2019, https://www.democratand chronicle.com/story/news/politics/albany/2019/03/20/why-school-funding -new-york-still-major-fight/3139023002.

21. Interview with Laurence Spring, March 11, 2019; New York Advisory Committee to the US Commission on Civil Rights, *Education Equity in New York*, 140.

22. Peter Goodman, March 5, 2019, "The (Maryland) Kirwan Commission: Is It Time for New York State to Investigate Changing School Funding Formulas as Well as Educational Governance and Priorities?," *Ed in the Apple*,

https://mets2006.wordpress.com/2019/03/05/the-maryland-kirwan
-commission-is-it-time-for-new-york-state-to-investigate-changing-school
-funding-formulas-as-well-as-educational-governance-and-priorities.
23. Cashin, *The Failures of Integration*, 268.
24. Jim Malatras, *Uneven Distribution of Education Aid within Big 5 School Districts in New York State* (Rockefeller Institute of Government, November 14, 2018), https://rockinst.org/wp-content/uploads/2018/11/11-13-18 -School-Spending-in-NYS_FINAL.pdf.
25. Eliza Shapiro and K. K. Rebecca Lai, "How New York's Elite Public Schools Lost Their Black and Hispanic Students," *New York Times*, June 3, 2019, https://www.nytimes.com/interactive/2019/06/03/nyregion/nyc-public -schools-black-hispanic-students.html.
26. Jose Vilson, "The New York City School Controversy Shows Why Standardized Testing Is Broken," *Vox*, March 22, 2019, https://www.vox.com /first-person/2019/3/22/18276408/new-york-city-stuyvesant-high-school -brooklyn-tech-science.
27. Plaintiffs' Corrected Third Amended Complaint, Connecticut Coalition for Justice in Education Funding, Inc. v. Rell, 295 Conn. 240 A.2d (Conn. 2010), http://ccjef.org/wp-content/uploads/CCJEF-v-Rell-Plaintiffs-Corrected -Third-Amended-Complaint-Jan-7-2013.pdf; Alana Semuels, "Good School, Rich School; Bad School, Poor School," *Atlantic*, August 25, 2016, https://www.theatlantic.com/business/archive/2016/08/property-taxes-and -unequal-schools/497333.
28. Semuels, "Good School, Rich School; Bad School, Poor School."
29. Plaintiffs' Corrected Third Amended Complaint, *Rell*.
30. Matthew Kauffman and Edmund H. Mahony, "State Supreme Court Overturns Sweeping Ruling in CCJEF Education Funding Lawsuit," *Hartford Courant*, January 18, 2018, https://www.courant.com/news/connecticut /hc-news-ccjef-education-ruling-20180117-story.html.
31. Kauffman and Mahony, "State Supreme Court Overturns Sweeping Ruling in CCJEF Education Funding Lawsuit."
32. The Connecticut Supreme Court did not acknowledge the state's racially segregated landscape and certainly did not assert that law requires formal equality. Instead the Connecticut Supreme Court legitimized systemic educational inequality between rich schools and poor ones by stressing that "court's primary focus should be on the adequacy of educational inputs . . ." See Connecticut Coalition for Justice in Education Funding, Inc. v. Rell, 327 Conn. 650, 706 (2018). Once the state showed that it had met the "minimally adequate" standard, the courts had no further role to play in the policy judgments involved in allocating resources for education; Kauffman and Mahony, "State Supreme Court Overturns Sweeping Ruling in CCJEF Education Funding Lawsuit."
33. Roger L. Kemp, "Chapter 6: Fundamental Orders of Connecticut (January 14, 1639)," in *Documents of American Democracy: A Collection of Essential Works*, ed. Roger L. Kemp (Jefferson, NC: McFarland, 2010), 37.
34. Jason Reece, Samir Gambhir, Jilian Olinger, Matthew Martin, and Mark Harris, *People, Place and Opportunity: Mapping Communities of*

Opportunity in Connecticut (Connecticut Fair Housing Center, November 2009), https://www.ctfairhousing.org/wp-content/uploads/People-Place-and -Opportunity.pdf. The Othering & Belonging Institute at UC Berkeley, which john a. powell now heads, continues to refine the methodology and tools of opportunity mapping to enable similar mapping of regions across the country. See Othering & Belonging Institute, "Opportunity Mapping Project," https://belonging.berkeley.edu/opportunity-mapping-project, accessed February 20, 2021.

35. Reece et al., *People, Place and Opportunity*, 5.

36. "Mayor's Office," West Hartford, https://www.westhartfordct.gov /government-services/mayors-office, accessed October 5, 2020.

37. Interview with Phil Tegeler, October 10, 2020, notes on file with the author.

38. Katie Roy, "Lawmakers Are Jeopardizing School Funding Equity—Again," *CT Mirror*, May 13, 2019, https://ctmirror.org/category/ct-viewpoints /lawmakers-are-jeopardizing-school-funding-equity-again.

39. Luke Broadwater, "Maryland School Funding Legislation Calls for $1 Billion over Two Years to Start Meeting Kirwan Goals," *Baltimore Sun*, March 4, 2019, https://www.baltimoresun.com/politics/bs-md-kirwan-bill -20190304-story.html.

40. Liz Bowie and Talia Richman, "Civil Rights Groups Ask Court to Force Maryland to Spend Hundreds of Millions More on Baltimore Schools," *Baltimore Sun*, March 8, 2019, https://www.baltimoresun.com/maryland /baltimore-city/bs-md-lawsuit-aclu-20190307-story.html.

41. Memorandum of Grounds, Points, and Authorities in Support of Plaintiffs' Petition for Further Relief, *Bradford v. Maryland State Board of Education*, https://www.aclu-md.org/sites/default/files/bradford_memoranduminsupport ofpetition.pdf.

42. "Climate Change: Creating an Integrated Framework for Improving School Climate," Alliance for Excellent Education, August 2013, https://all4ed.org /wp-content/uploads/2013/09/HSClimate1.pdf.

43. Dan Goldhaber, Lesley Lavery, and Roddy Theobald, "Uneven Playing Field? Assessing the Teacher Quality Gap Between Advantaged and Disadvantaged Students," *Educational Researcher* 44, no. 5 (2015): 293, doi: 10.3102/0013189X15592622.

44. C. Kirabo Jackson, "Student Demographics, Teacher Sorting, and Teacher Quality: Evidence from the End of School Desegregation," *Journal of Labor Economics* 27, no. 2 (2009): 213.

45. P. Iatrarola and L. Stiefel, "Intradistrict Equity of Public Education Resources and Performance," *Economics of Education Review* 22, no. 1 (2003): 77, doi:10.1016/S0272–7757(01)00065–6; Hamilton Lankford, Susanna Loeb, and James Wyckoff, "Teacher Sorting and the Plight of Urban Schools: A Descriptive Analysis," *Educational Evaluation and Policy Analysis* 24, no. 1 (2002): 54–55, doi:10.3102/01623737024001037; Marguerite Roza et al., "How Within-District Spending Inequities Help Some Schools to Fail," *Brookings Papers on Education Policy* 7 (2004): 202, https:// www.jstor.org/stable/20067269; Ross Rubenstein, "Resource Equity in the Chicago Public Schools: A School-Level Approach," *Journal of Education*

Finance 23, no. 4 (1998): 487, https://www.jstor.org/stable/40704039; Kenneth Shores and Simon Ejdemyr, "Pulling Back the Curtain: Intra-District School Spending Inequality and Its Correlates," *SSRN Electronic Journal* (2017): 3, doi:10.2139/ssrn.3009775.

46. John R. Logan, Elisabeta Minca, and Sinem Adar, "The Geography of Inequality: Why Separate Means Unequal in American Public Schools," *Sociology of Education* 85 (2012): 287–301.

47. Schleicher, *Preparing Teachers and Developing School Leaders for the 21st Century.*

48. Erica Frankenberg, Jongyeon Ee, Jennifer B. Ayscue, and Gary Orfield, "Harming Our Common Future: America's Segregated Schools 65 Years After Brown," Civil Rights Project, May 10, 2019, https://www.civilrights project.ucla.edu/research/k-12-education/integration-and-diversity/harming -our-common-future-americas-segregated-schools-65-years-after-brown /Brown-65-050919v4-final.pdf.

49. "Dismissed: America's Most Divisive Borders," *EdBuild*, https://edbuild .org/content/dismissed, accessed October 14, 2020.

50. Nancy McArdle and Dolores Acevedo-Garcia, "Consequences of Segregation for Children's Opportunity and Wellbeing," paper presented at A Shared Future: Fostering Communities of Inclusion in an Era of Inequality, a national symposium hosted by the Harvard Joint Center for Housing Studies, April 2017, 8.

51. Raegen Miller and Diana Epstein, *There Still Be Dragons: Racial Disparity in School Funding Is No Myth* (Center for American Progress, July 5, 2011), https://www.americanprogress.org/issues/education-k-12/reports /2011/07/05/9943/there-still-be-dragons.

52. "Projections of Education Statistics to 2026 Forty-Fifth Edition," US Department of Education, April 2018, https://nces.ed.gov/pubs2018/2018019.pdf.

53. John A. Powell, "The Tensions Between Integration and School Reform," *Hastings Constitutional Law Quarterly* 28 (2001): 655.

54. Brown v. Board of Education of Topeka, 347 U.S. 483, 493 (1954).

55. Appellate Brief for Appellants, *Brown v. Board of Education of Topeka*, 11, https://www.naacpldf.org/wp-content/uploads/Oliver-BROWN-Mrs-Richard -Lawton-Mrs-Sadie-Emmanuel-et-al-Appellants-v-BOARD-OF-E-1.pdf.

56. Josephine Sedgwick, "25-Year-Old Textbooks and Holes in the Ceiling: Inside America's Public Schools," *New York Times*, April 16, 2018, https://www .nytimes.com/2018/04/16/reader-center/us-public-schools-conditions.html.

57. Noliwe Rooks, *Cutting School: Privatization, Segregation, and the End of Public Education* (New York: New Press, 2017).

58. "Redlining Louisville: Racial Capitalism and Real Estate," https://www.arc- gis.com/apps/MapSeries/index.html?appid=a73ce5ba85ce4c3f80d365 ab1ff89010, accessed February 1, 2021; Gil Corsey, "Once a Booming Strip of Black Business, Wall Street Faded from Louisville's Memory for Failed Urban Renewal," last updated February 27, 2020, https://www.wdrb.com /in-depth/once-a-booming-strip-of-black-business-walnut-street-faded-from -louisvilles-memory-for-failed/article_fc600e82–580f-11ea-9ea5–638cf333 c542.html.

59. Century Foundation, *Louisville, Kentucky: A Reflection on School Integration* (September 15, 2016), https://production-tcf.imgix.net/app/uploads/2016/09 /03193859/louisville-kentucky-a-reflection-on-school-integration.pdf.

60. Elizabeth Gillespie McRae, *Mothers of Massive Resistance: White Women and the Politics of White Supremacy* (New York: Oxford University Press, 2018), 4.

61. Parents Involved in Community Schools v. Seattle School District No. 1, 551 U.S. 701 (2007).

62. Semuels, "The City That Believed in Desegregation"; Genevieve Siegel-Hawley, "City Lines, County Lines, Color Lines: The Relationship Between School and Housing Segregation in Four Southern Metro Areas," *Teachers College Record* 115 (2013): 1, 12, 14.

63. Siegel-Hawley, "City Lines, County Lies, Color Lines," 1, 24; see also Karl E. Taeuber, "Housing, Schools, and Incremental Segregative Effects," *Annals of American Academy of Political and Social Science* 441, no. 157 (1979).

64. Alana Semuels, "The City That Believed in Desegregation," *Atlantic*, March 27, 2015, https://www.theatlantic.com/business/archive/2015/03/the -city-that-believed-in-desegregation/388532.

65. Semuels, "The City That Believed in Desegregation."

66. "Redlining Louisville: The History of Race, Class, and Real Estate," Redlining Louisville, Louisville/Jefferson County Information Consortium, December 14, 2017, https://www.lojic.org/redlining-louisville-news.

67. "Redlining Louisville: Racial Capitalism and Real Estate"; Brentin Mock, "Louisville Confronts Its Redlining Past and Present," *Bloomberg CityLab*, February 21, 2017, https://www.citylab.com/equity/2017/02 /louisville-confronts-its-redlining-past-and-present/517125; "City Begins Community Conversation to Combat Redlining," *City News*, February 14, 2017, https://louisvilleky.gov/news/city-begins-community-conversation -combat-redlining; "Redlining Community Dialogue," Louisville, KY, gov-ernment website, https://louisvilleky.gov/government/redevelopment -strategies/redlining-community-dialogue.

68. "Housing Needs Assessment," Louisville, KY, government website, https: //louisvilleky.gov/government/housing-community-development/housing -needs-assessment.

69. Savannah Eadens, "Viral Photo Shows Line of White People Between Police, Black Protesters at Thursday Rally," *Louisville Courier Journal*, https://www.courier-journal.com/story/news/local/2020/05/29/breonna -taylor-photo-white-women-between-police-black-protesters/5286416002.

70. Semuels, "The City That Believed in Desegregation."

71. Gregory Acs, Rolf Pendall, Mark Treskon, and Amy Khare, *The Cost of Segregation National Trends and the Case of Chicago, 1990–2010* (Urban Institute, March 2017), 18–24, https://www.urban.org/sites/default/files /publication/89201/the_cost_of_segregation_final_0.pdf.

72. Raj Chetty et al., "The Opportunity Atlas: Mapping the Childhood Roots of Social Mobility," National Bureau of Economic Research Working Paper Series, October 2018, https://www.nber.org/papers/w25147.pdf.

73. Richard H. Sander et al., *Moving Toward Integration*.

74. R. A. Lenhardt, "Localities as Equality Innovators," *Stanford Journal of Civil Rights & Civil Liberties* 7 (2011): 265, 269, 291; see also Olatunde C. A. Johnson, "The Local Turn; Innovation and Diffusion in Civil Rights Law," *Law & Contemporary Problems* 79 (2016): 115.

CHAPTER 7: NEIGHBORHOOD EFFECTS

1. Lakia Barnett's self-published books are available for purchase on Amazon and her streaming radio show, *Facing Purpose*, can be found online and through her public Facebook page; see http://streaminginspiration.net /?page_id=26328, accessed October 3, 2018.

 2. Justin Jouvenal et al., "D.C. Family Homeless Shelter Beset by Dysfunction, Decay," *Washington Post*, July 12, 2014, https://www.washingtonpost.com /local/dc-family-homeless-shelter-beset-by-dysfunction-decay/2014/07/12 /3bbb7f50-f739–11e3-a3a5–42be35962a52_story.html?noredirect=on.

 3. Eloise Pasachoff, "Special Education, Poverty, and the Limits of Private Enforcement," *Notre Dame Law Review* 86 (2011): 1413–93; "A Guide to the Individualized Education Program," US Department of Education, https://www2.ed.gov/parents/needs/speced/iepguide/index.html, accessed August 12, 2019.

 4. Alison Bell, Barbara Sard, and Becky Koepnick, "Prohibiting Discrimination Against Renters Using Housing Vouchers Improves Results," Center on Budget and Policy Priorities, December 10, 2018, https://www.cbpp .org/research/housing/prohibiting-discrimination-against-renters-using -housing-vouchers-improves-results.

 5. "Garfield Elementary School," District of Columbia Public Schools, http:// profiles.dcps.dc.gov/scorecard/Garfield+Elementary+School.

 6. Peter Bergam et al., "Creating Moves to Opportunity: Experimental Evidence on Barriers to Neighborhood Choice," Harvard University (2020), https://scholar.harvard.edu/files/lkatz/files/cmto_paper.pdf.

 7. See generally Elizabeth Julian, "Making the Case for Housing Mobility: The CMTO Study in Seattle," *Poverty & Race* 28, no. 2 (2019): 10, https:// prrac.org/newsletters/may-aug2019.pdf.

 8. "The Opportunity Atlas," *Opportunity Insights*, https://www.opportunity atlas.org, accessed November 10, 2018. See also Emily Bardger and Quoctrung Bui, "Detailed Maps Show How Neighborhoods Shape Children for Life," *New York Times*, October 1, 2018, https://www.nytimes .com/2018/10/01/upshot/maps-neighborhoods-shape-child-poverty.html.

 9. Maury Elementary School," *GreatSchools*, https://www.greatschools.org /washington-dc/washington/28-Maury-Elementary-School.

10. "Maury Elementary School," District of Columbia Public Schools, http:// profiles.dcps.dc.gov/scorecard/Maury+Elementary+School.

11. John R. Logan and Brian J. Stults, "The Persistence of Segregation in the Metropolis: New Findings from the 2010 Census," US2010 Project (2011).

12. Patrick Sharkey, "Neighborhoods and the Black-White Mobility Gap," Economic Mobility Project, Pew Charitable Trust (2009).

13. Robert J. Sampson, "Durable Effects of Concentrated Disadvantage on Verbal Ability Among African American Children," *Proceedings of the National*

Academy of Sciences 105, no. 3 (2008): 845–52; Geoffrey T. Wodtke, "Neighborhood Effects in Temporal Perspective: The Impact of Long-Term Exposure to Concentrated Disadvantage on High School Graduation," *American Sociological Review* 76 (2011): 713.

14. Carolyn E. Cutrona, Gail Wallace, and Kristen A. Wesner, "Neighborhood Characteristics and Depression: An Examination of Stress Processes," *Current Directions in Psychological Science* 15, no. 4 (2006): 188–92.

15. Gary W. Evans and Pilyoung Kim, "Childhood Poverty, Chronic Stress, Self-Regulation and Coping," *Child Development Perspectives* 7, no. 1 (2013): 43–48.

16. Douglas S. Massey, "Why Death Haunts Black Lives," *Proceedings of the National Academy of Sciences* (2017). See also Sampson, *Great American City*.

17. Liam Downey and Brian Hawkins, "Race, Income, and Environmental Inequality in the United States," *Sociological Perspectives* 51, no. 4 (2008); Robert J. Sampson and Alix S. Winter, "The Racial Ecology of Lead Poisoning: Toxic Inequality in Chicago Neighborhoods: 1995–2013," *Du Bois Review: Social Science Research on Race* 13, no. 2 (2016); Matthew Desmond and Monica C. Bell, "Housing, Poverty, and the Law," *Annual Review of Law and Social Science* 11 (2015).

18. Desmond and Bell, "Housing, Poverty, and the Law," 22; Liam Downey, "Environmental Racial Inequality in Detroit," *Social Forces* 85, no. 2 (2006); Paul Mohai and Robin Saha, "Racial Inequality in the Distribution of Hazardous Waste: A National-Level Reassessment," *Social Problems* 54, no. 3 (2007); Jeremy Pais, Kyle Crowder, and Liam Downey, "Unequal Trajectories: Racial and Class Differences in Residential Exposure to Industrial Hazard," *Social Forces* 92, no. 3 (2014).

19. Brad Plumer and Nadja Popovich, "How Decades of Racist Housing Policy Left Neighborhoods Sweltering," *New York Times*, August 24, 2020, https://www.nytimes.com/interactive/2020/08/24/climate/racism-redlining -cities-global-warming.html?action=click&module=Top%20Stories &pgtype=Homepage; Jeremy S. Hoffman, Vivek Shandas, and Nicholas Pendleton, "The Effects of Historical Housing Policies on Resident Exposure to Intra-Urban Heat: A Study of 108 US Urban Areas," *Climate* (2020): 6, https://www.mdpi.com/2225-1154/8/1/12/htm.

20. Massey, "Why Death Haunts Black Lives," 1–2. See also Bruce McEwen and Elizabeth Norton Lasley, *The End of Stress as We Know It* (Washington, DC: Joseph Henry Press, 2002); Julia Burdick-Will et al., "Converging Evidence for Neighborhood Effects on Children's Test Scores: An Experimental, Quasi-Experimental, and Observational Comparison," paper prepared for the Brookings Institution, Project on Social Inequality and Educational Disadvantage, 2010; Greg J. Duncan and Richard J. Murnane, *Whither Opportunity? Rising Inequality, Schools, and Children's Life Chances* (New York: Russell Sage Foundation, 2011); Patrick S. Sharkey and Robert J. Sampson, "Violence, Cognition, and Neighborhood Inequality in America," in *Social Neuroscience: Brain, Mind, and Society*, ed. Russel K. Schutt, Larry J. Seidman, and Matcheri S. Keshavan (Cambridge,

MA: Harvard University Press, 2015); Belinda L. Needham et al., "Neighborhood Characteristics and Leukocyte Telomere Length: The Multi-Ethnic Study of Atherosclerosis," *Health Place* 28 (2014); Mijung Park et al., "Where You Live May Make You Old: The Association Between Perceived Poor Neighborhood Quality and Leukocyte Telomere Length," *Plos One* 10, no. 6 (2015); Arline T. Geronimus et al., "Race/Ethnicity, Poverty, Urban Stressors and Telomere Length in a Detroit Community-Based Sample," *Journal of Health and Social Behavior* 56, no. 2 (2015).

21. Olga Khazan, "Being Black in America Can Be Hazardous to Your Health," *Atlantic*, July/August 2018, 77–86.

22. Kelly M. Bower et al., "The Intersection of Neighborhood Racial Segregation, Poverty, and Urbanicity and Its Impact on Food Store Availability in the United States," *Preventative Medicine* 58 (2014): 2, 4.

23. Christopher Muller, Robert J. Sampson, and Alix S. Winter, "Environmental Inequality: The Social Causes and Consequences of Lead Exposure," *Annual Review of Sociology* 44 (2018).

24. Virginia Gordan, "Lawsuit: State's Emergency Manager Law Discriminates Against Black Communities," NPR: Michigan Radio, December 6, 2017, https://www.michiganradio.org/post/lawsuit-states-emergency-manager-law -discriminates-against-black-communities.

25. Paul Egan, "Flint Water Mystery: How Was the Decision Made?" *Detroit Free Press*, November 21, 2015, https://www.freep.com/story/news/politics /2015/11/21/snyders-top-aide-talked-flint-water-supply-alternatives /76037130.

26. Melissa Denchak, "Flint Water Crisis: Everything You Need to Know," National Resources Defense Council, November 8, 2018, https://www.nrdc .org/stories/flint-water-crisis-everything-you-need-know; Merit Kennedy, "Lead-Laced Water in Flint: A Step-by-Step Look at the Makings of a Crisis," *The Two Way*, NPR, April 20, 2016, https://www.npr.org/sections /thetwo-way/2016/04/20/465545378/lead-laced-water-in-flint-a-step-by -step-look-at-the-makings-of-a-crisis.

27. Mona Hanna-Attisha, "Elevated Blood Lead Levels in Children Associated with the Flint Drinking Water Crisis: A Spatial Analysis of Risk and Public Health Response," *American Journal of Public Health* 106, no. 2 (2016): 283–86; "Flint Water Advisory Task Force: Final Report," Office of Governor Rick Snyder, State of Michigan (March 2016), 6; Josh Sanburn, "Flint Water Crisis May Cost the City $400 Million in Long-Term Social Costs," *Time*, August 8, 2016, http://time.com/4441471/flint-water-lead-poisoning -costs.

28. *The Flint Water Crisis: Systemic Racism Through the Lens of Flint* (Michigan Civil Rights Commission, February 17, 2017).

29. Khazan, "Being Black in America Can Be Hazardous to Your Health," 82.

30. Muller, Sampson, and Winter, "Environmental Inequality," 11.

31. Samantha Gross, "What Is the Trump Administration's Track Record on the Environment," *Brookings*, August 4, 2020, https://www.brookings.edu /policy2020/votervital/what-is-the-trump-administrations-track-record-on -the-environment; "Environmental Protections on the Chopping Block,"

Environmental Integrity Project, https://environmentalintegrity.org/trump
-watch-epa/regulatory-rollbacks, accessed October 15, 2020.

32. Peter Jamison, "'Pure Incompetence,'" *Washington Post*, December 19,
2018, https://www.washingtonpost.com/graphics/2018/local/dc-opioid
-epidemic-response-african-americans/?utm_term=.8f119fdaceoa&wpisrc
=nl_buzz&wpmm=1.

33. David Leonhardt, "What Does Opportunity Look Like Where You Live?,"
New York Times, May 13, 2020, https://www.nytimes.com/interactive
/2020/05/13/opinion/inequality-cities-life-expectancy.html?smid=tw-share.

34. Massey, "Why Death Haunts Black Lives," 2.

35. See generally Ibram X. Kendi, *How to Be an Antiracist* (New York: Random House, 2019).

36. Caitlin Flanagan, "They Had It Coming," *Atlantic*, April 4, 2019, https://
www.theatlantic.com/ideas/archive/2019/04/what-college-admissions
-scandal-reveals/586468. See also "College Admissions Scandal: Complete
Coverage on a Brazen Scheme," *New York Times*, https://www.nytimes
.com/news-event/college-admissions-scandal.

37. Raj Chetty, Nathaniel Hendren, and Lawrence F. Katz, "The Effects of
Exposure to Better Neighborhoods on Children: New Evidence from the
Moving to Opportunity Experiment," *American Economic Review* 106,
no. 4 (2015).

38. Chetty et al., "The Effects of Exposure to Better Neighborhoods on Children," 856; Lawrence F. Katz, Jeffrey R. Kling, and Jeffrey B. Leibman,
"Moving to Opportunity in Boston: Early Results of a Randomized Mobility Experiment," *Quarterly Journal of Economics* 116, no. 2 (2001); Susan
Clampet-Lundquist and Douglas S. Massey, "Neighborhood Effects on
Economic Self-Sufficiency: A Reconsideration of the Moving to Opportunity Experiment," *American Journal of Sociology* 114, no. 1 (2008); Jeffrey
R. Kling, Jeffrey B. Liebman, and Lawrence F. Katz, "Experimental Analysis of Neighborhood Effects," *Econometrica* 75, no. 1 (2007).

39. Chetty et al., "The Effects of Exposure to Better Neighborhoods on Children," 889; James F. Rosenbaum et al., "Can the Kerner Commission's
Housing Strategy Improve Employment, Education, and Social Integration for Low-Income Blacks?," *University of North Carolina Law Review*
71 (1993): 1530, showing that "the employment rates of suburban moves
surpassed those of city movers, particularly for those who had never before
had a job."

40. Heather Schwartz, *Housing Policy Is School Policy: Economically Integrative Housing Promotes Academic Success in Montgomery County, Maryland* (New York: Century Foundation, 2010), 33–34.

41. Quentin Brummet and David Reed, "The Effects of Gentrification on the
Well-Being and Opportunity of Original Resident Adults and Children,"
Federal Reserve Bank of Philadelphia, https://doi.org/10.21799/frbp.wp
.2019.30, accessed October 15, 2020.

42. Nancy McArdle and Dolores Acevedo-Garcia, "Consequences of Segregation for Children's Opportunity and Wellbeing," paper presented at A

Shared Future, a symposium hosted by the Harvard Joint Center for Housing Studies, 2017, 4–5.

43. McArdle and Acevedo-Garcia, "Consequences of Segregation for Children's Opportunity and Wellbeing," 8.

44. Eric A. Hanushek and Steven G. Rivkin, "Harming the Best: How Schools Affect the Black-White Achievement Gap," *Journal of Policy Analysis and Management* 28 (2009): 366–93; Hamilton Lankford, Susanna Loeb, and James Wyckoff, "Teacher Sorting and the Plight of Urban Schools: A Descriptive Analysis," *Educational Evaluation and Policy Analysis* 24 (2002): 37–62; Roland G. Freyer and Steven D. Levitt, "Understanding the Black-White Test Score Gap in the First Two Years of School," *Review of Economics and Statistics* 86 (2004): 447–64; Dennis J. Condron, "Social Class, School and Non-School Environments, and Black-White Inequalities in Children's Learning," *American Sociological Review* 74 (2009): 673–708.

45. James Coleman, "Equality of Educational Opportunity," *Equity and Excellence in Education* 6, no. 5 (1968); Cashin, *The Failures of Integration*, 83–126; Richard D. Kahlenberg, *All Together Now: Creating Middle-Class Schools Through Public School Choice* (Washington, DC: Brookings Institution Press, 2001).

46. John R. Logan, Elisabeta Minca, and Sinem Adar, "The Geography of Inequality: Why Separate Means Unequal in American Public Schools," *Sociology of Education* 85, no. 3 (2012): 2.

47. Jonathan Guryan, "Desegregation and Black Dropout Rates," *American Economic Review* 94, no. 4 (2004); Rucker C. Johnson, "Long-Run Impacts of School Desegregation & School Quality on Adult Attainments," National Bureau of Economic Research, working paper (2011); David A. Weiner, Byron F. Lutz, and Jens Ludwig, "The Effects of School Desegregation on Crime," National Bureau of Economic Research, working paper (2011); David J. Deming, "Better Schools, Less Crime?," *Quarterly Journal of Economics* 126, no. 4 (2011).

48. Gary Orfield, John Kucsera, and Genevieve Siegel-Hawley, "E Pluribus . . . Separation: Deepening Double Segregation for More Students," Civil Rights Project, September 2012, 6–11, https://civilrightsproject.ucla.edu /research/k-12-education/integration-and-diversity/mlk-national/e-pluribus . . . separation-deepening-double-segregation-for-more-students. See also Myron Orfield and Thomas Luce, "America's Racially Diverse Suburbs: Opportunities and Challenges," Institute on Metropolitan Opportunity, July 20, 2012, 39, https://www.law.umn.edu/sites/law.umn.edu/files/metro -files/diverse_suburbs_final.pdf.

49. See chapter 8 discussion of the school-to-prison pipeline.

50. Sharkey, *Uneasy Peace*, 181–82; Tracy Meares, "Simple Solutions? The Complexity of Public Attitudes Relevant to Drug Law Enforcement Policy," in *Crime Control or Justice: The Delicate Balance*, ed. Darnell F. Hawkins, Samuel L. Myers, and Randolph N. Stone (Westport, CT: Greenwood Press, 2003); see also chapter 5 of this book.

51. See, e.g., Wilson, *The Truly Disadvantaged.*
52. See, e.g., Robert D. Putnam, "Crumbling American Dream," *New York Times*, August 3, 2013, https://opinionator.blogs.nytimes.com/2013/08/03/crumbling-american-dreams.
53. Stephen B. Billings, David J. Deming, and Jonah E. Rockoff, "School Segregation, Educational Attainment and Crime: Evidence from the End of Busing in Charlotte-Mecklenburg," National Bureau of Economic Research, working paper (2012). See also Ray Fishman, "Brown v. Board Reduced Crime," *Slate*, April 9, 2013, https://slate.com/business/2013/04/desegregation-and-crime-resegregation-has-led-to-a-spike-in-violent-crime.html.
54. Sampson, *Great American City.*
55. Sharkey, *Uneasy Peace*, 159.
56. James Forman Jr., "The Society of Fugitives," *Atlantic*, October 2014, https://www.theatlantic.com/magazine/archive/2014/10/the-society-of-fugitives/379328; David M. Kennedy, Anne M. Piehl, and Anthony A. Braga, "Youth Violence in Boston: Gun Markets, Serious Youth Offenders, and a Use-Reduction Strategy," *Law and Contemporary Problems* 59, no. 1 (Winter 1996): 147–96.
57. María B. Vélez, Christopher J. Lyons, and Wayne A. Santoro, "The Political Context of the Percent Black-Neighborhood Violence Link: A Multilevel Analysis," *Social Problems* 62, no. 1 (2015): 107.
58. Vélez et al., "The Political Context of the Percent Black-Neighborhood Violence Link," 107–8.
59. See generally Velez et al., "The Political Context of the Percent Black-Neighborhood Violence Link," 110; Sharkey, *Uneasy Peace*; Sampson, *Great American City.*
60. Chetty et al., "Race and Economic Opportunity in the United States: An Intergenerational Perspective," working paper (2018), 7. See also Emily Badger et al., "Extensive Data Shows Punishing Reach of Racism for Black Boys," *New York Times*, March 19, 2018, https://www.nytimes.com/interactive/2018/03/19/upshot/race-class-white-and-black-men.html?mtrref=www.google.com&gwh=8DDB4E003D42D99234C49C002EBD769A&gwt=pay&assetType=REGIWALL.
61. Sheryll Cashin, "In Shepherd Park, We're Working Toward a Racially Diverse Eden," *Washington Post*, August 25, 2017, https://www.washingtonpost.com/opinions/in-shepherd-park-were-making-it-up-as-we-go-along/2017/08/25/acb4db8c-8766–11e7-a50f-eod4e6eco70a_story.html.
62. Chetty et al., "Race and Economic Opportunities in the United States," 7.
63. William Julius Wilson, *The Truly Disadvantaged*, 135, 264–67; Alexander, *The New Jim Crow*, 6–7.

CHAPTER 8: SURVEILLANCE

1. "1,017 People Have Been Shot and Killed by Police in the Past Year," *Washington Post*, updated July 1, 2020, https://www.washingtonpost.com/graphics/investigations/police-shootings-database/?itid=lk_inline_manual_5.
2. "2018 Hate Crime Statistics," Criminal Justice Information Division, Federal Bureau of Investigation, https://ucr.fbi.gov/hate-crime/2018/topic-pages

/victims. In 2018, there were 5,155 victims of race/ethnicity/ancestry motivated hate crime. 47.1 percent were victims of crimes motivated by offenders' anti-Black of African American bias. The second largest group (20.1 percent) are victims of antiwhite bias.

3. Eyder Peralta and Cheryl Corley, "The Driving Life and Death of Philando Castile," NPR, July 15, 2016, https://www.npr.org/sections/thetwo-way/2016/07/15/485835272/the-driving-life-and-death-of-philando-castile.

4. Interview with Dr. Darryl Atwell, March 9, 2020, notes on file with author.

5. Elijah Anderson, *The Cosmopolitan Canopy: Race and Civility in Everyday Life* (New York: W. W. Norton, 2011), 249; Anderson, "The Iconic Ghetto," 8.

6. Robert J. Sampson and Stephen W. Raudenbush, "Neighborhood Stigma and the Perception of Disorder," *Social Psychology Quarterly* 67, no. 4 (2004): 337, https://www-jstor-org.proxygt-law.wrlc.org/stable/3649091?seq=2#metadata_info_tab_contents.

7. Anderson, "The Iconic Ghetto," 17.

8. Derek Hawkins, "Fort Worth Police Officer Fatally Shoots Woman in Her Home While Checking on an Open Front Door," *Washington Post*, October 13, 2019, https://www.washingtonpost.com/nation/2019/10/13/fort-worth-police-officer-fatally-shoots-woman-her-home-while-checking-an-open-front-door.

9. Errin Haines, "Family Seeks Answers in Fatal Police Shooting of Louisville Woman in Her Apartment," *Washington Post*, May 11, 2020, https://www.washingtonpost.com/nation/2020/05/11/family-seeks-answers-fatal-police-shooting-louisville-woman-her-apartment.

10. "Racial Disparities in D.C. Policing: Descriptive Evidence from 2013–2017," May 13, 2019, last updated July 31, 2019, https://www.acludc.org/en/racial-disparities-dc-policing-descriptive-evidence-2013-2017.

11. Peter Hermann, "Study Finds Disproportionate Number of Black People Arrested in D.C.," *Washington Post*, May 14, 2019, https://www.washingtonpost.com/local/public-safety/study-finds-disproportionate-number-of-black-people-arrested-in-dc/2019/05/14/92cf2d26-735a-11e98be0-ca575670e91c_story.html?utm_term=.bd0686584ab9.

12. See chapter 4.

13. Illinois v. Wardlow, 528 U.S. 119 (2000); see also Terry v. Ohio, 392 U.S. 1 (1968).

14. John Sullivan et al., "Four Years in a Row, Police Nationwide Fatally Shoot Nearly 1,000 People," *Washington Post*, February 12, 2019, https://www.washingtonpost.com/investigations/four-years-in-a-row-police-nationwide-fatally-shoot-nearly-1000-people/2019/02/07/0cb3b098-020f-11e9-9122-82e98f91ee6f_story.html; Alexi Jones and Wendy Sawyer, "Not Just 'A Few Bad Apples': U.S. Police Kill Civilians at Much Higher Rates Than Other Countries," Prison Policy Initiative, June 5, 2020, https://www.prisonpolicy.org/blog/2020/06/05/policekillings.

15. Odis Johnson Jr. et al., "How Neighborhoods Matter in Fatal Interactions Between Police and Men of Color," *Social Science and Medicine* 220

(2019): 227, https://doi.org/10.1016/j.socscimed.2018.11.024; Michael
Siegel et al., "Residential Segregation and Black-White Disparities in Fatal
Police Shootings at the City Level, 2013–2017," *Journal of the National
Medical Association* 111 (2019): 580–87, doi:10.1016/j.jnma.2019.06.003.

16. Ed Chung, "The Trump Administration," Center for American Progress,
April 13, 2017, https://www.americanprogress.org/issues/criminal-justice
/news/2017/04/13/430461/trump-administration-putting-doj-policing
-reform-efforts-risk.

17. US Department of Justice, Civil Rights Division, *Investigation of the Baltimore City Police Department* (2016), 26, https://www.justice.gov/crt/file
/883296/download.

18. US Department of Justice, *Investigation of Baltimore*, 65–66.

19. US Department of Justice, Civil Rights Division and US Attorney's Office,
Northern District of Illinois, *Investigation of the Chicago Police Department* (2017), 31, https://www.justice.gov/opa/file/925846/download.

20. US Department of Justice, *Investigation of the Chicago Police*, 143.

21. US Department of Justice, *Investigation of the Chicago Police*, 146.

22. Butler, *Chokehold*, 74–75.

23. George L. Kelling and James Q. Wilson, "Broken Windows: The Police
and Neighborhood Safety," *Atlantic*, March 1982, https://www.theatlantic.
com/magazine/archive/1982/03/broken-windows/304465, accessed July 12,
2020.

24. K. Babe Howell, "Broken Lives from Broken Windows: The Hidden Costs
of Aggressive Order-Maintenance Policing," *NYU Review of Law & Social
Change* 33 (2009): 276, https://academicworks.cuny.edu/cgi/viewcontent
.cgi?article=1166&context=cl_pubs; K. Babe Howell, "The Costs of 'Broken Windows' Policing: Twenty Years and Counting," *Cardozo Law Review* 37 (2016): 1062–64, https://heinonline-org.proxygt-law.wrlc.org/HOL
/Page?collection=journals&handle=hein.journals/cdozo37&id=1128&men
_tab=srchresults.

25. Al Baker et al., "Beyond the Chokehold: The Path to Eric Garner's Death,"
New York Times, https://www.nytimes.com/2015/06/14/nyregion/eric
-garner-police-chokehold-staten-island.html.

26. "Analysis of New NYPD Stop-and-Frisk Data Reveals Dramatic Impact on
Black New Yorkers," American Civil Liberties Union, published Nov. 26,
2007, http://aclu.org/racialjustice /racialprofiling/33095prs20071126.html.
See also Jeffrey Fagan et al., "Street Stops and Broken Windows Revisited:
The Demography and Logic of Proactive Policing in a Safe and Changing
City," in *Race, Ethnicity, and Policing: New and Essential Readings*, eds.
Stephen K. Rice and Michael D. White (New York: New York University
Press, 2009), 336.

27. Howell, "The Costs of 'Broken Windows,'" 1068.

28. The Editorial Board, "The Legacy of Stop-and-Frisk in New York's Marijuana Arrests," *New York Times*, May 14, 2018, https://www.nytimes.com
/2018/05/14/opinion/stop-frisk-marijuana-nyc.html.

29. Ashley Southall, "Scrutiny of Social-Distance Policing as 35 of 40 Arrested
Are Black," *New York Times*, updated May 29, 2020, https://www.nytimes

.com/2020/05/07/nyregion/nypd-social-distancing-race-coronavirus.html; Ben Kesslen, "NYPD to No Longer Enforce Wearing Masks Absent 'Serious Danger,' Mayor Says," *NBC News*, May 15, 2020, https://www.nbc news.com/news/us-news/nypd-no-longer-enforce-wearing-masks-absent -serious-danger-mayor-n1207931.

30. US Department of Commerce, Census Bureau, *QuickFacts: New York City, New York*; *Kings County (Brooklyn Borough), New York* (2020), https:// www.census.gov/quickfacts/fact/table/newyorkcitynewyork,kingscounty brooklynboroughnewyork/PST045219.

31. "Mapping Prejudice," https://www.mappingprejudice.org; PBS, "Jim Crow of the North," Twin Cities PBS Original, 56:45, aired February 25, 2019, https://www.pbs.org/video/jim-crow-of-the-north-stijws, accessed July 26, 2020.

32. Myron Orfield and Will Stancil, "George Floyd and Derek Chauvin Might as Well Have Lived on Different Planets," *New York Times*, June 3, 2020, https://www.nytimes.com/2020/06/03/opinion/george-floyd-minneapolis -segregation.html; Adam Minter, "In George Floyd's City, Inequalities Are Everywhere," *Star Tribune*, June 9, 2020, https://www.startribune.com/in -george-floyd-s-city-inequalities-are-everywhere/571133202; David Leonhardt and Yaryna Serkez, "What Does Opportunity Look Like Where You Live?," *New York Times*, May 13, 2020, https://www.nytimes.com /interactive/2020/05/13/opinion/inequality-cities-life-expectancy.html.

33. Richard A. Oppel Jr. and Lazaro Gamio, "Minneapolis Police Use Force Against Black People at 7 Times the Rate of Whites," *New York Times*, June 3, 2020, https://www.nytimes.com/interactive/2020/06/03/us /minneapolis-police-use-of-force.html?action=click&module=RelatedLinks &pgtype=Article.

34. Interview with Jason Kise, June 15, 2020, notes on file with the author.

35. Oppel Jr. and Gamio, "Minneapolis Police Use Force."

36. Casey Kellogg, "There Goes the Neighborhood: Exposing the Relationship Between Gentrification and Incarceration," *Themis: Research Journal of Justice Studies and Forensic Science* 3 (2015): 178, 185–86, https://scholar works.sjsu.edu/cgi/viewcontent.cgi?article=1031&context=themis; Mischa-von-Derek Aikman, "Gentrification's Effect on Crime Rates," *Urban Economics*, last visited December 11, 2017, https://sites.duke.edu/urban economics/files/2014/04/Gentrification%E2%80%99s-Effect-on-Crime -Rates.pdf; Ayobami Laniyonu, "Coffee Shops and Street Stops: Policing Practices in Gentrifying Neighborhoods," *Urban Affairs Review* 54 (2017): 898–930, https://doi.org/10.1177/1078087416689728.

37. Oppel Jr. and Gamio, "Minneapolis Police Use Force."

38. Orfield and Stancil, "George Floyd and Derek Chauvin."

39. Paul Hirschfield, "Lethal Policing: Making Sense of American Exceptionalism," *Sociological Forum* 30 (2015): 1111, doi:10.1111/socf.12200, accessed July 19, 2020.

40. Forman, *Locking Up Our Own*; John R. Logan and Deirdre Oakley, "Black Lives and Policing: The Larger Context of Ghettoization," *Journal of Urban Affairs* 39 (2017): 1031–46, doi:10.1080/07352166.2017.1328977.

41. Butler, *Chokehold*.
42. Duneier, *Ghetto*.
43. Wacquant, "Deadly Symbiosis," 95.
44. James Baldwin, *The Fire Next Time* (New York: Dial Press, 1963), 7.
45. James Baldwin, "Fifth Avenue, Uptown," *Esquire*, July 1, 1960, https://classic.esquire.com/article/1960/7/1/fifth-avenue-uptown, accessed July 19, 2020.
46. Howell, "The Cost of 'Broken Windows,'" 1062–64.
47. US Department of Justice, Civil Rights Division, *Investigation of the Ferguson Police Department* (2015), 9, https://www.justice.gov/sites/default/files/opa/press-releases/attachments/2015/03/04/ferguson_police_department_report.pdf.
48. Fagan and Ash, "New Policing," 134.
49. Fagan and Ash, "New Policing," 41–42.
50. "District Shatters Traffic and Parking Ticket Records and Stands to Rake in Record Breaking Ticket Revenue," John Townsend, American Automobile Association, published February 19, 2020, https://cluballiance.aaa.com/public-affairs/press-release/?rdl=midatlantic.aaa.com&Id=6d0b4879-5fa1-46f8-bf47-3f3a41658e15.
51. "Racial Disparities in D.C. Policing."
52. Elizabeth Jones, "The Profitability of Racism: Discriminatory Design in the Carceral State," *University of Louisville Law Review* 57 (2018): 61, https://heinonline.org/HOL/LandingPage?handle=hein.journals/branlaj57&div=8&id=&page=; Rose M. Brewer and Nancy A. Heitzeg, "The Racialization of Crime and Punishment: Criminal Justice, Color-Blind Racism, and the Political Economy of the Prison Industrial Complex," *American Behavioral Scientist* 51, no. 5 (2008): 625–44.
53. Bernadette Atuahene, "Predatory Cities," *California Law Review* 108, no. 1 (February 2020): 107–82, https://heinonline-org.proxygt-law.wrlc.org/HOL/P?h=hein.journals/calr108&i=107; Bernadette Atuahene, "The Scandal of the Predatory City," *New York Times*, June 11, 2020, https://www.nytimes.com/2020/06/11/opinion/coronavirus-cities-property-taxes.html?smid=tw-share.
54. Joanna C. Schwartz, "Police Indemnification," *New York University Law Review* 89, no. 3 (2014): 913, https://www.nyulawreview.org/wp-content/uploads/2018/08/NYULawReview-89-3-Schwartz.pdf. Between 2006 and 2011, taxpayers in 44 large metro areas paid out more than $735 billion to victims of police misconduct.
55. "Million Dollar Blocks," https://chicagosmilliondollarblocks.com/#section-4, accessed July 23, 2020. Emily Badger, "How Mass Incarceration Creates 'Million Dollar Blocks' in Poor Neighborhoods," *Washington Post*, July 30, 2015, https://www.washingtonpost.com/news/wonk/wp/2015/07/30/how-mass-incarceration-creates-million-dollar-blocks-in-poor-neighborhoods.
56. Jason P. Nance, "Students, Security and Race," *Emory Law Journal* 63, no. 1 (2013): 28–29, https://law.emory.edu/elj/_documents/volumes/63/1/articles/nance.pdf.

57. Melissa Diliberti, Michael Jackson, Samuel Correa, Zoe Padgett, and Rachel Hansen, *Crime, Violence, Discipline, and Safety in U.S. Public Schools: Findings from the School Survey on Crime and Safety: 2017–18* (Washington, DC: US Department of Education, National Center for Education Statistics, 2019), https://nces.ed.gov/pubs2019/2019061.pdf. See also Sandra Black, Laura Giuliano, and Ayushi Narayan, "Civil Rights Data Show More Work Is Needed to Reduce Inequities in K-12 Schools," *White House Blog*, December 9, 2016, https://obamawhitehouse.archives.gov/blog/2016/12/08/civil -rights-data-show-more-work-needed-reduce-inequities-k-12-schools; Stephen Sawchuk, "What Districts Should Know About Policing School Police," *Education Week*, October 1, 2019, https://www.edweek.org/ew/articles/2019 /10/02/what-districts-should-know-about-policing-school.html.

58. Megan French-Marcelin and Sarah Hinger, *Bullies in Blue: The Origins and Consequences of School Policing* (American Civil Liberties Union, April 2017), https://www.aclu.org/report/bullies-blue-origins-and-consequences -school-policing.

59. "We Came to Learn," Advancement Project and Alliance for Educational Justice, https://wecametolearn.com/?emci=5f211b14–47a5-ea11–9b05 –0155d0394bb&emdi=5728ac94–8da5-ea11–9b05–0155d0394bb &ceid=2360859#assaultat-map, accessed July 24, 2020.

60. Moriah Balingit et al., "Fueled by Protests, School Districts Across the Country Cut Ties with Police," *Washington Post*, June 12, 2020, https:// www.washingtonpost.com/education/2020/06/12/schools-police-george -floyd-protests.

61. "Black Agenda 2020," Black to the Future Action Fund, published February 2020, https://black2thefuture.org/wp-content/uploads/2020/02/Black Agenda2020.pdf, 22–24.

62. Jim Newell, "The Thin Blue Line Is in Retreat," *Slate*, June 8, 2020, https:// slate.com/news-and-politics/2020/06/police-reform-is-popular-now.html, citing Monmouth University Polling Institute national poll on the George Floyd protests.

63. Nicole Chavez, "Pennsylvania Senator Calls for Investigation into Golf Course That Called Police on Black Women," CNN, April 29, 2018, https://www.cnn.com/2018/04/29/us/pennsylvania-golf-course-black -women/index.html; David Williams, "Someone Called Police on an African-American Politician While She Campaigned in Her Wisconsin District," CNN, September 21, 2018, https://www.cnn.com/2018/09/20/us /wisconsin-candidate-police-trnd/index.html.

64. Brandon Giggs, "Living While Black: Here Are All the Routine Activities for Which Police Were Called on African-Americans This Year," CNN, December 28, 2018, https://www.cnn.com/2018/12/20/us/living-while-black -police-calls-trnd/index.html.

65. Elijah Anderson, "The White Space," *Sociology of Race and Ethnicity* 1 (2015): 13, doi: 10.1177/2332649214561306.

66. Richard Fausset and Rick Rojas, "Where Ahmaud Arbery Ran, Neighbors Cast Wary Eyes," *New York Times*, May 22, 2020, https://www.nytimes .com/article/satilla-shores-ahmaud-arbery-killing.html.

67. Khushbu Shah, "Ahmaud Arbery: Anger Mounts over Killing of Black Jogger Caught on Video," *Guardian*, May 6, 2020, https://www.theguardian.com/us-news/2020/may/06/ahmaud-arbery-shooting-georgia.

68. Khushbu Shah, "Ahmaud Arbery Killing: Man Called 911 to Report 'Black Male Running' Prior to Shooting," *Guardian*, May 7, 2020, https://www.theguardian.com/us-news/2020/may/07/ahmaud-arbery-killing-man-called-911-report-black-male-running-shooting.

69. Michael Brice-Saddler and Cleve R. Wootson Jr., "Ex-Detective Charged in Death of Ahmaud Arbery Lost Power to Make Arrests After Skipping Use-of-Force Training," *Washington Post*, May 14, 2020, https://www.washingtonpost.com/nation/2020/05/13/ex-detective-accused-death-ahmaud-arbery-lost-power-make-arrests-after-skipping-use-of-force-training.

70. Richard Fausset, "Two Weapons, a Chase, a Killing, and No Charges," *New York Times*, published April 26, 2020, updated May 17, 2020, https://www.nytimes.com/2020/04/26/us/ahmed-arbery-shooting-georgia.html.

71. Mihir Zaveri, "Man Who Fired at a Black Teenager Asking for Directions Is Convicted," *New York Times*, October 13, 2018, https://www.nytimes.com/2018/10/13/us/jeffrey-zeigler-brennan-walker-trial.html; Jasper Scherer, "Fla. Loud Music' Murder: Firing into Car Full of Teens Playing Rap Music Not 'Self-Defense,' Court Rules," *Washington Post*, November 18, 2016, https://www.washingtonpost.com/news/morning-mix/wp/2016/11/18/fla-loud-music-murder-firing-into-car-full-of-teens-playing-rap-music-not-self-defense-court-rules; Greg Botelho, "What Happened the Night Trayvon Martin Died," CNN, updated May 23, 2012, https://www.cnn.com/2012/05/18/justice/florida-teen-shooting-details/index.html#:~:text=Trayvon%20Martin%20walked%20into%20a,the%20clerk%2C%20then%20walked%20out.

72. Giffords Law Center and SPLC, "'Stand Your Ground' Kills: How These NRA-Backed Laws Promote Racist Violence," SPLC, splcenter.org, 15–16. https://www.splcenter.org/sites/default/files/_stand_your_ground_kills_-_how_these_nra-backed_laws_promote_racist_violence_1.pdf.

73. "Georgia: Concealed Carry Reciprocity Map & Gun Laws," US Concealed Carry Association, https://www.usconcealedcarry.com/resources/ccw_reciprocity_map/ga-gun-laws.

74. US Commission on Civil Rights, *Examining the Race Effects of Stand Your Ground Laws and Related Issues* (Washington, DC: USCCR, 2020), 16–17, https://www.usccr.gov/pubs/2020/04-06-Stand-Your-Ground.pdf.

75. Frances Robles, "The Citizen's Arrest Law Cited in Arbery's Killing Dates Back to the Civil War," *New York Times*, May 13, 2020, https://www.nytimes.com/article/ahmaud-arbery-citizen-arrest-law-georgia.html.

76. *An Act to Amend Article 4 of Chapter 4 of Title 17 of the Official Code of Georgia Annotated*, Georgia General Assembly, 2019–2020 Regular Session, H.B. 1203, *Georgia Congressional Record*, http://www.legis.ga.gov/Legislation/en-US/display/20192020/HB/1203.

77. Jacey Fortin, "Congress Moves to Make Lynching a Federal Crime After 120 Years of Failure," *New York Times*, updated February 28, 2020, https://www.nytimes.com/2020/02/26/us/politics/anti-lynching-bill.html.

78. Deborah N. Archer, "The Housing Segregation: The Jim Crow Effects of Crime-Free Housing Ordinances," *Michigan Law Review* 118, no. 2 (2019): 207–8, https://search-proquest-com.proxygt-law.wrlc.org/docview /2309261491?accountid=36339.

79. Archer, "The Housing Segregation," 199.

80. Archer, "The Housing Segregation," 199–200.

81. Archer, "The Housing Segregation," 199–200, 207.

82. Archer, "The Housing Segregation," 214.

83. Matthew Desmond and Nicole Valdez, "Unpolicing the Urban Poor: Consequences of Third-Party Policing for Inner-City Women," *American Sociological Review* 78, no. 1 (2013): 117–41, doi:10.2307/23469211.

84. J. Brian Charles et al., "How Police and Anti-Crime Measures Reinforce Segregation," *Governing: The Future of States and Localities*, January 23, 2019, https://www.governing.com/topics/public-justice-safety/gov-segregation -police.html, citing "Armadillos: Starting a Trend," Peoria Police Department.

85. Complaint filed by Hope Fair Housing Center against City of Peoria, 16, August 10, 2017, https://www.relmanlaw.com/media/cases/723_Complaint .pdf.

86. Sandra Park and Linda Morris, "Dialing 911 Can Get You Evicted," American Civil Liberties Union, published April 18, 2019, https://www.aclu.org /blog/womens-rights/violence-against-women/dialing-911-can-get-you -evicted.

87. "Remarks by the President at One Strike Crime Symposium," updated March 28, 1996, https://clintonwhitehouse6.archives.gov/1996/03/1996 -03-28-president-remarks-at-one-strike-crime-symposium.html; US Department of Housing and Urban Development, *Meeting the Challenge: Public Housing Authorities Respond to the "One Strike and You're Out" Initiative* (Washington, DC, 1997), https://www.ncjrs.gov/pdffiles1/Photocopy /183952NCJRS.pdf.

88. Kathryn V. Ramsey, "One-Strike 2.0: How Local Governments Are Distorting a Flawed Federal Eviction Law," *UCLA Law Review* 65, no. 5 (June 2018): 1146–99, https://heinonline.org/HOL/P?h=hein.journals/uclalr65&i =1204; Dept. of Housing and Urban Dev. v. Rucker, 535 U.S. 125 (2002).

89. Elena Goldstein, "Kept Out: Responding to Public Housing No-Trespass Policies," *Harvard Civil Rights-Civil Liberties Law Review* 38, no. 1 (Winter 2003): 215–46, https://heinonline.org/HOL/P?h=hein.journals/hcrcl38&i=221.

90. Charles et al., "How Police and Anti-Crime Measures Reinforce Segregation."

91. "311 Reports in SF by Neighborhood 2008–2016," Anti-Eviction Mapping Project, http://www.antievictionmappingproject.net/311.html, accessed July 26, 2020; Abdallah Fayyad, "The Criminalization of Gentrifying Neighborhoods," *Atlantic*, December 12, 2017, https://www.theatlantic.com /politics/archive/2017/12/the-criminalization-of-gentrifying-neighborhoods /548837; Mona Lynch et al., "Policing the 'Progressive' City: The Racialized Geography of Drug Law Enforcement," *Theoretical Criminology* 17 (2013): 335–57, https://doi.org/10.1177/1362480613476986.

92. Lynch, "Policing the 'Progressive' City"; Manissa M. Maharawal, "Black Lives Matter, Gentrification and the Security State in the San Francisco Bay

Area," *Anthropological Theory* 17 (2017): 338, 347, 349, https://doi.org
/10.1177/1463499617732501.

93. Rebecca Solnit, "Death by Gentrification: The Killing That Shamed San
Francisco," *Guardian*, March 21, 2016, https://www.theguardian.com/us
-news/2016/mar/21/death-by-gentrification-the-killing-that-shamed-san
-francisco; Adam Hudson, "The Bleaching of San Francisco: Extreme Gentrification and Suburbanized Poverty in the Bay Area," *Truthout*, April 27,
2014, http://www.truth-out.org/news/item/23305-the-bleaching-of-san
-francisco-extreme-gentrification-and-suburbanized-poverty-in-the-bay;
Steven Rosenfield, "Is Gentrification Fueling Police Brutality in San Francisco?," *AlterNet*, May 15, 2015, https://www.alternet.org/civil-liberties
/gentrification-fueling-police-brutality-san-francisco; see also Butler, *Chokehold*, 75, "As neighborhoods in San Francisco became wealthier and
whiter, calls to police for non-emergency reasons like reporting loitering
increased almost 300 percent."

94. Casey Kellogg, "There Goes the Neighborhood: Exposing the Relationship
Between Gentrification and Incarceration," *Themis: Research Journal of
Justice Studies and Forensic Science* 3 (2015): 178, 185–86, https://scholar
works.sjsu.edu/cgi/viewcontent.cgi?article=1031&context=themis; Mis-
cha-von-Derek Aikman, "Gentrification's Effect on Crime Rates," *Urban
Economics*, last visited December 11, 2017, https://sites.duke.edu/urban-
economics/files/2014/04/Gentrification%E2%80%99s-Effect-on-Crime
-Rates.pdf; Ayobami Laniyonu, "Coffee Shops and Street Stops: Policing
Practices in Gentrifying Neighborhoods," *Urban Affairs Review* 54 (2017):
898–930, https://doi.org/10.1177/1078087416689728.

95. Joscha Legewie and Merlin Schaeffer, "Contested Boundaries: Explaining
Where Ethnoracial Diversity Provokes Neighborhood Conflict," *American
Journal of Sociology* 122, no. 1 (2016), https://jlegewie.com/files
/Legewie-Schaeffer-2016-ContestedBoundaries.pdf; see also Tanvi Misra,
"Yes, 311 Nuisance Calls Are Climbing in Gentrifying Neighborhoods,"
Bloomberg CityLab, October 18, 2018, https://www.bloomberg.com
/news/articles/2018–10–18/in-new-york-city-gentrification-brings-more
-311-calls.

96. Lam Thuy Vo, "They Played Dominoes Outside Their Apartment for Decades. Then the White People Moved In and Police Started Showing Up,"
BuzzFeed, June 29, 2018, https://www.buzzfeednews.com/article/lamvo
/gentrification-complaints-311-new-york.

97. Sam Levin, "Racial Profiling Via Nextdoor.com," *East Bay Express*, October 7, 2015, https://www.eastbayexpress.com/oakland/racial-profiling-via
-nextdoorcom/Content?oid=4526919.

98. Maria R. Lowe, "Who Looks Suspicious? Racialized Surveillance in a
Predominately White Neighborhood," *Social Currents* 4 (2016): 34–50,
https://doi.org/10.1177/2329496516651638.

99. Kim Lyons, "Amazon's Ring now reportedly partners with more than
2,000 US police and fire departments," The Verge, January 31, 2021,
https://www.theverge.com/2021/1/31/22258856/amazon-ring-partners
-police-fire-security-privacy-cameras; see also Drew Harwell, "Doorbell-

Camera Firm Ring Has Partnered with 400 Police Forces, Extending Surveillance Concerns," *Washington Post*, August 28, 2019, https://www
.washingtonpost.com/technology/2019/08/28/doorbell-camera-firm-ring
-has-partnered-with-police-forces-extending-surveillance-reach.

100. Caroline Haskins, "Amazon's Home Security Company Is Turning Everyone into Cops," *Vice*, February 7, 2019, https://www.vice.com/en_us
/article/qvyvzd/amazons-home-security-company-is-turning-everyone
-into-cops.

101. Drew Harwell, "Federal Study Confirms Racial Bias of Many Facial Recognition Systems, Cast Doubt on Their Expanding Use," *Washington
Post*, December 19, 2019, https://www.washingtonpost.com/technology
/2019/12/19/federal-study-confirms-racial-bias-many-facial-recognition
-systems-casts-doubt-their-expanding-use.

102. MIT Media Lab, "Gender Shades," YouTube video, 4:59, February 9,
2018, https://www.youtube.com/watch?v=TWWsW1w-BVo&feature
=emb_title; Joy Buolamwini and Timnit Gebru, "Gender Shades: Intersectional Accuracy Disparities in Commercial Gender Classification," *Proceedings of Machine Learning Research* 81 (2018), 1–15, http://proceedings
.mlr.press/v81/buolamwini18a/buolamwini18a.pdf.

CHAPTER 9: ABOLITION AND REPAIR

1. Wayne Drash and Tawanda Scott Sambou, "Paying Kids Not to Kill,"
CNN Health, May 20, 2016, https://www.cnn.com/2016/05/19/health
/cash-for-criminals-richmond-california/index.html.

2. Drash and Sambou, "Paying Kids Not to Kill."

3. "Number of Deaths in 2020," Gun Violence Archive, https://www.gun
violencearchive.org/query/14cood51–0b8d-4dd6-a71e-0caa61f54155
/map, accessed August 30, 2020; George Kelly, "Richmond Police Share
New Details in Fatal April Shooting: Video Shows Vehicle Sought by In-
vestigators in City's First Homicide of Year," *East Bay Times*, August 13,
2020, https://www.eastbaytimes.com/2020/08/13/richmond-police-share
-new-details-in-fatal-april-shooting.

4. Richard Gonzales, "To Reduce Gun Violence, Potential Offenders Offered
Support and Cash," NPR, March 28, 2016, https://www.npr.org/2016/03
/28/472138377/to-reduce-gun-violence-potential-offenders-offered-support
-and-cash.

5. Richard Wright, *12 Million Black Voices* (New York: Basic Books, 2008), 61.

6. Gonzales, "To Reduce Gun Violence"; Tim Murphy, "Did This City Bring
Down Its Murder Rate by Paying People Not to Kill?," *Mother Jones*, July/
August 2014, https://www.motherjones.com/politics/2014/06/richmond
-california-murder-rate-gun-death.

7. Lesley McClurg, "Richmond Gun Violence Drops by Half After Offenders Get Support . . . Including Cash," KQED, September 19, 2019, https://
www.kqed.org/science/1947571/richmond-gun-violence-drops-by-half
-after-offenders-get-support-including-cash.

8. Murphy, "Did This City Bring Down Its Murder Rate by Paying People
Not to Kill?"

9. Brianna Calix, "'Somebody's Going to Get Killed.' Can Fresno Find Money for Program That Cuts Gun Violence?," *Fresno Bee*, June 4, 2019, https://www.fresnobee.com/news/local/article231254513.html, citing "The Solution," https://www.advancepeace.org/about/the-solution.

10. Drash and Sambou, "Paying Kids Not to Kill."

11. Ellicott C. Matthay et al., "Firearm and Nonfirearm Violence After Operation Peacemaker Fellowship in Richmond, California, 1996–2016," *American Public Health Association* 109, no. 11 (2019): 1605–11, doi:10.2105 /AJPH.2019.305288.

12. Rachel Huguet et al., "Cost Benefit Analysis: Operation Peacemaker," University of Southern California, Sol Price School of Public Policy, https:// www.advancepeace.org/wp-content/uploads/2017/04/6-USC_ONS_CBA .pdf, accessed August 16, 2020.

13. Jason Corburn and Amanda Fukutome-Lopez, "Outcome Evaluation of Advance Peace Sacramento, 2018–19," 10, UC Berkeley Institute of Urban and Regional Development, published March 2020, https://www.advance peace.org/wp-content/uploads/2020/04/Corburn-and-F-Lopez-Advance -Peace-Sacramento-2-Year-Evaluation-03–2020.pdf.

14. "ONS—The Office of Neighborhood Safety 2019," Advance Peace, https:// www.advancepeace.org/wp-content/uploads/2020/03/ONS_Impact2019.pdf, accessed August 16, 2020.

15. Corburn and Fukutome-Lopez, "Outcome Evaluation of Advance Peace Sacramento, 2018–19," 6.

16. Interview with DeVone Boggan, Washington, DC, July 9, 2020, notes on file with author.

17. John Eligon, Shaila Dewan, and Nicolas Bogel-Burroughs, "In the Wake of Covid-19 Lockdowns, a Troubling Surge in Homicides," *New York Times*, August 11, 2020, updated August 24, 2020, https://www.nytimes.com/2020 /08/11/us/homicides-crime-kansas-city-coronavirus.html; John D. Harden and Justin Jouvenal, "Crime Rose Unevenly When Stay-at-Home Orders Lifted. The Racial Disparity Is the Widest in Years." *Washington Post*, October 9, 2020, https://www.washingtonpost.com/graphics/2020/local /public-safety/crime-rate-coronavirus/?itid=hp-top-table-high.

18. Jessica Anderson, "The Coronavirus Pandemic and Surveillance Plane Have Not Stemmed Baltimore's Torrid Rate of Homicides This Year," *Baltimore Sun*, June 30, 2020, https://www.baltimoresun.com/news/crime/bs-md-ci-cr -violence-20200630–7sns3jyi3rgojidvmx3gi6nxme-story.html.

19. German Lopez, "Trump Claims Crime Is Up in US Cities. The Truth Is More Complicated," *Vox*, updated August 27, 2020, https://www.vox .com/2020/8/3/21334149/trump-rnc-murders-crime-shootings-protests -riots.

20. Nicholas Bogal-Burroughs, "Baltimore Hopes Surveillance Planes Lower Crime, but Residents Fear Abuse," *New York Times*, updated June 3, 2020, https://www.nytimes.com/2020/04/09/us/baltimore-surveillance-planes -aclu.html.

21. See generally Dunbar-Ortiz, *An Indigenous Peoples' History of the United States*.

22. See generally Katherine Franke, *Repair: Redeeming the Promise of Abolition* (Chicago: Haymarket Books, 2019).

23. Angela Davis, *Are Prisons Obsolete?* (New York: Seven Stories Press, 2003), 107.

24. Angela Davis, *Abolition Democracy: Beyond Empire, Prison, and Torture* (New York: Seven Stories Press, 2005), 73.

25. Ruth Wilson Gilmore, "Abolition Geography and the Problem of Innocence" in Gaye Theresa Johnson and Alex Lubin, eds., *Futures of Black Radicalism* (Brooklyn, NY: Verso, 2017).

26. Emily Badger, "How Mass Incarceration Creates 'Million Dollar Blocks' in Poor Neighborhoods," *Washington Post*, July 30, 2015, https://www.washingtonpost.com/news/wonk/wp/2015/07/30/how-mass-incarceration-creates-million-dollar-blocks-in-poor-neighborhoods.

27. Badger, "How Mass Incarceration Creates 'Million Dollar Blocks.'"

28. Sara B. Heller, "Summer Jobs Reduce Violence Among Disadvantaged Youth," *Science 346*, no. 6214 (December 2014): 1219–23, 10.1126/science.1257809.

29. Bogal-Burroughs, "Baltimore Hopes Surveillance Planes Lower Crime"; Doug Donovan, "Billionaire Donors Laura and John Arnold Support Far More in Maryland Than Police Surveillance," *Baltimore Sun*, August 26, 2016, https://www.baltimoresun.com/maryland/baltimore-city/bs-md-arnolds-20160826-story.html; Tim Prudente, "Researchers Find Baltimore Spy Plane a Small Help in Crime Fight; Mayor to Make Decision on Program's Fate," *Baltimore Sun*, January 27, 2021, https://www.baltimoresun.com/news/crime/bs-md-ci-cr-spy-plane-preliminary-study-20210127-twux5fpjxzfahnnutmewysmalu-story.html.

30. bell hooks, "Love as the Practice of Freedom," in *Outlaw Culture: Resisting Representation* (New York: Routledge, 1994).

31. hooks, "Love as the Practice of Freedom."

32. hooks, "Love as the Practice of Freedom."

33. See generally David Dante Troutt, *The Price of Paradise: The Costs of Inequality and a Vision for a More Equitable America* (New York: NYU Press, 2014).

34. See for example, Catherine Coleman Flowers, "Mold, Possums and Pools of Sewage: No One Should Have to Live Like This," *New York Times*, Nov. 14, 2020, https://www.nytimes.com/2020/11/14/opinion/sunday/coronavirus-poverty-us.html.

35. Rebecca Morin, "Percentage Grows Among Americans Who Say Black People Experience a 'Great Deal' of Discrimination, Survey Shows," *USA Today*, updated June 11, 2020, https://www.usatoday.com/story/news/politics/2020/06/08/survey-higher-percentage-us-agree-black-people-face-discrimination/3143651001.

36. "Race and Social Justice Initiative," City of Seattle, https://www.seattle.gov/rsji, accessed August 28, 2020.

37. National League of Cities, "How Baltimore is Advancing Racial Equity: Policy, Practice & Procedure," January 21, 2019, https://www.nlc.org/article/2019/01/21/how-baltimore-is-advancing-racial-equity-policy-practice-procedure/.

38. "2020 Budgets Wins," Liberate MKE, https://www.liberatemke.com /campaign-results, accessed August 27, 2020.

39. "2020 Budgets Wins." Corrine Hess, "Milwaukee Considering Universal Basic Income Pilot Program," Wisconsin Public Radio, January 13, 2020, https://www.wpr.org/milwaukee-considering-universal-basic-income-pilot -program.

40. Audra D. S. Burch et al., "How Black Lives Matter Reached Every Corner of America," New York Times, June 13, 2020, https://www.nytimes.com /interactive/2020/06/13/us/george-floyd-protests-cities-photos.html; Larry Buchanan, Quoctrung Bui, and Jugal K. Patel, "Black Lives Matter May Be the Largest Movement in U.S. History," New York Times, July 3, 2020, https://www.nytimes.com/interactive/2020/07/03/us/george-floyd-protests -crowd-size.html.

41. Sarah Holder, "Stockton Extends Its Universal Basic Income Pilot," Bloomberg CityLab, June 2, 2020, https://www.bloomberg.com/news /articles/2020–06–02/stockton-extends-its-universal-basic-income-pilot.

42. Sigal Samuel, "Everywhere Basic Income Has Been Tried, in One Map," Vox, February 19, 2020, https://www.vox.com/future-perfect/2020/2/19 /21112570/universal-basic-income-ubi-map.

43. Mayors for a Guaranteed Income, "Resources," https://www.mayorsforagi .org/guaranteed-income, accessed February 19, 2021.

44. For prominent recent examples of arguments for reparations, see William A. Darity Jr. and A. Kirsten Mullen, From Here to Equality: Reparations for Black Americans in the Twenty-First Century (Chapel Hill: University of North Carolina Press, 2020); Coates, "The Case for Reparations"; Nikole Hannah-Jones, "What Is Owed," New York Times Magazine, June 30, 2020, https://www.nytimes.com/interactive/2020/06/24/magazine/reparations -slavery.html.

45. Franke, Repair.

46. Richard Rothstein, "A 'Forgotten History' of How the U.S. Government Seg- regated America," Fresh Air interview by Terry Gross, NPR, May 3, 2017, podcast transcript, 35:40, https://www.npr.org/transcripts/526655831.

47. Brown, The Black Butterfly, 231.

48. Clare Busch, "Philly Activists Occupy and Win Control of Vacant Homes," The Real News Network, October 13, 2020, https://therealnews.com/philly -activists-occupy-and-win.

49. "City Council Approves of Transfer of Central Area Senior Center and Fire Station to Black-led Organizations," Seattle Medium, November 4, 2020, https://seattlemedium.com/city-council-approves-transfer-of-central-area -senior-center-and-fire-station-to-black-led-organizations/.

50. Caroline Spivack, "Community Land Trusts Score Crucial Funds in City Budget: The $750,000 Will Go Toward Fostering a City Network of Land Trusts," Curbed New York, June 18, 2019, https://ny.curbed.com/2019/6 /18/18682466/nyc-community-land-trusts-funding-city-budget.

51. John Kamp, "Cities Offer Free Buses in Bid to Boost Flagging Ridership— Update," Dow Jones Institutional News, January 14, 2020.

52. Erica L. Green, "LeBron James Opened a School That Was Considered as Experiment. It's Showing Promise," *New York Times*, April 12, 2019, https://www.nytimes.com/2019/04/12/education/lebron-james-school-ohio.html.

53. "The Movement for Black Lives," https://m4bl.org, accessed October 14, 2020; "BLM's #WHATMATTERS 2020," Black Lives Matter, https://blacklivesmatter.com/what-matters-2020, accessed October 14, 2020.

54. Jemima McEvoy, "At Least 13 Cities Are Defunding Their Police Departments," *Forbes*, updated August 12, 2020, https://www.forbes.com/sites/jemimamcevoy/2020/08/13/at-least-13-cities-are-defunding-their-police-departments/#1edae09a29e3.

55. See, for example, Davis, *Are Prisons Obsolete*; Allegra McLeod, "Prison Abolition and Grounded Justice," *UCLA Law Review* 62 (2015): 1156, https://www.uclalawreview.org/wp-content/uploads/2019/09/McLeod_6.2015.pdf; Ruth Wilson Gilmore and James Kilgore, "The Case for Abolition," Marshall Project, June 19, 2019, https://www.themarshallproject.org/2019/06/19/the-case-for-abolition.

56. Alisha Ebrahimji, "San Francisco Official Proposes 'CAREN Act,' Making Racially Biased 911 Calls Illegal," CNN, updated July 8, 2020, https://www.cnn.com/2020/07/08/us/caren-act-911-san-francisco-trnd/index.html.

57. "Pandemic Remedies," Rutgers Center on Law, Inequality, & Metropolitan Equity, July 2020, https://static1.squarespace.com/static/5b996f553917ee5e584ba742/t/5f1ee1dace6f4a7166a7f34f/1595859425355/Pandemic+Essay+Series+7–24–20+%282%29.pdf.

58. Dylan Matthews, "Study: Cory Booker's Baby Bonds Nearly Close the Racial Wealth Gap for Young Adults," *Vox*, updated February 1, 2019, https://www.vox.com/future-perfect/2019/1/21/18185536/cory-booker-news-today-2020-presidential-election-baby-bonds.

59. Joseph R. Biden Jr., Inaugural Address, January 20, 2021, https://www.whitehouse.gov/briefing-room/speeches-remarks/2021/01/20/inaugural-address-by-president-joseph-r-biden-jr.

60. "Executive Order on Advancing Racial Equity and Support for Underserved Communities Through the Federal Government," January 20, 2021, https://www.whitehouse.gov/briefing-room/presidential-actions/2021/01/20/executive-order-advancing-racial-equity-and-support-for-underserved-communities-through-the-federal-government.

61. Joseph R. Biden Jr., "Remarks by President Biden at Signing of an Executive Order on Racial Equity," State Dining Room, January 26, 2021, https://www.whitehouse.gov/briefing-room/speeches-remarks/2021/01/26/remarks-by-president-biden-at-signing-of-an-executive-order-on-racial-equity.

62. "Executive Order on Advancing Racial Equity."

IMAGE CREDITS

INTERIOR

Page 13: W. Ashbie Hawkins: Unknown attribution: Public domain: Located in Antero Pietila, *Not in My Neighborhood: How Bigotry Shaped a Great American City* (Chicago: Rowan and Littlefield, 2010).

Page 13: George W. F: McMechen: George W. F: McMechen, 1905.

Page 18: "The Road to Nowhere": Photo by Jerry Jackson/Baltimore Sun Media: All rights reserved.

Page 33: Earl Andrews: Photo by Michael S. Williamson/*The Washington Post* via Getty Images.

Page 43: Hollenden Barber Shop: Cleveland Public Library/Photograph Collection.

Page 43: George A. Myers: Western Reserve Historical Society, Cleveland, OH.

Page 47: Greenwood burning: Tulsa riot, 1921, via *Common Dreams*, "The More Things Change: Tulsa's Race Massacre the History Books Turned Into a Race Riot," by Abby Zimet (2018).

Page 59: Burning buildings during Watts riots: *New York World-Telegram* via Library of Congress.

Page 67: Dorothy Gautreaux: Courtesy of BPI Chicago.

Page 150: Lakia Barnett: Photo by Sheryll Cashin.

Page 152: Student demographic charts: Courtesy of DC Public Schools.

Page 171: Dr: Darryl Atwell: Photo by Tyrus Ortega Gaines, courtesy of Darryl Atwell.

Page 196: DeVone Boggan: Courtesy of DeVone Boggan, Neighborhood Safety Director and Founding Director, Office Safety, Richmond, CA (2007–16).

INSERT

Map 1.1: US Census Data, 1940. Prepared by Social Explorer. Accessed 2020.

Map. 1.2: "Baltimore, MD," Mapping Inequality, September 21, 2020, http://dsl.richmond.edu.

Map 1.3: Courtesy of the Baltimore City Health Department, Community Health Assessment, September 20, 2017.

Maps 3.1 and 3.2: "Who Can Live in Chicago?" UIC Nathalie P. Voorhees Center for Neighborhood and Community Improvement, 2019.

Map 5.1: Courtesy of Paul A. Jargowsky. "The Architecture of Segregation (Online Appendix)." Century Foundation and Center for Urban Research and Education (CURE), Rutgers University, Camden, August 2015.

Map 5.2: Courtesy of Texas Low Income Housing.

Map 6.1: Connecticut Opportunity Index Map and Non-White Population, Jason Reece, Kirwan Institute, OSU. Used with permission of the Ohio State University.

Map 8.1: Minneapolis Race and Poverty. Prepared by Social Explorer. Accessed 2020.

INDEX

ABOUT THE AUTHOR

Sheryll Cashin has written five books that implicate the US struggle with racism and inequality. Her books have been nominated for the NAACP Image Award for Nonfiction (2015) and the Hurston/Wright Legacy Award for Nonfiction (2005, 2009, 2018) and selected as a *New York Times Book Review* Editors' Choice (2004). Cashin is the Carmack Waterhouse Professor of Law, Civil Rights and Social Justice at Georgetown University, where she teaches Constitutional Law and Race and American Law, among other subjects. She is an active member of the Poverty and Race Research Action Council. Cashin worked as a law clerk to US Supreme Court justice Thurgood Marshall and in the Clinton White House as an advisor on urban and economic policy, particularly concerning community development in inner-city neighborhoods. A contributing editor for *Politico Magazine*, she has written commentaries for the *New York Times*, *Los Angeles Times*, *Washington Post*, *Salon*, *The Root*, and other media. Cashin was born and raised in Huntsville, Alabama, where her parents were civil rights and political activists. She currently resides in Washington, DC, with her husband and twin sons.